THE WHITE PASS

THE WHITE PASS

GATEWAY TO THE KLONDIKE

ROY MINTER

UNIVERSITY OF ALASKA PRESS

Rasmuson Library Cataloguing in Publication Data

Minter, Roy, 1916–
The White Pass

Bibliography: p
Includes index.
ISBN 0-912006-26-9

1. White Pass and Yukon Railway – History.
2. Railroads – Yukon Territory – Construction.
3. Klondike River Valley (Yukon) – Gold discoveries.
I. Title.

HF2810.W48M56 1987

Published in Canada by: Published in the United States by:
McClelland and Stewart   University of Alaska Press
The Canadian Publishers   Signers' Hall
481 University Avenue   Fairbanks
Toronto, Ontario   Alaska 99775-1580
M5G 2E9

Printed and bound in Canada by John Deyell Co.

Printing of the United States edition of this book has been supported by funds provided to the University of Alaska Press from the Otto Geist Endowment.

*To the men and women who built the
White Pass and Yukon Railway
and made it run.*

CONTENTS

FOREWORD   *ix*

ACKNOWLEDGEMENTS   *x*

A NOTE ON NAME CHANGES   *xii*

INTRODUCTION   *13*

One
THE MYSTERY PASS   *19*

Two
THE MEN FROM ENGLAND   *34*

Three
A PAPER RAILWAY   *51*

Four
KLONDIKE GOLD   *69*

Five
THE PROMOTERS   *86*

Six
THE BATTLE OF THE PASSES   *111*

Seven
THE IRISH PRINCE   *127*

Eight
A CHANCE MEETING   *147*

Nine
LONDON GIVES THE NOD   *166*

Ten
BRACKETT'S BLUFF   *189*

Eleven
SHOOTOUT ON JUNEAU WHARF   *200*

Twelve
THE FIRST TRAIN   *218*

Thirteen
BLASTING THE GRADE   *236*

Fourteen
WINTER IN THE WHITE PASS   *249*

Fifteen
CRISES OF MEN AND MONEY   *266*

Sixteen
ON TO BENNETT CITY   *290*

Seventeen
HENEY'S SEVENTY MILES   *315*

Eighteen
THE BENT SPIKE   *335*

EPILOGUE   *356*

BIBLIOGRAPHY   *361*

NOTES   *367*

INDEX   *383*

MAPS

One

EARLY SEA ROUTES TO ALASKA AND THE YUKON 37

Two

THE BOUNDARY DISPUTE 53

Three

THREE COMPETING ROUTES 100

Four

THE CHILKOOT AND WHITE PASSES 124

Five

THE RAILWAY'S ORIGINAL GOAL 237

Six

FROM SKAGWAY TO WHITE PASS SUMMIT 267

Seven

FROM SKAGWAY TO WHITEHORSE 346

FOREWORD

I have been sitting here, reading Roy Minter's marvellous book and trying to figure out how many trips I made on the White Pass Railway before it suspended service in 1982. The figure, I think, comes to twelve. It was not enough. Twenty would not be enough; nor fifty. It is – or was – the single most spectacular one-day railway journey in Canada. I'm glad that on my last trip on that dramatic narrow-guage line, I was able to take my children with me. It is an experience that no one may ever know again and one that they will come to treasure.

My parents made the trip before me. I remember my father telling me how, when the winter was very hard, the men sometimes had to leave the coaches and walk across the trestle bridges on foot. How many other railways can lay claim to that statement?

But then, the White Pass was always unique as a railway. What other railway paid for itself out of its fares by the time it was finished? Canadian history – and American history, too – is full of dreadful stories about shoddy railway financing, company failures, last-minute government subsidies. Thus, the story Roy Minter tells is quite different from most railway epics.

It is, of course, a marvellous narrative. It is also important as history. The author has done his homework, dug deeply, and placed on the record a great deal of material that is new and would otherwise have been lost. I thought I knew a good deal about the building of the White Pass line, but much of what is here I find both fresh and surprising.

The tragedy, of course, is that the railway is no more. Unless someone with a flair for adventure starts it up anew, none of us will ever again be able to cross the great trestle of Dead Horse Gulch, or gaze out of the windows and look down on the actual Trail of '98 – a slender pathway worn by thousands of prospectors' boots. Those of us who have had that experience enjoyed a unique and unforgettable privilege. The rest will have to be content with enjoying the book.

Pierre Berton, KLEINBURG, ONTARIO, MARCH 1987

ACKNOWLEDGEMENTS

This book has been in the works, on and off, for the past twelve years, although serious research extends back even further. The delay in its completion was not lack of interest, but the need to earn a living while financing and pursuing the research, and writing the manuscript.

Many people helped me to find my way through the labyrinth of research. Some of us were strangers at the start, but as a result of a continuing association and a shared interest in Alaska and Yukon history, deeply cherished friendships have developed.

I am deeply indebted to Pierre Berton for his generous foreword, and to Gordon Bennett of Parks Canada for his advice and encouragement, as well as the information I obtained from his book, *Yukon Transportation: A History*. The observations of Dr. Kenneth Coates, University of Victoria, who read a draft of my manuscript, were of immense value. Marvin Taylor, Executive Vice-President of the White Pass and Yukon Corporation, was unstinting in his support. In addition to providing many of his company's engineering drawings, he patiently answered more questions by mail and in person than any author has a right to expect. I owe a great debt of gratitude to Les Rimes of West Vancouver whose critical comments and sharp pencil added clarity to the text. A very special thanks to Carl Mulvihill, a local Skagway historian, who never failed to extract urgently required information from what he calls his "shoe box filing system." And to Peter Shackleton, my thanks for producing seven excellent maps.

I am grateful to Paul Taylor, an Alaskan engineer whose knowledge of the White Pass railway grade and the weather conditions within the pass, helped recreate the construction scene. Many thanks to Associate Professor J.L. Wise, Alaska Climate Center, University of Alaska, who also provided information on weather conditions. Professor R.G. Bucksar (retired), and Professor Clarence C. Hulley, were most helpful in the early stages of the project. Edwin Bearss's Historic Resource Study for the Klondike Gold Rush National Historical Park was a valuable source of information.

Willard Ireland, Kent Haworth, and John Bovey, past and present Provincial Archivists, Victoria, B.C., rendered sterling service during my early years of research as did A.J. Helmcken, Victoria, B.C., and John R. Cummings, of Walla Walla, Wash. Thanks also to Steven Hites and Rand E. Snure who generously provided me with copies of their personal research material.

I also acknowledge my indebtedness to many people who provided information on the principal people who played major roles in the railway construction drama. I list them following each principal's name. TANCRED: Sir Henry Lawson-Tancred, Bart., Mary Lawson-Tancred, Christopher Lawson-Tancred, Dr. and Mrs. H. Denis White, Lorna Gibbs, Rev. Ken Holder, and Brian and Pamela Tyler, all residents of England. GRAVES: Brian Graves, Vancouver; Roy Graves, San Diego; Gudrun Sparling, Whitehorse, Yukon. HAWKINS; Mason Hawkins, Nicki J. Nielsen, Anchorage, Alaska. HISLOP: Robert Wood, Cambridge, Ont; Helenita Harvey, Salmon Arm, B.C. HENEY: Michael J. Heney, Toronto; Mrs. G.T. Heney, and Judge and Mrs. Frank Dunlap, Ottawa; John J. Heney, Nepean, Ont; Dr. M.J. (Joe) Heney and Alice Murchison, Vancouver; Walter Sweet, Altin, B.C.; W.F. Baxter, North Surrey, B.C.; Dick Racine, Long Beach, Cal; and Archie Shiels, Bellingham, Wash. MOORE: Robert L. Spude, Regional Historian, National Park Service, Anchorage, AK; D.A. Gestner, Seattle. BRYDONE-JACK: Faith Rendell, Jack Rendell, and Mrs. Katherine Rendell, Cal; Frances Brydone-Jack, Victoria, and Vaughan Brydone-Jack, Vancouver, B.C. STRETCH: Michael Butler, Mrs. Wm. P. Butler, Seattle; and William M. Hainsworth, Auburn, Wash. CLOSE BROTHERS: Company Secretary, Terence D. Cansick, and the officers and staff of Close Brothers Limited, all residents of London, England, who gave me their board room for a week, a pile of early documents to study, and tea and biscuits twice a day; A.H. Martens and J.R. Close, both of London, and Clifford J. Rogers, Seattle. F.H. WHITING: Robert Whiting, Denver. FOY: Dr. Dwight McNair Scott, Philadelphia.

I also extend my heartfelt thanks to the following: Dinah Forbes of McClelland and Stewart for her patience, kindly advice, and for the sensitive and perceptive editing she applied to my manuscript; Christa Goncalves who typed and retyped my drafts of the manuscript in a brave effort to keep up with the changes; Dariya Bagnall who organized my Notes and Sources; Jean Martin-Smith who produced the final narrative on her word processor; and Nora Agabob, whose constructive criticism and unfailing support helped me through many difficult moments during the preparation of the manuscript.

A deep bow to staff members of the following organizations: Alaska Historical Library, Juneau, Alaska; The James Jerome Hill Reference Library, and the Minnesota Historical Society, St. Paul, Minnesota; Northwest History Section, Vancouver Public Library; National Archives and Records Service, Washington,

D.C.; Public Records Office, and Companies House, London, England; Public
Archives of Canada, Ottawa; Colorado State Historical Society and Colorado State
Museum, Denver; Seattle Public Library; United States Department of the Inte-
rior, Washington, D.C.; and Anchorage, Alaska; United States Board of Geogra-
phic Names, Washington, D.C.; Yukon Archives, Whitehorse, Yukon. Special
Collections, University of Washington Libraries, Seattle.

Finally, I express my gratitude to Bill Roozeboom, who worked so diligently to
restore and print the Barley plates; to Jeffrey P. Balabanov, of Continental
Explosives Ltd., Vancouver, B.C., who gave me a quick course in the characteris-
tics of black powder and dynamite; and to the following people who provided
support in a variety of ways: Bill Braden, Rosemary and Jonathan Donald, Vera
Baker, Glen Gordon, Historical Section, R.C.M.P., Bill Ferro, A.J. Helmcken,
Gordon Martin, R.C. Beaumont, F.G. Downey, A.P. Friesen, F.D. Smith, D.H.
Sladden, Jim and Flo Whyard, Brian Wilson, Andrew (Budge) Jukes, Christine
Dickinson, Rosemary Monk, Stuart Wright, Helen Baker, and Glen E. Robertson
for his permission to quote from *Soapy Smith: King Of The Frontier Con Men*,
written by his father, Frank C. Robertson, and to Beth Kay Harris, co-author of
the book.

There are others who helped – too many to mention – but they know the
depth of my gratitude through our correspondence, or by my personally offered
thanks when, by good fortune, our paths have crossed.

A NOTE ON NAME CHANGES

Whether to use modern or original place names always presents a problem when
writing history. I decided to use the modern names of towns, except when they
are mentioned in actual quotes. Michael J. Heney, for instance, called modern-day
Carcross "Caribou Crossing," or "Caribou" for short. The name Carcross did not
exist in his day – as Caribou Crossing does not exist in ours. It would therefore be
inaccurate and improper to change Heney's quote by making him use a name
that did not exist in his time. The same applies to "White Horse," a two-word
name for the Yukon's capital city of Whitehorse. I have used Whitehorse in the
narrative, but have left it as "White Horse" when extracting quotes from the
historical record. The decision in this case was made more difficult in that during
the construction of the railway "White Horse" was also referred to as "Closeleigh," and appeared by this name on maps of the day. Lake Bennett was often
referred to as "Bennett," as was the important gold rush community that grew
up around the Lake's southern tip. As it increased in size, it was often called
Bennett City. I have used both Bennett and Bennett City to describe the town.
The lake is always referred to as Lake Bennett in the narrative.

INTRODUCTION

The construction of the White Pass and Yukon Railway stands as a world-class engineering accomplishment involving British financing, American engineering, and Canadian contracting.

The first time I saw the railway in action I knew that I had stumbled on to something special. That was in 1955, when I was posted to Whitehorse by the Canadian Army for duty with the North West Highway System – the military command that maintained the Alaska Highway and its ancillary facilities.

Shortly after arriving, I was invited to ride on the railway to the port of Skagway, Alaska, a Klondike gold-rush boom town that was the operational headquarters of the railway and the Yukon's ice-free port of entry.

During that six-hour train ride, I discovered that the railway, as well as the majestic White Pass, was steeped in Klondike gold-rush history. Just one hundred feet from my coach window I could see a narrow, twisting, rock-strewn path that had been scuffed out of the hillside and along the floor of the valley by the pounding feet of sourdoughs who were bent on reaching the Klondike to make their fortune before the gold ran out.

By the tens of thousands they came, making their way through the White Pass, an awe-inspiring mountain gap that was sculptured by the eternal upheavals of the land and the relentless flow of the ice-age glaciers as they ground their way to the sea.

After that magnificent ride I was hooked on the White Pass, the railway, and the whole northern scene.

This book took root on that trip, although I did not know it at the time. I jotted down a few notes, and later began seriously to research the conception and construction of the railway and the gold rush that brought it into existence.

It soon became evident that the building of the railway had been an epic northern event, involving financiers, engineers, politicians, and promoters who resided in London, Washington, D.C., Ottawa, Seattle, Victoria, Juneau, and

Dyea – most of whom had worked to untangle a myriad of financial, legal, engineering, and legislative problems associated with the enterprise.

When construction began, Skagway and the White Pass were bursting with gold-rush activity – some of it legal, some of it illegal, all of it muscular, lusty, and strenuous. It was within this environment that the railway was built. For the twenty-five months of its construction it was surrounded by an ever-changing stream of frontier life that sometimes helped and sometimes hindered the men who were blasting out the roadbed from Skagway to White Pass summit and along the shore of Lake Bennett to Whitehorse on the Yukon River.

Not everyone cheered its progress. It was regarded as a serious rival by the owners of existing transportation systems operating through the White Pass and the Chilkoot Pass, as well as by some Skagway residents who saw no advantage in supporting a railway that wanted to transport the gold seekers and their freight out of town as soon as they arrived.

There were schemers in Dyea who condemned the railway and extolled the virtues of the Chilkoot Pass as the only reliable route to the Yukon interior. And there were the White Pass packers, with their strings of horses and mules, who saw the railway as their nemesis.

The railway, therefore, was not the only White Pass story. It was one of many stories. But it did emerge as the principal transportation system after it created its corporate structure, fought off its competitors, and completed the construction of its line in a sub-arctic environment a thousand miles from the closest source of supply.

The pages in this book focus on that period of the railway's history – the time when it was conceived, organized, and built.

That the railway continued to operate after its completion for almost eighty-five years is another story. It can be said, however, that throughout those years it accomplished more than anyone should expect from an international narrow-gauge railway that is only one hundred and ten miles long. But ever since the completion of its first mile of track, its family of companies, known collectively as the White Pass & Yukon Route, has played a prominent role in the development and support of virtually every industrial and commercial enterprise in Skagway, Alaska, the Yukon, as well as adjacent mining areas in northern British Columbia. In addition to its year-round railway operations, these White Pass "route companies" served the Yukon's mines and communities with a large fleet of sternwheel riverboats throughout the ice-free summer months – an inland marine operation that continued until the early 1950s.

Throughout World War I, the 1920s and 1930s, the White Pass & Yukon Route maintained its presence, although the level of northern business remained low during the Great Depression. During the 1930s it added an air arm to its roster of northern services. White Pass Airways flew from its own airstrips across the coast range between Skagway and Whitehorse, and north to Dawson City and Mayo. Its fleet included Ford Tri-Motor airplanes, a Boeing 247D twin engine all metal monoplane, a variety of float- and ski-equipped bush planes in season, and a Condor biplane, which, at that time, was the largest passenger-carrying aircraft in Canada.

Soon after the start of World War II, plans for the contruction of a highway to Alaska as a defence measure were completed and accepted by the governments of Canada and the United States. Almost overnight, the White Pass & Yukon Route found itself once again embroiled in a northern drama – the construction of the Alaska Highway. Hundreds of thousands of tons of United States Army equipment, machinery, and supplies, as well as battalions of troops, were transported by rail from Skagway to Whitehorse. The demands on the railway were so heavy that its locomotives, rolling stock, and grade were leased to the United States Army for the duration of the war.

Highway construction began in March 1942, and in the incredibly short time of nine months the 1,420 mile military tote road was completed from Dawson Creek, British Columbia, to Big Delta, Alaska.

In the early 1940s White Pass Airways was sold to a company formed by Grant McConachie, which, in later years, became part of Canadian Pacific Airlines.

Besides assisting in the rapid construction of the Alaska Highway, the White Pass & Yukon Route constructed military airports at Watson Lake, Whitehorse and Snag. These three airports, which were built under contract, were part of the North West Staging Route project, which facilitated the direct delivery of United States fighters and bombers to the Soviet Union in support of the Soviet war effort.

In the early 1950s the company introduced the container concept of freight handling – a transportation technique that has since been adopted world-wide. In 1955 it launched the motor vessel *Clifford J. Rogers*, the first vessel in the world designed and built from the keel up as container ship. During the same year, the railway was converted to diesel and the company was operating a completely integrated ship-train-truck containerized transportation from Vancouver to all points in the Canadian Northwest. Within ten years, the *Clifford J. Rogers* was replaced by an ultra-modern container-tanker ship christened the *Frank H. Brown*, honouring the White Pass president who conceived the integrated container system and set it in motion. Two years later the *"Brown"* was joined by her sistership, the M.V. *Klondike*.

The railway, although currently shut down, is still visible. Every year thousands of tourists arrive in Skagway and Whitehorse, and many of them are fascinated with the railroad's past, and its vivid and colourful association with the Klondike gold rush of 1897 and 1898.

"Who built the railroad, and why?" they ask. And they wonder about the people who "punched that railway along those high cliffs in the White Pass." "What happened in the pass during the gold rush?" asks another, "and who found it?"

This book was written to answer those questions, and to provide an intimate look at what has been described as "the greatest little railroad in the world."

Roy Minter, DECEMBER 22, 1986

THE CONSTRUCTION OF
THE WHITE PASS
AND YUKON RAILWAY

This great piece of work has
been accomplished without a
dollar's aid from any
government or any concession
except the right-of-way,
which had no possible value
without the railway. It is
no disparagement to other
mountain railways to say that
the construction of the
White Pass & Yukon is among
the most brilliant feats of
railway engineering, in view
of the tremendous difficulties
to be encountered and the
shortness of the time in which
the work was done.

Victoria Colonist
DECEMBER 2, 1900.

One

---◆---

THE MYSTERY PASS

O N MAY 13, 1887, the Pacific Steamship Company sidewheel steamer *Ancon*, commanded by Captain J.C. Hunter, steamed out of Victoria harbour into Haro Strait.[1] At Turn Point she changed course and headed north up the Strait of Georgia towards Lynn Canal, Alaska, nine hundred miles to the north.

Aboard were George Mercer Dawson and William Ogilvie, two prominent Canadian government surveyors who had been instructed by the Honourable Thomas White, Minister of the Interior, to explore the region of the Canadian North-West Territories drained by the Yukon River. The survey was to determine the position of the 141st meridian, the international boundary between the Canadian Northwest and Alaska, and to obtain geological, topographical, and general information about the Yukon district, a vast and virtually unexplored region stretching from the northern boundary of British Columbia to the Arctic Ocean, and from the Mackenzie Mountains in the east to Alaska in the west – 186,299 square miles of potential wealth that was often described as "the British Empire's furthest north."

There was a sense of urgency about the expedition. Placer mining along the Yukon River had been attracting prospectors since the early 1880s. Now, hundreds of gold-seekers were entering Alaska and the Yukon district via St. Michael, and travelling up the Yukon River to the gold camps. Others were landing at Dyea, crossing the Chilkoot Pass to the headwaters of the Yukon River, and rafting down north to the creeks that held promise of gold.

This growing influx had brought into question the location of the 141st meridian, which was designated in 1825 by the Treaty of St. Petersburg as the boundary line between Russian and British possessions in the far northwest region of North America.[2]

Ogilvie, commenting on the expedition, said that the venture was set in motion by correspondence to the Canadian government from west coast Canadian and American businessmen, and from local western governments, regarding gold mining in the Yukon district. "This correspondence," he said, "had continued for several years and became so serious that it induced governmental action."[3] Should gold or other mineral wealth be discovered there, it would be in Canada's interest to ensure that the area was internationally recognized as Canadian territory, and that its administration was firmly in Canadian hands.

Thomas White, Minister of the Interior, had entrusted the overall direction of the expedition to Dr. George Dawson, Assistant Director, Geological Survey of Canada, a public servant who, at age twenty-five, had already earned an outstanding reputation for his report on the mineral resources of Canada along the 49th parallel. He was held in the highest regard by the mining fraternity and was often described as one of the greatest scientists Canada had produced.[4]

With two assistants, Richard George McConnell and James McEvoy, Dawson was to mount a two-pronged thrust into the North, covering the Stikine, Pelly, and Liard rivers and portions of the Richardson Mountains and the Mackenzie River valley. The Yukon River segment of the expedition was given to William Ogilvie, who had completed extensive mapping expeditions throughout Canada's western prairie.

Ogilvie's orders were to enter the Yukon district via the Chilkoot Pass and gather geological and topographical information, as well as measure by instrument the traverse of the route from the head of Lynn Canal to the Yukon River and along the line of the river to the 141st meridian. It would, therefore, be Ogilvie's task to conduct the first Canadian attempt to fix the precise location of the 141st meridian.[5]

Time was short and Ogilvie's impatience mounted as the *Ancon* wallowed north through the Inside Passage, "excelling herself in slowness," he observed, as the ship discharged freight and passengers along the way. The delays were frustrating, but the days were still pleasurable as they watched the deeply notched Pacific Coast slide by. This was a voyage along a seemingly endless coastline of fjords and mountains – a gigantic seascape displaying an exhilarating mixture of power and serenity, sunshine and thunder.

Captain Moore, a supernumerary member of Ogilvie's party, watched the ship's progress with an experienced eye. The coast of British Columbia held few mysteries for him. Since his arrival in Victoria in the spring of 1858, he had sailed the rivers, lakes, and coastal waterways of the North, winning and losing three fortunes while operating steamboats, building trails under government contract, and searching for gold. He was vigorous, courageous, headstrong, and competitive, and his battles for the lion's share of the freighting business against friend and foe had made him a west-coast legend in his own time.

He was born in Emden, Germany, in 1822, where he had received little formal education before venturing to the New World. Alaska District Judge, Melville C. Brown, once described him as "a man of great determination and possessing a vigorous intellect." He had participated in gold rushes in California, Oregon, and the Cassiar district in northern British Columbia, where he discovered gold on Dease Creek.

While working his Cassiar claims and operating a steamboat service between Victoria and the Cassiar gold-fields, he noted that many miners were travelling north to the tip of Lynn Canal where they entered the Yukon interior via the Chilkoot Pass. There they were panning for gold on the sandbars of the Upper Yukon, Big Salmon, Little Salmon, Pelly, Hootalingua, and Stewart rivers. Their interest in the region intrigued him and led him to prophesy that one day gold would be found in huge quantities in the Yukon valley.

Captain Moore had urged his son, William, known as "Billie," to enter the Yukon district in 1886, to explore the country, assess its potential, and search for gold. Billie landed at the Indian community of Dyea at the tip of Lynn Canal, crossed the Chilkoot Pass, and rafted down the Yukon River to the gold-bearing creeks. This was the year gold was discovered on Fortymile River in the Yukon interior. Billie, who had been joined by his brother, Bernard, rushed to the new gold-field and staked and worked a claim.[6]

At age sixty-five, Captain Moore still moved with the easy gait of a man half his age, a fact noted by Ogilvie when Moore called on him in Victoria to apply for a position as a labourer with the survey party. At first Ogilvie was reluctant to hire him but agreed when Moore explained that he wished to remain with the party only as far as necessary to meet his two sons, Billie and Bernard.[7]

After he had crossed the Chilkoot Pass on his way into the interior in 1886, Billie had written to his father about an Indian he had met, Skookum Jim, who "could talk a good deal of Chinook jargon," and who had found that by way of the Skagway River there was a longer route through the mountains but not so high a pass to cross.[8] Skookum Jim would not provide Billie with any further information, protesting that a great evil would befall him if he said any more.

For centuries the Chilkoot branch of the Tlingit Indian Nation had controlled the Chilkoot Pass, which they called *Vlekuk*. The pass, one of their greatest resources, provided the Chilkoots with a natural route between the great Mother River in the interior and their community of Dyea on the coast. So great was the Chilkoots' control over the pass, and so complete was their monopoly on packing goods through it, that they would not permit their own kinsmen, the Chilkats, to use it. The name of their coastal village, "Dyea," is Chilkoot for *to pack* or *to load*.

The Chilkoots were determined to protect their monopoly by suppressing all knowledge of a nearby pass. Anyone who revealed its existence would be subject to severe retribution by the Chilkoots – a fact well known to Skookum Jim. But, despite this taboo, he defied the Chilkoots and revealed the existence of this secret pass to Billie Moore – a pass rumoured to be lower than the steep and rocky pass the Chilkoots so carefully guarded.[9]

Nothing could have excited Captain Moore as much as this information about a mysterious low pass leading into the Yukon district, where he prophesied a major gold-field would eventually be discovered.

He had received Billie's letter late in the fall of 1886, too late in the season to investigate the matter of the pass for himself. Besides, a series of disastrous business decisions had left him financially destitute. He had even lost his home. His only remaining assets were his inexhaustible store of energy and his unshakable belief in his ability to surmount any obstacle that stood in his way. The mystery of the low pass, not money, was his preoccupation as the *Ancon* steamed north.

After eleven frustrating days at sea, the ship turned into Lynn Canal, a gigantic trench created by some prehistoric upheaval that left in its wake a narrow ribbon of water stretching eighty miles from the Pacific Ocean to the canal's northern tip.

Ogilvie and his party arrived at Haines Mission, Alaska, the ship's most northerly port of call, at dawn on May 24, 1887. The weather was cold, and it was pouring with rain.[10]

The surveyors and their freight were landed and at eleven that morning the ship backed away, leaving Ogilvie and his party on the threshold of their exile. Fourteen months would pass before they received news from the outside world. As the *Ancon* dipped her flag and blew a farewell whistle, Ogilvie confessed that he could not swallow and that he suffered "a moisture in my eye that would not dry as long as the *Ancon* was in sight."[11]

The party's freight was loaded into two boats belonging to a trader and towed twenty miles to Dyea. There the party was greeted by Captain John Jerome Healy and George Dickson who, with Edgar Wilson, operated the Healy and Wilson Trading Post. Healy, one-time boss of a whisky fort on the Montana-Canadian border and sheriff of Couteau County, had, with partner Dickson, been trading with the Indians and supplying gold-seekers since the middle eighties. Their trading post was not an impressive site. A few clapboard buildings, a log hut or two, and Captain Healy's schooner, *Charlie*, were the only visible signs of civilization. Although Dyea did not rate a dot on the maps of the day, it was home to the Healys, Dickson, Wilson, and 138 Indians.[12]

Behind the Indian village, which spread across the tidelands and into the forest beyond, was the entrance to the Chilkoot Pass - the historic Indian trade route from tidewater to the interior. From the village the trail followed the banks of the Taiya River, climbing through the coastal benchlands to the foot of an awesome mountain barrier. This alpine massif stood like a huge grey fortress – silent and hostile. Through it zigzagged a jagged gap, which had been shaped by the eruptions of nature, the crushing weight and abrasive power of glacial action, and later honed by the eternal movement of ice, wind, and water. This was the Chilkoot Pass, formed by a million years of natural turmoil. In the summer it was a tough but manageable mountain pack trail, but in winter it became an accursed abomination of snow, ice, rock, and terror.

Once he had established his camp, Ogilvie set about organizing his expedition into the Yukon interior and becoming acquainted with the local terrain. He was particularly interested in the matter of the low pass he had heard about while the *Ancon* was unloading freight at Juneau. Some of his Juneau informants were of the opinion that a low pass did exist, but when pressed for specific information they admitted that they had never personally seen it.[13] This came as no surprise to Captain Moore. He, like Ogilvie, had heard a good deal of speculation about the pass during the *Ancon*'s stay in Juneau, but he could not confirm its existence. It did not take him long to realize, however, that the only fact of any consequence about the pass was in his own pocket – the year-old letter from his son, Billie, informing him that Skookum Jim had actually crossed the pass but, fearing retribution from the Chilkoot Indians, would not reveal its location.

Healy and Dickson admitted to Ogilvie that they had heard of the pass but could not – or would not – provide any information on which a reasonable judgement could be made. Since their future business depended on selling supplies to travellers heading across the Chilkoot they were as reluctant as their Indian neighbours to reveal its location. They did, however, suggest that Ogilvie discuss the question with George Carmack and his brothers-in-law, Skookum Jim and Tagish Charlie.[14]

George Carmack, a United States Navy cook, had jumped ship at Juneau in 1885 and was now living part of the year at Dyea and part along the lakes and rivers of the interior. He had learned the language of the local Indians and had gained considerable influence over the Indians who occupied the Yukon interior and who accepted him as one of their own. Carmack's wife, Kate, a member of the Tagish Indian band, was the daughter of the Chief, which enhanced Carmack's stature in the northern Indian communities. But because of his tendency to boast about his exploits, he was not well liked by the mining fraternity. Behind his back, and at times to his face, he was derisively referred to as "Siwash George," a sobriquet he found in no way objectionable.[15]

His brother-in-law, Skookum Jim, was well-known in the Dyea area and throughout the Yukon interior. He was a strong, handsome, and able man, a good friend and companion to Carmack, and a hunter of considerable local fame. Once, after being attacked by a wounded brown bear, he rammed his empty rifle down its throat and stoned it to death with a rock, emerging from the fray victorious though bloody and exhausted.[16]

Ogilvie approached Carmack and Skookum Jim at Dyea. They both confirmed that a low pass did exist and told him about its main features and location. Ogilvie decided to have the pass examined. Years later Ogilvie stated that:

> the prosecution of my survey required my own immediate attention, and also that of all the members of my party who had any experience in survey work. I could therefore spare no man to go through the pass and report on it but Captain Moore. Consequently I decided to send him provided I could find someone to accompany him who knew the route. After much hesitation Skookum Jim agreed to go, but only on the condition that the trip be kept secret from the Chilkoot Indians, as he feared interference from them.[17]

Captain Moore's experiences at Dyea appear to have parallelled those of Ogilvie. "When we arrived at Dyea," Moore recalled, "I hunted up ... Skookum Jim who had informed my son Billie the previous fall of a low-lying pass through the mountains a few miles from the Chilkoot Pass." During this conversation, Skookum Jim told Moore that he had actually travelled over the mountains from Tagish Lake by way of the low pass and had reached tidewater five miles east of Dyea at the site of a deep-water bay that the Indians called *Skagua* (later spelled Skagway), meaning *home of the north wind*.[18] Moore learned that the pass was much easier to travel across than the Chilkoot and that it was timbered much of the way.

Moore had already observed that the difficulty of packing supplies over the tortuous Chilkoot Pass would hinder any major developments in the Yukon interior, and from all reports the possibility of building a successful wagon road through it seemed highly unlikely.

Moore quickly made ready to search for the low pass, and Ogilvie turned to his primary responsibility of moving his survey crew and seven tons of supplies across the Chilkoot. A spell of dank and dirty weather caused a frustrating delay, but finally, on June 6, 1887, the survey party, supported by 120 Indian packers, started the long and arduous struggle up the Chilkoot Pass towards the summit and on to Lake Bennett.[19]

MOORE AND SKOOKUM JIM watched Ogilvie and his party disappear into the coastal forest and then pushed off in a canoe and paddled five miles to the southeast. They pulled their canoe onto the beach at the most northerly tip of Lynn Canal, well out of reach of the twenty-five-foot tides that flood the canal's upper reaches, and examined the landscape stretched out before them. The surrounding mountains were half-hidden in the summer mists, but they could see the blue-white masses of glacial ice and miles of fractured peaks and ridges – lonely, windswept, and forbidding. Through the valley to the north tumbled a silt-laden river, which in eons past had spread its deposits across the valley, creating a giant triangle of land with its apex at the foot of the mountain and its broad base leading into the sea. Heavy growths of spruce and hemlock, cottonwood, pine, and birch mantled the valley floor and the sides of the encircling mountains. Driftwood littered the muddy beach, and above high water the shoreline was covered with waving clumps of coarse grass. Long-abandoned Indian fish camps, campfires, old bear and fox traps, and axe blazes on the trees told of previous but tentative occupations of the valley. The silence was broken only by the grunting of porcupines and flights of Old Squaw ducks that skimmed across the valley and with a rustle of wings splashed down in the bay.[20]

Moore and Skookum Jim made their way through the pristine forest towards the mountains. Dense underbrush slashed their clothes and ripped their skin as they cut their way through the thick growth and climbed over and around masses of tangled and rotting windfalls. Fording swollen streams added to their miseries, but they finally emerged in a jagged granite-walled valley that zigzagged into a land that seemed to stand on end. They inched their way around the cliffs and box canyons, yelling to be heard above the roar of the river. As they made their way, Moore made note of places where a wagon road could be built. The slow and brutal climb drained them of their energy, and they paused on a high granite bluff from where they could trace the tangled route they had taken and contrast it with the calm blue waters of Lynn Canal that lay far below.[21] Beyond the canal rose mountain peaks and glaciers in a stunning and colourful tapestry.

At times on their journey, Moore stopped to take compass bearings and estimate the distances they had travelled. He entered each piece of information into a notebook as he had been instructed by Ogilvie, but his records later failed to meet Ogilvie's high standards. "I found that he had not completed the survey in a way I had expected," Ogilvie observed.[22] But record-keeping held little interest for Moore, who regarded himself as a practical man. In his opinion, filling up pages with notes would contribute nothing to the task at hand. It was a foot-slogging job, and as they tramped on, the major mysteries of the pass vanished in the late spring air.

They were close to the summit now, and etched in the sky-high horizon they could see their goal – an open rocky notch. On the third day of their struggle they clambered through the gap and entered the broad rock-strewn uplands that lay behind the summit of the pass.

Before them lay miles of fractured granite that had been crushed during the ice age, leaving behind an awesome and chaotic landscape. Together they strode some twenty miles through the splintered outcrops to Lindeman Lake where, on the tenth day of their arduous trek, they rejoined Ogilvie and his party, who were moving towards Lake Bennett, seven miles to the north.[23]

Moore told Ogilvie that a wagon road could be built through the mystery pass from tidewater to Lake Bennett and that even a railroad could be constructed when the need arose, which, according to Moore, would not be too far in the future. Ogilvie knew Moore had considerable experience of building roads through the mountainous regions of northern British Columbia and accepted his opinion. "From all the information I could get," Ogilvie later wrote, "I concurred with him and so reported."[24]

Ogilvie incorporated all of Moore's information into his survey and, because the expedition into the Yukon district had been authorized by the Honourable Thomas White, Canadian Minister of the Interior, he named the new route into the Yukon district the "White Pass."[25]

EVIDENCE OF past boat-building activities was everywhere apparent as Ogilvie stood at the southern tip of Lake Bennett. Tree stumps, piles of sawdust, and abandoned whip-saw platforms clearly indicated that many prospectors had already travelled over the Chilkoot Pass.

Miners and prospectors were coming to the North in greater numbers every year. In twos and threes they came – the gold-seekers, the opportunists, and many from that footloose fraternity of adventurers who wander through the outbacks of the world.

To Moore the signs were clear. Now that he had crossed the newly named White Pass and had recognized its potential as a major transportation route into the Yukon district, he was anxious to return to Skagway and explore the land there. But he was also aware of his obligation to remain with the Ogilvie party until he found his sons, Billie and Bernard.

Moore set about constructing a scow that, with two Peterborough canoes, would carry Ogilvie's survey party and its seven tons of supplies down the Yukon River to the international boundary area where they would set up winter camp. A few large trees were found and whip-sawed into lumber. Moore framed the twenty-foot scow and spiked the boards to it. But all the while, he thought of the pass. The deep-water bay, the miners, and the prospects of a major gold strike in the interior offered a combination of opportunities he could not ignore. The pass had suddenly become the central theme of his existence, and he was determined to return to Skagway Bay and stake land there as soon as he found his sons.

On July 11, 1887, the scow was finished, and on the following day the advance party pushed off, the scow's long sweeps keeping her steady to the wind. Ogilvie followed with the main group in the two Peterborough canoes.[26]

Slowly the surveyors made their way to the northern tip of Lake Bennett, through Nares Lake to Tagish Lake, and on to Marsh Lake where they entered the Yukon River.

During the slow voyage down the river, Moore talked endlessly of developing a transportation route into the Yukon interior and drove Ogilvie and his surveyors to distraction. Ogilvie reported Moore was convinced "the White Pass would reverberate with the rumble of railway trains carrying supplies, and its peaks and valleys would echo and re-echo to their signal whistles," and that "his transportation system would bring supplies in to the miners and carry out their golden stores to the treasure marts of the world."[27]

Ogilvie's condescending remarks ignored Captain Moore's record of proposing government action with respect to the North. On February 12, 1883, Moore had written to British Columbia's Lieutenant-Governor, C.F. Cornwall, seeking government aid to mount an exploratory and prospecting expedition into the Yukon district via the Yukon River estuary. "I feel convinced," he wrote, "that there are large deposits of gold at the headwaters of the Yukon River."

Even at that early date, Moore had grasped the significance of the Yukon district and its relationship to Victoria. "This extensive area of Canadian Territory," he wrote, "although in such close proximity to Victoria . . . is unknown and lies unproductive, whereas, if explored and prospected, it might develop a source of wealth to the Province and be of great commercial value to this city."

Although he was proposing to enter the Yukon district via the mouth of the Yukon River, he had heard of the Chilkoot Pass route. "To make the exploration effective," he wrote, "it is proposed that some of the exploring party be detailed to proceed by the Chilcot river [sic] and over a portage to the Lewes [Yukon] River and down into the Yukon district, with the view of obtaining . . . information about the country and the best mode of communication for transmission of mails, merchandise, and for travel when navigation of the Yukon River by being frozen is stopped."

His letters failed to generate support or encouragement from either the provincial or federal governments, despite his plea that "the Dominion Parliament be called upon to contribute in aid of this undertaking . . . to the extent of $6,000."[28]

Now that he had located the mysterious pass, he was impatient to stake 160 acres of land at Skagway, including sea frontage for a wharf.

Much to Moore's annoyance, the party moved at a snail's pace as it carried out its instrumentally measured traverse along the river towards the 141st meridian. Ogilvie was continually forced to remind Moore that the surveyors "could not and would not" move any faster. Moore's impatience was understandable. "The Lord knows where those damn boys of mine are or what they are doing," he exclaimed to Ogilvie, who now regarded Moore as a problem and a bore.[29] But they were both about to find relief.

On the morning of August 12, 1887, Moore noticed four men in a boat poling up the Yukon River, with his son, Bernard, standing at the stern. Bernard already had seen the surveyor's barge and canoes tied to the bank on the opposite side of the river. He heard his father shouting, and through the overhanging willows he saw him running towards his boat. Bernard had never been so happy to see anyone in his life for he had become terribly homesick and was determined to leave the North before the onslaught of winter.[30] He explained to his father that Billie had decided to spend the winter at Fortymile and probably would not return to Victoria until late the following year.

Moore told Ogilvie he wished to return to the coast with his son. With concealed glee, Ogilvie thanked him for his work and wished him a safe journey. Moore transferred his gear to Bernard's boat and the following morning they waved good-bye to Ogilvie and set off upstream.

The weather was hot; the air was black with mosquitoes. Hardly a day went by when they did not meet a boatload of miners heading north to the gold strike at Fortymile. As they met each northbound boat, there would be a brief exchange of information, equipment, and views, and then they would part. For twelve days they poled up the river, finally arriving at Whitehorse Rapids where they portaged their boat and supplies past the turbulent white water and on to Miles Canyon. At the head of the canyon they met a group of miners from Quebec heading out, and Father Pascal Tosi and two other priests heading in – three missionaries who had been dispatched to assist Archbishop Seghers with his apostolic work in Alaska. The traffic was becoming heavier now. But there was one weak link in the route – the overland haul from the sea to Lake Bennett. Captain Moore was convinced that he had the answer to that.

THE WIND SHRIEKED down Windy Arm off Tagish Lake and the waves thundered onto the beach. Moore and his son huddled in their tent. They were alone. The other three occupants of the boat had left for Dyea, bent on making their way to the world outside before the onset of winter. Under the flapping canvas Bernard listened to his father proclaim his belief that one day there would be an important gold strike in the North. He predicted that an army of gold-seekers would flood into the Yukon interior, spilling along the rough and ready routes created by nature. Some were doing it now, he insisted, although the present trickle would be nothing compared to the number of miners who would come after the gold was found. The present route over the Chilkoot, Moore explained, was slow and inefficient. What was needed was a good trail with fair grades, one that could be improved to accommodate pack horses, and later a wagon road. Once Lake Bennett is reached, he said, "there are no further obstructions for a sternwheel river steamer, excepting the Whitehorse rapids and Miles Canyon, round which a tramway can be built, a distance of three miles. From there a steamer can proceed to the Bering Sea."[31] The key to reaching this inland waterway would be an organized transportation system through the White Pass to connect Lake Bennett, the accepted head of Yukon River navigation, to Skagway Bay, some forty miles to the south.

Skagway Bay had fathoms of deep water and, unlike Dyea, no tidal flats stretching hopelessly into the sea. Ocean-going ships would be able to berth at a proper wharf to discharge their cargoes. Behind the bay was a broad flat land where a town could be built. It would become the staging area, the transfer point from ships to wagons or trains. Their first job, he insisted, would be to hurry to the deep-water bay and stake 160 acres of land – the amount allowed by the land laws of the United States. The next two steps would be to build a wharf for the ships that were bound to come and then blaze a trail through the new pass to the Yukon interior.

They broke camp the following morning and sailed to the head of Windy Arm on Tagish Lake, hoping to discover a useful water course that would lead into the general vicinity of the White Pass. They found nothing except thick fog and heavy rain. For four days in a leaking boat they fought biting northern winds and Lake Bennett's choppy waves, arriving exhausted at the lake's southern tip on September 4, 1887.[32] Because their supplies were dangerously low, they chose to return to tidewater via the more familiar Chilkoot Pass. They cached their boat, lashed their equipment high in a tree, and struggled on with only the barest of necessities.

Within a day they had reached the summit of the Chilkoot, soaked to the skin and miserably cold. The wind blasted through the cut, driving sleet and snow before it in blinding sheets. Father and son, faces stinging under the onslaught of a million wind-borne barbs, stumbled through gullies and creeks, where not a stick of wood or a dry chip could be found.

"Darkness was upon us now," Bernard later wrote, "and we were cold, hungry and wet to the skin and our blankets were soaked. We lay down in the rain and sleet in a clump of willows on the wet soggy ground near a creek, and shivered and steamed ourselves till the morning, without fire or hot drink." It was September 6, 1887, Bernard's twenty-second birthday.[33]

IT WAS QUIET at the Healy and Wilson Trading Post at Dyea. Mrs. Healy had trimmed the lamps for the evening and ground the coffee for tomorrow's breakfast. It was only six o'clock but the night had already crept in with the evening mist at half past four. Mrs. Healy could read the signs of winter. It had been raining all day at sea level and blowing hard from the southeast. If the temperature dropped, as it surely would, the rain would turn to snow and soon winter would be upon them. It was the way of the North, where the seasons change with startling suddenness.

The door of the post burst open and Moore and his son staggered in. They had eaten nothing but a few hardtack biscuits since crossing the Chilkoot summit. Their grub box was empty. At the trading post they told how, after stumbling across the bleak rock-strewn Chilkoot and fording rain-swollen streams, they reached the Taiya River where, by luck, they found a canoe. They had paddled downstream and had just arrived at Healy and Wilson's trading post, soaking wet and ravenously hungry. Mrs. Healy, known throughout the North as "the miners' and travellers' friend," provided them with a piping hot supper, which was consumed without conversation or interruption. "Never before had a meal tasted as good as this one," Bernard wrote. Because it was a special occasion, Mrs. Healy gave them some of her precious red currant jam made from berries she had picked and preserved.[34]

After dinner Healy listened intently to the Moores' tale of adventure. Except for the disquieting news about the crossing and naming of the White Pass, their stories were not unusual.

Like Moore, Healy had faith in the future of the land beyond the mountains. He, too, was sure that something was going to happen in the Yukon district, and when it did, he reasoned, his trading post would become a major base of supply. Already he and Wilson were the keepers of the gate to the interior, and regardless of what Moore and his son had to say about their White Pass route, he was convinced that keepers of the gate they would remain. Moore disagreed. He argued that the future of the Yukon interior could not depend on the narrow Chilkoot mountain trail. Not even mules could negotiate its tortuous grades. What was needed, Moore insisted, was a wagon road through the White Pass, starting at Skagway, where deep-sea ships could discharge their passengers and freight directly on to a proper wharf – unlike Dyea, where freight and passengers would have to be transferred from ship to the muddy beaches by barges and small boats. He was sure that the wagon road through the White Pass would be only a start. Later there would be a need for a railroad.[35]

They argued into the night. They became good friends, but both of them knew that one of them would be proved right and one of them would be proved wrong.

The following morning, Captain Moore and Bernard loaded a borrowed canoe and headed down Lynn Canal, arriving in Juneau after paddling ninety-five miles in eighteen hours and forty-five minutes. There, they bought supplies on credit and headed back to Skagway, arriving on October 29, 1887. They paddled up a creek for about a quarter of a mile and set up camp at the foot of a bluff.

They had arrived at the site of Moore's dream. Moore gazed around him and announced to his son and the silent wilderness, "Here we will cast our future lots and try to hew out our fortune. I fully expect before many years to see a pack trail through this pass, followed by a wagon road, and I would not be at all surprised to see a railroad through to the lakes."[36]

The next morning a thin layer of ice whitened the mouth of the creek. After a hasty breakfast, they paddled to the middle of the bay where, with a weighted cod line, they took soundings throughout the day. They confirmed that the rocky shoreline beneath the high granite bluff along the east side of the bay was the ideal location for their wharf. In the days that followed they began to build the wharf's foundation crib. They felled trees and rolled the trimmed logs to the wharf site where they were shaped, fitted, and bolted into place. As the crib rose in height, they filled it with heavy rocks to protect it from the tides and surging sea.

One day, Healy and Wilson arrived from Dyea. They could not conceal their interest in Moore's wharf, although they continued to insist that the gateway to the Yukon interior would always be through Dyea and the Chilkoot Pass. They pleaded with both of the Moores to abandon their White Pass scheme before they lost all of their remaining money, even their sanity. "It will never amount to anything as a route for supplies or traffic for the interior," Healy shouted, "and I feel sorry for you wasting your time here."[37]

The Moores stubbornly rejected Healy's and Wilson's critical comments, but they were forced to admit that their project would eventually require substantial capital. A way would have to be found to attract the interest of one or more governments. As well, they would need to induce financiers to invest in their proposed White Pass transportation scheme.

They reconnoitered the valley and posted notice of location for 160 acres of land, and beneath the east bluff they measured off a 600-foot strip of foreshore for their wharf. Finally, on November 12, 1887, they laid the foundation logs for a sixteen-by-sixteen-foot cabin, which they planned to complete the following year.

"We fully made up our minds to return early in the spring of 1888 and resume our work," Bernard recorded, "but to build our wharf out into any depth of water, a pile driver would be necessary, and this we could not think of getting because we had no funds to procure one."[38] As winter set in the Moores left Skagway and travelled to Juneau where they booked passage on the steamer *Sardonyx* bound for Victoria, arriving there dead broke on December 2, 1887.

During the next eight years, Captain Moore and Bernard shuttled from job to job, sometimes in Alaska, sometimes in British Columbia. Bernard worked in sawmills, canneries, and mines, while Captain Moore piloted ships, built boats, transported freight, and fished in Alaska waters for ten cents a fish.

The Moores' White Pass dream remained suspended between hope and reality: too far advanced to stop, but without the financial base to proceed. Skagway and the White Pass had consumed much of their energies and all of their savings, yet they had failed to generate any interest in the White Pass or to obtain any financial support.

Occasionally they were able to visit Skagway, sometimes together, sometimes alone. Throughout these years, despite occasional doubts, their fundamental belief in their property never diminished, and their promotion of the White Pass never ceased.

Two

THE MEN FROM ENGLAND

RNEST EDWARD BILLINGHURST, an English civil engineer associated with the Victoria law firm of Drake, Jackson, & Helmcken, had been keeping a close watch on mining activities in Alaska and the Yukon district for months. They appeared to be the sort of developments that might interest Charles Herbert Wilkinson, an agent for the British Columbia Development Association, Limited, who was due to arrive from England to investigate investment opportunities for himself and his British associates.

The "Syndicate" – the term used by Wilkinson for the British Columbia Development Association – had been incorporated in London on December 14, 1895, just two weeks before his departure for New York, San Francisco, and Victoria. Its principal shareholders included businessmen, members of the professions, British military officers, and gentlemen of independent means, including His Highness, Francis Duke of Teck, whose daughter later became Queen Mary when her husband was crowned George V. At the shareholders' initial deliberations in London, they had agreed that the West Coast of Canada was ripe for investment and development. The Syndicate's Memorandum of Association set out a long catalogue of objectives, the main ones being, "To develop the resources of British Columbia and to promote commercial and financial enterprise," as well as "organize and conduct the colonization of suitable emigrants from Great Britain and other countries."[1]

Billinghurst was in western Canada to prepare information for the Syndicate on resource-based business and investment opportunities. In this he was guided by Drake, Jackson, & Helmcken, who also acted as the Syndicate's legal counsel. During the course of his research, he had obtained a copy of N. Belleau Gauvreau's report on his explorations in the northern areas of British Columbia.

Gauvreau and his survey party, which included Captain Moore, had left Victoria on May 13, 1892, on the instructions of British Columbia's Surveyor-

34

General. They had sailed north on the steamer *Mexico*, arriving at Wrangell, Alaska, five days later. From there Gauvreau and his party of surveyors had travelled up the Stikine River on the steamboat *Alaskan* to Telegraph Creek where, with three men and six pack horses, they had carried out a track-survey of the Stikine valley and the White Pass. The White Pass survey had been conducted by one of Gauvreau's subordinates, who reported that the White Pass was impractical as a route to the interior. Gauvreau had endorsed this view in his report, stating that any trail would have to be cut from miles of solid rock and that "by the end of September this trail would be practically closed during the winter months because the excessive snow would make it too dangerous to use."

Billinghurst's views on the White Pass appeared to be equally pessimistic, as he drew point after point from Gauvreau's report. There was no question that Gauvreau saw little merit in the White Pass, observing that the "mountain sides are formed of slides, and the summit of the pass is treeless and desolate."[2] But Billinghurst had read of Captain Moore's exploits and opinions in the local newspapers and arranged to meet with him. During their discussion, he asked Moore for his personal knowledge of the White Pass and his opinion of Gauvreau's report.

Captain Moore detested the contents of Gauvreau's report because they refuted his own opinions about the White Pass. Moore was inclined to be testy at the best of times, but if anything was designed to send him into a rage, it was the section of the Gauvreau Report that dealt with the White Pass. Moore, with the assistance of a lawyer, had written a letter to British Columbia's Lieutenant-Governor, Edgar Dewdney, that was highly critical of Gauvreau's conclusions. "Mr. Gauvreau," his letter stated, "has never been through the pass himself and only derived his information concerning it from others. His report is, in many respects, erroneous and misleading and I am strongly at variance with what he sets forth."[3]

In many respects Moore's critical observations were justified, but because Gauvreau had been unwell and under severe pressure to complete his work before the end of the summer season, it had not been unreasonable for him to have sent his assistant, Omer Poudrier, to examine and report on the White Pass. Moore's implied suggestion that Gauvreau had acted unprofessionally by not personally examining the pass was unfair. Moore himself had examined the same pass for Ogilvie and all of his opinions and observations were included in Ogilvie's report and, rightly or wrongly, they had become part of the record.

Moore claimed that the Gauvreau Report was an inaccurate description of the White Pass, and he set out to convince Billinghurst that it was the most practical route to the Yukon interior. He dismissed the Stikine River route out of hand. "That river is one of the worst rivers for navigation in British Columbia." The Taku route was, in his opinion, hardly worth consideration. "The mouth of the Taku," he said, "is generally never free of icebergs." Moore admitted that the Chilkoot Pass was the shortest, "But it's the most dangerous of all. It has an altitude of 3,600 feet, and it's covered with perpetual snow." He also emphasized that this route had no harbour, just a long mud beach that would force steamers to lie at anchor in the open channel about two miles off shore. He insisted that the Yukon interior could never be adequately served by the Yukon River route via St. Michael. "You are looking at a 1,600 mile trip up the river by steamboat and . . . you can only run the riverboats when the river is free of ice."

Billinghurst listened quietly as Moore explained that there were two principal trading companies, both American-owned, working on the Yukon River, the Alaska Commercial Company and Captain Healy's North American Transportation & Trading Company, which Healy with a group of Chicago financiers had recently organized. They supported both the Alaskan and Yukon miners, he said, by bringing supplies *up* the river by steamboat from St. Michael during the few months when the river was not frozen over. "The earliest a miner can expect to receive his freight would be around the tenth or twentieth of June," Moore said, "his supplies having been shipped from San Francisco or Seattle the previous year. This means that the goods have been more than ten months in transit, and probably stored all winter in some warehouse at St. Michael, or stuck in the hold of a late-starting steamboat that got frozen-in three hundred miles up stream."

The two American trading companies could hardly expect an enthusiastic endorsement from Moore. Their riverboats operated out of St. Michael by travelling *up* the Yukon River. Moore's plan was to enter the Yukon district from Skagway, cross the White Pass, and haul freight and passengers by steamboat *down* the Yukon River to the Canadian gold camps and, if possible, on into Alaska. The Skagway-White Pass route would, he was convinced, provide a far superior and more economical freight service to the Yukon district and "with my plan it would be controlled by British interests, not American!"[4]

As he sketched the various alternative routes, he carefully weeded out any of their redeeming features, emphasizing a long catalogue of horrors the hapless miners would face if they chose any other route than the White Pass.

"There will be problems," he said. "The Alaska portion of the White Pass

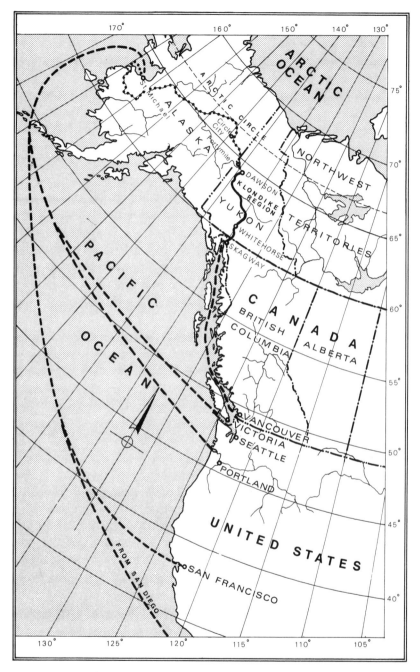

EARLY SEA ROUTES TO ALASKA AND THE YUKON
During the 1880s and 1890s, thousands of tons of mining supplies were
transported from West Coast ports to St. Michael, Alaska. In the summer
months, the freight was taken by sternwheel riverboats to the gold camps
along the Yukon River.

route will require very heavy construction work. Beyond the summit there are swamps that will have to be corduroyed, and timber for corduroying is scanty near the summit."

The advantages of the White Pass, according to Moore, far outstripped the disadvantages, which he regarded as relatively minor. First on Moore's list of five specific advantages was the undeniable fact that the White Pass was the most practical route for the construction of a pack trail from tidewater to the headwaters of the Yukon River. "Once the trail is completed to the navigable sources of the river, sternwheel riverboats can be brought into service," he said.

His second advantage was that the White Pass was an all-land route. There would be no need for canoes. His third advantage was that the trek from Skagway to Lake Bennett via the White Pass would not exceed forty miles, far less than any of the other routes, with the exception of Chilkoot Pass, which in Moore's opinion had no future – the hostile terrain making the construction of a usable wagon road through it virtually impossible. The fourth advantage on Moore's list was that the White Pass trail could be used for a much longer period in the season than any other route.

"My fifth advantage is that the White Pass possesses tidewater facilities for ocean-going vessels that can go right to the foot of the pass at Skagway, and land cargo any season of the year." Combined, his five advantages embodied his entire argument and showed that the irrepressible Captain Moore possessed a fundamental understanding of transportation economics. "For these five reasons," he argued, "the White Pass route would be the shortest and cheapest route for the transportation of supplies to the interior."[5]

Not all of Moore's information about the White Pass or the other routes was accurate. He had his mind set on the White Pass, which he truly believed would become the Yukon's primary transportation route, eventually connecting the Yukon to the sea through an ice-free port at Skagway Bay. He exaggerated, and at times he was a bore. But he was dedicated to the northlands and he never abandoned his belief that one day there would be a great gold rush to the Yukon River valley. The miners, he reasoned, would flood north to Skagway, where they would be greeted by the merchants and saloon-keepers who would be obliged to erect their buildings on his 160 acres of land.

"The Yukon basin," he told Billinghurst, "will be the largest gold producing country that has yet been discovered on the Pacific coast. . . . It's all through the valley," Moore argued, drawing more on faith and hope than facts. When facts were unavailable, he simply fell back on his dreams and spoke of them as if they were reality. "Out of the forty rivers emptying into the main Yukon there is not one that does not carry gold. Good prospects have been found along the

Yukon valley for roughly 1,900 miles, but until people have confidence that there will be ample supplies of the necessities of life, the Yukon's population will be limited."[6]

No reasoned discussion about the White Pass could avoid the question of the boundary. Moore insisted that as far as he was concerned both Skagway Bay and the White Pass were in Alaska, and in recognition of this he and his son had applied to American authorities for their 160 acres of land – not to Canadian officials in Ottawa. He attested that he had never heard of a British subject exercising any authority along the shores of Lynn Canal or at any point in the mountains north of Dyea and Skagway Bay.[7]

The whole Lynn Canal-White Pass area was still claimed by both Canada and the United States. In recent years some progress towards a resolution was being made. In November 1892, Canada and the United States had agreed to conduct a joint survey of the Alaska Panhandle the following year. This agreement resulted in eleven survey parties – four American and seven Canadian – working in predetermined field areas in the coastal mountains from Unik River in the south to Lynn Canal in the north.

By 1895, both Canadian and American surveyors had produced maps of the Panhandle delineating their respective boundaries, which to a large extent supported their own country's interpretation of the 1825 Treaty of St. Petersburg. Early in 1896 the maps were virtually complete and available to the governments of Canada, Britain, and the United States. The hope of resolving this issue evaporated as rancour and distrust refuelled the debate – a situation that left confusion and not a little bitterness in its wake.[8]

It was clear that the construction of a trail or a wagon road through the White Pass to the Yukon River would be a difficult and expensive undertaking. But Billinghurst was impressed by Moore's vision and thought that Moore's Skagway-White Pass proposals were worthy of further consideration. His immediate task was to produce a report based on Moore's information and the contents of his own file. He had little time. Wilkinson would be arriving in Victoria from London, England, in less than two weeks, seeking investment opportunities in British Columbia – a colonial frontier the Syndicate's shareholders regarded as a land of great opportunity, and the gateway to the Orient.

CHARLES HERBERT WILKINSON arrived in Victoria by steamer from San Francisco in January 1896 – the last leg of his journey from London.

Sailing ships and tall-funnelled steamers cluttered the piers along the shoreline and from them came the heady aroma of the harbour, a mixture of timber, tar, horses, and the sea. Lines of wagons loaded with cedar and fir lumber were backed up to the main street waiting to deliver their loads to the cavernous holds of the sailing ships. This was the pattern of Victoria's commercial life – ships and the sea. It was a welcome sight to Wilkinson. It aroused his business instincts.

Besides dabbling in finance, Wilkinson was an experienced contracting engineer who specialized in the construction of light railways and the development of electrical traction. In 1892, however, during the construction of the Bray and Enniskerry Railway in Ireland, he had been forced into bankruptcy by a series of financial misfortunes beyond his personal control. During the following three years, his solicitor constantly advised him to apply for discharge, a suggestion that he refused to accept. "I wish to come out of the bankruptcy court as I went in – with clean hands," was his persistent reply.

Early in 1895, Wilkinson had been approached by a London solicitor who offered him an opportunity to earn a substantial commission by arranging a loan of £450,000 for the British Columbia Development Association, Limited, an amount required for possible investments in British Columbia. Wilkinson accepted and induced a London business friend to underwrite the entire loan.

The Syndicate's directors were impressed, and when they began their search for an agent to handle their affairs in British Columbia, Wilkinson headed their list. Now, after only a few weeks' employment as a principal agent, Charles Herbert Wilkinson, an undischarged bankrupt, had arrived in Victoria to conduct the Syndicate's affairs.[9]

Wilkinson had no difficulty in picking Billinghurst out of the crowd at the foot of the gangway. He was well acquainted with the Billinghurst family in England, particularly Ernest's brother, Henry Farcome Billinghurst, who was involved in the Syndicate's affairs in Britain.

As they drove by horse-drawn cab to the hotel, Victoria came into sharper focus. There was a great deal of mud but the sidewalks gave the street a sense of order and design. An open electric tramcar rumbled along the street, carrying townspeople and Royal Navy sailors from the British naval base at nearby Esquimalt. Ship chandlery shops, lumber mills, commission stores, and wholesale warehouses dotted the main thoroughfares. Several impressive church spires split the horizon and the city's new Board of Trade Building loomed over Bastion Square. Telephone poles, heavy with cross arms and wire, parallelled the streets, although the telephone itself was still regarded by some as a tedious intrusion that, mercifully, would not last.[10] The city was very much alive and displayed a unique mixture of influences: the forest and the sea, business and government – the whole creating an atmosphere that was half Victorian and half new frontier. And in its midst rose the new provincial legislative building, as beautiful and impressive a structure as any on the North American continent.

Their cab passed the Victoria Theatre and stopped on the corner of Broad and View streets. Wilkinson and Billinghurst entered the Driard, the city's most luxurious hotel, said to be second in elegance only to the Pacific Hotel in San Francisco.

It had been a long and tedious journey for Wilkinson. Now, his task was to determine where to place the Syndicate's funds, and he looked to Billinghurst to help him do that.

THERE WAS LITTLE DOUBT in Wilkinson's mind that Billinghurst was sincere in his belief that Moore's proposals for the White Pass should be investigated, but he had already decided that the whole concept was painfully lacking in detail, despite Billinghurst's impressive file on the subject. On the surface the scheme looked promising, but he was aware that even well-intentioned people are capable of going off half cocked.

Despite Billinghurst's optimism, Wilkinson was not convinced that the number of miners travelling from the head of Lynn Canal to the headwaters of the Yukon River justified the construction of a simple pack trail through the White Pass, let alone a road or a railroad. Yet, if the number of miners increased as a result of a major gold discovery, the prime investors in Moore's White Pass transportation scheme would be in a position to reap a handsome profit, and finding profitable investments was his sole reason for being in western Canada. Further, Wilkinson knew he was in a good position as Moore was virtually broke and had little to bargain.

"If the White Pass is the only place to build a wagon road, or a railroad," Wilkinson wondered, "why do the miners still elect to tramp over the Chilkoot Pass?"

Drawing on Moore's arguments, Billinghurst explained that the Chilkoot Pass had been the Indian's traditional route into the interior country and, in recent times, had been promoted for business reasons by the proprietors of Healy and Wilson's trading post at Dyea. While the Chilkoot is shorter, Billinghurst went on, it is said to be much steeper and higher than the White Pass, and neither a road nor a railroad could be built through it. He explained that Moore was convinced that the eventual discovery of gold was a certainty, and the only place to build a trail or a wagon road or a railroad to support the coming rush to the gold fields would be through the White Pass.

Wilkinson could not conceal his lack of enthusiasm. He had come to the conclusion that Moore and his son Bernard were chasing rainbows and that Billinghurst was on the verge of taking leave of his senses. To start with, there were too many unanswered questions. Who owned the land around the tip of Lynn Canal – Britain or the United States? Where was the international boundary line between Alaska and British Columbia to be located? What about the existing transportation facilities? Was it reasonable to expect that the Moores' plan to outflank two well-established Yukon River transportation companies operating out of St. Michael could possibly succeed? Gold rush or no gold rush, where was the business that could possibly justify the expense of Moore's White Pass project?

Although Wilkinson had quickly grasped the significance of the proposal, he found it vague and perplexing. Yet he could not deny that the whole scheme had an element of adventure. The great British companies in India and South Africa had earned their original shareholders huge returns on their investments. Was it possible that a great northern company, operating in the Dominion of Canada's western sub-arctic regions could accomplish the same? An exciting idea, but at this stage all of his information was second-hand. To obtain a better understanding of the proposal, he asked Billinghurst to arrange a meeting with Moore.

Wilkinson then turned his attention to other promising areas for investment, travelling to the Kootenay and Cariboo regions of British Columbia. There he investigated mining opportunities – gold and coal. Along the coast he saw possibilities in forest management, logging, sawmills, and lumber. Beyond the coastal mountains he found gaps in the transportation system he believed could be closed by constructing light railways that would connect remote southern British Columbia communities to the Canadian Pacific Railway's main line. But the proposal that intrigued him most of all was Moore's railway to the mysterious Yukon – an enigma about which he had virtually no facts at all.

CAPTAIN MOORE WAS seventy-four when he met Wilkinson, yet his energy belied his years. He was still headstrong, aggressive, and ambitious. When he met with Wilkinson, Billinghurst, and H. Dallas Helmcken, QC, he covered in even greater detail the information he had given Billinghurst during their first meeting. The broad sweep of his plan to develop a competitive transportation system to supply the Yukon interior country emerged with greater clarity. His maps, his stabbing finger, his knowledge of the northern country, his sheer persistence brought the White Pass plan into much sharper focus.

As the meeting progressed, however, Wilkinson became aware of Moore's inclination to generalize when details were lacking. Sometimes he spoke of a pack trail through the White Pass. At other times he referred to a road, or a wagon road, and occasionally a railroad. Clearly, Moore saw his White Pass transportation route as a progressive undertaking, with events dictating the speed of its ultimate development.

There was a certain logic in what Moore had to say, which Wilkinson understood despite his doubts. Meeting the colourful and persistent Moore was an experience in itself, as he had the capacity to give the project a dimension that neither Billinghurst nor his file of papers could convey.

"I tell you that away up there, surrounding the headwaters of the Yukon River, 2,000 miles from its mouth, there is a grand and beautiful land, but it's barred to all but the most hardy men because there are no trails into the region."[11]

Moore, of course, was overstating his case. There were already primitive but well-established trails and routes into the Yukon district, and some 1,500 prospectors were working its sandbars and creeks – especially those on Fortymile River. And in Alaska, Circle City was growing month by month. Moore, who claimed that all but the hardiest of men would be barred from the North, had assured Billinghurst that there would soon be 30,000 miners toiling in the Yukon district. "It is not to my personal advantage to speak in glowing language of the place," he said, "for land is there for the asking. I have nothing to boom. But I know of no part of the world where there are such boundless possibilities for young men."[12]

The facts as Wilkinson saw them at the conclusion of the meeting were now reasonably clear. The Yukon district was attracting increasing numbers of miners each year. At present, those operating in the Yukon district bought most of their commercial supplies from the Alaska Commercial Company and John Healy's North American Transportation & Trading Company, both of which were based in St. Michael near the mouth of the Yukon River. But this supply source was limited because the Lower Yukon River in Alaska, served from St. Michael, was closed by ice for approximately seven months of each year. On the other hand, the Upper Yukon River in the Yukon district was closed only six months of each year because of the earlier ice break-up in the river's upper region. This gave any supply and freighting system operating on the Upper Yukon River a distinct advantage.

The Chilkoot Pass remained a competitive deterrent to opening up the White Pass, but its future was limited because neither a road nor a railway could be constructed through it without, as Moore is said to have stated, "building a tunnel eleven miles long."[13] Besides its physical advantages, the White Pass route offered the possibility of supplying miners working in Canadian territory through a Canadian-controlled transportation system. Later, this system would be in a good position to serve Alaskan communities along the Lower Yukon River, thereby challenging the two established American transportation companies that now held a virtual monopoly on both Alaskan and Yukon passenger freight service.

Should this grand scheme proposed by Moore ever materialize, Skagway would become the key link in the chain – and, according to Moore, he controlled 160 acres of Skagway land that spread across the entrance to the White Pass itself. Anyone using the White Pass would have to cross Moore's land. The plan made sense, although Wilkinson was forced to admit that there would be difficult problems to overcome – sovereignty being one of the most serious. The immediate question, however, was the likelihood of Moore's predicted gold rush. Unless gold was discovered in quantity, none of the routes into the North would prosper for long.

It was now clear to Wilkinson that the key to the success of Moore's plan was the discovery of a major gold-field in Alaska or the Yukon interior. Should this occur, the development of a transportation system through the White Pass could generate substantial profits for its investors. After conferring with Billinghurst and Helmcken, Wilkinson concluded that the Syndicate's interests could best be served by investing a modest sum in Moore's White Pass project. For this support, he insisted that Moore be required to sign over a substantial interest in his Skagway land and wharf.

He subsequently proposed this possibility to Moore, who accepted the idea without argument. From Moore's point of view, this was not the time to haggle over details. It was the first convincing expression of faith he had received since he first conceived the White Pass transportation plan in 1887.[14]

The following two days were spent assessing Moore's plan. But, apart from what Moore had told Wilkinson and Billinghurst, they actually knew nothing about the pass itself. Before a decision of any consequence could be made, Wilkinson decided that someone with engineering experience and a good pair of legs must travel north to examine the Chilkoot Pass and the White Pass and return to Victoria with an unbiased report. Because Billinghurst was the only one present who possessed Wilkinson's two basic qualifications, he was instructed to leave as soon as possible and inspect the two passes. On his return he was to provide a report on which a reasoned decision could be based.[15]

BILLINGHURST LEFT VICTORIA for Alaska early in March 1896. After a short stop at Juneau, where he made a number of inquiries, he arrived at Dyea and found accommodation at Healy and Wilson's trading post. The country was very much as Moore had described it: the flat beachlands; the incredible mountain barrier pierced by the two passes that had become the subject of government reports, correspondence, and meetings, as well as a source of conflict between miners and packers, entrepreneurs and governments, Moore and Gauvreau. Tents dotted the landscape. A few miners and their Indian packers were preparing for the long and difficult climb to the Chilkoot summit.

After hiring a guide, Billinghurst faced the mountains and entered the forest north of Dyea. The trail led up the Taiya River and into a forty-foot-wide canyon that wound and twisted for four miles. Here he first became conscious of the grade. At the end of the canyon, huge mountain spurs blocked his view of the summit. As they pushed on, he noticed a number of fresh snowslides, which suggested potential danger to miners and packers. So far he had found no sign of a natural grade suitable for the construction of a wagon road, let alone a railway. The trail was so difficult that even pack horses could not be used beyond the lower regions.

Small groups of miners and packers were coming and going. Mounds of supplies covered with freshly fallen snow were piled here and there along the way, their owners having returned to a lower camp to manhandle another 100-pound pack up the frozen trail. It was back-breaking work. It did not take Billinghurst long to realize that the winter way across the Chilkoot was a frigid snowbound trail of pain, chilblains, and sweat. Moore's description appeared to be close to the truth.

Right from the early days, it had been said that some miles are longer than others on the Chilkoot, and so they seemed to Billinghurst as he approached the head of the valley. In the distance rose a sheer wall of solid ice and rock that appeared to bar the way to the summit. Gradually the grade became steeper until it reached an angle of thirty-five degrees, forcing him at times to climb on all fours. As he gained altitude, the horizon slowly lowered, finally revealing at the summit a broad blue backdrop of snow-covered mountains. To the south he could see the thrust of the Taiya valley stretching to the head of Lynn Canal and the sea. To the north lay Moore's domain of endless opportunities, his land of gold.

Billinghurst searched the landscape. The clouds pressed against the peaks and the mists billowed and swirled through the valleys. It was cold and desolate. As he surveyed the scene, he was satisfied that Moore's assessment was correct. A railroad could not be built through the Chilkoot Pass unless someone financed the construction of a long tunnel through the mountain beneath the pass itself.

He turned and retraced his steps, arriving at Dyea with his packer after an absence of four days, convinced that the Syndicate should not invest one penny in the Chilkoot Pass.

Billinghurst then travelled by canoe to Skagway Bay. There he found everything very much as described by Moore: the cabin, the half-completed wharf, the sheltered deep-water harbour. After inspecting Moore's land, he and his packer entered the Skagway River valley and headed for the summit of the pass, fourteen miles in a direct line to the north. Unlike the Chilkoot Pass, the White Pass offered no established trail, and while the overall grade was less onerous than the Chilkoot, it was still heavy going, and much of it had to be climbed on snowshoes. He avoided the surrounding hills and cliffs by following the course of the Skagway River. Soon, some of the advantages of the White Pass became apparent. There did not appear to be any serious obstacles barring the way – at least not along the lower levels. As they snowshoed further into the pass, Billinghurst could find none of the barriers described by Gauvreau in his report, although it was much more difficult than he had imagined from Moore's description. Thousands of tons of granite would have to be blasted from the cliffs and mountain spurs before a railway could be built through it.

On the other hand, a wagon road could be punched through faster and for far less cost than a railway. And it could be ready to transport miners' freight and supplies through to Lake Bennett months before railway construction had reached the summit of the pass.

At the White Pass summit, Billinghurst looked south towards the sea. The bewildering maze of natural features again cast shadows of doubt across his mind. Ice-crusted mountain peaks joined by jagged saw-tooth ridges seemed to fill the sky. Glaciers shouldered their way through the mountain massifs, and below them the snow flowed in blue-white folds to the timberline and on into the coastal forest. Viewed from the summit, the White Pass, with its flying buttresses of rock, its sheer cliffs rising hundreds of feet from the valley floor, its chaotic piles of splintered granite, its gorges, gaps, chasms, and rifts, seemed invincible. And through all of this must be carved a smooth and gradual grade, much of it constructed during the dark and frigid months of winter under dangerous and exhausting conditions.

The wind swirled the snow into rock-hard drifts. Ice crystals hung in the air. It was cold and silent and forbidding. The problems seemed insurmountable. Billinghurst was comforted somewhat by the knowledge that he was not charged with the responsibility of deciding whether or not to proceed with the project. His job was to check Moore's report and to determine by personal survey the better of two routes from tidewater to the head of river navigation. Billinghurst and his guide shouldered their packs and started their descent to Skagway Bay.

From what he had seen and experienced, he was confident that the White Pass was superior to the Chilkoot Pass in every respect. He recognized that constructing a railway through it would be a demanding, difficult, and costly task, but he believed that, if attacked yard by yard, it could be conquered by competent surveyors and engineers, provided the project was properly financed – and given a nod from Lady Luck.

WILKINSON AND HELMCKEN were impressed with Billinghurst's report. The young engineer was observant, articulate, and enthusiastic about the role he was playing in assessing the relative merits of the two main passes that connected the Yukon valley to the sea. According to Billinghurst, a successful wagon road would never be built through the Chilkoot Pass, let alone a railroad. He could find nothing to recommend it. As a packer's trail it was acceptable, but the Chilkoot Pass was incapable of development as a heavily mechanized transportation artery.

On the other hand, Billinghurst reported, the White Pass appeared to offer better opportunities for the construction of a wagon road or a railroad. He acknowledged that there would be difficulties – some of them of a most serious nature – but none that could not be overcome by innovative surveyors and engineers. There was a natural grade through the pass, which also had the advantage of being hundreds of feet lower than the Chilkoot. He described both harbours in considerable detail and recommended that, if deep-sea ships were to be served, the Skagway harbour location would prove to be far superior to the muddy tidal flats of Dyea.

While in Skagway, he had inspected the Moore wharf and cabin and had decided that much heavy construction would be required before Skagway could offer terminal facilities to ocean-going freighters and passenger ships. He had paced off most of Moore's land and found that it was perfectly situated to accommodate Moore's townsite. In fact, everything Moore had said about the Chilkoot Pass, Dyea, Skagway Bay, and the White Pass was substantially correct. On the basis of available evidence, plus what he had seen with his own eyes, Billinghurst cast an unreserved vote for the White Pass.[16]

Wilkinson was now satisfied that he could rely on Moore's information on the relative merits of the White Pass and Chilkoot Pass. There now appeared to be little doubt that if a wagon road or a railway was to be constructed from Lynn Canal to the interior country, it should be built through the White Pass – not the Chilkoot. One nagging question, however, was Moore's predicted gold rush. When was it going to happen? Or was it already under way?

During Billinghurst's absence in the North, Wilkinson had examined these questions and he was encouraged by the increasing number of miners moving into Alaska and the Yukon district every year. There was also constant talk of gold, and while Moore's strike had not yet materialized, the persistent rumours of gold along the Yukon, Stewart, and Pelly rivers could not be ignored. Fortymile River itself had been a gold-producer of considerable stature since 1886. St. Michael, at the mouth of the Yukon River, was flourishing to such an extent that the municipal fathers of Juneau had become apprehensive about their city losing its position as the North's major business centre. To protect their interests, they had asked the United States federal government to construct an overland road from Juneau to the Yukon interior. The *Juneau City Mining Record* commented, "In consequence of a wholesome dread to fight the strong current up the Yukon River, from St. Michael, a road to the interior will help Juneau grow quite populous."

The Alaska Commercial Company was extending its river services year by year, and now the North American Transportation & Trading Company, which had been operating on the Yukon River for less than four years, was giving the Alaska Commercial Company its first effective competition. Sternwheel riverboat construction was increasing to keep pace with the growing business generated by the miners. Alaska gold production was growing year by year. Early in 1896, the Alaska Commercial Company alone had shipped $1.5 million in gold to San Francisco through its Circle City store. Circle City itself now boasted of more than three hundred log cabins, and its stature was such that the *Chicago Daily Record* had dispatched reporter Omer Maris there solely to keep its Midwest readers informed about the handsome profits being gleaned by enterprising Americans who were willing to head north, don a wool shirt, a miner's hat, and muck for gold.[17] Many early Alaskan gold-seekers referred to Circle City as "the Paris of Alaska" because, besides two huge warehouses, it sported a music hall, two theatres, eight dance halls, and twenty-eight saloons.

Across the border, the Canadian community of Fortymile was flourishing. It had a store where one could buy anything from beans to paté de foie gras and tinned plum pudding. A log opera house, complete with a troupe of dance girls from San Francisco, offered nightly entertainment, and ten saloons provided the citizens with "steamboat" whisky or locally distilled hootch for fifty cents a shot. Paris fashions were on sale at the dressmaker's shop, and a bawdy house known locally as the Cigar Factory offered the lonely miners comfort for an ounce or so of gold.[18] Since July 1895, Inspector Charles Constantine of the North-West Mounted Police, with two officers, a customs collector, and twenty NCOs and men, had firmly established an official Canadian presence in the community of Fortymile and its environs. And an upswing in river traffic could not be ignored. The North American Transportation & Trading Company had already established Fort Cudahy across the river from Fortymile, and the Alaska Commercial Company was strongly established in Fortymile itself.

The answer was becoming clear to Wilkinson. The annual increase in gold production in Alaska and the Yukon district was bound to fuel business activity during the coming years. Given this possibility, why transport the Yukon district's supplies all the way to St. Michael and *up* the Yukon River against the current when they could be transported more quickly through the White Pass and *down* the Yukon River to Fortymile and beyond into Alaska?

After just three months of investigation, Wilkinson listed his recommendations on investment opportunities in a letter to the directors of the Syndicate, dated April 12, 1896. He regarded a number of the investment opportunities as singularly attractive, but, in his opinion, the construction of a light railway from Lynn Canal to the head of Yukon River navigation at Lake Bennett would be the best investment of all. This was his prime recommendation – a railway to serve the thousands of square miles of Canadian and American northern territory that he predicted would become one of the great gold-producing areas of the world.[19]

Wilkinson had, so far, fully justified the confidence placed in him by the Syndicate's directors. After only a few months of inquiry, he was in a position to submit a comprehensive report, which targeted business opportunities in widely diversified areas of British Columbia, Alaska, and the Yukon interior. But, despite his accomplishments, he was troubled by a nagging sense of unease. While in Victoria he had learned that other transportation men were aware of the growing activities in the North and were already assessing the possibility of constructing their own railways through the White Pass to the

Yukon interior, the most prominent being Captain John Irving of the Canadian Pacific Navigation Company, with whom Wilkinson had become friends.

To avoid being out-manoeuvred by Irving or anyone else, Wilkinson decided that the Syndicate's interests needed to be protected by the incorporation of three separate companies. The first would be an American company authorized to operate a railway through the White Pass from Skagway Bay to the international boundary which, when settled, would form the border between Alaska and British Columbia. The second company, formed under the laws of British Columbia, would authorize railway operations across the northwest corner of the province. The third company, incorporated under the federal laws of Canada, would authorize railway operations from the northern border of British Columbia into the Yukon interior. He reasoned that after forming the companies and obtaining the necessary authorities from Washington, D.C., Ottawa, and Victoria, there would be no doubt that the Syndicate had established prior rights to construct and operate a railway from salt water on the Pacific Coast to the Yukon interior via the White Pass and Lake Bennett.

He decided to set the plan in motion on his own initiative, without any reference to the Syndicate's directors. In his opinion, interminable correspondence with London would simply invite delay. And any delay could upset a scheme that was beginning to germinate in the deepest reaches of his mind.

Three

A PAPER RAILWAY

ITHIN TEN DAYS of dispatching his list of suggested investments to
London, Wilkinson was in Seattle conferring with officials of the
Great Northern Railway and the Seattle law firm of Burke, Shepherd
& McGilvra. His objective was to determine the *sine qua non* of the
construction and operation of a railway across a strip of land north of
Lynn Canal that was claimed Alaskan territory by the United States.

He was advised by the solicitors that he could incorporate a company in any
state of the union and then apply to the United States government for the land
required for railway shops, stations, freight yards, and a railway right-of-way.
He was also assured that there would be no need to apply for a charter: the
Articles of Incorporation, when signed and filed in accordance with the law,
would constitute the charter of the company.[1]

The next pressing problem was to reach an accord with Captain Moore, a
responsibility Wilkinson assigned to Billinghurst. During May 1896, Billinghurst and Moore reached an agreement that provided the Moores with limited
financial support for the development of their wharf and land in Skagway. The
funds were to be advanced by a group of investors whom Billinghurst refused
to identify. The extent of the investment, Moore was advised, would be limited
to the amount required to complete current construction and would not exceed
$1,450 for the purchase of two horses, two cows, and 6,000 feet of rough
lumber. In addition, the Moores would receive moneys sufficient to employ five
men at Skagway for the rest of 1896. In consideration of these funds, Moore
promised to have the land surveyed and to obtain a valid title. He also agreed
to deliver a mortgage to Billinghurst to secure this and any future financial
support.[2]

Through this agreement, a 75-per-cent interest in the Moores' Skagway
assets eventually came under the control of the Alaskan and North Western
Territories Trading Company, an as yet unincorporated entity that had been

hastily organized on behalf of the Syndicate by Wilkinson, with the assistance of D. Noble Rowan, a West Virginia businessman who had substantial connections and influence in Washington, D.C.

With the Moore agreement completed, Wilkinson returned to Seattle to confer with lawyer H.G. Struve and draw up Articles of Incorporation for the Pacific and Arctic Railway and Navigation Company. The objects of the company, which was subsequently formed under the laws of the State of Washington, were to locate, construct, equip, and operate a railroad and telephone and telegraph lines from Skagway to Summit Lake at the top of White Pass – the point selected as the probable location of the international boundary.

The boundary question, unfortunately, was an unresolved issue that would plague Wilkinson for months to come. Where was it to be? Would Skagway be in Canada or the United States?

The Treaty of St. Petersburg, signed in 1825 by Great Britain and Russia, failed to describe accurately the boundary between the 141st meridian and the Portland Canal – a line roughly parallelling the coast of southeast Alaska, which would, when established, create the Alaska Panhandle. Disagreement over the interpretation of the words "sinuosities" and "headlands" – two treaty words describing the location of this specific section of the boundary – had escalated into a continuing dispute between Canada and the United States. Acting on Canada's behalf, Britain still claimed that, under the terms of the treaty, the boundary should intersect Lynn Canal some fifty-five miles south of Skagway. This would place both Skagway and Dyea within Canada – although all of this disputed territory was firmly occupied and held by the Americans.[3] The United States, having purchased Alaska from the Russians in 1867, insisted that the treaty of St. Petersburg placed Skagway and Dyea well within Alaska. Some Americans, however, claimed that the boundary should be marked as far north as the southern tip of Lake Bennett.[4] Wilkinson and his advisers decided that the Pacific and Arctic Railway and Navigation Company and the two yet-to-be incorporated Canadian companies must obtain rights and charters capable of maintaining their validity regardless of where Canada and the United States finally drew the international boundary line.

Wilkinson then returned to Victoria, where he completed his initial assessment of British Columbia business opportunities for the Syndicate. He also laid plans with Helmcken to incorporate a railway company under the laws of British Columbia, again setting out the difficulties associated with the border question. Should Skagway be recognized as a Canadian port, it would be situated in British Columbia. The Pacific and Arctic Railway and Navigation

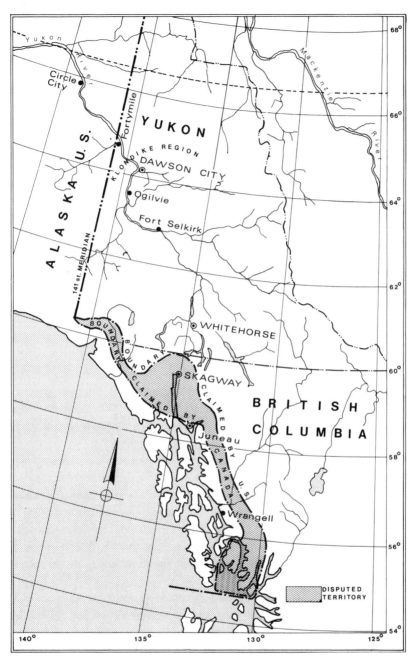

THE BOUNDARY DISPUTE

Throughout the last two decades of the nineteenth century, the precise location of the international boundary south of the 141st parallel was in dispute, generating political tensions between Canada, Great Britain, and the United States. The dispute was not resolved until 1903, three years after the railway was completed.

Company would then be unnecessary, and Washington, D.C., would no longer be a factor in Wilkinson's White Pass railway scheme.

WITH THE FINANCES provided by the Syndicate's Alaskan and North Western Territories Trading Company, the Moores made steady progress with their land developments in Skagway. They slashed clearings out of the forest for a sawmill, a trading post, and a warehouse. The first cabins were erected – one for Bernard and his young family and one for Captain Moore.

To support his wife and his Victoria residence, Captain Moore contracted with the Canadian postmaster general to complete three mail trips to and from Fortymile during the spring and summer of 1896. He had left Dyea on August 29 on the last of his three trips and had arrived at Fortymile during the second week in September.[5] There he learned that, during the previous month, George Carmack and his two Indian companions, Skookum Jim and Tagish Charlie, had discovered gold on Rabbit Creek, a tributary of the Klondike River.

William Ogilvie, who was waiting at Fortymile for instructions from Ottawa, had witnessed the local rush to Rabbit Creek. Throughout the winter of 1895-96, he had been engaged in surveying the 141st meridian and had completed his season's work on April 12.[6] His departure at that time, however, had been delayed by spring floods on the Yukon River. While Ogilvie waited for the high water to subside, Moore had arrived in Fortymile on one of his early trips with the Canadian mail.

A letter to Ogilvie from his department chief informed him that the Canadian government was negotiating with the United States government to appoint a joint commission that would establish the international boundary from the Pacific Ocean to the High Arctic. The letter further informed Ogilvie that he had been appointed Canadian representative on the joint commission and that he was to remain in the Yukon district and await further instructions. "This precluded all thought of going out till fall, if not later," wrote a somewhat forlorn Ogilvie.[7]

He had waited anxiously all summer for further direction but none came until the middle of September, when Moore arrived on the last of his three mail trips. The long-awaited letter from Ottawa informed him that the boundary negotiations with the United States had failed to produce an agreement and that he was to return to Ottawa "with all possible dispatch."[8]

But on the day of his departure the central Yukon district was struck by a violent storm that lasted for three days. Ogilvie was forced to cancel his departure, and by the end of October, winter had set in.

As a result of these two delayed departures, Ogilvie was among the first to learn of the gold strike on Rabbit Creek and was one of the few official observers of the tumultuous days that followed.

Some three weeks after the gold strike, Ogilvie, on September 6, 1896, dispatched a letter to Canada's surveyor general via the Alaska Commercial Company's riverboat *Alice*. "I am very pleased to inform you that a most important discovery of gold has been made on a river known here as the Klondike. You can fancy the excitement here. It is claimed that from $100 to $500 per day can be made off the ground that has been prospected so far."[9]

Moore's arrival at Fortymile within a month of the gold strike was another extravagant intrusion of fate. The discovery was a vindication of his prophecies about gold in the Yukon. Nearly ten years had passed since he had predicted that there would be a major strike in the Yukon River valley. Now, in the late summer and early fall of 1896, he was present to witness the unfolding of the predictions he had repeated to the point of boredom. Judging from the frantic activity, his predictions had all come true. But it would be months before news of the discovery would reach the outside world.

Locally, the discovery was expected. During the summer of 1896 an estimated 300–500 miners had worked in the Yukon district.[10] They were strung out along the creeks and rivers that lace the Yukon valley, working the sandbars, digging, panning, searching, moving from place to place, all the while alert to snippets of gossip about gold-bearing gravel in newly explored gulches, rivers, and creeks.

These early miners simply *knew* that the gold was there. It would only be a matter of time, they reasoned, before someone would strike it rich. Bob Henderson from Big Island, Nova Scotia, had already panned out $600 in gold on Quartz Creek, a tributary of the Indian River. Some miners were even aware of his latest strike on Gold Bottom Creek, where he panned out $750 in gold – the first gold of any consequence gleaned from a creek that flowed into the Klondike River.[11] It was Henderson who had set Carmack and his two companions on the road to discovery. During a chance meeting at Carmack's fish and logging camp at the confluence of the Yukon and Klondike rivers, Henderson, honouring the miners' code, invited Carmack to join him on Gold Bottom Creek and stake a claim. Twenty days later, after completing their fishing and logging operations at the camp, Carmack, Jim, and Charlie had made their way up Rabbit Creek and across a steep divide to Henderson's claim on Gold Bottom. Meeting with little success there, they decided to return to the mouth of the Klondike via Rabbit Creek after first promising Henderson that they would send a message to him if they discovered gold. On their return journey to their fish and logging camp, they found the gold on Rabbit Creek.

Carmack, Jim, and Charlie stood transfixed; three pairs of eyes riveted on the grains of gold that curved around the bottom of the pan. This was not the usual smudge of colour. This was a clean line of gold that they could touch and move around with their fingers – a quarter of an ounce worth four dollars in cold hard cash.[12]

The following day, they tested the gravel to find the richest area to stake. After choosing their ground, they argued about who would stake Discovery Claim. Under Canadian mining law, no man could stake more than one claim in a mining district, the only exception being the discoverer, who was permitted to stake two claims side by side. Carmack staked two claims for himself because, he later insisted, he discovered the gold. According to Jim, however, the two Discovery claims were staked by Carmack only because he had convinced Jim that an Indian would never be recognized as a discoverer. The matter was finally resolved by all agreeing that Carmack would stake and record Discovery Claim and assign a half interest in it to Jim, a compromise strongly suggesting that Jim's subsequent contention that he was the one who discovered the gold was probably correct. Having settled on this plan, Carmack staked Discovery Claim and Number One below Discovery Claim on the morning of August 17, 1896. Number Two below Discovery was staked for Charlie and Number One above was allotted to Jim.[13]

The gold they had panned was carefully poured into a spent Winchester rifle cartridge, and after a final examination of their claims, they hoisted their packs and set off for their camp at the mouth of the Klondike River, eleven miles away.[14]

A short distance downstream they encountered four hungry Nova Scotians who had been prospecting all summer without success. They told Carmack that they had heard rumours of Henderson's strike and asked him if he knew where it was. Carmack said that he did, but boasted that he knew of a far better location and to prove it he showed them the cartridge filled with gold. After receiving directions, David McKay, Harold Waugh, Daniel McGilvray, and David Edwards scrambled up Rabbit Creek and staked claims that eventually earned them a fortune.[15]

Suddenly the land was alive with men. Two days later, on August 19, Edward Monahon and Gregory Stewart staked on Rabbit Creek, and the following day

D. Edwards, J. Moffat, D. Robertson, and C. Kimball arrived on the scene and hammered in their stakes. By August 22, just five days after Carmack had staked Discovery Claim, fifty men were wandering about on Rabbit Creek staking claims or looking for Henderson's camp on Gold Bottom.[16]

At the mouth of the Klondike River, Carmack, Jim, and Charlie prepared their raft of logs for the trip down the Yukon River to the sawmill at Fortymile. But already they were becoming concerned by the number of men heading for Rabbit Creek. Jim returned to Rabbit Creek to guard their claims, while Carmack and Charlie rafted their logs to Fortymile.

On the way, Carmack told his story to everyone he encountered. A few who knew him called him a damn liar and brushed his yarn aside. But new arrivals, eager for any story that held a few dollars' worth of hope, bundled up their outfits and headed for Rabbit Creek. When some demanded proof, Carmack would pour the gold from his Winchester cartridge.[17] There was the proof, he would shout. They would regret it if they did not believe him!

As soon as he arrived at Fortymile, Carmack headed for Bill McPhee's saloon and announced to the crowd at the bar that he was the bearer of good news. "There is a big strike up the river," he exclaimed. Most of those present did not believe him. They had heard Carmack's boastful yarns before and, because so many of them had proved false, were inclined not to believe this latest story. Sensing their disbelief, he pulled out his rifle cartridge with a flourish, emptied the gold onto the bar scales, and shouted, "How does that look to you?"[18]

The men gathered close to scrutinize Carmack's gold. Could there be truth in his wild and implausible tale? The gold looked different from Miller Creek gold, or the gold from Davis Creek or Glacier Creek. It was different in texture, colour, and shape. It must have come from *somewhere*.

A hush spread through the bar. One by one, the miners moved toward the door and out into the night. The surrounding cabins quietly emptied and the neighbouring saloons grew quiet as Carmack's tale of gold spread through the community of Fortymile. Drunks were rolled from the bunks by their partners or returned to the land of the living with a well-aimed bucket of water. Outfits piled up on the river banks as men gathered around the boats. In ones and twos and threes they embarked. Each boat slowly pulled upstream beneath the willows that dipped into the grey waters of the Yukon River. The rush to the Klondike from Fortymile had started. George Washington Carmack was the man of the hour in the fading summer days of August 1896.[19]

The miners from Fortymile were among the first to disturb the silence of the Klondike valley, but others soon followed as the news of the strike on Rabbit Creek spread up and down the Yukon River valley. Within a matter of days, the irresistible pull of gold had exerted its terrible influence. Miners paddled and poled along the Yukon River to the mouth of the Klondike. Abandoning their boats and rafts, they wallowed through a growing sea of mud along the banks of Rabbit Creek, their shouts shattering the peace of the surrounding hills. They pounded in their stakes. They argued and cursed, and some even prayed as they frantically searched the wooded landscape for ground that looked rich, panned rich, and had been blessed by Midas himself. Each new arrival compounded the confusion. A nightmare staking spree saw the same ground claimed by one, then another, and again by a third. Some claims overlapped, some were jumped. Conflict spread the length and breadth of the valley.

Many oldtimers had their doubts. The valley was too wide for gold, they said. But to the frenzied stakers, future prospects looked so promising that at a miners' meeting they changed the name of the creek from Rabbit to Bonanza – a name more fitting for a creek they believed would produce millions in gold dust and nuggets.[20]

Throughout September gold fever rampaged through the Upper Yukon valley, infecting every camp and cabin and producing a kind of insanity in everyone it touched. By the end of the month, newly named Bonanza Creek was staked solid from its source to its confluence with the Klondike River, a distance of fourteen miles.

The rush intensified. Miners, scrambling to stake, flooded along a tributary of Bonanza – first called "Bonanza's Pup," but soon to become known as Eldorado Creek. At the time, no one realized that Eldorado was the richest placer creek in the world. Virtually every claim from Number One to Number Forty on Eldorado would be worth half a million dollars and many would be worth more. Claim Number Sixteen alone was to produce more than $1.5 million in gold.[21]

There is little doubt that Carmack was responsible for starting the stampede out of Fortymile. Ironically, despite his intention to uphold the miners' code and tell everyone about the gold strike, he did not make any effort to inform Henderson, who was still working his claim on Gold Bottom Creek.

By the time Henderson heard of the strike from wandering miners, it was too late. All the land on Bonanza and Eldorado had been staked solid from end to end. Henderson, the first man to find gold in quantity in the Klondike, received little recognition for his work and none of the wealth.

Captain Moore did not participate in the initial rush to Bonanza Creek. His prime objective was to hurry home with news of the Klondike strike – information that would be vital to Wilkinson's Syndicate. At Circle City he delivered a consignment of United States mail on behalf of an American mail carrier, who had been turned back near Lake Bennett by a party of Indians he had angered. At Circle City, however, Moore found he could go no further. Rapidly forming ice had stopped steamboat transportation on the Lower Yukon River for the season. Unable to reach St. Michael, Moore, now in his seventy-fifth year, obtained a dog team and fought his way back along the river trails from Circle City to Fortymile, a distance of 260 miles.[22]

At Fortymile, he repaired his sleigh and dog harness and headed up river to the Chilkoot Pass and Dyea. There he would wait for a steamship to Victoria and home. Before leaving Fortymile, Ogilvie had given him a letter to his department chief in Ottawa providing further information about the discovery of gold in the Klondike valley – a report that failed to impress anyone in government circles.[23]

AFTER NINE MONTHS in Canada, Wilkinson left Victoria in September 1896 to return to London. He first stopped in Ottawa to familiarize himself with the action required to incorporate a federal company capable of constructing and operating a railway within the Yukon district, and to become acquainted with government ministers and civil officials, who eventually would be involved in the company's incorporation by an act of Parliament.

His second stop was in New York for a meeting with D. Noble Rowan regarding the Alaskan and North Western Territories Trading Company's investment in the Moores' Skagway land. He then embarked for England, arriving in Southampton on October 28, 1896.

At a special meeting of the Syndicate's directors in London during November 1896, Wilkinson explained the business options he had outlined in his dispatches from British Columbia. After quickly dispensing with them, he moved to his main subject – a railway to connect the Yukon district to the sea. With the aid of a large map he drew the directors' attention to the established transportation route from the West Coast ports of Canada and the United States to Circle City and Fortymile, via St. Michael and the Yukon River. He explained the relative positions of the Chilkoot Pass and the White Pass and their routes to the head of Yukon River navigation at Lake Bennett.

He dealt at length on the Moores' Skagway lands, the deep water of Skagway Bay, which meant it could accommodate large steamers, and the superiority of the White Pass over the Chilkoot Pass as a means of reaching the broad uplands beyond the coastal mountains. And he spoke of the growing realization that there were potential fortunes in gold within the boundaries of Alaska and the Canadian Northwest.

At first the directors were unimpressed. Some shook their heads in disbelief while others simply laughed at the idea of building a railway to serve what they considered a desolate, frozen wasteland.

Wilkinson was neither disappointed nor surprised at their reaction. The directors' failure to grasp the significance of building a railway through the White Pass was not unexpected, particularly as its future appeared to rest on the realization of an old man's dream. The very name "Alaska" evoked the popular vision of endless miles of ice and snow and frozen rivers. To ask a sane man to consider financing the construction of a railway in such a hostile environment was to the directors a preposterous suggestion. Wilkinson's enthusiasm failed to carry the day. The directors' response was a resounding "no."

Wilkinson was not unhappy. Rather, he was relieved when his railway proposal was rejected. He had already anticipated that possibility, and their refusal to participate gave impetus to an idea that had been forming in his mind for weeks. He suggested that, as they did not want to undertake the construction of the railway, they might consider optioning the charters to himself or his nominees. The directors agreed and invited him to submit his proposal in writing. Wilkinson did so on January 7, 1897, stating that he agreed to purchase all of the Syndicate's interests in the White Pass, together with any future benefits that might be derived from negotiations with the governments of the United States, Canada, and British Columbia pertaining to mail contracts, land grants, mining royalties, subsidies, and the construction of a light railway over the White Pass from Lynn Canal to Lake Bennett.[24]

He also advised the Syndicate that he had received confirmation from Billinghurst that the Pacific and Arctic Railway and Navigation Company had been incorporated in the U.S.A. This was only the first link in a three-link chain, but it was nevertheless a tangible asset, even though its value was doubtful without the necessary charters and authorities to construct the railway.

The Syndicate could hardly reject Wilkinson's proposal. Had its financial position been stronger, it might have undertaken the construction of the railway itself, but it was already fully committed. "These properties are readily afforded to you for the reason that our hands are tied by want of capital for such large enterprises, and on the faith of your statements and our confidence in your intention to deal fairly with us," Walter Townsend, the Syndicate's general manager, told Wilkinson during the option negotiations.[25] The directors had also reasoned that optioning the railway companies to Wilkinson could produce a tidy profit should Captain Moore's gold rush become a reality. Through Wilkinson's agreement with the Moores, the Syndicate had acquired an interest in Skagway, and the movement of gold-rush supplies through the White Pass could only enhance the value of the Syndicate's holdings there.

For these reasons, the Syndicate accepted Wilkinson's preliminary proposal. The whole scheme still depended on the incorporation of the Canadian federal and provincial companies, which, with the Pacific and Arctic Railway and Navigation Company, would create a packet of government charters the Syndicate's directors estimated should be worth some £30,000, or $150,000 – a figure that Wilkinson accepted as the price he would have to pay.[26] But without the two Canadian links, the railway scheme would be virtually worthless.

Wilkinson suggested that, because of the importance of the two Canadian companies, someone with intimate knowledge of the railway plan should leave immediately for Canada to represent the Syndicate and, when necessary, act independently in its interests. The directors could think of no one better qualified to represent them in Canada and assist in the incorporation of the two companies than the man who had sought an option to buy them – Wilkinson himself. They agreed that the enabling charters would be obtained in the name of the Syndicate and that all expenses would be to the Syndicate's account.

Wilkinson embarked for Canada early in February 1897, again as the paid agent of the Syndicate, with instructions to obtain a British Columbia charter for the proposed railway and to assist the Syndicate in incorporating a federal company in Ottawa.

Both Wilkinson and the Syndicate's directors regarded the incorporation of the federal company as the key to the success of the entire undertaking. They visualized the company holding unlimited powers as did the great colonial trading companies that dominated huge areas of Britain's expanding empire. Their company would not only build a railway, it would govern the Yukon district. The powers they sought would, if granted, give them the authority to collect royalties, distribute the mail, recruit and direct its own police force, and generally administer the affairs of the Territory.

ON HIS ARRIVAL in Canada, Wilkinson faced three major problems. The first two – the formation of the federal and provincial railway companies – were well known to the Syndicate's directors. The third problem, which was not fully understood by the directors, involved the American government, the only authority that could provide the Pacific and Arctic Railway and Navigation Company with a right-of-way, a fact that Wilkinson had not emphasized during his meetings in London. He had not been deliberately devious. He had been led to believe by Struve in Seattle that the Syndicate could procure a right-of-way simply by applying to the United States General Land Office in Washington, D.C.

After visiting Ottawa, where he conferred with the Syndicate's council, Francis H. Chrysler, QC, Wilkinson left for the West Coast. He met with Struve in Seattle to resolve the Alaska right-of-way issue and instructed him to prepare an application to the United States General Land Office for a railway right-of-way from Lynn Canal to the Canadian frontier – wherever that might be. He also instructed the Pacific and Arctic Railway and Navigation Company's three trustees, C.L. Webb, M. McMicken, and A.B. Stewart, to name Billinghurst company engineer and commission him to survey the White Pass for the location of the railway line.

In Victoria, he arranged with Helmcken to take the necessary legal and political action required to incorporate a company in British Columbia empowered to construct a railway from a point on, or near, Lynn Canal to the province's northern border with the Yukon district.

On March 26, 1897, John Patton Booth, a member of the British Columbia Legislative Assembly, presented a petition to the House on behalf of Charles Herbert Wilkinson, Henry Coppinger Beeton, and Adolph Drucker, all of the City of London, and Ernest Edward Billinghurst of Victoria, praying for the incorporation of the British Columbia-Yukon Railway Company.[27] After three weeks in committee, the Bill was passed on April 22, 1897.[28]

In London, the Syndicate's directors had been busy ever since Wilkinson had departed for Canada. During the early months of 1897, they had been preparing to incorporate a Canadian federal company – a firm in which they hoped to retain an interest. Its objects were to "construct and operate a railway . . . from a point in British Columbia . . . near the head of Lynn Canal, thence across the White Pass, and then northerly and westerly by the most feasible route to Fort Selkirk." This proposed railway would run approximately 400 miles. The old Hudson's Bay fur-trading post at Fort Selkirk was chosen as the railway's northern terminus because of its convenient location as a freight transfer point between the proposed railway and the riverboats operating out of St. Michael on the Lower Yukon River.[29]

George W. Mitchell, a prominent figure in Ottawa and a spokesman and adviser to the Syndicate, was doing everything in his power to promote the

Syndicate's railway and to help Wilkinson by opening political doors. To these ends he made a direct appeal to Prime Minister Laurier seeking a government-guaranteed return on any capital invested in the Syndicate's northern transportation concept.

"We ask no money from the government," Mitchell wrote on March 27, 1897, "simply a guarantee of 3% on $1,250,000 for which we will build the line, place ten steel steamboats and 50 barges on the Yukon, and open 9,000 miles of river tributaries and 192,000 square miles of territory rich in gold." The Syndicate's transportation scheme was, Mitchell stated, "an eminently practical one and broad and patriotic in its scope and character," although "it is utterly impossible to get a shilling in London without a guarantee. But once I show the people at home that they have *at last* made a paying thing in Canada, the surplus millions will pour in." In case there was any doubt in Laurier's mind about Wilkinson's social status, Mitchell wrote, "I need only refer you to the *London Morning Post* where Mr. Wilkinson's dinner for His Highness, the Duke of Teck, is mentioned. And further letters are on their way from London now from the Hon. Joseph Chamberlain introducing Mr. Wilkinson to yourself."[30]

Despite Mitchell's appeal to Laurier, the Syndicate gained neither the financial investment nor the government support it sought. Without a government guarantee of a return on invested capital, London investors refused to take the risk. Wilkinson, however, with Mitchell's help, was progressing rapidly with the formation of the federally incorporated company required for transportation operations in the Yukon.

The federal company's name first appeared on the House of Commons order paper of April 23, 1897, the day after the British Columbia-Yukon Railway Company had been incorporated in Victoria. The House read and received the petition of "His Highness, Francis Duke of Teck, Grand Cross of the Most Honourable Order of the Bath, White Lodge, Richmond, in the County of Surrey, and others, of Great Britain and other places; praying for an Act of Incorporation under the name of The British Yukon Chartered Company."[31] The list of supporting petitioners included fifteen members of the British House of Commons and many leading London bankers, as well as Wilkinson, Billinghurst's brother Henry, John Henry Escolme, who was also Managing Director of The Alaskan and North Western Territories Trading Company, and Richard Byron Johnson, the Syndicate's chairman.[32]

On May 21, 1897, the bill to incorporate the company was introduced to the Canadian House of Commons by Duncan Cameron Fraser, Liberal Member of Parliament for Guysboro, Nova Scotia. The bill was relentlessly hammered by most members, who opposed granting the extensive powers the petitioners sought. The Duke of Teck found himself described in Canadian newspapers as a "British capitalist" who had discovered a way to repeat "in a modified and strictly legitimate fashion" the triumphs of the great British Charter companies of India and Africa and the Hudson's Bay Company of Canada. While described as a capitalist, the Duke was never regarded as a notable financier. He was, however, father-in-law to the heir apparent and, in view of this, his petition was regarded as a matter of extreme importance.[33]

The adventurous nature of the company's enterprise, and the Duke's connection with it, became front-page news after it was learned that the company not only planned to explore the Yukon district but was working to obtain a Canadian government charter giving it the power to *govern* the area. The company was proposing a grand scheme, and it became the object of wide speculation. What were the Duke and his associates up to? Central News of London was advised by an inquisitive British Columbia newsman's telegram that the Duke of Teck "has asked the Canadian government to allow him and his company to govern the Canadian gold fields in the Yukon district. The British Columbia press is rather outspoken on the subject and says that this is the most paralyzing proposal ever presented to any modern government."[34]

Central News promptly contacted the Duke and asked him to comment on Canadian concerns over the extensive powers his company was seeking. He replied that he did not belong to any company, but that he was interested in The British Yukon Chartered Company. He said he had "asked some members of the Canadian government to support it. That is all." Many readers could only agree with the *Victoria Daily Colonist* of May 15, 1897, when it said that "it does not seem to be plain just what he means to say."

Public opinion was on guard, but it was not opposed to the construction of the railway. "If any English company desired to build a railroad line up in the Arctic, no one in Canada will say no," wrote the *Colonist*'s Ottawa correspondent. But the powers the company sought had created a great deal of suspicion. The questions the Canadian House of Commons had to decide were how far the granting of the Charter would affect the rights of private prospectors, and whether under any circumstances the power to govern should be delegated to a private company.

Despite support from some members of the House, opposition to the bill continued to mount. Those who were obstructing the measure claimed that the company was asking for a virtual monopoly and that, if the bill passed in its present form, it would eliminate competition, set whatever rates it liked, and strangle private enterprise.[35]

To prevent the matter becoming a serious national issue, the Syndicate's legal counsel, Francis H. Chrysler, agreed, after consultations with Wilkinson, to drop all of the provisions that would give the company police, postal, and other administrative powers over the Yukon district. They also agreed to drop the word "Chartered" from the company's name and that it would henceforth be called the British Yukon Mining, Trading and Transportation Company. They also agreed to drop all clauses that would permit the company to purchase existing northern companies with its own shares. In addition, sections related to property would be amended to limit the company's land to its actual requirements and the clause enabling the company to sell water would be struck out. A clause providing a time limit for the start and completion of the railway was added, this being two years from the passage of the bill to start construction, and five years from the passage of the bill to complete the railway.[36]

The Act to incorporate the British Yukon Mining, Trading and Transportation Company was passed by the Canadian Parliament on June 29, 1897.

The springs were now wound and the legal wheels set in motion. In only eighteen months the Syndicate, through Wilkinson, had created an asset of considerable potential wealth. But grants of rights and charters for possible exploitation were not unusual at the time. Railways were frequently incorporated before there was sufficient traffic to warrant their construction. Their real value would be realized only if the surrounding country boomed into prominence or was developed by legitimate enterprise. Either way, Wilkinson and the Syndicate were ready. The grand design was complete.

While Wilkinson was engaged in Ottawa, the American trustees of the Pacific and Arctic Railway and Navigation Company had moved on June 9, 1897, to secure a right-of-way through public lands of the United States. The trustees' application, however, raised a serious question: did the provisions of the United States land laws apply to the District of Alaska?

After a lively exchange of letters and telegrams, the Secretary of the Interior, Cornelious N. Bliss, concluded that, other than mining laws, which were in full force, "Nothing contained in the ... Act shall be construed to put in force in Alaska the general land laws of the United States."[37]

The Right Of Way Act of 1875 was regarded as part of the general land laws of the United States, but its provisions had never been extended to the District of Alaska. It was clear that they did not apply to railway builders seeking a right-of-way through Alaska's rugged coastal mountains. Wilkinson and the

Pacific and Arctic Railway and Navigation Company had hit their first serious snag.

ON JUNE 10, 1897, John Henry Escolme arrived in Victoria from Ottawa, where he had been assisting Wilkinson with the formation of the federal company. He had been dispatched from London by the Syndicate to take over the development of the Moores' Skagway land. The Syndicate's directors had reasoned that, if Wilkinson was successful in his efforts to build the railway, and if the current Yukon gold flurry became a major gold-field, the Syndicate could, for a relatively small investment, profit from its control of the land at the tip of Lynn Canal – a potential asset not included in Wilkinson's option. Escolme was charged with the responsibility of developing Skagway and promoting the White Pass as the most logical route into the Yukon interior.

When he arrived in Victoria, Escolme announced to the press that he had been sent out from England by the Syndicate to undertake the preliminary development work connected with the Syndicate's recently acquired interests in Alaska, British Columbia, Washington, and the Yukon district. This work, he said, included establishing a general supply depot at Skagway and opening trading posts along the trail from Skagway into the Yukon interior. "The White Pass is the most practical key to the Yukon," Escolme said. "It is our intention to run steamers to Skagway and these will connect with a railway to Lake Bennett where steamers will again be used." He assured his listeners that the White Pass trail was already being slashed out and improved. "Our company's intentions are to do a general trading and transportation business, and as travel into the Yukon is constantly increasing we expect it will be remunerative." Probably because the hammering the federal company received in Ottawa was fresh in his mind, he assured the journalists present that, "We have general powers, but no special powers that any other corporation could not get."[38]

Escolme and party, which included Billinghurst, left Victoria for Skagway on June 15, 1897, one month before news of the Klondike gold strike reached the United States. At Skagway they started their survey of Moore's property, the White Pass, and the region's mining potential.

Billinghurst left the party and returned to Victoria on July 3. He reported that Moore and the growing numbers of gold-seekers had already mucked out a trail of sorts from Skagway to the summit of the pass, although much work remained to be done before it could be regarded as a legitimate trail capable of accommodating heavy traffic. But, he said, "There are no engineering difficulties in the way for the trail which has been cut along the west side of the river."

He also revealed that, within a week, a group of surveyors under his supervision would start to survey the route for the proposed railway from Skagway to the summit and on to Lake Bennett. He was confident that business activities would continue to increase through the Skagway route and that the White Pass was superior to the Chilkoot Pass in every respect – an opinion that was gaining some support.[39]

Herbert Rice, a Juneau packer who had moved large quantities of goods over the Chilkoot trail, had announced after examining the White Pass that he would abandon the Dyea-Chilkoot route and start using Moore's trail.[40] The movement of men and materials into the Yukon district over both trails was now a major operation. The presence of gold in the Klondike was becoming better known, although the influx of miners had not yet exploded into anything approaching a stampede. An immense amount of supplies had been taken into the interior during May and June of 1897, including sheep and other livestock. Billinghurst witnessed much of this activity during his trip to Skagway with Escolme.

Even at this early date, Billinghurst could see a compelling need to establish Canadian customs officers at the summits of both passes. "As it is now," he stated on his return from the North, "the conditions are altogether favourable to the Americans. The Canadians have no customs officer at the summit to charge duty on goods from the United States, but American authorities, already established at Dyea and Skagway, are very careful to see that Canadian goods crossing American territory either pay duty, or that expenses are paid for a customs officer to accompany the bonded goods to the frontier, a decidedly expensive and troublesome procedure."[41]

This problem would plague the movement of goods into the Yukon for months to come. Victoria and other coastal cities were already losing Yukon trade, and it was in the interest of all Canadian West Coast cities to press the Canadian government for customs officers at strategic locations.

Wilkinson now felt reasonably confident about the eventual growth of business along the Yukon River valley, although he accepted the fact that optimum results for the projected railway would not be realized without a substantial increase in the production of gold. The most hopeful sign of this happening was the increase in the number of miners and prospectors headed into the Yukon district during the spring. But Moore's report of the discovery of gold in the Klondike River valley – news that was now some six months old – had yet to be confirmed. Opinions on the extent of the discovery and its effect on the future of the railway and the Skagway developments could only be regarded as speculative at best. There was still serious doubt about Moore's story. Moore could never resist embroidering a tale if it served his purpose. His enthusiasm, as always, was suspect. Wilkinson pondered. Was the news of the strike simply the exaggeration of a minor discovery, or was it an event of major importance, fully justifying Moore's impassioned dream?

Wilkinson found Billinghurst's reports encouraging, but he was troubled by a lack of specifics. Certainly, business was developing as he had predicted it would, but there remained a disturbing doubt that these predictions might not be fully realized. If Moore's reported gold strike was true, however, it would provide the Syndicate with a solid peg on which to hang its corporate hat.

The undertaking must be capable of convincing London's hard-headed financiers that the railway scheme through the White Pass had merit. If Wilkinson failed to convince them, all the arguments in the world would not induce them to part with a penny. He knew that further progress could not be made without a substantial infusion of capital. Clearly, this was the next and most pressing item on Wilkinson's agenda. It was time to return to London to pick up his option. Only then would he be in a position to raise the capital required to construct the railway.

Four

---◆---

KLONDIKE GOLD

THE ALASKA COMMERCIAL COMPANY steamer *Excelsior* wallowed through the Pacific swell and, on July 16, 1897, turned into the waters of San Francisco Bay. A long wisp of smoke trailed from her single black funnel leaving a dirty smudge on the western horizon. Rust-pitted, grimy, and stained, she looked as tired and tattered as her passengers, who only a few weeks before had been scrabbling for gold on Bonanza and Eldorado creeks in the Yukon district. Unshaven and sea-weary, they were returning to civilization and the bright lights of San Francisco still wearing their battered miners' hats and mud-caked clothes – a gaunt and motley mob of prospectors with weather-beaten faces and $750,000 in Klondike gold.[1]

The ship eased into her berth at the foot of Market Street, but no one took much notice of her arrival. The gangplank was lowered and the miners disembarked, many of them staggering under the weight of heavy bundles, boxes, and bags. They looked like the remnants of a defeated battalion. But this was not defeat. This was victory.

For the first few hours, neither the miners nor their gold attracted much attention, although a few nuggets were passed from hand to hand. Sensing a story, newspaper reporters were soon on the scene, but San Francisco editors had yet to grasp the significance of the unfolding events. That night, while the routine news of the *Excelsior*'s arrival was sent out by wire to the eastern newspapers, the full story of miners and their gold began to emerge. By the following morning, two newspapers, the *Chronicle* and the *Call*, gave the Klondike gold strike banner headlines. The following day, Hearst's *San Francisco Examiner* plunged into the fray, and by noon the headlines in all the San Francisco papers screamed the story of the Klondike. Beneath them ran stories of the richest gold strike in mining history, which had been made during the late summer of the previous year.[2]

Within a day of the *Excelsior*'s arrival in San Francisco, the steamer *Port-*

land berthed at Seattle with sixty-eight miners and some $800,000 in gold.[3] More than 5,000 people crammed the dock to greet the ship. "Show us the gold!" they shouted, and along the ship's railing a line of waving miners hoisted their bulging sacks and started to cheer, "Hurrah for the Klondike."[4] The emotional temperature was rising. Talk of gold was on everybody's lips. News of the gold swept through the streets like a raging prairie fire and the *Seattle Post Intelligencer*'s banner fanned the flames. GOLD! GOLD! GOLD! it screamed, "68 Rich Men On The Steamer Portland! STACKS OF YELLOW METAL," and in the story were the inspired lines that would race around the world, accelerating pulses wherever they appeared: "At 3 o'clock this morning the steamer Portland, from St. Michaels for Seattle, passed up [the] Sound with more than a ton of solid gold on board."[5]

Virtually overnight, news of the Klondike spread throughout the world, its impact growing with each press run. Gold fuelled the emotional fire, and the media fanned the flames.

But not everyone was impressed. Commenting on the news from San Francisco, the New York *World* warned its readers to be wary of the headlines announcing the discovery of gold in the Yukon district. It reported that there were well-informed men who regarded the reports as exaggerated. To support its view, the paper interviewed J. Hobart, associate editor of the *Engineering and Mining Journal*, who said, "Yes, I have read these stories but, to be frank, I do not credit them. Our information, which is detailed and positive, makes it impossible for me to accept the roseate announcement that the Yukon River runs over a bed of virgin gold."

Hobart went on to suggest that even if the Yukon gold-fields proved to be rich it would mean very little to the world. "Only the hardiest and most experienced miners could hope to prosper in that desolate land. For eight months of each year no work can be done. The long winter is of Arctic-like severity. Into four months the miner must crowd a year's work."[6]

Hobart was wrong on two counts: the length of the winters, and the Klondike's reserves of gold. In any event his warnings were unheeded. Gold-fever was rampant and there was no stopping it.

A few days after her arrival, the *Portland* returned to Alaska with fifty-eight first-class and ninety-eight second-class passengers. A former state governor and a general were among them. On the docks close to 1,500 passengers clamoured for passage out of Seattle to the North. The steamers *Queen*, *Mexico, City of Topeka,* and *Al-Ki* were booked to sail by August 5. The *City of Seattle* and the *City of Kingston* were hurriedly pressed into service to handle the overflow. People piled aboard anything that would float.

One steamer, the *Willamette*, a coal carrier commanded by veteran navigator Captain Holmes, had been quickly converted to a passenger ship by the construction of rough, wooden berths in the hold where, a few hours previously, tons of bulk coal had been stowed. Two hundred passengers, sixty horses and mules, and several hundred tons of freight were taken aboard at San Francisco. From there she sailed for Seattle where 600 passengers and 240 horses and mules were loaded aboard, along with hundreds of tons of additional freight. The *Willamette* left Seattle with little more than standing room only for most of the passengers and her decks piled high with bales of hay, equipment, and general freight.[7]

As the demand for shipping space increased, more steamers were diverted from their regular coastal runs to transport the growing army of men who had visions of a land carpeted with golden nuggets. Every vessel was booked beyond capacity, many of them dangerously overloaded. The eastern papers reported that the Klondike strike already eclipsed anything that had happened in the California rush of '49. "Big strike in the Klondike," the newsboys shouted, and, if proof was needed, there were men in Seattle with bulging pokes of gold and nuggets as big as walnuts.

Victoria, Vancouver, Portland, and Tacoma were propelled into the madness. Every transportation company on the West Coast was besieged for information. Government offices, newspapers, and stores were inundated by mobs wanting information about routes, custom duties, mining laws, supplies, equipment, and conditions in the far-off Klondike. Men quit their jobs, left their families, delayed weddings, mortgaged their homes, and headed for the Klondike. Ministers, doctors, lawyers, clerks, and labourers, all looking the same under miners' hats, assembled their outfits and joined the throng. Stock companies were formed, and the public was invited to invest in a variety of Klondike mining schemes that held promise of huge rewards without having to stir from home or job. The papers were filled with good advice, bad advice, and terrifying stories of hardships on the trail.

But still the gold-seekers came by the thousands, pouring into the ports to plunge into the human vortex. Nothing stopped them. It seemed they were driven by something more than gold, perhaps by the sheer drama of joining a stampede greater than any the world had ever seen before. Perhaps it was just a search for adventure that propelled them into the unknown. Whatever the reason, the gold had been found and, just as Moore had predicted, the horde was on its way. The Klondike fuse had been lit.

News of the Klondike reached Ottawa as Wilkinson was preparing for his return trip to London. It could not have arrived at a better time. Now, when he approached the London money market for financial support for the railway, he was confident he had something specific to offer – the prospect of the Yukon district becoming one of the great gold-fields of the world. Armed with newspapers carrying stories of the Klondike strike and confirming telegrams from Struve, Helmcken, and Billinghurst, he left for New York, where he met with D. Noble Rowan, and then, on August 4, 1897, he sailed for England.

He was convinced the news from the Klondike would make a difference. Surely it would persuade the Syndicate's directors to re-examine the Yukon railway scheme. If, as a result, they decided to invest in the railway he would be assured of full participation in the project and a substantial share of the profits. On the other hand, if the directors still refused to become involved, Wilkinson could exercise his option and, with the help of influential friends in London and Manchester, build the railway himself.

WITHIN TWO WEEKS of the *Portland*'s arrival with news of the Klondike strike, the vanguard of a gold-crazed army of miners had left Seattle for the North. Like a swarm of starving locusts they plunged across the beaches of Skagway and Dyea, trampling everything in sight.

Moore watched helplessly as they swept in from the sea to invade his Skagway lands. The horde was ruthless, unthinking, and in a hurry. Down went his trees, leaving a field of jagged stumps in a sea of mud. In went their stakes, as plot after plot of choice land was wrenched from his acres. Up went their tents as frantic men sought shelter from the relentless wind and rain. The miners had arrived, and they were tearing Moore's dream to bits.

Soon a ragged row of tents stretched across the beachlands, and from a hundred smouldering campfires a threatening cloud of wood smoke spread through the valley. Still the ships came, the captains quickly dumping their passengers and cargoes ashore, each eager to make another trip and more profit while the fever raged.

In a matter of days, Skagway had become a hodge-podge of tents. Piles of tarpaulin-covered freight sprawled across its muddy beach. As each ship dropped anchor, passengers were dumped into rough barges and towed ashore. Horses and mules were shoved off the ships into the bay. Most of them were rounded up as they emerged from the sea, but others, terrified by the noise and activity, stampeded through the jumble of tents and freight, creating havoc wherever they galloped. The shouts of cursing men echoed and re-echoed across the valley, and ships' whistles, braying mules, and barking dogs added to the din. There was no system, no shipping official to oversee the delivery of goods to their rightful owners, just barge after barge of supplies and equipment flung ashore to be picked over and manhandled by a mob of would-be miners who had landed on a strange and hostile shore.[8]

A twisting, muddy, stump-filled road wound through Skagway from the beach into the forest beyond, and along its edges rough log buildings were already taking shape. Frame buildings of rough lumber and canvas served as hotels and stores. The Pack Train saloon was already in business, selling illegal hootch at two-bits a shot and cigars at the same price. An enterprising doctor had established an apothecary shop in a tent, and large painted canvas signs advertised eating houses that served eggs, hotcakes, bacon, and beans. Outside one restaurant a sign announced that "CUSTOMERS NOT IN GOOD FINANCIAL STANDING WILL BE REQUESTED TO MAKE A DEPOSIT BEFORE ORDERING EGGS." It was a rough, untidy street and its salient feature was mud. They called it "Broadway" and along it, day and night, moved an endless parade of wagons, men, pack animals, dogs, and even a few venturesome women garbed in shocking knee-length dresses and high leather boots.

Already some discouraged men had given up. They had seen the quagmires and cliffs along the trail leading out of Skagway to the White Pass, and they had thrown up their hands in despair. They had returned to Skagway with tales of unbelievable hardships and the loss of outfits when their pack horses had fallen off the sheer granite walls into the valley below – seventeen dying in one place alone. For these beaten men, the venture had suddenly become a nightmare of physical torture and suffering.

"This is the worst trail I have ever seen for the distance," one man cried, "and I predict that if the rains keep up it will be impossible to get a horse over." Others, faced with these appalling conditions, bartered away their outfits and caught the next boat south.

Almost every man was armed with a revolver, some with a repeating rifle. One packer exclaimed, "There are more double-action revolvers and inexperienced men around here to the square foot than any place I've ever been."[9]

Other gold-seekers, after landing, saw opportunity staring them in the face. One look, and they grasped the significance of Skagway as a gateway to the Klondike. There would be no trail, no panning for them, they reasoned. The town itself would be their Bonanza. They would mine the miners as they passed through on their way north, and again when they returned from the Klondike with their pokes bulging with gold. Someone had to build the town, and if a tidy profit could be gained in the process, so much the better. Others could have the trail. They would stay and build the stores, saloons, theatres, and dance halls. The rest pushed on toward the pass. Men bowed with heavy packs, heavily laden pack horses, dogs, burros, and even a team of oxen made a discordant caravan through the White Pass, all struggling and scraping and bumping their way over and around stumps and through the mud that was the everlasting curse of the trail.

The first shiploads of miners had arrived in Skagway on July 26, 1897, and within a month the trickle had become a flood of men and animals pushing and shoving its way into the Skagway valley, leaving confusion and hostility in its wake. There was no order. No authority. No design. Too much was happening too fast. More saloons were springing up along the rutted main street. Beyond the Pack Train, the Bonanza had opened up for business, followed by The Grotto, The Nugget, and the Klondike Saloon. The gamblers were already spinning their wheels and rattling their dice, while the innocent marvelled at what they saw. And through the noise and laughter came the tinkling notes of an out-of-tune piano beating out the popular ragtime songs of the day, each chord competing with the crack of the broad axe, the rasp of the crosscuts, and the ring of a hundred busy hammers. Before the year was out, there would be twenty-five saloons in Skagway where a man could knock back all the red-eye whisky he could hold and gamble until his money belt was flat. For diversion there were girls with names like The Virgin, Sitting Maud, Lil Davenport, Mollie Fewclothes, Babe Wallace, and Ethel the Moose.

In an attempt to establish some sort of order out of the prevailing chaos, a gold-seeker named Dave McKinney called a meeting of stampeders to "set up the town" and "impartially settle" land disputes. The committee decided to lay out the town in blocks of twelve lots each fifty feet by a hundred feet. The streets were to be sixty feet wide except for Broadway, the main street, which was to have a width of eighty feet.[10] The committee appointed Frank H. Reid, a bartender in the Klondike Saloon, as surveyor. Reid, in the course of his duties, had acquired a set of survey instruments from a down-and-out engineer who was heading for the gold-fields. Exhibiting his ready wit, Reid took the instruments and nominated himself City Engineer. John U. Smith, the United States Commissioner for the District of Alaska, was appointed Recorder of Town Lots – a duty he badly handled, resulting in many angry meetings of protest.

Solomon himself might well have declined an invitation to join the committee. The problems it faced were endless, and Skagway's first citizens were confused, suspicious, angry, and vocal. No one was more angry than Captain Moore and his son Bernard. Miners in boatload after boatload arrived at Skagway, stormed ashore, and raised their tents wherever they chose. They thrashed through the Moores' land, ignoring the indignant complaints as well as the authority of the recently convened land committee. There was no one the Moores could turn to for protection or advice. They cursed and called everyone within earshot "trespassers," but the stampeders paid no attention to them or to the boundaries of the property they claimed.

Overnight, signs appeared on trees, stumps, and hand-driven stakes, serving the dual purpose of establishing ownership and warning off any who had designs on lots that were already claimed. "THIS LOT," stated one such notice, "100 FEET ALONG THE TRAIL BY 50 FEET WEST, LOCATED AND IMPROVED BY J. MURPHY, AUG. 14, '97. SEE MY NOTICE ON STAKES AT N. AND E. END OF LOT." Another stated tersely, "THIS CLAIM, 50' BY 100' IS CLAIMED BY J.H. FOOT." It was not taking the townspeople long to establish ownership of their chosen property, nor to select alternate lots should their claims be located on a street reserve.[11]

Reid advised Bernard Moore to "stake out" a few acres of land before he and his father were overwhelmed by the stampeding miners. As a result of Reid's foresight, a large tract of land was staked around the Moores' original log cabin location and a second tract around their sawmill operation. Unfortunately, neither tract included the wharf bunkhouse, where Captain Moore and his wife lived.[12]

The final blow to Moore came when it was discovered that, according to Reid's survey, the bunkhouse occupied a plot of land that was to become the intersection of Fifth and Main streets – right in the middle of Skagway. Captain Moore watched with mounting anger as a crew of men approached his bunkhouse home with their stakes and lines. He confronted the surveyors and asked what they thought they were doing. The leader replied that they were surveying the street as laid down by the plan approved by the citizens' committee. The irate, jut-jawed Moore spat out a prolonged and exquisite stream of riverboat invectives, leaving little doubt about his low opinion of the citizens, committee, and all the assorted claim jumpers who were defiling his lands. Shaking with anger, he told them that he had been in Skagway before the lot of them had ever heard of Alaska, and that he had no intention of budging for the citizens' committee, the surveyors, or any other Johnny-come-lately.

Despite Moore's provocative outburst, the members of the committee remained calm. One committeeman called out that they were all reasonable men and offered the seething Moore twenty-four hours to make up his mind to move. Moore rejected the offer and slammed the door to the bunkhouse, leaving his wife weeping on the steps.

Two days later, Moore watched as a noisy mob carrying sledges, peaveys, saws, and wrecking bars approached his home. In a blind rage he snatched up a steel bar, opened the door, and charged, swinging wildly as he went. He thrashed out at one man who was about to drive his axe into the Moores' front door. The bar came down with a bone-crunching thump on the axeman's arm. With a cry of pain he turned and fled, followed by the rest, who saw retreat as the only course to take in face of Moore's monumental wrath.[13] The first battle of Skagway was over, leaving Moore the apparent winner. But the sheer weight of numbers and events finally persuaded Moore to move into temporary hotel quarters while the citizens' committee moved his house to a plot near the waterfront, where it reverted to a bunkhouse for the Moores' workers.

Moore was not alone in his concern for the fate of his lands. It was also a worry for Escolme, who had recently arrived at Skagway to take up his duties as manager of the Syndicate's White Pass transportation project. His job was to complete the Moore wharf in Skagway harbour, improve the Skagway townsite, and develop the trail through the White Pass. Now, with the arrival of the hordes, Escolme found himself in the centre of the biggest mess he had ever faced in his life. Quite aside from the colossal task of building the wharf and improving the trail, he faced the summary occupation of Moore's land, in which the Syndicate had a 75 per cent interest. The land had been invaded by strangers who were ignoring Moore's and Escolme's demands that they clear off.

Despite these land problems and an alarming shortage of funds, Escolme pressed on with the immediate task of completing the wharf and improving the trail to the White Pass summit. But his claim that the White Pass was superior to the Chilkoot Pass was not borne out by the thousands of prospectors who used it during the fall of 1897.

"The opening of the White Pass as a summer trail was not a blunder – it was a crime," said Tappan Adney, a correspondent who had been commissioned by Harper and Brothers publishers and the *London Chronicle* to furnish news and pictures of the gold rush to the Klondike. "Where there are no rocks there are boggy holes. It is all rocks and mud – rocks and mud." In addition to the masses of gold-seekers who were temporarily bivouacked in Skagway, Adney guessed that some 5,000 miners and 2,000 horses were spread out along the trail between Skagway and Lake Bennett. No one bothered to keep track of steamer arrivals. "A steamer arrives," Adney reported, "and empties several hundred people and tons of goods into the mouth of the trail, and the trail absorbs them as a sponge drinks up the water."[14]

The trail was now in constant use. Just north of the beach, it entered the tangled underbrush of the forest, winding around a series of waterways, quagmires, and rock outcrops until it reached the foot of a steep hill. From there, it zigzagged to the hill's summit, where it passed into a ravine pitted with muddy holes. At the far end of the ravine, the trail mounted the slope of the mountain, whose smooth rocky ledges sloped away from the cliff's sides, providing only the barest of footholds. Following a series of perpendicular cliffs, the trail climbed from terrace to terrace and then plunged down the side of Porcupine Ridge to a narrow gorge. Here, the trail crossed a rough pole bridge constructed by Moore and the packers. On the other side of the gorge, the trail climbed steep rock ledges that were slippery with trampled mud.

Stage by stage, the trail rose and dipped as it followed the undulating banks of the Skagway River. Some six miles from the summit, it crossed the river by a second bridge, which afforded a spectacular view of the surrounding mountains. "Near here a stream of water comes down the mountainside out of the clouds," Adney wrote, "and before it is half-way down it divides into several more streams, which find their way into the Skagway [River] in a dozen places." He claimed that the least sentimental of the gold-seekers could not avoid admiring the beauty of this shimmering cascade, later to become known as the "Bridal Veil Falls."

The trail continued along the bank of the Skagway River over broken rock, boulders, and bogs. The last few miles to the summit were a nightmare for the gold-seekers, the packers, and for their animals. Creeks tumbled down the mountainside, crossing the trail in fords twenty- to thirty-feet wide. Horses and men plunged into the frigid waters, which were often chest deep. Twice more the trail crossed the Skagway River and then climbed a narrow, rocky ledge that wound up a sharp incline of broken rock to the summit.

Many of the gold-seekers soon became discouraged. They were dirty and muddy from head to foot, wet, tired, and disheartened. Outfits were packed to the summit and then abandoned. Tents, piles of supplies, exhausted horses, boats, and lumber were strewn along the trail in utter disorder. When night fell, the weary army of men dropped to the ground to sleep, using their coats for pillows and their broad-brimmed hats to shelter their faces from the rain.

The horses and mules suffered most. Some were owned by gold-seekers, who had purchased them in Skagway, but most had been brought in by the non-Indian packers, who had followed the stampeders to the White Pass. Overloaded and often underfed, the horses were lashed on by their inexperienced, inconsiderate, and sometimes brutal owners. Adney, a sensitive observer, said, "the White Pass trail will be paved with the bones of horses. As many as have come in alive, just as many will bleach their bones by the pine trees and the gulches – for none will go out."

From morning to night it was man against man, man against nature, and man against himself. One man said, "I was in the Salmon River mining excitement in Idaho, but I've never seen anything on the coast like this." A mining engineer from California reported, "I have never seen people act as they do here. They have lost their heads and their senses."[15]

Their desire to reach the gold-fields of the Klondike was turning Skagway and the White Pass into a madhouse, its inmates imprisoned by time and the bleak buttresses of solid granite. There seemed to be no chance to escape from the torture of the White Pass. Many said that Skagway and the White Pass trail had been totally misrepresented by Escolme and Moore, as well as all the other experts who appeared on the scene offering bad advice. Begrimed, unshaven, and weary, the frustrated Klondike-bound miners began asking if there was a better way to cross the mountains into the Yukon interior. Some began making anxious inquiries about Dyea and the Chilkoot Pass.

"All who enter Chilkoot Pass leave truth behind," said one newspaper. A seasoned ship's officer explained to his eager passengers, "There be Skagway, and over there be the flats of Dyea. You can take your choice – Chilkoot Pass or White Pass – and I guess they're both bad enough."[16]

Deciding which trail to take was a major preoccupation of the gold-seekers during their tedious voyage up the coast. The horrors of the White Pass were becoming common knowledge, but experts were ever present who would tell spine-tingling stories about the Chilkoot Pass and the special terrors *it* held in store for all who chose it. Choosing which pass to climb was a dilemma. The Chilkoot had been used for a much longer time than the White Pass, but the White Pass was lower and Skagway offered superior unloading arrangements. On the other hand, the White Pass was a series of ups and downs, whereas the Chilkoot was shorter, steadier, although steeper and higher. All the factors were considered, mulled over, and argued until the sea-borne miners threw up their hands in frustration. One thing was certain, when they arrived at the head of Lynn Canal a decision would have to be made, and no matter which trail they picked, by the end of the first day they would be certain that they had made a colossal blunder and had chosen the wrong one.

Like Skagway, Dyea now sprawled from the beachlands into the woods beyond. Where before there had been a few log huts and hovels, buildings were beginning to appear along the muddy roadway that trailed off into the forest. The landscape was crowded with tents of all shapes and sizes, piles of supplies, lumber, boats, among which wandered dogs and horses. Through it all stampeded the army of miners who, like those on the White Pass trail, were intent on getting their outfits to Lindeman Lake or Lake Bennett before the onslaught of winter. There, where the two trails joined, they would build their boats and await the coming of spring. Then, when the ice went out, they would float down north together as one mighty armada to the Klondike.

It was a profitable time for the Chilkoot Pass Indian packers. Their route was the most popular, despite the growing interest in the White Pass. They were shrewd, hard bargainers, who knew the value of money. They were small, muscular, and strong. Robert Kirk, a Klondike observer, reported seeing one Indian near the Chilkoot summit packing 250 pounds of flour on his back.[17] They were in constant demand, receiving their packing instructions from a heavy-set Indian who lived in a dilapidated Dyea cabin. Over his door was a large sign stating that its owner was Isaac, "Chief of the Chilkoots."

Everyone was searching for something: a horseshoe, dry wood, lost friends, a doctor, supplies, or a good deal with a packer. The general feeling was that the Chilkoot Pass would become the superior trail, particularly during the summer or fall months. When the ground was frozen during winter, perhaps the White Pass trail would be the one to take. No one was sure. In the meantime there was food to cook, horses to load, and packs to prepare. Some gold-seekers were confident, knowing their inner strength would be equal to the task, others were frightened and unsure. And there were the nameless, faceless men who hovered around the edges of the crowd, hoping to escape the turmoil and return to civilization with their dignity intact. Other frightened men stuck it out, crossed the Chilkoot, and were never frightened again.

Following the muddy road that bordered the western bank of the Taiya River, the Chilkoot army marched northward out of Dyea in disordered ranks, up past Finnegan's Point, along a gravel creekbed, through the gloomy canyon, and on to a corduroy road. Finally they reached Sheep Camp, fourteen miles from the sea. Bad weather, sodden clothes, and unremitting labour soon separated the weak from the strong. While the waverers returned to relative safety, the strong pushed on. Others flopped on the floor of Sheep Camp's only hotel to sleep and regain their strength. By dawn they were up preparing to tramp on into the gorge-like valley. The trail was rough and rose with each step towards Stone House. Here it bore to the right and grew steeper. Their breathing became laboured and their legs grew weary. Pack straps cut into their shoulders. Ahead was a solid wall of jagged grey rock, the final agony, the last great barrier that rose abruptly to meet the sky.

"They start to climb a narrow foot trail," Adney recorded. "The packers and packs disappear. There is nothing but the grey wall of rock and earth. But look ... the mountain is alive. A continuous moving train is zigzagging across the towering face of the precipice, up, up into the sky."[18]

Archie Burns had also watched them tramp up the face of the last man-killing, thirty-five-degree incline. In his opinion the struggle was too great. What was needed, he thought, was a mechanical hoist that would pull the thousands of tons of supplies from the bottom of the incline to the summit of the Chilkoot Pass. Perhaps there should be a series of aerial tramways, he speculated, that stretched to the summit all the way from Dyea. It could be a very profitable undertaking. Furthermore, it might establish once and for all the supremacy of the Chilkoot Pass over the White Pass.

WILKINSON ARRIVED in London on August 11, 1897. He was glad to be back. There was a sense of order about England that he found necessary for the full enjoyment of life. Wilkinson and those with whom he associated were gentlemen of Victorian enterprise, the upper middle class of a nation that was imperial, rich, and magnificent. Everything had its place. Business, the law, the navy, the army, labour, politics, and the Throne all maintained a sensible balance in the grand scheme of things, and those who would disturb it were in the minority. From this island flowed a stream of ideas, people, and commerce to the far corners of the globe, protected along the way by the world's most powerful navy. The leaders of this majestic isle understood the power and the glory of an expanding empire on which the sun never set. They also knew the value of a pound.

After protracted discussions with Wilkinson, the Syndicate's directors confirmed that they were unable to undertake the railway project. They agreed that the best course was to transfer to Wilkinson all the rights and powers belonging to the American company and the two Canadian companies "so far as these rights relate to the construction and maintenance of a railway." For these rights it was finally agreed that Wilkinson would pay to the Syndicate £10,000 on January 9, 1898, and £20,000 on the following May 9, for a total of £30,000.

In addition, Wilkinson agreed to pay the Alaskan and North Western Territories Trading Company £1,000 per annum as rent for a railway right-of-way across the company's Skagway land. Further, he agreed to provide the Syndicate £14,000 of fully paid-up debentures in the British Yukon Mining, Trading and Transportation Company when it had been financed.[19] But Wilkinson was virtually penniless and was supported mainly by his wife's money. Now he required £10,000 immediately and had also to find an additional £20,000 to meet the final option payment.

While many of Wilkinson's contacts were well placed in London's financial circles, they thought that his proposal to construct a railway in remote Alaska to support an obscure gold strike on some God-forsaken creek was sheer madness. To ask them to underwrite the cost of his £30,000 option was, in their minds, proof that the Syndicate's directors and Wilkinson were out of touch with reality. With one exception, the financiers who occupied the oak-panelled offices of Victorian London could not be induced to part with a penny. The one exception was William Brooks Close of Close Brothers & Company, a British financial house with solid connections and substantial interests in the United States.

William Brooks Close came from a family with a long history of banking and commerce in Britain. His great-grandfather, William Brooks, with his partner, Roger Cunliffe, had established the Cunliffe and Brooks Bank of Manchester in 1792.

Later, Brooks's son, Samuel, consolidated the bank's prestige during a financial panic in the early years of the nineteenth century. To reduce a run on his bank, Samuel brought in sacks of corn, covering the corn in each sack with a layer of gold sovereigns. The sacks, apparently bulging with gold, restored the confidence of the bank's nervous customers. By this ploy, the bank weathered the storm.

William Brooks Close, Samuel's grandson, was equally inventive. In 1878 he sailed for the United States and later invited his two brothers, James and Frederick, to join him there. British investments in North America were on the increase, and he was confident that this flow of capital, when combined with the energy and ingenuity of the American people, would create opportunities for substantial profits for himself and his two brothers. This resulted in the formation of an American branch, Close Brothers & Co. – a slight name change to keep the American branch distinct from the London office.

Close Brothers' American operations suffered a severe blow when Frederick Close, who looked after the company's investments, was killed while playing polo. Fortunately, an associate of the partners, Samuel Haughton Graves, was in the United States and, as he was thoroughly familiar with all of the major American transactions, was invited to take control of all Close Brothers' North American business. With Graves acting as chief executive officer in the United States and William Close providing overall direction from London, Close Brothers' North American operations continued to expand and prosper.[20]

Through friends in London, William Close had heard of Wilkinson's search for funds to finance his option with the Syndicate. He decided to look deeper into the Alaska railway scheme. Subsequent talks with the Syndicate's chairman provided him with the details of the Syndicate's railway companies, rights, and charters, and he was impressed with what he heard.

On November 4, 1897, Wilkinson was introduced to Close by Edwin Midgely, an influential friend of Wilkinson's who had agreed only the day before to raise the cash required to finance the option, but not without payment. Midgley insisted on getting 36 per cent of the substantial profits expected from the public share issue planned for the British Yukon Mining, Trading and Transportation Company – a demand Wilkinson accepted without argument.

As a result of Midgely's introduction, Wilkinson met Close with the hope of obtaining his financial support. With the aid of a number of large maps, which had become an indispensable part of his promotional equipment, Wilkinson described the topographical features of Alaska and the Yukon district to Close and a few of Close's most intimate associates. He demonstrated how Lynn Canal, Skagway, and the White Pass formed a giant gateway to the navigable waters of the Yukon River and the Klondike gold-fields. He embellished his presentation with photographs taken by Billinghurst and dramatic North American newspaper gold-rush stories. Wilkinson's pitch was both riveting and logical. He impressed everyone present. Close's interest rose as Wilkinson sketched the relationships of the three companies and the provisions of their rights and charters. Close absorbed the information with well-concealed excitement. Here was an opportunity for profit with little risk, if Wilkinson was desperate enough to meet his terms.

After several more meetings, Close was satisfied that Wilkinson's railway proposal was worthy of support but had decided that Close Brothers would limit its investment to £10,000, the amount Wilkinson required to meet his first option payment to the Syndicate. In return, Wilkinson and Midgely agreed to transfer to Close Brothers £25,000 in fully paid ordinary shares and £25,000 in fully paid preference shares in the British Yukon Mining, Trading and Transportation Company. They further agreed to Close Brothers' demand that, should Wilkinson fail to retire his £10,000 loan or transfer the £50,000 in shares by April 9, 1898, Close Brothers, as "lenders," would have the right to sell the three company charters or to finance, develop, and construct the railway itself.[21]

It was a paralysing agreement. Yet, Close Brothers' involvement was highly speculative and they had a responsibility to protect their interests. Indeed, Close Brothers' solicitors wrote to Close on December 15, 1897, stating:

We have given anxious consideration to the whole subject. We think that to put down the £10,000 in the hope of getting the £50,000 (face value) of shares would be a very highly speculative venture. Money might be made out of it but we do not think the odds are fair odds. If you hedged by bringing in a number of friends we think that you might feel afterwards that your friends had not got as good a prospect as their risk entitles them to have. On the whole, we think you had better say that, unless you can be brought in on a wholly different footing which will give you . . . much more effectual command, you must let the thing alone.[22]

Close ignored this advice. Three days after receiving it, he wrote to nine of his friends setting out the conditions of Wilkinson's option on the railway to the Klondike district in the Yukon, and offering them an opportunity to invest in the scheme.

There is going to be an enormous rush to the Klondike region and . . . those who own the 44 miles of this railroad, which in time may be extended to Dawson City, will, I believe, for years to come have an investment paying enormous dividends.

My firm have undertaken to find £10,000 to enable Mr. Wilkinson, lately the agent for the British Columbia Development Association, Limited, to secure an option on the railway. Mr. Wilkinson, recognizing the railway's manifold advantage . . . recommended its development to the Syndicate. They declined to become involved but accepted his request for an option on the undertaking.

My firm have the right to take over the control of the contract if . . . the debenture capital and other moneys required to give full effect to the contract are not sufficiently provided for, and if we think it desirable we are to have the right to sell the option for whatever price we choose to ask.

Should you care to join in the venture, I shall be prepared to let you share to the extent of £1,000 neither more nor less. I am offering this to nine friends who are large investors with my firm. I shall take £1,000 myself personally, so as to take a similar risk to that which I recommend my friends to take.[23]

While Close Brothers had agreed to provide the Syndicate with £10,000 as part payment of Wilkinson's £30,000 option, at the end of December 1897, £20,000 had still to be found. It was not yet due, but Wilkinson could not move ahead with what he called the "big finances" to build the railway until he had at least found the money required to cover his option. Without it, he had little chance of attracting the additional investment needed to build the railway. Close did not move. He was biding his time.

During the past two months, huge sums of money had been discussed, and relationships between Wilkinson, Midgely, and the Syndicate had become strained. Countless meetings had taken place, and the correspondence between individuals, groups, and their respective solicitors had been voluminous. Share transfers, verbal understandings, written agreements, and contracts filled the days. And these in turn were changed, restructured, agreed to, modified, and changed again. The only tangible development was Close Brothers' £10,000 part payment on Wilkinson's £30,000 option. The rest was nothing but words.

Close Brothers were interested in the eventual construction of the railway, but they would not undertake to finance the project on their own. To make their position abundantly clear, they had stated to Wilkinson that they would do everything in their power to find the capital to float the enterprise but, "as ordinary Commission Agents ... without undertaking any pecuniary liability whatever."[24] But Close Brothers' reluctance to become involved in the railway was not fooling Midgely. He had come to the conclusion that Close was much more interested in the scheme than he was leading everyone to believe. Acting on his intuition, Midgely cautioned Wilkinson about Close. "I am distinctly of the opinion that we should let Mr. Close slide. I think our railway is so good for him that we may fall back on him at any time."[25]

At this stage there was a certain ambivalence in Close's thinking. If Wilkinson raised the additional £20,000 option payment and launched the project with outside financing, Close Brothers would be repaid the £10,000 loan, plus receive £50,000 worth of paid-up shares in the railway company – all of this without putting up another shilling. On the other hand, if Wilkinson failed to repay the loan Close Brothers could take over the three railway companies and sell them, or build the railway themselves.

It was during Close's assessment of these two courses that Midgely announced he had found a new source of financing – the Exploration Company, Limited of London. Faced with this turn of events, Close decided to leave the financing of the railway to others. He told Midgely that the negotiations with the directors of the Exploration Company had his approval.

On completion of preliminary discussions with Exploration Company, Midgely presented its directors with a formal offer on January 27, 1898, stating:

My friends are willing to make over to your Company all the authorized share capital and debentures of the British Yukon Mining, Trading and Transportation Company, the British Columbia-Yukon Railway Company, and the Pacific and Arctic Railway and Navigation Company holding a right-of-way through Alaskan Territory to be used by the railway; also an agreement with the Alaskan and North Western Territories Trading Company for terminal rights and lands. The Exploration Company, Limited, to form a new company to be registered in England with a capital of £1,250,000 in ordinary shares.... Your company to accept or reject this offer on or before February 11, 1898.[26]

Four days before the Exploration Company received Midgely's offer, however, Hamilton Smith, one of Exploration's associates, left London for Canada to organize a railway to the Yukon.

Close was incensed when he learned of Smith's departure. Should Smith gain political support in Canada and establish himself as a legitimate contender in the Yukon railway stakes, he might conceivably outflank the Wilkinson-Syndicate railway. Further, if Exploration Company's directors chose to reject the option offered by Midgely, it could destroy investor confidence in the White Pass railway scheme. Both of these possibilities could jeopardize the construction of the railway – and the repayment of Close Brothers' £10,000 loan.

Close told Wilkinson that "when Hamilton Smith gets to Ottawa there will be any number of people connected with the c.p.r. and other interests who will make it their business to crab [sic] our route." He emphasized that the whole White Pass railway proposal was in danger of disintegration. "It will be impossible to place the deal if once it is refused by the Exploration Company." He insisted that Wilkinson embark immediately for Ottawa "to see that justice is done to the White Pass."[27]

Wilkinson left three days later for Canada on the transatlantic liner, *Teutonic*, the first ship out.

William Close was beginning to take charge.

Five

THE PROMOTERS

HROUGHOUT THE FALL and winter of 1897-98 Skagway and Dyea boomed and swaggered in traditional frontier style. Already Skagway had the edge over Dyea, which could offer only three or four saloons and a hotel – all of them awash in a sea of tents. Skagway now boasted thirty-five restaurants, ten hotels, and enough saloons and brothels to satisfy the most insistent demands of a gold-crazed army on the move. It was a tough, rip-roaring town with more than its share of con men, stick-up artists, and drunks. While admitting that Skagway possessed "many fine fellows of whom a country could be proud," Governor Brady of Alaska was realistic enough to warn the Secretary of the Interior that, "if toughs arrive in large numbers, the United States must be ready to rush troops to Lynn Canal."[1]

Brady's assessment was fully endorsed by Alexander Macdonald, a sophisticated and worldly Britisher, who wrote, "I have stumbled upon some tough corners of the globe during my wanderings beyond the outposts of civilization, but I think the most outrageously lawless quarter I have ever struck was Skagway."[2] Captain Henry Mann, an arctic explorer, who slept fitfully in Skagway for six nights, reported that "there was shooting on the streets every night."[3] Major Samuel B. Steele, Superintendent of the North-West Mounted Police, observed that Skagway "was about the roughest place on earth, with its gambling halls, dance hall pianos, crashing bands, and the hard, cracked voices of the singers wailing amidst shouts of murder, cries for help, and the sharp staccato crack of gunfire."[4]

Skagway never slept. Day and night the sounds of ribald laughter and debauchery echoed along the trail to the summit, where the occasional stampeder would be found sprawled lifeless across his sled, powder burns on his back and his pockets inside out. Life was far from peaceful in Skagway. Tired and penniless men begged in the muddy streets for the price of a meal and a warm place to flop. There was no official civic government, only a self-appointed citizens' council, which had little authority. There was no police force, only a deputy United States marshal, who supplemented his income by befriending the thugs and sharing in their loot. He stoutly resisted any suggestion that a police force be established. "Other cities are over-governed," he would argue, "but Americans, when left to their own resources, are disposed to do the right thing."⁵

Dyea was suffering the same agony as Skagway, its miseries rooted in overcrowding, disease, poor sanitation, high living, and crime. The whole northern end of Lynn Canal was rapidly becoming a moral blot on the Alaskan landscape. Both cities needed time to build normal community facilities, establish their local governments, create a sense of order, and purge themselves of the unsavoury elements that were destroying any hope of civic pride.

"It seemed God couldn't care, seemed God wasn't there," wrote Joaquin Miller, the "Poet of the Sierras," when writing about the men and women who were fighting and brawling their way through Skagway and across the White Pass. But it appears that God did care. The Reverend Mister Robert McCahon Dickey, a Presbyterian, arrived in Skagway in October, 1897. Seventy of the faithful showed up for Dickey's first church service held in Burkard's Hall, hurriedly hired for the purpose. Within a month he had built a church, aided by the devout of seven denominations and a goodly number of sin-stained sourdoughs who, no doubt, hoped their contributions would move the angels to stamp "paid" on their overdrawn heavenly accounts.

"Take a day off and go to church," urged the newly established *Daily Alaskan*, and the people of Skagway responded in such numbers that four services had to be arranged. Episcopal Bishop Rowe, wearing his robes of office, was present. He praised the citizens of Skagway for their united effort in building an interdenominational church. Years ahead of his time in thought, he stated that "one strong church in a community can do many things that could not be done by three or four struggling rival congregations."

Father O'Neil, a recent arrival, responded to Dickey's invitation to conduct a service for Roman Catholics. The good father was so overcome by the congregation's enthusiastic welcome that he dramatically thrust his prepared sermon into the potbellied heater and proclaimed "the sermon will make more heat in the burning than it ever could in the preaching." He then, extemporaneously, gave a thundering oration on unity, liberty, and charity. As he stepped down from the hastily built pulpit, a Jewish gold-seeker who stood at the back of the hall called out, "I'm not a Christian, but . . . I count it a happiness to have had a small share in the building of this Synagogue!"⁶

Building the church was a community effort. Most people chipped in, including the gamblers and the prostitutes. At a fund-raising social, the Reverend Doctor Yukum of the American Episcopal Church delivered a rousing address that helped raise $200. He was assisted by the entertainment talent of Skagway, which included an instrumental trio known as the "Mountain Flats," Professor Trenaman, who swung his Indian clubs, Mr. Cadman's trick dog, and selections on the gramophone provided by William Ogilvie, who was passing through Skagway on his way to the Yukon district with Clifford Sifton, Canadian Minister of the Interior. The Lord might well have been pleased with the Reverend Mr. Dickey's accomplishments. Indeed, Dickey's life so inspired Dr. Charles William Gordon of St. Stephen's Church, Winnipeg, better known by his pen name, Ralph Connor, that he patterned his preacher after Dickey when he wrote his famous novel *The Sky Pilot*.[7]

But around Dickey's oasis of respectability and brotherly love swirled an ever-growing mass of men and women – the good and the bad, the legitimate and the illegitimate, the tough, the weak, and the tender. It was magnificent and it was hopeless. There was courage, crime, poverty – and disease. Spinal meningitis rampaged through Skagway and along the trails to the Klondike during the spring of 1898. Each local death was duly recorded in Skagway's Inquest Book. And with the passing of each week the cemetery north of town grew in importance, particularly to the hungry, who could earn the price of a meal or a drink or two by digging graves for those who had succumbed to the plague.

KLONDIKE-BOUND MINERS had arrived at the head of Lynn Canal in such huge numbers during the summer and fall of 1897 that Skagway had become a serious bottleneck. Unloading hundreds of passengers and thousands of tons of freight was not a serious problem, but transporting this mass of people and material from Skagway to the White Pass summit was. Moore's trail was too rough, too narrow, and the packers, with their trains of plodding mules, could not cope with the hordes of gold-seekers. Unless an answer to this nagging problem could be found, Skagway's position as a gateway to the gold-fields would soon become the object of continent-wide ridicule. There had to be an immediate solution. Joseph Hayes Acklen, a lawyer from Nashville, Tennessee, and a former congressman, was convinced that he had the answer.

He offered nothing new, simply another proposal to build a wagon road through the Chilkoot Pass or the White Pass to the head of navigation at Lake Bennett. He was well aware of the Syndicate's work to breach the White Pass, but he was convinced that with solid local support, combined with his influence in Washington, D.C., he could push a road through to successful completion before anyone else.

Acklen had discussed the transportation situation at length with George Augustus Brackett, businessman and railroad contractor, while they travelled to Skagway on the steamer *City of Seattle* in the fall of 1897. Brackett was on his way to meet his son James, who had gone north on the barque *Shirley* with a shipment of horses, cattle, and hardware, which he and his father planned to sell to the gold-seekers. This undertaking, they hoped, would help to restore the Brackett fortune, which had been seriously depleted by a number of business failures.

Acklen's meeting with Brackett had been a chance shipboard encounter. During the *City of Seattle*'s slow journey northward, they talked about the chaotic freighting and transportation conditions at Skagway and Dyea and the endless problems faced by the shiploads of stampeders. Acklen argued that the rapid construction of a good wagon road through one of the passes was the immediate answer and invited Brackett to join him in a survey of both passes – an undertaking Acklen believed could lead to a profitable business. Brackett was hesitant but finally agreed to join Acklen's survey and to determine the most favourable route for a wagon road to the Yukon interior.

The survey led Brackett to conclude that the Chilkoot Pass offered the most promising route and, as a demonstration of his faith in Dyea's future, he purchased several lots near the centre of town. Acklen, however, strongly favoured Skagway and the White Pass. These contrary views signalled the end of the Brackett-Acklen surveys, leaving each free to go his independent way.

Acklen's enthusiasm for the White Pass soared even higher when he learned that a local civil engineer, Norman R. Smith, had completed an independent survey for a wagon road from Skagway to Lake Bennett. Acklen sought out Smith and told him that he was interested in the development of such a road. Smith confirmed that he had been working on his survey for some time, that it was now complete, and that a road through the White Pass could be constructed with little difficulty and at minimal cost. Smith further suggested that, as they were both seeking ways to unsnarl Skagway's huge freighting problem, they should act together. Acklen quickly agreed.

Their first move was to discuss the matter with three local citizens, Dr. R.B. Runnalls, a prominent Skagway physician, Charles E. Kelly, a lumber merchant and property owner, and hotel-owner David Samson. A further eight Skagway citizens were invited to join them at an exploratory meeting held at Kelly's home, where Acklen, assisted by Smith, outlined the wagon-road proposal. After much discussion, those present resolved to form a company to build the road – to be followed, if possible, by a railway. Acklen then and there drew up a promoters' agreement, which was signed by everyone attending the meeting. Their company, when incorporated, was to have capital stock of $300,000. The sixteen promoters, who included three of Acklen's Nashville friends, voted to retain $150,000 of this public investment for themselves, presumably to cover the time they had spent on the proposal. Once they had this agreement, they each contributed $180 to a pool.[8]

The moment for the road seemed right. Escolme had made little progress in upgrading the Moore trail from Skagway to the summit. As a result, the townspeople of Skagway were unimpressed when he told them that he would have a few miles of railway built through the pass by fall.

Escolme's promise was based more on speculation than fact. Wilkinson's efforts to attract financial support for the railway had met with little success – other than the Close Brothers & Co.'s £10,000 loan. But despite these dismal prospects, Escolme pressed on, speaking confidently of the number of stampeders who were using his trail, and all the while hoping that the promised financial support from London would materialize.[9] To his credit, he had not been idle. Ignoring the Syndicate's restraining letters, he had spent a considerable sum on Moore's wharf, the construction of the sawmill, and improvements to parts of the Moores' Skagway property – most of which had been overrun by the stampeders. Nonetheless, everything seemed to be going wrong for Escolme, the Moores, and the Syndicate. The wharf and sawmill were showing a good profit, much to the Moores' satisfaction, but the trail through the White Pass, as originally laid out by Captain Moore and Bernard, was incomplete and, in places, impassable. And it was on the integrity of the trail that Skagway's future as a port of entry to the Yukon interior and the Klondike gold-fields depended.

Events were closing in on Escolme, and he was feeling the pressure. Frustrated miners were demanding a more satisfactory method of transporting their supplies and equipment across the pass. The trail had failed them and they made no bones about their dissatisfaction. The continuing boundary problems only added to Escolme's troubles. "Now our Skagway land is disputed territory," he lamented, "and it is still being administered by American authorities."[10]

Further confusion was created by D. Noble Rowan, one of Escolme's immediate superiors and president of the Alaskan and North Western Territories Trading Company. Escolme was predicting the start of the railway during the coming fall at the same time that Rowan was seeking permission to build a road along the same route. On July 26, 1897, Rowan had written to the United

States Secretary of the Interior, Cornelius N. Bliss, requesting permission to "construct a wagon road from Skagway through the White Pass to Lake Bennett, or to the border line between Alaska and British Columbia."[11]

Escolme, as well as representing the London Syndicate, was also managing director of Rowan's company, which was tied to the Syndicate through investment, directorships, and agreements. Although they ostensibly represented the same interests, Escolme and Rowan were sending out different signals, possibly because of the primitive communications between New York and Skagway or, more probably, because of conflicting policies emanating from the three Syndicate offices in London, New York, and Victoria, British Columbia.

Just twelve days later, on August 7, 1897, Rowan again wrote to the United States Secretary of the Interior, claiming that his company had now completed a *trail* from Skagway to the summit of White Pass "entirely at its own cost." Because he was anxious to recoup his company's outlay, he requested authority to "levy a small toll, say one cent a pound on goods going over the trail."[12] This was the trail the Moores had started and now the target of the miners' frustration and anger.

Neither of Rowan's letters produced the desired results. In fact, Secretary Bliss did not possess the authority to grant either of Rowan's requests because the land laws of the United States did not yet apply to the Territory of Alaska, and until they did, permission to build trails, roads, or railways, or to charge tolls, could not be granted by anyone in Washington, D.C. Whoever built such a facility and charged tolls would be operating outside of the law.

The Moores' own lamentable trail had been constructed without authority but, cursed or not, it was serving a purpose, and it held promise for the future. Now Acklen's road threatened to upset the Syndicate's plans, and there was nothing that either Escolme or the Moores could do about it.

Acklen knew the law, but he was confident that he could circumvent any difficulties the United States federal government might pose. It was his intention to travel to Washington, D.C., as soon as his business in Skagway was finished and use his considerable political influence to ensure that no legislation was passed contrary to the interests of his wagon-road proposal. That he had political influence, there could be no doubt. He had practised law in Nashville and Memphis and was actively involved in public life and private business. As a Democrat he had been elected to the 45th and 46th Congress of the United States, later declining a judgeship in the Federal District Court of Louisiana, a position tendered by President Hayes.[13] With his impressive background, Acklen, at the age of thirty-eight, was in a position to identify the centres of political power in Washington. He had reason to believe that his

White Pass wagon-road project would be protected by his friends in government and advanced by a wide range of investors with whom he was well acquainted.

Both Acklen and Norman Smith had studied the quality and capacity of the Moore trail that Escolme claimed now belonged to the Alaskan and North Western Territories Trading Company. This claim was hotly contested by the packers, who argued that the Moores and Escolme had done little more than improve a trail already scuffed out of the rocky terrain by the plodding feet of packers and miners. Moore countered by claiming that he alone had cut the original trail from Skagway Bay to the entrance of the pass, long before the packers arrived with their freight rates and strings of braying mules.

The Moores could claim credit for establishing the first general route through the pass, but they could not rightly claim to have established a recognizable trail complete with bridges, rock cuts, and corduroyed roads through the mud pits and swamps. It was only when Escolme arrived that serious trail improvements began. By the time his upgrading program was under way, however, the miners and the packers had already organized their own trail, part of it nothing but detours across better ground, and part of it following the original trail established by the Moores. Given the work contributed by the Moores, as well as the miners and packers, there is little doubt that both sides were justified in claiming to be the creators of the trail. To Escolme and the Syndicate, however, must go the credit for improving the trail by incorporating the best features of the work completed by the Moores and the improvements that had been made by the miners and packers.

By July 1897, Escolme had spent $10,000 on the trail, although he admitted that the main reason that the Syndicate had undertaken the work was to prospect for a railway. "But even when the railroad is done," he said, "there will be many miners who will continue to use the trail. Our desire is to help them get their supplies across the pass at a reasonable cost."[14]

It was impossible to find two miners who could agree on the condition of the trail. "It is good for about four or five miles," claimed one group of miners, "but after that hell begins." Discouraged men returned to Skagway telling of the brutal hardships they had suffered. They told of horses falling right and left over the cliffs and of the agony of the climb to the summit. Experienced men blamed both the trail and the general lack of competence that was evident everywhere. "They came from desks and counters," said one miner, "and they have never packed nor are they accustomed to hard labour."[15]

It mattered little what was said. The experienced and the inexperienced had been thrown together on a dangerous trail that twisted and turned and wormed its way between rocky outcrops, broken granite, tree stumps, and moss-covered boulders. Broken and jagged and at times awash in water, it was crowded with thousands of men who pounded it to pieces as they struggled north with hundreds of tons of equipment and supplies. Blockades and delays were a daily occurrence, adding to the frustration and ill-temper of the miners and packers wending their way to the summit, nearly 3,000 feet in the sky.

Acklen had observed it all. He was not interested in who should be credited for building the trail. The clear fact remained that there was still no road, and he was determined to do something about it. He could find nothing wrong with the Moores' original transportation plan, but he criticized the lack of boldness in the Syndicate's method of carrying it out. It seemed to Acklen that the Syndicate had attempted to upgrade the Moores' original pack trail both to encourage gold-seekers to accept Skagway as their port of entry and to provide a service trail for surveying a wagon road and later a rail route. In Acklen's view, the Syndicate had ended up with neither one thing nor the other. The trail in its present state was clearly hopeless as a means of moving freight in quantity and, unless huge amounts of capital could be found and invested in the project, neither the Syndicate's wagon road nor its railway would ever materialize. From what he had heard in Skagway, he could not imagine the Syndicate's London office financing either a road or a railway.

What was needed immediately, Acklen had concluded, was neither a trail nor a railway, but a first-class wagon road; the railway would come later. A wagon road, if constructed *now*, could provide the means to move many more tons of freight each day, and it would be easy and cheap to construct. He was confident that investors would quickly recover the road's costs by charging a toll, whether authorized or not. By moving quickly, Acklen hoped to beat both Dyea and the Syndicate to the punch.

Dyea entrepreneurs had not been asleep. A Boston capitalist, Thomas Nowell, had already announced that his recently incorporated Dyea-Klondike Transportation Company would construct an electric-powered transportation system to haul freight from his company's wharf at Dyea to Lindeman Lake, a distance of thirty-five miles. The scheme involved surface haulage along a wagon road to an aerial tramline that would swing freight through the air clear to the summit of Chilkoot Pass. This announcement was followed by a statement from The Pacific Coast Steamship Company that its recently incorporated subsidiary, the Alaska Railroad & Transportation Company, would also construct an aerial tramline – this one to be powered by a gasoline engine to transport freight up the final incline. While these two tramlines were being launched, a third was being organized. On October 13, 1897, a group of

Tacoma businessmen with interests in the North filed documents with the United States Secretary of the Interior to incorporate the Chilkoot Railroad & Transport Company. Hugh C. Wallace, a feisty official of the Washington and Alaska Steamship Company and Dodwell, Carlo & Co. of Tacoma, was named president of the tramline, and G.B. Pearce, general manager of the Northern Pacific Railroad, was named vice-president. The list of investors included bankers, transportation officials, and an assortment of industrialists, including millionaire Samuel S. Bush from Louisville, Kentucky, who stumbled onto the project while on an Alaskan holiday.

Wallace's plan was to construct a short horse-drawn, wooden-tracked railway out of Dyea and a nine-mile aerial tramline designed to transport 120 tons of freight each day from Dyea to the Chilkoot summit and over the top to Crater Lake, a quarter mile into what many regarded as Canadian territory. On the performance of this major tramline, which was to have the longest single aerial span in the world, would rest Dyea's claim to be the Klondike's principal port of entry.

The idea of using mechanical hoists to move freight over the Chilkoot Pass was not new. In the spring of 1895, Peter H. Peterson, an inventive ferry operator from Juneau, had devised and built a system for hauling freight up the steep and final incline to the Chilkoot summit. It consisted of a rope that ran through a series of poles and pulleys from the foot of the incline to the summit of the pass. Attached to each end of the rope were five canvas-wrapped sealskin bags. Peterson's plan was to load the top five bags with snow, which would then slide down to the foot of the incline. This gravity-induced snow-power, Peterson claimed, would provide the energy required to haul the lower five bags, loaded with miners' supplies, up the incline to the summit. Bernard Moore, who had been hired by Peterson to help build the hoist, argued that it would not work. Ignoring young Moore's advice, Peterson pressed on, but, as predicted, the snow-powered hoist failed to move a single pound of freight to the Chilkoot summit.[16]

Undaunted, Peterson tried again the following year. This time he dispensed with the cumbersome seal skins and substituted two wooden boxes mounted on steel runners. The principle was the same, but the technology was improved. A stout rope was passed through a pulley at the top of the pass and a sleigh-mounted box fixed to each end. The box at the bottom of the steep incline was filled with freight while the box at the top was loaded with snow. Then, to add weight, Peterson himself would climb into the snow-filled box – along with anyone else who was handy. With this added weight, the top box would start down the incline, pulling the freight-loaded box to the summit. It worked somewhat better than the sealskins. At least the packers, who contracted to use Peterson's improved hoist, could now struggle to the mountain summit unencumbered by heavy packs.[17] Although both of Peterson's hoists failed to live up to expectations, to him must go the credit for first hauling freight to the summit of Chilkoot Pass by mechanical means.

In the spring of 1897, Archie Burns, an experienced gold-seeker from Fortymile and Circle City, developed a practical horse-driven winch to pull loaded freight sleighs up the final steep incline from the Scales to the summit. By December the same year, he had dispensed with the horse and had installed a steam-powered drum. This, in turn, was replaced by a gasoline engine, which was said to be capable of hauling five tons of freight to the summit each day.

Peterson and Burns had led the way, but now three modern aerial tramlines were under construction on the Chilkoot Pass. Acklen knew that he had a fight on his hands to attract investors to his White Pass wagon road, although he later confidently wrote, "the more thought I have given the matter, the better I am satisfied that our wagon road must be a far safer and better paying investment than the wire tramway over the Chilkoot Pass." He was sure of success and he was confident that his wagon road would be only the beginning. "If the wagon road pays, and it certainly should," he boasted to Brackett, "we will have money enough on hand to go into the railroad business in the spring of 1898, or early summer."[18]

There was no doubt in his mind that his wagon road would meet and defeat any local competition, and that Skagway would win the day over Dyea. But on paper, it did not look quite that simple. The Syndicate, the three aerial tramlines, and Acklen's wagon road were not the only proposals to overcome the colossal Klondike transportation snarl.

The *Toronto Mail and Empire* reported in January 1898, that, in addition to the Syndicate charters, "Already twenty-one applications have been made to Canadian governments for the incorporation of various railway enterprises all of which have the Klondike for their goal." Ten of the twenty-one projected companies asked for powers to build and operate railways to the Yukon, to deal in land, mining, and properties, and to own and operate smelters. Several wanted the right to "build, acquire, and operate wagon roads, and collect tolls." Others sought authority to operate "sawmills, vessels, wharves and docks, telegraph and telephone lines, deal in water power, divert rivers and streams, acquire timber rights, and act as express companies." Most of the applicants had never been near the Yukon, but they recognized opportunity when they saw it. Some of them were foreign promoters who had never even set foot on Canadian soil, but they sketched their projects on the primitive northern maps

The newspaper story that triggered the mad rush to the Klondike.
AUTHOR'S COLLECTION

Thousands of gold seekers stormed the beaches of Skagway Bay on their way to the goldfields during the summer of 1897.

Mud, rain, and optimism characterized Skagway's early days.

Within weeks of the spampeders' arrival, Skagway's entrepreneurs managed to turn a
scattering of tents into a town.

(Above) Thousands of horses and mules were used to pack the miners' supplies over the White Pass trail.

(Right) The pack animals were overworked, underfed, and brutalized. Most ended their days at the bottom of Dead Horse Gulch.

(Below) George Brackett's wagon road north of Skagway.

North of White Pass summit, the foot-slogging army of sourdoughs hauled their heavily loaded sleighs towards Lake Bennett—some of them harnessing the wind.

Thousands of would-be miners bypassed Skagway and landed on the muddy beaches of nearby Dyea.

From Dyea, a seemingly endless line of stampeders made their way to Lake Bennett via the infamous Chilkoot Pass.

At Bennett, they built their boats and rafts and, when the ice broke up in the spring of 1898, they set sail on Lake Bennett, heading north to the Yukon River and the Klondike.

Eldorado Creek in the heart of the Klondike was, foot for foot, the richest gold-bearing creek in the world.

Klondike gold ready for shipment to the mints of Canada and the United States.

(Right) Captain William Moore.

(Below) Bernard Moore.

George Brackett

Charles Herbert Wilkinson

Ernest Edward Billinghurst

Sir Thomas Tancred, Bart.

William Brooks Close

Samuel H. Graves

Erastus Corning Hawkins

Michael James Heney

John Hislop

Robert Brydone-Jack

Supt. Frank Herbert Whiting

Dr. Fenton B. Whiting

Skagway before the start of railway construction.

Broadway, where the builders began the grade.

Behind the grades came the rail-laying gangs.

Jefferson Randolph "Soapy" Smith (hat in hand) at the bar of his Skagway saloon.

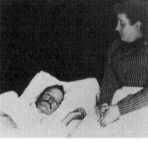

A fatally wounded Frank Reid became a Christian after putting a bullet through Soapy's heart.

At Soapy's funeral, the Rev. Mr. Sinclair said: "His remains lie there, cold and still in solitary death, no worthy mourner near his bier, no tears of sorrow shed."

Bargeloads of construction supplies were picked up by work trains operating on rough tracks across Skagway's beach.

Moore's Wharf. Its operation was the cause of much ill will between Captain Moore and officials of the railway, tracks of which were squeezed between the dock and the bluff on the right.

Engine No. 2, the first locomotive to operate in Alaska.

Railway graders at work north of Skagway.

With nothing but picks, shovels, horses, and brawn, the builders drove the railway
toward the summit of White Pass.

of the day and submitted them with supporting documents to the appropriate Canadian officials.

The Caribou Cassiar Railway applied to build a line from the Canadian Pacific Railway at Ashcroft, British Columbia, to Teslin Lake and follow the Hootalinqua and Yukon rivers to Dawson City and the Klondike. The British-Columbia Northern Railway also proposed to start at Ashcroft but "follow the Fraser River valley to the headwaters of the Stikine River," and on to Fort Selkirk.

Some companies selected Edmonton as a likely place to start. The Northern and Yukon Railway proposed to lay tracks from Edmonton to the Peace River and on to Dawson via Teslin Lake and the Yukon River. One group proposed to build from Edmonton, "with no particular route in view and to issue paid up promoters' stock." Another gave notice of its intention to build from Edmonton to the Peace River, "and then to the Yukon by the most practical and feasible route." None of the Edmonton railway proposals matured.

"Most of the railway magnates of the time," reported the *Toronto Mail and Empire*, "were of the opinion that the Pacific coast offered the most rewarding route to the Klondike."

The Lynn Canal and Dalton Railway mapped a route from a point near Dyea northward along the Dalton Trail to Fort Selkirk. The Stikine and Dresden Company proposed to start at Wrangell and follow the Stikine River to Telegraph Creek and on to Fort Selkirk by way of Teslin Lake. Skagway or Dyea was to be the southern terminus for the Yukon and Pacific Railway, which planned to construct a route to Lake Bennett and then continue down the Yukon River by boat to Dawson. A railway with nearly the same name, the Pacific and Yukon Railway, chose a route that would start "somewhere at the head of Lynn Canal," then travel over the Chilkat Pass to Dalton Post on the Alsek River, then on to Five Fingers Rapids and down the Yukon River to the gold-fields. Another line was projected from Portland Canal to Telegraph Creek on the Stikine River and on to Dawson via Teslin Lake and the Yukon River. Still another charter sought to build through the White Pass from the head of Lynn Canal and on to the Hootalinqua River.

"To avoid any scarcity of railroads," declared *The Mail and Empire*, "the British Pacific Railway proposes to build a railroad from the coast with branch lines meandering through the Cassiar and Yukon districts." Delighting in the North's profusion of railway schemes, the paper concluded its Klondike transportation survey by stating, "The trails, passes and valleys will echo with the shriek of iron horses very soon, if the applications to Parliament afford any indication of the number of railroads about to be built. The present plans, if executed, would make Dawson City the most important railway centre in the world."[19]

At the same time, the United States government authorities were being approached for permits to build railways from the coast of Alaska into the Canadian Yukon district interior – all designed to support the Klondike gold rush. The attractive combination of adventure, gold, and profits had fired the imagination of transportation men throughout Canada and the United States, as well as a number of overseas business tycoons. The Alaska and Northwestern Railway also made several proposals to the Canadian government, offering to build a railroad over the Dalton Trail, provided the company received a 6,400-acre grant of land for each mile of track built. An alternate offer was to construct a railroad from the Stikine River for an outright land grant of one million acres.

Because there was a fundamental difference between Canadian and United States railway policy, the Canadian government received many more applications for railway permits and charters than the government of the United States. Canada had started making large grants of land to railway builders about the same time the United States had stopped. By the mid-1890s, however, after granting some 56 million acres of federal and provincial lands to transportation projects, Canada proposed to modify its policy. The new approach envisaged aid in the form of cash subsidies and guaranteed interest on borrowed capital. Indeed, Wilkinson had already reported to the Canadian government that he had been unable to raise sufficient funds in London to construct the Syndicate's proposed railroad through the White Pass without government assistance.[20]

Because of the growing Klondike madness, the proper administration of the Yukon district and the transportation panic were two major problems placed before the recently elected Liberal government headed by Sir Wilfrid Laurier. His newly appointed Minister of the Interior, the Honourable Clifford Sifton, had hardly settled in his office when the full impact of the Klondike landed on him.

Sifton left Ottawa early in September 1897, to conduct a personal survey of the Yukon district's mining and transportation situation and the influence U.S. customs regulations were having on the freighting of Canadian-produced goods and supplies across the Alaska Panhandle. He visited Skagway, arriving there on October 8, and travelled through parts of the White Pass, the Chilkoot Pass, and the Lake Bennett district. After two weeks of investigation, he announced that the Yukon district's transportation needs could best be met by constructing an all-Canadian route, possibly through the Stikine River valley.

Sifton's decision to promote an all-Canadian route was supported by the findings of W.T. Jennings, a civil engineer whom Sifton had dispatched to northern British Columbia early in September 1897, with instructions to assess all the coastal passes leading to the Yukon interior, paying particular attention to the Stikine River valley. Jennings's survey party examined five possible rail routes: the Stikine valley, the White Pass, the Chilkoot Pass, the Chilkat Pass, and a possible route inland from the northern tip of Taku Inlet.

His surveys complete, Jennings returned to Wrangell, Alaska, where he had the good fortune to meet Sifton on his way back to Vancouver. During their voyage south together, Jennings told Sifton of his survey. He said that, with proper financial support, a 165-mile railway between a Stikine River port and Teslin Lake could be built and operating by September 1898, "provided all arrangements are made and the location determined by April 1898." The cost of constructing the railway, Jennings said, would be $4 million, including the cost of one major bridge. Should the railway idea be rejected, Jennings suggested that a good wagon road could be constructed along the same general route in ninety days for $1,400 per mile.[21]

Sifton liked what he heard. Undoubtedly he had already been influenced by his own personal observations as well as the opinion of Major James M. Walsh, the Yukon Commissioner, who had been urging the Canadian government to support the construction of an all-Canadian route into the Yukon interior via the Stikine valley and Teslin Lake. "Let us find a harbour," Major Walsh had written, "and Skagway and Dyea will return to what they were a year ago."[22]

The construction of an all-Canadian route was not a new idea. The Yukon Order of Pioneers, at a meeting at Fortymile in 1896, had asked the Canadian government to authorize the construction of a railway from Taku Inlet to Teslin Lake or Atlin Lake.[23] The absence of any diplomatic solution to the boundary question or uncontested Canadian access to the port of Skagway had forced Sifton to consider seriously such proposals for the development of port and transportation facilities free of United States influence.

Sifton's endorsement of the all-Canadian route proposal, however, appeared to contradict his earlier views about the future of the Klondike gold-fields. He could see that the Yukon district was experiencing a boom, but he did not believe that it would be a substantial or continuing source of wealth. "The Yukon is not the same as any other gold mining country in the world," he had stated, "and the difference consists of the fact that it is good for nothing except mining, which in all probability will be temporary."[24] Now, after seeing the

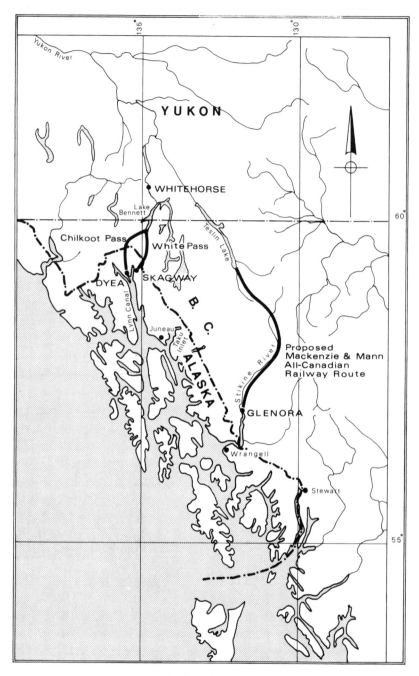

THREE COMPETING ROUTES

*The White Pass route faced fierce competition, not only from the trail and
the aerial tramlines through the neighbouring Chilkoot Pass, but also
from a scheme to build a railway via the Stikine Valley from Glenora,
B.C., to Teslin Lake.*

situation for himself and hearing Jennings's report, Sifton reversed his opinion and advocated the construction of a railway to the Yukon interior via the Stikine River and Teslin Lake.

Once back in Ottawa, Sifton's newly found enthusiasm for the construction of an all-Canadian route soon became Canadian government policy. Contractors were chosen to build a railway from Telegraph Creek at the head of navigation on the Stikine River to Teslin Lake. They were William Mackenzie and Donald Mann, two energetic and influential Canadian railway men, who had already seen the possibility of carving out a railway empire that would eventually serve the Orient through the northern British Columbia port of Prince Rupert. The contract was raised in the Department of the Interior by an act of executive volition and hastily signed by the contracting parties for ratification by Parliament when it reconvened in the New Year. The haste in which the contract was prepared and signed generated a considerable amount of adverse comment in the press. While admitting the urgency of the matter and the documented need for an all-Canadian route to the Klondike, *The Monetary Times* observed that "Parliament, under the circumstances, can scarcely consider the contract on its merits . . . its only function being to assent to a bargain already made."[25]

Under the terms of the contract, the government-sponsored, all-Canadian railway to the Yukon was to be built, equipped, and operating before September 1, 1898. Mackenzie and Mann agreed to deposit a $250,000 performance bond and guaranteed the construction of a port and railway terminus at the head of navigation near Telegraph Creek on the lower Stikine River. A further contract provision granted Mackenzie and Mann 25,000 acres of land *per mile* of operating railway as well as land in the Klondike area bordering 960 miles of creeks.

"The land," reported the *Victoria Colonist*, "is to be so located that the government and Mackenzie and Mann will have alternate blocks of land six miles by three miles." All of the land granted was to be subject to a royalty on gold of one per cent instead of the 10 per cent required of miners working in the Yukon district.[26]

Detailed location surveys for the railroad were started by Mackenzie and Mann. Soon loads of construction material and railway rolling stock were deposited at the southern terminus of the proposed railway on the Stikine River, and a horse trail was hacked along the general line of the route.

Acklen was not fully aware of the Mackenzie and Mann all-Canadian-route contract and the scramble for Canadian and United States charters to build railways into the Yukon district, but he could recognize local competition when he saw it. In Skagway, opposition to his wagon road was growing. He knew that the packers would be against his wagon road because of the toll they would have to pay if they used it, and he had plans to ensure that they would pay, handsomely.

Surprisingly, even a few of Skagway's businessmen opposed the construction of the wagon road, giving it no more support than they were offering the Syndicate's railway project. For them, it was a matter of business survival. They were earning fat returns from the hundreds of stampeders who were trapped in Skagway by conditions along the trail and anyone who planned to break the transportation bottleneck was not, in their opinion, working in Skagway's interests.

Other, more enlightened members of Skagway's growing business community recognized that their town's future depended on the long-term development of reliable port and overland transportation facilities. Acklen approached these progressives and urged that together they take action to resolve the transportation problem in anticipation of a good profit. But, he insisted, they would have to act fast. He had already learned that a group of West Coast capitalists had incorporated The Skagway and Lake Bennett Tramway Company Limited for the purpose of constructing a horse-drawn tramway through the White Pass, using cars five-feet wide and eight-feet long. "The cars," stated company engineer Basley A. Webster, "will be capable of carrying three tons pulled by one horse on the level and three horses on the heavier grades."[27]

Acklen's biggest concern was that the Syndicate would suddenly come to life and throw his wagon-road project into disarray. Already there were persistent rumours of reviving Syndicate activity, and subsequent events fully justified his fears. In November 1897, he had learned that Wilkinson had entered into an agreement with the Alaskan and North-Western Territories Trading Company, the American company that controlled the Moores' Skagway land. The agreement stated that Wilkinson intended to proceed with the construction of a railway from Skagway to White Pass summit, where it would connect with the British Columbia-Yukon Railway, and that the line would be built and running by July 1, 1899.[28]

As a result of this agreement, Escolme's public statement that he expected to see a few miles of track built by fall gained some credibility. To Acklen this turn of events was cause for worry. He wanted to see the transportation bottleneck broken, but he was determined to be the one to break it and reap the rewards. Wilkinson was not his only problem: across the peninsula at Dyea, the Chilkoot Railroad & Transport Company and The Dyea-Klondike Transportation Company were starting work on their respective aerial tramlines and were actively soliciting contracts to haul freight from Dyea to the Chilkoot summit.

With competition springing up all around him, Acklen and his Skagway shareholders could no longer delay incorporating their wagon-road company. Acklen hired a small local work force to start the construction of two bunk-houses and then left for Seattle accompanied by Norman Smith.

By coincidence, George Brackett was travelling south to Seattle on the same ship. Once again, Brackett and Acklen fell into conversation about Skagway's transportation problems. This time, Acklen and Smith both urged Brackett to become actively involved in the wagon road. Finally, after much persuasion, Brackett agreed to lend his name to the enterprise, but because of a lingering commitment to the Chilkoot Pass and Dyea, he refused to take any stock in the company until he had returned to Skagway and had personally examined the White Pass route. Should he find the route incompatible with his perception of what a good wagon route should be, his name would be removed from the company directorate.

In Seattle, Acklen, Brackett, and Smith visited John Hartman, an aggressive lawyer, and on October 13, 1897, the trio filed to incorporate the Skagway & Yukon Transportation & Improvement Company. Hartman was enthusiastic about the road's prospects and assured Acklen that he was convinced there was no better business proposition in the North than the proposed wagon road. He did, however, register a doubt about Norman Smith. "The only thing that I am apprehensive about is that the survey may not be correct."[29]

Acklen at once prepared to leave Seattle for Washington, D.C., to seek political support for his road and to contact the eastern money markets for investment capital. Before leaving, he explained to Norman Smith that his position would be untenable should he represent the survey as correct to his eastern colleagues if, in truth, it were not so. Smith, with hackles rising, told Acklen that he had nothing to worry about; the survey was correct. Acklen accepted Smith's somewhat heated assurances, but to protect his position he made Smith sign an affidavit attesting to the correctness of the survey. As a final precaution, Acklen had Smith questioned by F.C. Farnham, a civil engineer, who later informed Acklen that he was satisfied that Smith had completed a proper survey for the wagon road through the White Pass. With these assurances, Acklen left for the East feeling justified in attaching full faith and credibility to Smith's survey.[30]

With Farnham's assurance that Smith's survey was valid, Brackett finally accepted the post of vice-president and general manager of the project at a salary of $500 a month.[31] After purchasing construction materials and equipment and arranging for the shipment of a 250-foot steel bridge on the barque *Shirley*, Brackett left Seattle for Skagway together with the controversial Smith.

Brackett was eminently qualified to manage the project. He had been raised as a drover and cattleman and, at the outbreak of the United States Civil War in 1861, when only twenty-five years old, he contracted to furnish the army of the Potomac with beef. Later he crossed the central plains with General Sibley, where he provided the United States Army with transportation and supplies during the Indian campaigns of 1863.

After the war, he displayed an interest in milling and became the first president of an association of Minnesota millers. By 1866, he was contracting supplies and equipment for the great railways that were sweeping across the central plains towards the Rockies and the Pacific Ocean ports. This provided him with a decade of intense activity and a modest fortune. But more importantly, it brought him into contact with many of North America's leading railway tycoons and political figures. His work with the railways included supplies, transportation, construction, and reconnaissance expeditions as far as the Missouri River. With a number of business associates, he successfully bid on a contract to construct the first section of the Northern Pacific Railway from St. Louis to Fargo and, later, a contract for the second section from Fargo to Bismarck. These led to construction contracts with the Great Northern Railway. By 1881, he had arrived in Canada, where he built a section of railway west of Winnipeg for the Canadian Pacific.[32]

Brackett was also well versed in civic administration. He had served as an alderman in Minneapolis, and for one term had been the city's mayor. Now in his sixty-first year, he was a tall, thin, modest man with a greying beard and a clean-shaven upper lip, which led many people to remark on his striking resemblance to Abraham Lincoln. His wide-ranging activities included many public charities, which he often personally financed.

His involvement in so many diverse activities led one of his fellow citizens to claim that the phrase, "Let George do it," was inspired by Brackett, whose voluntary work ranged from sending food to the victims of the Johnstown flood in 1887 to being a leading organizer of the 1892 Republican convention.

When he returned to Skagway on November 6, 1897, Brackett discovered that the work ordered by Acklen early in October was at a virtual standstill. One fifty-bunk house had been completed, but the second was barely under way. He soon put his finger on the trouble. At a hastily called meeting of the local backers, he found "a great deal of boom enterprise – all stock and no money."[33] He told the backers that he would not take hold of the enterprise until he could, in good conscience, prove to prospective investors that the wagon road was a sound undertaking with good prospects for profit. To place things on a firmer financial footing, Brackett insisted that each of the promoters put up an equal amount of cash. He assured them that, because of his growing involvement, he would invest his share and become a shareholder.

Putting up their own money was not exactly what the Skagway promoters had in mind, but because Brackett would not take charge of the construction unless they did, they reluctantly accepted his demands. Brackett re-started construction of the road the following day, but only five of the promoters produced their promised cash. With such minimal financial support, it soon became clear that Acklen's wagon-road company was no better off financially than the Syndicate.

Within twenty-four hours of re-starting construction Brackett was rocked by some appalling news. Norman Smith's survey was a fraud. Not a single stake or elevation existed. Livid, Brackett confronted Smith, who finally admitted that he and two associates had run a line from Skagway to Bennett in five days using a pocket compass, a Canadian map, and "some good guessing as to the character of the country."[34]

Lesser men might have quit on the spot, but Brackett immediately struck off into the mountains to survey a line of his own. By November 12, he was satisfied that his new route would justify proceeding with construction as planned. His route would follow the Skagway River as far as possible, with an extreme grade of 8 per cent and an average grade of 4 per cent for the whole distance. The route question had finally been settled locally. Although still shocked by Smith's chicanery, Brackett at least now knew where he stood and he could still justify his previous claims that "a wagon road can be built with a railroad to follow later."[35]

The incident confirmed Brackett's suspicions of Smith, which had clouded their relationship from the beginning. When Acklen had first learned of the hostility between two of his senior officials, he had written to Brackett expressing the hope that "you and Mr. Norman Smith will work in harmony, as any differences at the outset will seriously militate against ultimate success." Brackett had swallowed his resentment at the time and had devoted his full attention and energies to the completion of the road. "He was determined to complete the road," wrote reporter W.A. Croffut, "through the dark defiles and up the frowning acclivities."[36]

By the middle of November 1897, Brackett had seventy-five men on the payroll, including Norman Smith, whose removal had yet to be authorized by Acklen. Construction was well advanced, as the rock work had proved to be much easier than predicted. Gangs of men hired locally were operating at several points, each opening up several hundred feet of road and working to join the completed sections together. Despite Brackett's energetic management, insufficient finances meant that paying bills was a nightmare. Each payday occasioned a frantic search for funds. Brackett's own salary went unpaid. The $300 monthly salaries of Norman Smith and D.M. Brown, superintendent of timber works, came out of Brackett's own pocket, despite his contempt for the perfidious Mr. Smith.

DURING THESE FINAL MONTHS of 1897, Skagway became the focal point of discussions, plans, and activities in widely separated parts of the world: Wilkinson, Close, and the Syndicate in London; Sifton, Mackenzie, and Mann in Ottawa; Acklen in Washington, D.C., and Nashville; attornies Struve and Hartman in Seattle; Helmcken and Billinghurst in Victoria; Chrysler in Ottawa; and Moore and Escolme, who shuttled back and forth between Seattle, Vancouver, and the North. This raw, rambling, gold-rush boom town had become a free enterprise transportation target, the hub of international intrigue. In three countries, players battled for control of the flow of freight in and out of the Klondike gold-fields – an enterprise that would, with a little luck, earn them each a fortune.

Jefferson Randolph "Soapy" Smith cared little about transportation, other than a set of wheels to keep him ahead of the law. He arrived in Skagway late in the fall of 1897, and he was pleased with what he saw. The one thing that he could not abide was law and order and, much to his satisfaction, there was little evidence of either. His qualifications as a get-rich-quick artist were already apparent, and in certain circles he was considered one of the most accomplished bunco artists of his day.

Smith was born in 1860 at Noonan, Georgia. His family had sired three lawyers, three doctors, a minister, and a farmer. His mother, who was known for her beauty, held hopes that her son, Jeff, would choose the ministry as his vocation, and to this end she set about giving him a Christian upbringing. One can imagine her disappointment when, in his late teens, his itchy fingers and compelling curiosity propelled him from Georgia to the rangelands of the Lone Star State. There he became an expert horseman and found, to his surprise, that the world was full of suckers. He was not particularly handsome, but he possessed a deep and mellow voice and a commanding presence, two attributes that set him above the men who frequented the dance halls and gambling joints of Texas.

He was twenty-five when he left the South and rode into Leadville, Colorado, full of bravado and determined to find a sure and painless way of emptying the pockets of the innocent. By chance he became acquainted with a virtuoso of the shell game, known throughout the West as "Old Man Taylor." At Soapy's silky urgings, Taylor taught him the art of manipulating three walnut shells and a rubber pea with such dexterity that the ever-missing pea was soon providing Smith with a handsome living in Leadville's best hotel.

He later moved to Denver, where he graduated from the shell game to selling soap – at a substantial profit. His game was to purchase a stock of soap, cut each bar into four miniature squares, and wrap each square in plain white paper. After setting up his satchel and tripod on a street corner, he would attract a crowd with his convincing manner and sonorous voice. "Friends," he would purr, "this is the finest soap ever compounded. It was concocted in my own laboratory and manufactured in my own factory. My mission in life is to get people to use soap, and I'm willing to pay you for it."

He would then take several squares of soap from his satchel and, in full view of the crowd, wrap each square in a high-denomination bill – some twenties, a few fifties, and one or two hundreds. He then covered both the soap and the bill with a new white paper wrapper and tossed the squares back into his satchel, which was full of "unbilled" soap. The onlookers were then invited to step forward and, for only five dollars, buy a bar of soap on the chance of picking a bar wrapped in a bill. The first man to buy invariably won a twenty- or a fifty-dollar bill, which he dutifully returned to Smith later in the day for a cut of the take. Encouraged by his luck, others would surge forward waving their five-dollar bills.

It was only a matter of time before he was arrested for running a confidence game in broad daylight on the streets of Denver. Unable to remember the name "Jefferson Randolph," but aware that his prisoner had been selling soap, the policeman recorded the arrest by writing "Soapy" Smith on the police blotter, and by that name Jefferson R. Smith eventually became known throughout Canada and the United States.[37]

Soapy Smith was a born leader, a trait he discovered on the streets of Denver, where he organized crooks and drifters into a disciplined army ready to do his bidding and receive his protection. He had influence with some politicians and city officials who were on his payroll. He was observant, articulate, and convincing – three sterling qualities that brought him several sizeable fortunes, which he gambled or gave away. "Money has no value except to back a good hand," he would say. Despite his contempt for wealth, he devoted most of his life to the relentless pursuit of plunder, using his genius to rally the forces of crime around his shoddy banner of corruption. Yet, he was an amazing rascal with a philosophical turn of mind. "A gambler," he once said, "is one who teaches and illustrates the folly of avarice; he is a non-ordained preacher on the vagaries of fortune and how to make doubt a certainty."[38]

Making doubt a certainty became increasingly difficult for Smith as the years flew by. Denver became thoroughly fed up with his criminal activities. One escapade ended in his arrest for attempted murder of Colonel John Arkins, manager of *The Rocky Mountain News*. The paper had brought its editorial guns to bear on Smith and his gang, revealing the cutthroat tactics they employed in their unceasing efforts to maintain control of the city. Now, Colonel Arkins had a fractured skull, and the citizens of Denver were appalled.

"The *News* has opposed this scoundrel," thundered the plucky paper. "It has pointed out that he has supreme control over the lesser scoundrels. It has exposed his methods and drawn his plots into the light of day. It has urged that he could not daily pursue his career of robbery unless with the knowledge and consent of the authorities. The answer to this was a blow in the darkness of night – a murder in all but success."[39]

Smith never came to trial. He slipped out of town and headed for Creede, a boisterous mining town in southeast Colorado near the headwaters of the Rio Grande. There he established the Orleans Club in competition with Bob Ford, the man who shot Jesse James. It has been said that no frontier town was more wide open than Creede. "It's day all day in the daytime," wrote Cy Warman, editor of the *Creede Candle*, "and there is no night in Creede."

Smith numbered amongst his friends such underworld aristocrats as the "Reverend" John Bowers, "Shoot-your-eye-out" Jack Vermillion, "Troublesome Tom" Cady, "Old Man" Tripp, and "Slim Jim" Foster, to name a few. He controlled events from the shadows and influenced the mighty with his charm. In Washington, D.C., he met many of the nation's most prominent citizens and lawmakers, including senators, businessmen, and editors. "They were charmed with him," wrote his cousin Edwin Bobo Smith, a Washington, D.C., newspaperman, "and they never seemed to tire of his company."[40] Despite his infamous behaviour, he tended to regard himself as a paragon of virtue. Yet his outrageous activities did nothing to help cast him in the noble mould he sought during his short but turbulent life. "The way of the transgressor is hard to quit," he would say as he set out on yet another caper that held promise of wealth or influence.[41] Year after year he went on crossing and recrossing the line that separates good from evil in his fruitless attempt to be all things to all men. This was the incredible Soapy Smith who, while gambling, would confound his fellow players by gently singing his favourite Sunday school hymn, "Jesus Wants Me For A Sunbeam."[42]

Throughout his larcenous career in an underworld of his own making Smith never quite abandoned his dream of one day becoming a man of national importance. "Jeff . . . had a brilliant mind and could achieve being President of the United States," Edwin Bobo Smith is reported to have said. But the exceptional ability of both Smith and his father "was apparently diminished by their alcoholism, the only members of the family to have suffered this affliction."[43] Instead of becoming the president of the United States, Smith achieved the distinction of becoming one of the first racketeers in the West.

While in Washington, D.C., during the fall of 1897, Smith announced that he was giving up his crooked ways and was going to "seek an honourable fortune in the frozen Alaskan country." He said that he would return to Washington after gaining his fortune and establish himself as a respectable hotel owner. News of the Klondike was on everybody's lips. "This," he said, "is my last opportunity to make a big haul. Alaska is the last west. I know the character of the people I shall meet there, and I know I'm bound to succeed with them."[44]

Somewhere along the way, his good intentions were contaminated by the dark chemistry of his soul. Gathering up two of his trusted lieutenants, "The Reverend" Bowers and "Doctor" W.H. Jackson, he headed for the West Coast where all three boarded a ship that would take them to Skagway.

As the northern tip of Lynn Canal came into view, Smith quickly grasped the significance of Skagway's unique location. It was not only the natural gateway to and from the Yukon valley, it was a staging area, entertainment centre, transfer point, gold camp, and a hub of commercial enterprise. But best of all, it was totally unorganized and a thousand miles from significant United States law enforcement agencies. And ambling along its muddy streets were thousands of *cheechakos* in bright new mackinaws, innocent and ready for the plucking, and boatloads more arriving every day. He could hardly believe his eyes. He had stumbled into a bunco paradise. All he had to do was set up his court and crown himself king.

Skagway's underworld soon bowed to his authority. Under Smith's sure and experienced hand they operated happily without fear of interference from the local marshal. He convinced many of Skagway's respectable citizens that he was the town's prime stabilizing influence because, he said, he had a way of dealing with crooks!

By late 1897, Skagway was in Smith's pocket. He had quickly flim-flammed his way into almost every local enterprise that would turn a legal or illegal dollar. His intricate crime machine operated around the clock, pumping out con jobs, protection deals, knifings, and armed hold-ups. He no longer avoided violence. "Get it while the getting's good," he used to say, and his gang of thugs would knock back their drinks and slink off into the night to do their worst. As well as saloons and gambling joints, he operated the Reliable Packers, a Merchants Exchange, and a Telegraph Office where, according to the advertisement, you could send a telegram anywhere in the world for five dollars, although no telegraph facilities existed! Yet the suckers came, paid their money, and within an hour or so they would receive a suitably worded reply – collect.

His activities, however, did not go unnoticed. A news item from Seattle reported: "Officers from the steamer *Noya* from Skagway today reported conditions of lawlessness at Skagway beyond description. Soapy Smith and his gang are in full control. Law-abiding people do not dare say a word against them. Hold-ups, robberies, and shootings are part of the routine."[45]

Smith was now king, crowned with a broad-brimmed miner's hat. This was the man who posed as a friend of law and order. He seemed to have everyone duped – except Frank Reid, the town surveyor. He and a few of his friends had been watching Smith for a long time, and they were deeply troubled by what they saw.

Six

THE BATTLE OF THE PASSES

WHILE BRACKETT STRUGGLED in the mountains during November 1897, Acklen toured the eastern United States and the offices of investors and legislators in Washington, D.C. His major problem was that, until Congress extended the provisions of the U.S. land laws to apply to Alaska, there was no way anyone could obtain a right-of-way for a road to move freight through federal lands without Congressional approval. But Acklen was a former congressman, and he was not without political friends who offered their sympathetic ears as he described the transportation problems at Skagway and his plan to overcome them.[1]

As citizens of the United States, Acklen argued, Alaskans had a right to expect the consideration and support of their federal government. Alaska's first need, he explained, was the development of transportation, and this could only be accomplished by a government edict granting him a right-of-way from Skagway to the White Pass summit – should the boundary be established there. Such right-of-way, he assured Washington officials, "would afford the easiest access to Dawson City to relieve the wants of Americans who may suffer there during the coming spring from the scarcity of provisions."[2]

He proposed that the United States Secretary of War should establish a military presence at Skagway. "This," he wrote to Brackett, "would further the ends we have in view."[3] And the ends he had in view were to overcome the transportation debacle, control the Klondike lifeline through Skagway, and become a millionaire.[4]

Nothing specific was accomplished at Washington during Acklen's visit there, as Congress was not due to meet until December. He had, however, successfully advanced the argument among his political friends that transportation through the White Pass was in complete disarray, that his company was capable of sorting out the mess, and that he was entitled to "those rights which we have acquired by possession." There is little doubt that if the Moores or

Wilkinson or the packers had heard Acklen's "rights by possession" argument, they would have been enraged. Claiming "rights by possession" was sheer impertinence, but no one in Washington knew how far Acklen was stretching the truth. "I think it of great importance that such action should be taken at Washington, D.C., as will unquestionably secure us . . . those rights," Acklen wrote to Brackett without any evidence of shame or remorse.[5]

Brackett was determined to build the wagon road whether Washington granted a right-of-way or not. He knew he could not afford to wait for the government to act, although without government sanctions there would be neither guarantees nor protection for the enterprise. Acklen was of the same opinion and urged Brackett to push construction to the limit and build the first bridge as quickly as possible. "These bridges . . . must be so constructed as to admit of being used later for a narrow gauge railroad," he advised Brackett. "This in my judgment will insure the success of the enterprise and place us in a position to command outside capital."[6]

Bold statements and bravado, however, do not pay bills, and Acklen's quest for investment capital met with little success during his swing through the East. It seemed that doubts about the integrity of Smith's survey had reached New York and other financial centres.

Acklen, far from the local scene and without detailed knowledge of Smith's confession to Brackett, continued to defend the survey. He argued that the engineering profiles clearly demonstrated that a wagon road could be constructed through the pass and that, in due course, he and his associates would use it to build a narrow-gauge railway. Despite Acklen's calming assurances, the rumours persisted in eastern political and financial circles that Smith's survey was both faulty and incomplete. Acklen was finally forced to admit that "Someone has evidently written out here conveying the information that the survey of our road up the Skagway river is not to be relied upon, and that the grade is one which can never be used for railroad purposes. I am thus far unable to trace this down, but it has seriously hampered me in my plans."[7]

Acklen had no alternative but to clarify the veracity of Smith's survey. On November 25, he telegraphed the superintendent of the wagon road's timber works, D.M. Brown, who was on a purchasing trip to Seattle. "EASTERN MONEY IS CONDITIONED UPON CORRECTNESS OF SMITH'S SURVEY. WAS SMITH'S SURVEY ABSOLUTELY CORRECT? WIRE ANSWER." Brown replied, "SMITH MADE NO SURVEY. ADMITS THAT NOW. DOES NOT EVEN KNOW ROUTE."[8]

Acklen was crushed. His enterprise, entered into with such clarity of purpose, was falling apart and slipping from his grasp. He was too far removed from Skagway to exercise direct control and there was, unknown to him, a growing opposition to his influence within the company because of his inability to fill the empty treasury.

In an attempt to raise money, company treasurer Samson had sailed to Seattle with $125,000 worth of blank stock, which, he had assured the Skagway promoters, he would quickly sell, even promising to send $50,000 to them within three weeks.

In Seattle, Samson learned of Brown's wire to Acklen denouncing Smith's survey and flew into a rage. He then added to the mounting confusion by wiring Acklen that a proper survey *had* been made and to ignore the information provided by Brown. He concluded by asking Acklen to scrape up as much money as possible and forward it immediately so that the payroll could be met. In reply, Samson received a terse telegram from Acklen's secretary stating that Acklen was very ill. "OVERWORK AND WORRY FROM PRESENT STATE OF YOUR COMPANY THE CAUSE."[9] The telegram further stated that neither Acklen nor anyone else would invest in the road until there was absolute assurance that a proper survey had been made.

Samson responded by convincing the company's directors in Seattle that Acklen should be purged from the company, describing him as "a wrecker of whatever he undertakes and an all around fraud; a man without means and a man with a very scaley reputation."[10]

The directors met on December 4, 1897, and on the pretext that a stock transfer to Acklen had been improperly conveyed, stripped Acklen of his power and authority in the company. The directors' support of Samson in purging Acklen indicates an alliance with George Brackett, who now found himself in charge of the project but without financial support from the original Skagway promoters or Acklen himself. Brackett also was beginning to have serious reservations about Samson, who had failed to sell a dollar's worth of stock or to raise money by any other means – including an attempt to borrow from the Washington National Bank.

For reasons known only to himself, Brown, on learning of Samson's loan application, had informed the bank that no proper survey for the road existed and that he had serious doubts about Samson's personal integrity. Forewarned, the bank told Samson that it could find little to recommend the granting of a loan. Accepting defeat, and unable to sell stock or obtain a loan, Samson cut and ran, taking with him the last $800 in the company's treasury – an amount he claimed the company owed him for services rendered. He was neither seen nor heard of again.[11]

The future of the Skagway & Yukon Transportation & Improvement Company looked bleak indeed. If the wagon road was ever going to be built, there was only one man who could do it – George A. Brackett.

Brackett reviewed the situation with the Skagway promoters, who gave him little encouragement and virtually no financial support. It was then that the company's president, T.M. Word, announced that he wanted all the money he had invested in the project refunded – and if he didn't get it, he would obtain a court order and have the work stopped.[12] Brackett, who was now determined to see the matter through, dug into his own savings, paid off Word, and accepted his resignation.

Now uncontested head of the company, Brackett turned his back on the shambles created by the original promoters and faced the mountain barrier. He was determined to build the road, and he was confident that he could raise the funds required to pay the drawer full of bills he had inherited, as well as finance future construction. The road was needed and he took advantage of every opportunity to promote it as *the* route to the Klondike. "This road," he proclaimed, "is bound to accommodate the great bulk of travel to the gold country and it will give a decided impetus to the human tide which is finding its way to the pass."[13]

Brackett expected to recover his investment and to reap huge profits in the near future. These prospects fired his enthusiasm. The future looked bright. The hordes of miners arriving in Skagway grew week by week as rumour fed on rumour.

While in Victoria on a business trip during late October, Brackett had met Sir Charles Tupper, recently defeated Conservative prime minister of Canada. Sir Charles himself, Brackett discovered, was organizing an expedition to the gold-fields and Brackett knew Tupper's comments would carry a great deal of weight. "The Syndicate," Sir Charles informed Brackett, "is very dilatory in its movements in regard to opening up roads to the Yukon," and that "there would be from England alone not less than 100,000 people." The manager of the Bank of Montreal in Victoria told Brackett that he had a similar report from England, and no one placed the number of people coming from England at less than 100,000.

Brackett doubted the accuracy of these figures – a judgement that proved to be substantially correct.[14] Nevertheless, at the time, they represented thousands of tons of potential freight, and each ton would produce a handsome profit. His eyes fixed on the prospect of these profits, Brackett was more than ever determined to build the road. He alone would raise the money. He alone would spearhead the mountain road through the rocky defiles of the White Pass.

BRACKETT SOON HAD 100 men on his payroll, most of them miners who had gone broke in Skagway. They were quickly formed into gangs and dispatched to strategic locations along the line of road construction. The draw on his personal funds was immediate and heavy. Besides the costs of tents, tools, provisions, and construction supplies, Brackett was forced to pay the pack-train operators twenty cents a pound to transport this heavy freight to the work camps high in the pass.

As late autumn set in, Brackett wisely decided to concentrate on completing the heavy rock work in the upper reaches of the pass before freeze-up. When the early December snowstorms blasted down from the mountain peaks, he directed his gangs to work back towards Skagway and the sea, where the frigid grip of winter was less intense.

By the middle of December, Brackett had completed eight miles of road. But he still had neither a franchise nor Washington's authority to build the road or charge a toll, and he was concerned.

"Now as to the franchise," he wrote his friend, United States Senator Cushman K. Davis, "I will take the matter up when the road has been finished, trusting that you can keep the Senate from passing bills in favour of anyone who has not been on the ground or built an inch of road, when my company has had the courage to come here and complete the road without asking for a franchise."[15] Brackett was worried about Moore and Escolme and Rowan, all of whom had applied to Washington for permission to construct a wagon road through the White Pass to the unofficial boundary at the summit. "I shall, therefore, rely on the Senate to hold off any new companies until such time as I can give the matter attention and ask for the necessary legislation."

In his letter, Brackett also told Davis of his complete disenchantment with Acklen, informing him that Acklen and his eastern friends had been removed from the company, "they not having taken the proper steps to aid this under-taking." He also warned Davis that Acklen was still urging Washington officials to assist him in obtaining a franchise to which, in Brackett's view, he had no right. "He is entitled to no consideration whatever until he has at least come here and rendered some assistance in this great work," Brackett wrote. "I must ask you, therefore, to protect my interest as far as he is concerned." The mistrust was running deep. Brackett's fear was that, after he had financed and built the road, Acklen would grab the franchise through the influence of powerful friends in Washington.

By December 20, 1897, the wagon-road project was flat broke and facing a mound of unpaid bills – including the payroll, now one week overdue. Brackett called his workmen to a meeting where he took them wholly into his confidence. He confessed that he could not pay their back wages, but he promised that, if they would stay on the job, their time sheets would become promissory notes he would redeem as soon as he could raise the cash. They believed him and stayed almost to a man. Brackett left for Seattle in search of investors. There he placed his project before several Seattle business leaders, but his belief in Alaska and his wagon road failed to elicit any expressions of interest, let alone offers of money.

These were dark days for Brackett, and he was almost on the point of giving up, when he decided instead to return to Skagway and face his unpaid workers. Some of his friends pleaded with him to stay out of the North for his own protection. The men who were waiting for their wages would eventually turn ugly, they warned, and make life dangerous for him. Brackett would not hear of it. "They have treated me fairly and frankly," he said, "and I propose to go back and face them and tell them the exact situation."[16]

That same, depressing day a friend named Macauley from Victoria offered to mortgage his house and lend Brackett $5,000 without security. Brackett gratefully accepted the offer, took the money, and sent it to his son, James, in Skagway to pay the long-suffering workers. Shortly after this windfall, he received a telegram from James J. Hill, president of the Great Northern Railroad, who, in response to Brackett's written appeal for financial support, invited him to visit him in St. Paul. With rising spirits, Brackett boarded a train for the East to raise capital and solidify his political support.

Brackett was still convinced that, given a few breaks with weather and finances, he could finish the road by the end of January or early February 1898 and turn the debt-ridden enterprise into a money-maker. His main problem was a lack of capital, a situation Brackett made clear in a final blistering letter to Acklen before leaving Seattle on December 29, 1897:

> To sum up the whole question, I find that I have been drawn into a company, the treasurer having taken the larger portion of the funds, the engineer a fraud, yourself refusing to respond financially as I had reason to believe you would, and now the president has demanded of me the money that he had put in, thereby making me the loser of some thousands of dollars. . . . You can imagine my feelings to be more than

three thousand miles from home and any moneyed center, with two hundred and twenty-five men building a road that you gentlemen put me in charge of. Now I have but one thing to do. Either lose every dollar I have invested, or push the work to completion. Whatever troubles have been placed on you, I can multiply it by twenty, and I'm still on my feet, here to complete the road, pay the bills, and when I'm through, to leave a clear record. I leave tonight, to get the balance of the money that shall pay the debts of this boomed-to-death company.[17]

Having got that off his chest, Brackett left for Minneapolis to confer with his old contracting associates and his eastern political friends. In Minnesota, Brackett contacted newspaperman and ex-congressman, Colonel William S. King, an old associate and political ally. Brackett outlined the nature of his undertaking in Alaska, his desperate search for cash, and his need for legislation that would legalize his project. King must have blinked when Brackett asked for such extensive help, but he did not flinch. After discussing Brackett's problem, King went to Montreal to meet with another of Brackett's friends, Sir William Van Horne, president of the Canadian Pacific Railway, for whom Brackett had worked during his railway-contracting days.

King gave Van Horne a report on Brackett's plight, which included his need of cash to continue construction of the wagon road and his hope that the Canadian government could be induced to grant Brackett authority to extend his road into Canada from the White Pass summit to the head of Yukon River navigation. In support of his argument, King pointed out the overall benefits of the wagon road to Canada and Canadian trade. Van Horne discussed the matter with Richard B. Angus, a CPR director, and Thomas G. Shaughnessy, a CPR vice-president, and on January 7, 1898, he telegraphed Brackett's Seattle office:

HAVE SEEN KING. ANGUS, SHAUGHNESSY AND MYSELF WILLING TO PUT FIVE THOUSAND EACH IN YOUR ENTERPRISE ON SUCH BASIS AS YOU THINK FAIR. WE HAVE SUCH CONFIDENCE IN YOU THAT DETAILS CAN BE ARRANGED LATER.[18]

The eastern trip was starting to produce results.

King then left Montreal for Washington, D.C., to promote legislation that would provide Brackett with authority to construct his road and collect tolls. When King arrived in the capital, he found that Congressman John F. Lacey of Iowa had already introduced a bill to extend the United States land laws to the Territory of Alaska. This was exactly what Brackett and others wanted –

including Wilkinson, Rowan, and Escolme, who still clung to the hope that the Syndicate's transportation enterprise would prevail.

The White Pass and the Chilkoot Pass were becoming transportation battlegrounds. Backers of both passes were fighting each other to control the lucrative freighting business. Within the Chilkoot Pass three aerial-tramway projects vied with each other, while the Indian packers fought unsuccessfully to protect their traditional monopoly. Within the White Pass the struggle continued between the Syndicate, Brackett, and the pack-train operators. Here, Brackett was emerging as the winner.

Lacey's bill to extend the land laws to Alaska passed the House on January 21, 1898. It was then referred to the Senate committee on public lands, where it was debated and subsequently forwarded with amendments to the floor of the Senate. It was not yet law, but for the first time since Brackett embarked on his long and involved odyssey, he had reason to feel encouraged by the developments in Washington.

Lacey's bill was a matter of some concern to Close Brothers of London, who were preparing strategies to protect the £10,000 loan they had made to Wilkinson. Should Congress extend the land laws to Alaska, and Brackett – or others – successfully file for a right-of-way through the White Pass before the Syndicate, Close Brothers' loan would be in jeopardy. Whoever cornered the right-of-way would control the pass, and Brackett seemed to have a distinct edge over his competitors as a result of his hard work, personal investment, and the influence of his Washington-based political contacts. Wilkinson and Close Brothers had every reason to be concerned.

During his stay in the East, Brackett wasted no opportunity to extol the glories of Alaska and the riches of the Canadian Yukon. To hear him describe the North and its future would lead one to believe that the great sweep of the Alaska-Yukon landscape had been blessed by heaven itself.

"While Horace Greeley told the young men of this country to go west," Brackett said while being interviewed by the *Minneapolis Journal*, "he predicted that wealth and population of Minnesota would be multiplied by twenty. I firmly believe that the same will apply to Alaska. The wealth is there and that is what will draw people from all parts of the globe."[19]

As Brackett prepared to leave the *Journal*'s editorial room, he displayed a handful of large Klondike nuggets, one of them worth twenty-one dollars. The reporter gazed at the gold in wonder. "They are throwing these away up there," said Brackett, pocketing his nuggets with an amused smile.[20]

In St. Paul, Brackett conferred with James J. Hill, the railroad executive who had telegraphed him in Seattle suggesting that they discuss Brackett's money problems. Hill was unable to generate any interest among his railway associates or business friends, but he demonstrated his personal belief in Brackett by presenting him with a cheque for $15,000 without asking for any security other than his note.[21]

Brackett returned to Seattle early in January 1898. From there he wrote to Van Horne thanking him for his $15,000 and urging him to obtain a charter from the Canadian government that would authorize the extension of the wagon road into Canada. As well, Brackett explained, he would need additional financial help.[22]

On January 13, Van Horne telegraphed Brackett in Vancouver:

> MINISTER INTERIOR SAYS GO AHEAD WITH YOUR WAGON TO LAKE BEN-
> NETT AND HE WILL SEE THAT YOU ARE NOT INTERFERED WITH.[23]

With this information, Brackett laid plans to send a survey crew into Canada to plot a route from White Pass summit to Lake Bennett. His idea was to build a sled road across the hard-packed snow that could handle the thousands of tons of freight piled up all along the route. Later, if the money could be raised, the sled road could be upgraded to a wagon road. "Had I the money at my command to build the road to Bennett," he wrote to Van Horne, "I would push it through regardless of cost as it is really essential that it should be done."

Brackett was particularly concerned about the number of people who were pouring into the Pacific Northwest. "The situation as it exists in Seattle frightens me," he wrote to Van Horne, explaining that the city was packed solid with would-be prospectors heading for the gold-fields, although there were no facilities to move them beyond Skagway "except what little I have done in constructing a wagon road."[24]

Transportation was chaotic. Moving freight and passengers to Skagway and Dyea from Seattle, Vancouver, San Francisco, and other West Coast ports was often a frustrating exercise. The steamship operators made it all look simple by avoiding any mention in their advertisements of the searching, the wrangling, and the countless delays caused by their sisyphean struggle with mountains of freight – all of it destined for Skagway or Dyea in overloaded, overcrowded, and overworked ships.

As soon as he arrived back in Skagway, Brackett was confronted by this pandemonium. Dumps of freight lined the beaches, and through them and around them swarmed scores of harassed and bewildered gold-seekers, many of whom were unfit for the task they faced. The men displayed all the signs of an army in full retreat. But they muddled on as men do when faced with the unexpected – some with courage and good humour, some with fear and sullen discontent. They struggled across the beaches and on into the mountains, looking like a long and ragged line of ghostly hunchbacks as, laden down with packs, they shuffled towards the summit, their eyes fixed on the jagged, snow-draped horizon beyond which lay the promised land.

From the day he returned to Skagway, Brackett worked virtually non-stop on his wagon road, which he now estimated would reach the summit during the first week of February. He also tackled Skagway's fledgling *ad hoc* city council, which had no legal right to exist. Legal or not, he talked the council members into granting him a railway right-of-way along Runnalls Street. He also completed his examination of the land beyond the summit and established a route for his proposed Canadian extension to Lake Bennett.

By letter and telegram, both Brackett and his lawyer, John Hartman, continued to press Van Horne to extract a charter from the Canadian government that would not only permit Brackett to extend his road into Canada but also authorize him to charge and collect tolls. Van Horne responded by stating that he doubted if the Canadian government was in a position to examine Brackett's request as the current parliamentary session was well-advanced and it was already too late to introduce special legislation on Brackett's behalf.

He added, however, that Brackett should be satisfied with the Minister's assurance that his road construction on the Canadian side would not be interfered with. As to the matter of tolls, Van Horne urged Brackett to cover his Canadian construction costs by increasing his toll charges on the Alaskan side – a suggestion that Brackett rejected out of hand.[25]

Brackett had, in fact, reached an impasse. He did not have authority to build a road or to charge tolls in either Canada or Alaska. He knew there would be serious resistance to the unauthorized tolls he planned to charge packers who used his road on the Alaskan side, let alone increasing the freight charges to cover the cost of extending his road into Canada.

The imprecise status of his road and the lack of enabling legislation on either side of the boundary – all compounded by a constant and frantic search for funds – forced Brackett to delay the construction of the Canadian extension and concentrate on completing the road on the Alaskan side of the summit. His financial resources at this stage, however, simply could not support his plans. Time was passing, costs were mounting, and by the end of January 1898, construction had consumed every dollar he had raised during his trip to the East.

By early February, his road still was not finished, and he owed $10,000 in back wages in addition to many outstanding accounts with local Skagway suppliers. Throughout this difficult period, he kept Van Horne fully apprised of developments, particularly the desperate financial state of his company. Just one month after his initial approach to the CPR's president, Brackett was forced to ask Van Horne if he and his friends could provide him with additional funds until the road was completed and the toll situation clarified.

During the first week in February, Brackett made a hurried trip to Seattle in search of more funds. His first call was to John Hartman's law office, where he was relieved to find a bank draft from Van Horne for $7,500. During the following few days he raised an additional $8,500 from individual investors, many of whom had been lined up by Hartman before Brackett's arrival. He returned to Skagway on February 13th with this new money, paid his workers their back wages, and retired his outstanding local debts.

Once again, the project had been saved by the last-minute infusion of funds by friends and associates, who, time and again, demonstrated boundless faith in Brackett and his road, which they expected would eventually provide them with a tidy profit.

Throughout February the tonnage of freight and single outfits manhandled through the White Pass dramatically increased. In one three-day period, eight steamers unloaded 2,500 passengers and thousands of tons of freight at Skagway and Dyea, blocking the wharves and muddy streets of the two overwhelmed northern ports. Day and night the White Pass trail was alive with men bent on reaching Lake Bennett in time to build their boats and rafts before spring break-up. The long, disorganized, ragged line of men, dogs, horses, mules, and hand-pulled sleighs moved relentlessly towards the summit – some toiling up the old Moore trail. Other gold-seekers and packers used parts or all of Brackett's road, which appropriated much of Moore's original trail.

Although Brackett's road was emerging as the prime route through the pass, its intrusion on parts of their original pack trail had irked many of the packers. As a result, relationships between Brackett and the packers had become antagonistic. Accusations flew during March when Brackett imposed a charge of forty dollars for every ton of freight hauled over his road, although he had no legal right to do so.

Most packers accepted the existence of Brackett's road between Skagway and White Pass City – a temporary trail town – but a group of irate packers insisted that he had done nothing to justify collecting a toll between there and the summit. All Brackett had done, they said, was make a few improvements to a trail that they themselves had helped to blaze and had been using without interruption since the summer of 1897. Brackett refuted this argument, stating that he had provided the public with free access to what he called "the upper portions of my road" for such a long time that "they thought they owned it."

Some paid the toll. A few turned back in disgust. But soon the growing band of objectors avoided the toll charges by travelling up the frozen waters of the Skagway River – outflanking Brackett's toll collectors, who stood firmly by their gate. One packer, who had more than a hundred tons of freight to move across the summit, threatened to build a trail of his own. To forestall this possibility Brackett bribed him with a pass to pack from White Pass City to the summit without charge.[26]

Meetings, charges, and counter-charges fuelled the general uproar. When the packers confirmed that Brackett had no authority from Congress to build and operate a road across United States federal land, let alone collect tolls for its use, they occupied the road, tore down Brackett's recently installed toll-gate, and severely mauled the toll-gate keepers and guards.

Brackett demanded help from Colonel Thomas M. Anderson, the officer commanding the United States troops. Colonel Anderson, however, was fully aware that Brackett had no authorizing charter and declined to act on Brackett's behalf. Frustrated at every turn, Brackett boarded the first ship for Seattle, where he telegraphed his friend and Washington advocate, William S. King, for help.

King immediately visited the War Department and convinced its senior officials that a group of rowdy packers had seized Brackett's wagon road and had placed the area "in a state of terror." Secretary of War Russell A. Alger promptly telegraphed the military commander of the Department of the Columbia to have Colonel Anderson "take proper steps for the protection of persons and property." A copy of Alger's telegram in his pocket, Brackett returned to Skagway where he met with Colonel Anderson, produced his telegram, and invited the reluctant colonel to help him recover his road.[27]

Brackett now had the support of the army, but he still did not possess Congressional authority to charge tolls, although the Secretary of War's telegram and the presence of Colonel Anderson and his soldiers along the road and upper trail were convincing symbols of broad government approval of his enterprise.

At the entrance to the canyon just north of White Pass City, Brackett erected a new toll-gate and put a hard-nosed company agent in charge of a gang of thirty of his toughest workmen.

The defiant packers reacted by outflanking Brackett's gate. Brackett's agent countered the packers' move by instructing his gang of toughs to erect a fence from one side of the narrow canyon to the other, effectively barring the packers from the upper trail. Two hot-headed packers, who were determined to put Brackett's resolve to the test, attacked the gate and fence with axes, but they were quickly subdued, arrested, and subsequently fined for trespassing. For the time being, the dissident packers gave in and paid the toll. Brackett was finally in business – although his authority to operate was still bogged down in Congress.

While the toll issue was boiling, Brackett found himself faced with another serious problem involving Hugh C. Wallace, the president of the Chilkoot Railroad & Transport Company, who was building a nine-mile aerial tramline to the Chilkoot summit. Understandably, Wallace regarded Brackett's road and the port of Skagway as a major threat. Wallace had issued a series of circulars to southern shippers extolling the virtues of Dyea, the Chilkoot Pass, and his company's ability to transport any amount of freight they shipped to the Klondike via Dyea, a claim Brackett regarded as a deliberate misrepresentation of the truth.

"Through trickery," he wrote Van Horne, "Wallace secured Canadian government freight which is now stranded at Dyea, and yet he publishes the fact that the government had adopted that route as the only feasible route to be used."[28]

To defend himself against Wallace and to promote the use of his own road, Brackett had already asked three prominent transportation men to endorse his enterprise and, at the same time, bring the deficiencies of the Chilkoot trail to public notice. The men he chose were already biased in Brackett's favour. Their interests were largely centred in Skagway, and one of them, A.S. Kerry, was an original investor and promoter of the wagon road during the Acklen regime.

In a signed statement Kerry said, "To anyone wishing to make the trip into the interior of Alaska, either with heavy or light outfits, I can conscientiously recommend the wagon road as being a practical and easy way of getting in." He declared that "it is a very good mountain road, having been constructed in a most substantial manner. . . . Tons of drift bolts having been used . . . to bolt the abutment timbers under the bridges directly to the bed rock." He claimed the road was surfaced for the most part with granite that had been "pulverized with dynamite and hammers," and concluded by stating that he was pleased to endorse Brackett's road in order to counter the false reports being circulated by the promoters of the Chilkoot Pass.[29]

Transportation representative and packer, Joseph T. Cornforth, after stating that "the only reliance is by the wagon road over the White Pass," issued a devastating condemnation of the Chilkoot trail and those who championed its cause. "No line is in operation from Dyea to the summit of Chilkoot Pass," he

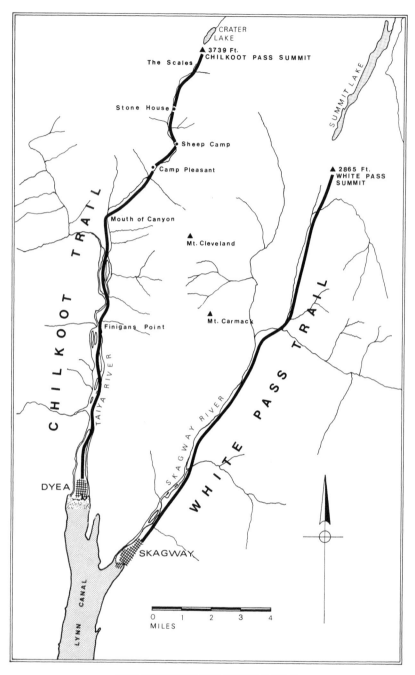

THE CHILKOOT AND WHITE PASSES
*Gold-seekers headed for the Klondike in 1897-98 had to choose between
the shorter, steeper Chilkoot Pass and the longer, lower White Pass. Most
early sourdoughs chose the Chilkoot. The White Pass was favoured only
after the wagon road and, later, the railway were built.*

said, adding that "no wires nor cables are strung on their aerial tram nor is the boiler set at Canyon City." He claimed that during late February and early March, between thirty-five and forty-five hundred tons of freight awaited transportation over the Chilkoot Pass, "a congestion that is daily increasing." Many caches of freight were lost from sight, he said, "having been buried many feet in the snow."[30]

Pierre Humbert, Jr., of the Humbert Transportation Company, stated that he had personally inspected the Brackett road and had found it well constructed with moderate grades. Like the others, he had nothing good to say about the Chilkoot trail. "The merchandise and goods landed at Dyea are piled in endless succession of ownership from Sheep Camp to The Scales, so the blockade this side of the Chilkoot Pass is complete." He was certain that eventually all travel to Bennett would use the Brackett road because "it is the cheapest, best and surest way of getting through."[31]

Brackett used these testimonials in an advertisement, which included a scathing open letter to Wallace that charged him with ignoring Skagway in his circulars. "By Skagway's intentional omission," Brackett wrote, "you have sought by cunning phraseology to make it appear a secondary place to Dyea, and you have employed all this to deceive the public in a manner that no common carrier had a right to do so."

Having publicly skewered Wallace, Brackett commenced to trumpet his own accomplishments. "With truth, right and nature on my side I have . . . completed the only available method of crossing the passes,. . . and today my wagon road . . . is pronounced by . . . those using it to be the best and only feasible route for reaching the lakes from the seacoast of Alaska." Brackett concluded his attack by stating his sincere wish that Wallace's aerial tramline was in fact completed and operating for there was, in his view, more than enough freight to keep them both busy. "I would like to see you working the line you say is 'now in operation' for . . . you would then be doing what you have for a long while falsely claimed you were doing."[32]

The *Skagway News* fired its own broadside at the "alleged tramline," accusing its principals of being guilty of the "most outrageous misrepresentation in announcing that their lines were completed from Dyea to Lindeman." The *News* asserted that no tramline from Dyea to Lindeman Lake had been completed and anyone who made a contrary statement "knows that he lies."[33]

Wallace retaliated with his own open letter to Brackett, which received wide circulation in Skagway and Seattle and other West Coast ports. "Your ill-tempered, gratuitous and unjustifiable attack on me . . . might properly be treated with the contempt which the motive that inspired it deserves," he wrote. He charged that Brackett had once strongly favoured Dyea, "but now your interests appear to colour your views and lead you to make untruthful statements about the Dyea trail ... which are picturesquely false."

He accused Brackett of falsely advertising that his road was complete. "You know that the wagon road is not finished and that you have done no road work of any kind beyond the summit." Brackett, in his opinion, should be consigned to the undying contempt of every honourable man. "Your shafts of abuse are pointless – your assumptions of truth a farce – your letter a tirade of misrepresentations, which are, in fact, but the senile wailings of a desperate and disappointed old man."[34]

Seven

———◆———

THE IRISH PRINCE

O N A DAY IN FEBRUARY 1898, the docks of Seattle were, as usual, tangled with people, miners, horses, and dogs. Gold fever was rampant, and it seemed as if the rush to the Klondike would never end. Along every pier and wharf throngs of people pushed past jagged islands of baled hay, sacked oats, and equipment and supplies. Outnumbering the miners, spectators, who had come to say good-bye to friends and relatives headed north to Skagway and Dyea, crowded the docks. Among them mingled the artful and the crafty, who were there to fleece the gold-seekers by selling them everything from patented electric belts that would restore a man's lost libido to devices that could sniff out gold from the darkest reaches of the earth. Still others had come just to stand and look and take in the wonder of it all. There were backslaps and handshakes, fraud and goodwill, laughter and tears, and all the while the ships vented smoke and steam and groaned against their lines as the heavy loads of freight were winched aboard.[1]

Michael James Heney hurried along the crowded dockside and boarded the 400-ton, Alaska-bound steamship *Utopia*. He surrendered his ticket, which he had purchased with borrowed funds, and made his way to the wheelhouse.[2] There he was welcomed warmly by his friend, Captain "Dynamite" Johnny O'Brien, a fearless Irish-American seafarer who was devoted to poker and given to singing ear-splitting renditions of "Sweet Rosie O'Grady" from the bridge of his ship.

Once under way, Heney's lifelong distrust of the sea surfaced. Every fibre in his body rebelled against its uneasy motion and its ominous depths. "Rivers I can abide," he once wrote to his father, "for they cut a decent path through the mountains. But the ocean is another matter," he added with melancholy premonition of his own death, "for it can not be trusted."[3]

His destination was Skagway. The town and its trail to the gold-fields had fascinated him ever since the arrival of the *Portland* at Seattle the previous July with more than a ton of Klondike gold. He had followed the crowd that day to Schwabaker's dock and had listened intently to the miners' tales of gold and the challenge of the wild northern landscape. He had heard them speak of the winds and the cold and the agony of climbing the mountain passes. He had listened to the miners argue about the merits of the passes and pack trails that led from Skagway and Dyea to Lake Bennett, forty-one miles to the north.

The land they said was rich in gold was known to Heney. During the spring of 1897, he had built a hydraulic gold-mining installation at Anchor Point on the west coast of Alaska's Kenai Peninsula. His contract called for the construction of a large ditch to carry water from an inland lake to a beach near Anchor Point. There, the lake water, under high pressure, was used to wash the beach sands in a largely unsuccessful mining operation, which produced only nine dollars an hour in gold.[4]

During the week following the *Portland*'s arrival, Heney had read everything about the Klondike that he could find. The newspapers had been filled with stories about Alaska and the stark tragedy of the trails that led to the Canadian gold-fields. The prospectors' stories had intrigued him, but his imagination had been fired by their transportation problems, not by their talk of gold. Many experienced northern merchants and gold-seekers had sworn that the Pacific Ocean-Yukon River route via St. Michael was the best way to reach the gold camps on the lower and upper reaches of the river. Certainly it offered relatively trouble-free transportation from Canadian and American Pacific Coast ports to the northern interior, but its use depended entirely on the season of the year and the amount of ice on the Lower Yukon River. The inefficiencies and general unreliability of this route held little appeal for Heney. Why not, he had reasoned, build one of the proposed railways from Skagway to the head of the Yukon River navigation?

A series of letters written to the *Seattle Post-Intelligencer* by Richard Harper Stretch supported this view. Stretch, a civil engineer, had been travelling through parts of southern Alaska and the Yukon interior assessing mining properties for potential investors. He wrote that he had been impressed by the land and the opportunities it offered as a producer of gold and base metals, but that he was dismayed by the restrictions on future development imposed by a lack of reliable transportation. Heney was impressed with Stretch's letters and later acknowledged that they were the most important factor in his decision to travel north and examine the situation for himself.[5]

Echoing the opinions of Moore, Stretch, Wilkinson, Brackett, and dozens of others, Heney believed that the construction of a railway through the mountains to Lake Bennett and beyond would shorten by 2,500 miles the distance miners entering the Yukon via St. Michael were now travelling. He offered nothing new. The problem was that no one was actually building the railway – despite all the newspaper stories about Brackett's wagon road that stated it would lead to the construction of a railway through the White Pass and about Wilkinson's plan, which appeared to be going nowhere.

Although it was true his plans were stalled, Wilkinson had never stopped promoting his White Pass transportation project. In early February 1898, he announced from Montreal that a group with which he was associated was ready to start construction. He claimed that the rail could be laid from Skagway to Lake Bennett in ninety days and the railway could be in full operation by July or August of 1898. He further declared that the track gauge would be 3 foot 6 inches and that the grade over the pass would not exceed 3 per cent.

"In areas where the grade is steepest," he explained to reporters, "we will be installing an Abt rail system which is a notched rail designed to grip a cog-wheel that forms part of the locomotive's driving system." He assured his listeners that "this type of system is used in the mountains of Europe with great success."[6]

Wilkinson had no mandate from either Close Brothers or the Syndicate to make such a statement. But he hoped that it would indicate to government officials and to Hamilton Smith's supporters that the three companies Wilkinson had organized were committed to build the railway. But it was clear from his description that he was no longer talking about a substantial railway from Skagway to Fort Selkirk but only a short mountain *tramway* through the White Pass to Lake Bennett.

Although the Syndicate in London had optioned the railway companies to Wilkinson, its directors were still promoting the railway. Only through its construction could the Syndicate's shareholders benefit from their interest in the Moores' Skagway lands. Without revealing that they had given an option to Wilkinson, the Syndicate announced to the American press that their group had "perfected arrangements for the construction of a transportation system from the head of Lynn Canal over the White Pass to a point on the Yukon River below Whitehorse Rapids." From railhead, the Syndicate said, the route would continue down the Yukon River to Dawson, employing riverboats in the summer and horse-drawn sleighs in the winter to transport freight and passengers to the gold-fields.[7]

Wilkinson's most immediate challenge was the Canadian government's new determination to develop an all-Canadian route to serve both northern British Columbia and the Klondike gold-fields. Wilkinson admitted this in his announcement, when he stated it had been the Canadian government's commitment to the Mackenzie and Mann, all-Canadian route to the Yukon interior via the Stikine River that had prompted him to announce the immediate start of railway construction through the White Pass.[8]

His concerns were justified. Mackenzie and Mann had only recently announced that, subject to final parliamentary ratification, their all-Canadian railway through the Stikine River valley would soon be under way. "We have three outfits enroute already and a line has been located," Mackenzie had stated. He predicted that his company would start rock-blasting during April 1898, and that, at the height of construction, at least 4,000 men would be employed. "The line," he said, "will be completed before September without a doubt or we should not have undertaken the job."[9]

HENEY TOOK ADVANTAGE of his days at sea to question those aboard the *Utopia* who had personal knowledge of the Chilkoot Pass, the White Pass, and the broad uplands that swept north beyond their summits. He inquired about conditions along the trails and the relative merits of Skagway and Dyea as ports of entry into the Yukon interior and the gold-fields. He heard opinions of Brackett's road and descriptions of the mountain terrain and its weather. Some he interviewed were thoughtful and reserved; others gave coloured and over-stated accounts. A few offered extravagant portrayals of precipitous, ice-encrusted mountain barriers that must be met and vanquished by anyone climbing through either pass. When railways were mentioned, most just shook their heads.

Heney was not deterred. He had heard similar stories before in his career as a railroad contractor. He was only twenty-three when he was dubbed "the boy contractor" by Seattle's railway fraternity, who recognized in him a resourceful railway builder who completed his contracts within budget and on time. Now aged thirty-four, he had neither work nor contracts.

He had no mandate. He had embarked on his northern venture represent-ing no one but himself. Except for a few borrowed dollars, he had neither technical nor financial support. His was to be a personal assault on the White Pass – a bold reconnaissance, which could lead to opportunity for himself and an end to the ongoing transportation muddle on the trails leading north from Skagway and Dyea.

Before leaving Seattle, he had discussed his proposed railway survey with Bronco Harris, a gruff-voiced railway construction foreman who had, over the years, become a Heney confidant and friend. Harris had a deep affection for

Heney, but he never ceased to wonder where he obtained his self-assurance, his sense of command, his intuitive understanding of complex engineering problems and his ability to overcome them, his concern for the feelings and well-being of his workmen who sweated in his tunnels and along his grades. From what hidden well did Heney draw his energy, his physical strength, his ability to inspire loyalty in those who worked closely with him? Harris did not understand the chemistry of the man. No one did. But his many friends and admirers knew that Michael J. Heney was equipped by his nature, his stamina, and his intellect to move mountains, and that whatever he did, he would do with style and grace.[10]

Like Heney, Harris had lived most of his life under canvas or in railroad bunkhouses. Although he had little formal education, he was a giant on a railroad grade. Clumping around on his wooden leg, he could make the men and the job move with a relentless rhythm.

Heney and Harris had laid a lot of steel together since the summer of 1879 when young Heney had run away from the family farm in the Ottawa Valley near Stonecliffe, Ontario, and headed for Lake Superior and the CPR construction camps. He was energetic and restless, and he rebelled against schools and their confining restrictions and demands. His lack of scholastic ambition disappointed his father, Thomas Heney, who had emigrated from Killashandrea, Ireland, with his bride, Mary, in 1854.[11]

Heney was determined to follow the footsteps of his uncle, John Heney, an energetic Ottawa merchant and entrepreneur who was also a construction contractor. During the late 1800s and on into the early years of the twentieth century, the elder Heney erected buildings and bridges as far west as Calgary and Battleford, and harbour installations and other works throughout Ontario, Quebec, and the Maritime provinces. In 1874, he and an associate won a contract to construct a fifty-mile section of the CPR, known as the Georgian Bay Branch. Litigation involving his partner and the federal government clouded this railway project, but the elder Heney continued for years to win important government contracts for the construction of marine facilities along the St. Lawrence River and the Atlantic seaboard.[12]

John Heney's accomplishments as a successful contractor gave Michael Heney the courage to ignore his father's wish that he remain in school. At age fourteen, he ran away and headed west to the railway construction camps, where he signed on as a mule skinner and grader.

During his first day on the grade, Heney discovered that mules have a will of their own and, at times, refuse to move on command. Blocked by Heney's contrary mule, the scrapers behind him were forced to stop. A bull of a man bellowed in the distance, and suddenly Heney was looking into the purple face of Bronco Harris, the grade foreman.

For all his fury, Harris was a kindly man, and he taught Heney how to handle himself on the grade. It was not long, however, before Heney was forced to part company with his mule and his new-found instructor. His elder brother, Peter, appeared one day and, with little ceremony, took him back to the family farm. Heney's first taste of freedom was over, but from that day forward, railroad construction would remain the prime passion of his life.

As the years passed, it became obvious to Thomas and Mary Heney that their son Michael ached to escape from the restricting influence of school-rooms, farm work, and hum-drum local employment. In June 1882, just four months short of his eighteenth birthday, they gave him their blessing and told him that he was free to leave home to find work. Once again he hurried west to the railway's construction front, now at Elkhorn, Manitoba, twelve miles east of the Saskatchewan border. There he found that Harris still presided over the grading operations. Heney asked for work and, after signing up, received a mule and scraper. He was soon promoted from grading to laying rail, which brought him a raise of a dollar a day.

Throughout the summer of 1882, he wrestled with railroad ties neatly placed at two-foot intervals along the grade. But all the while, he searched for a way to join the surveyors who were working their way west towards the Rocky Mountains and the setting sun. His chance came in March 1883, when John Stevens, an American survey engineer, was preparing to lead a railway survey party into British Columbia's Selkirk Mountains. Heney approached Stevens and asked for a job with the survey crew. But the ranks were filled. In any event, Stevens explained, he only hired men with survey experience. Sensing Heney's disappointment, Harris invited him to drive a team of horses in a wagon train that would soon be leaving Swift Current for Calgary with sup-plies for Stevens's surveyors.

The heavily loaded wagons travelled across more than 300 miles of roadless prairie, wallowing in the mud of the spring thaw. At Calgary the supplies were transferred from the wagons to pack mules, and the surveyors moved out towards the mountains. In low spirits Heney drove back towards the grade.

Shortly after the wagons left Calgary, a lone rider galloped up to the wagon-master and asked for the whereabouts of Michael Heney. The rider explained that one of the survey party's chainmen had been killed in a brawl and John Stevens wanted Heney to take the chainman's place. Heney seized this chance to join the surveyors.

The summer of 1883 was busy and productive for Heney, and he grasped every opportunity to learn the business of surveying a route for a railway.

In the spring of 1884, he accepted Stevens's invitation to join a crew surveying the last leg of the CPR railway from the interior of British Columbia to the Pacific Coast. During 1884 and 1885, he worked through British Columbia's mountains and along the Fraser River, all the while learning about costs, manpower, equipment, snowsheds, curvatures, and grades. He studied the properties of powder and dynamite, the science of blasting, and the precise calculations required to produce a drilling plan. He discovered how to analyse rock structures to calculate the exact explosive energy needed to blast a cliff into fragments, leaving the shattered rock in chunks small enough to be easily handled. He studied the construction of tunnels and the ways to control water seepage; how to slope a tunnel roof to facilitate ventilation; how to design the shoring required to prevent collapse. He learned about leadership, authority, and how to handle men. Everywhere he went, his presence was felt and his influence accepted. All along the line, he became known as "M.J." and "the Irish Prince" – two sobriquets that would remain with him for the rest of his life.[13]

HENEY STOOD on the bridge with Captain O'Brien as the *Utopia* steamed into Skagway Bay on March 31, 1898. A pall of blue smoke hung over the town, rising from the hundreds of chimney pipes that vented from a jumble of soot-stained tents, rough board buildings, log cabins, and canvas-covered lean-tos. Coastal steamships were busy discharging cargo at each of Skagway's three operating wharves. At Moore's wharf, four freighters and a large barge were unloading more than a thousand tons of general merchandise and thousands of feet of lumber. A fourth wharf was already serving scows and small ships, although it was still under construction.[14] Lines of heavily loaded, double-team wagons were moving back and forth along the docks, passing through canyons of masts, rigging, funnels, and yardarms, each rocking to its own cadence on a wind-driven tide. Seagulls screeched overhead. A dead horse floated out to sea.

Heney studied the scene, and what he saw confirmed what Captain O'Brien had told him. O'Brien was well acquainted with Skagway's waterfront problems, particularly with the ongoing dispute between the steamboat operators and Skagway's aggressive band of longshoremen.

During the first half of March, feelings had run high between the ship owners and the stevedores. "Pure unadulterated cussedness" was the cause, one newspaper claimed, citing a serious waterfront confrontation as an unhappy by-product of "civilization's onward march."

The longshoremen had claimed that, because of the high cost of living in Skagway, they could not work for less than seventy-five cents an hour. One captain had refused to employ them at this rate, hiring in their place forty local Indians who had agreed to work for less. A street fight had broken out between the Indians and the longshoremen, during which several shots were fired. The Indians, outnumbered four to one, had run to the wharf to seek the protection of the ship's captain – hotly pursued by some 200 hostile stevedores. Hearing the shouting and the shots, Skagway's two senior law enforcement officers, Marshal McInnes and Deputy Quinlan, had rushed to the wharf with drawn guns to quell the disturbance. Peace had been eventually restored, but during the mêlée Deputy Quinlan had distinguished himself by accidentally shooting himself in the foot.

The truce had been short-lived. The following day, Captain Hall of the steamship *Cleveland* had arrived with 200 passengers and a hold crammed with freight. He had experienced trouble with the longshoremen during his previous trip, and this time he had brought extra crewmen to unload his ship. As soon as the work began, however, a mob of enraged stevedores had quickly brought it to a halt.

In retaliation, Captain Hall had unlimbered an impressive-looking cannon, which he had thoughtfully mounted on the bridge of his ship, and had proceeded to load it in full view of the irate longshoremen and a growing crowd of spectators. Despite the menacing presence of the captain's loaded cannon, no one had budged. The longshoremen had stood firmly by their principles, and the hapless captain had stood by his gun. The standoff had continued until the timely arrival of Marshal McInnes who, for the second time in twenty-four hours, restored order by convincing the longshoremen that they should withdraw from the wharf and allow the *Cleveland* to unload her cargo, using her own crew.[15]

Heney grasped the significance of the waterfront as he listened to Captain O'Brien explain the layout of the harbour and the current labour tensions. If a railway was to be built, the efficiency and reliability of Skagway's waterfront would play a signal role during construction and subsequent operations.

As the ship approached the wharf, Heney saw the ragged line of debris and crab grass that marked the high tide around the perimeter of the bay. He estimated the slope of the beach and gauged the capacity of its surface to support the track that would have to be built to move construction equipment and railway rolling stock from ocean-going barges to the shore. Along the beach, where the wharves butted against the townsite, there were new clusters of wooden pilings that would, when braced, planked, and spiked, provide additional wharf space for the ever-increasing flow of freight.

The town was a jumble of match-box shacks and lumber-strewn streets. Black, tarpapered roofs stood out in sharp contrast to the unpainted, rough-cut siding of the buildings along Broadway and the piles of old and dirty winter snow. Large signs jutted out from many of the structures, one of the most prominent being a long black-and-white billboard atop the rusted corrugated iron roof of the St. James Hotel, a prominent Skagway establishment, which featured electric lights and individual room call bells and boasted of accommodating the town's most notable visitors.

Beyond the rooftops stood the infamous mountain barrier. Rising from a series of tree-clad bluffs just north of town, it stretched into the distance in diminishing shades of blue, reaching an elevation of 2,865 feet in seventeen miles. From his vantage point on the ship's bridge, Heney contemplated the gigantic saddles of granite that swept down from the surrounding snow-capped peaks and ridges, forming a rough, zigzag valley from the sea to the summit of the pass. Even from this distance, he could see that the path of a railway through these mountains would be dictated by these colossal spurs of rock, which interlocked and meshed like the teeth of two gigantic gears.

Heney disembarked and took a horse-drawn carriage to the St. James Hotel. Everywhere he looked, he saw activity and confusion. The gambling joints were operating in broad daylight, and around their swinging doors stood knots of men gazing aimlessly at the passing parade. Pack horses and mules loaded with sacks, boxes, and bales of hay plodded disconsolately along the rutted streets towards Liarsville, a convenient marshalling area and jumping-off camp just north of town. There, trail-wise sourdoughs told outrageous tales to bewildered newcomers about the horrors they faced on the White Pass trail.

Here and there along Skagway's main streets were piles of bottles and cans where tented cafés once stood, their owners now lured away by the call of the Klondike. Store fronts, businesses, and signs indicated the permanency of this new town, which now boasted more than 800 buildings, cabins, and shacks of infinite variety.[16]

Freight wagons rattled between the wharves and the town, the straining teams churning up the water-filled potholes and splattering the new wooden sidewalks with sawdust and mud. This was a town where transportation operated on raw horsepower, its commerce conducted by mackinaw-clad businessmen and cursing teamsters and fuelled by illegal beer, dried beans, and bales of hay. Through its crowded streets strode soldiers of the United States

14th Infantry Regiment, which had recently been dispatched from its Vancouver, Washington, barracks to help maintain order along the Chilkoot Pass and White Pass trails.[17]

There were people begging in the streets, some looking for a meal while others panhandled for the price of a locally brewed beer, which was bottled one day and sold the next. Other enterprising citizens illegally manufactured rum in stills of their own design, and a few local Indians produced rotgut beer from tubs of sugar, yeast, and flour. Amid all of this iniquity stood the church and the school, both claiming increasing attendance and a sobering influence on the community. The town's water system was now complete, and electricity produced by a recently installed Delco generating plant lit the newfangled street lamps, which sported tin wash tubs to reflect the light.

Heney registered at the St. James Hotel. His first task was to establish to his own satisfaction the relative merits of Skagway and Dyea as ports capable of handling large ocean-going freighters and passenger ships. A short overland journey to Dyea soon established its deficiencies. He noted that, while there were three wharves under construction at Dyea, they were far from completion and of questionable utility because of Dyea's flat, tide-swept, mud beaches and shallow water.[18] Skagway, on the other hand, had three operating wharves and a fourth under construction. Its harbour's deep waters enabled it to handle the largest ships on the coast. Nevertheless, more men entered the Yukon district through Dyea and the Chilkoot Pass than through Skagway and the White Pass because of the popular belief that the Chilkoot trail was superior to the White Pass trail, a view hotly contested by Skagway's packers and business leaders. If there was a preference for the Chilkoot Pass and trail, it would soon be reversed, argued some of the packers, now that Brackett's road was completed to White Pass City.

Dyea's answer to the wagon road was the three aerial tramlines still under construction, which could wrest the freight business from Skagway. Heney soon learned, however, that the construction of the aerial tramlines was handicapped for want of funds and by dubious management. Skagway offered goldseekers the option of a trail, a road, and the possibility of a railway operating between Skagway and the summit before the onslaught of winter.

Heney knew that building a railway through the White Pass would be an extremely labour-intensive undertaking, requiring a reasonably stable work force with an extensive range of skills. The work would be hard and hazardous, and because much of it would be constructed under sub-arctic weather conditions, any men employed in the railway's work gang would be tested to the limit. This knowledge gave Heney little comfort as he contemplated the unusually high cost and local shortage of skilled labour.

A further worry was that Brackett and the Skagway and Lake Bennett Tramway Company each controlled a separate right-of-way through Skagway, granted by Skagway's *ad hoc* council. This arbitrary action of the council was being hotly contested by the Moores and the Syndicate, who declared that by right of claim and extended occupation they jointly owned the land through which Brackett's road and the tramway ran.

It was soon clear to Heney that, before one yard of grade could be built or one rail laid out of Skagway, the builders would have to deal with a number of conflicts and legal problems. The most visible and immediate concern was Brackett's wagon road, which was far more advanced in both distance and quality than he had imagined. News reports about its progress in the *Seattle Post-Intelligencer* and the *Seattle Times* had extolled its virtues as a boon to Seattle industry and commerce. "It is not so much a wonderful piece of engineering as it is a herculean task on the eve of completion," the *Seattle Times* had commented a few weeks prior to Heney's departure for Skagway. "It is a magnificent piece of work, and it is as substantial and durable as the rock out of which it has been cut."[19] Brackett, who never seemed to have any trouble getting himself into print, said that anyone using his road would, under normal conditions, be able to pull one ton of freight with a double-horse team from Skagway to Lake Bennett and return in just four days.

Heney studied the route and quality of Brackett's road and observed its general acceptance by most of the packers and gold-seekers. He noted that its general condition was good, although it was marred in places by steep grades, particularly at Porcupine Hill, where two horses with a single sled loaded with only 400 pounds could barely climb to the top.

Brackett's road was now complete, except for the four-mile stretch between White Pass City and the summit. Here, the road was nothing more than the original pack trail, partially improved by Brackett's engineers. They had blasted away many of the jagged rock outcroppings that had made the trail north of White Pass City difficult and, in places, dangerous, but it still could not accommodate horse-drawn wagons or sleighs. The gold-seekers still had to stop at White Pass City, break their freight down into 100-pound packs, and load them on horses and mules for the onward journey to the summit.

Heney assessed the value of Brackett's road as a supply route to forward men, materials, and equipment to the railway's construction front. He did not regard the road as a serious threat to an operating railway, although he recognized it would have to be controlled or eliminated entirely if the railway was to operate free of competition.

Among the mountains, Heney was in his element. From the road he could see the character of the land and many of the valley's main features. He strode along the road, occasionally pausing to make notes: here climbing a rocky cliff to gain a fresh perspective, there descending into a snow-filled gulch to examine a water course or determine the stability of the rock. Around him rose the grey granite walls that partially blotted out the sun, leaving the east side of the valley cast in deep shadows.

On first view, the cliffs on the west side seemed to offer the best route for a railway. There, the rock appeared more solid, the way more clearly defined. The east side of the valley looked less attractive. There, the rock seemed less stable, and the general direction of the natural route was fragmented by a series of intersecting bluffs and valleys. On the eastern side, he could plainly see a series of rock-formed chutes, high on the cliffs, each containing thousands of tons of trapped snow in huge, hard-packed drifts, which could hurtle down without warning and cascade across the railway track when the snow changed to mush during the spring thaw. At one spot, fifteen miles north of Skagway, there was an almost perpendicular wall of granite, which had been ground smooth by the relentless action of ice-age glaciers. If the east side of the valley should be selected for the right-of-way, the railway grade would have to cross that bulging, hanging cliff that already was known as "Slippery Rock."

A thousand feet beneath Slippery Rock, Heney entered White Pass City, a rapidly growing frontier town at the northern end of the Brackett road. From there the original trail, which Brackett claimed he had improved, led on to the summit of the pass. The town was built on gently sloping bench lands that skirted the banks of the Skagway River. A number of bunkhouses, stores, and cafés were in business, and several corrals and barns had been erected for the stabling of hundreds of the pack animals that were employed along the trail. Freight could now be transported by wagon and pack train to the townsite. There, the wagon loads were transferred to the backs of the pack animals for the final four-mile push to the summit.[20]

On a smaller scale, White Pass City was a repeat of Skagway and Dyea – men, horses, harness, and mud. Piles of hay were stacked between the tents and rough log shelters, and the valley rang with the sounds of hammers and saws, barking dogs, neighing horses, and the frenetic shouts of men in a hurry. Looming over the town were the silent cliffs that shaped the valley, and beyond them rose the icebound mountains – inhospitable, commanding, and imperious. "It is a masterful piece of world building," commented J.A. Costello in an article for the *Seattle Times*. "The camp is a setting in a silver shield. Bejewelled in shimmering icicles, embedded in deepest snows, and overlooked by giants of purest white on every side."[21]

But not everything was white. Strewn beneath the snow along the trail were the carcasses of 2,000 pack horses. A thousand more would perish from starvation and overwork before winter was done. The way was littered with putrid snow, blood, and the stinking flesh of pack animals that had seared their lungs, broken their legs, or, from sheer exhaustion, had simply died where they dropped. Others had fallen to their deaths along the hellish trail. Strung together in trains of up to twenty, each carrying up to 400 pounds of freight on their backs, the horses were driven relentlessly to the summit. Their loads included lumber, knock-down boats, window frames, stoves, beds, machinery, benzine, boxes of general freight, and canned and dried food. The sharp edges of the wooden crates shifted with every step, causing abrasions and hip sores as big as a man's fist.

Bert Hartshorn, a trail-wise blacksmith, shook his head in despair as he watched the inhuman, callous brutality of the packers as they lashed their overloaded animals to the summit and oblivion. He did what he could. He shod their bleeding hoofs, but he could do little for their gashed and bruised legs or their oozing saddle sores. When they faltered, they were killed by their owners and left lying in the trail's frozen sump holes and creekbeds. Others were shot and pushed down the rocky inclines to lie legs up and spread-eagled in the snow – their ordeal over at last.

This was one of the Klondike trail's darkest chapters. The killing was endless, the misery complete. It turned men's stomachs, for it was virtually impossible to walk the White Pass trail of '97 and '98 without stepping on the rotting remains of a hundred slaughtered horses. "Most of them perished at the hands of gold-mad cheechakos who believed that a horse could work night and day on nothing but Saratoga chips,"[22] wrote newspaper correspondent Cy Warman. "I must admit that I was as brutal as the rest," wrote Jack Newman, a prominent White Pass packer, "but we were all mad – mad for gold, and we did things that we lived to regret."[23]

The hideous pack trains were maintained only by a constant supply of fresh horses from Seattle or Vancouver. Few animals survived more than two or three trips to the summit and beyond. Those that were not shot were left to starve. No one would waste ten cents worth of hay on a worn-out horse. Of the 3,800 pack animals that were taken north in 1897, only thirty survived. The rest died, leaving their flesh to rot and their bones to bleach in the summer sun.

Heney had seen the death of both man and beast on many a railway grade, but nothing to equal the almost wilful maiming and slaughter of animals he saw in the White Pass – one part of which was already known far and wide as Dead Horse Gulch.[24]

AT VIRTUALLY every point of the White Pass, Heney saw construction problems that would test the mettle and ingenuity of the most experienced railway contractors. He had already been warned by local engineers and transportation men familiar with the valley's formidable topographical features that a railway could not be punched through to the summit and that anyone who tried was bound to fail. Others predicted that, even if a railway was successfully completed, it would be unable to operate during the long winter months when rock-hard snowdrifts would block the right-of-way for weeks on end.

He was impressed by what he had seen and heard, but not surprised. In the days when he was still a neophyte railway builder, he had faced similar conditions during the construction of the CPR through the Rockies, but this was the first time he had been confronted with such a wide variety of engineering and construction problems crammed into a space of some twenty miles. There was more than just the ice-shrouded cliffs to consider. During the winter, temperatures could fluctuate between zero and fifty below. There were the long hours of winter darkness, the deep snows, the cruel winds. And there was the problem of supplies, as the closest commercial and industrial centre was a thousand miles to the south. The immensity of the task became abundantly clear to Heney as he climbed through the valley towards the summit of the pass.

Despite these obstacles, Heney was convinced that, with sufficient manpower, engineering, and financial support, a railway could be built through the pass to the summit. He was aware that others before him had faced the same mountains, the same barriers, the same weather conditions, and had confidently announced that they would build a railway through the White Pass to the Yukon interior – notably Moore, Billinghurst, Wilkinson, and Acklen. But Wilkinson's recent announcement from Montreal had convinced Heney that Wilkinson's Syndicate had neither the engineering ability nor the financial resources to construct a railway capable of handling the thousands of tons of freight pouring across Skagway's wharves.

Beyond White Pass City, Heney rejoined the seemingly endless line of men and horses thrusting north on their final assault on the summit. Traffic on the trail had increased as the days lengthened, but the weather was still treacherous. Towards the end of March, the gold-seekers were tormented daily by downpours of sleet, forcing those who had them to don oilskins to keep dry and reasonably warm. Those who had failed to bring waterproof clothing suffered miserably as they dragged their loaded sleighs through the freezing slush, or tramped on towards the summit with heavy packs and sinking morale.[25]

Heney strode on, gaining the summit of the pass where, for the first time, he came in contact with Canadian authorities operating in what they insisted was Canadian territory. For some time most of the gold-seekers and local Canadian officials had anticipated that the international boundary, when finally fixed, would bisect the White Pass trail at White Pass summit. Others hotly contested this opinion, including many influential Americans and local Skagway boosters, supported by the Skagway press.

To emphasize Canada's claim to the lands north of the White Pass and the Chilkoot Pass, the North-West Mounted Police had established border patrol camps at the summit of both passes during February 1898. Their symbols of authority at the White Pass were their badges and two British-made machine guns, an air-cooled Maxim and a water-cooled Nordenfelt, both of them capable of firing 500 rounds of .303 calibre ammunition per minute.[26] The police were there to show the flag, maintain law and order, and collect customs duties on goods entering Canada that had been purchased in the United States.

Before February, the only police post capable of inspecting American goods was on Tagish Lake, some sixty miles beyond the White Pass summit. There, the police, assisted by sub-collector John Godson, had been collecting customs duties since September 1897. Tagish Post, which also served as a North-West Mounted Police District Headquarters, was strategically placed on the great water course leading from Lake Bennett to the Yukon River. But the establishment of a post so far inland had led many Americans to believe that Canada had finally acknowledged that all of the lands between Tagish and the sea belonged to the United States. In response to mounting American pressure, North-West Mounted Police Superintendent Zackery T. Wood, officer commanding the Tagish District, reported to his superiors in Ottawa that the Americans had already elected mayors and justices of the peace at Lake Bennett and Lindeman Lake, which he emphatically stated were "eighteen miles on our side of the summit."[27]

Establishing the police posts at the summits was a bold move although some months would pass before tensions eased. The North-West Mounted Police faced the difficult task of collecting duties from American and other nationals – some 90 per cent of the gold-seekers – who were entering Canada with goods purchased in the U.S. or, in some cases, purchased in both Canada and the U.S. Lost invoices, incomplete documents, and a general ignorance of Canadian customs law by those seeking to enter Canada added to the daily confusion at the summit of the pass. Administering Canada's customs regulations under these circumstances was a never-ending and tedious task, which strained the resources of the White Pass detachment's establishment of one officer, four non-commissioned officers, and sixteen constables. Of these, one NCO and two constables did nothing but forage for firewood near Log Cabin, fourteen miles north of the barren White Pass summit.[28]

In addition to collecting customs duties, miners' licence fees, and timber dues, the police were obliged to settle disputes, attend to the injured, investigate deaths, act as coroners, look after the sick, regulate sanitary conditions, and deal with a dismal catalogue of crimes, which ranged from petty theft to murder. When necessary for the common good, they applied their own impromptu rules to control the mass movement of men and materials across the disputed boundary at the summit. That they discharged these arduous duties without serious incident was due in part to the traditions, training, and discipline of the force, and in part to the goodwill of the majority of American citizens who passed through Canadian police posts on their way to the Klondike.[29]

When Heney arrived at the summit of White Pass in early April 1898, traffic was so great that the whole summit was an unruly tangle of supplies and equipment. Strings of horses and knots of men trudged their way through a sea of frozen slush stained with manure and mud.

The weather was blustery, and the snow drifted in places to a depth of twenty feet. From his vantage point, Heney could barely trace the snow-covered folds of granite to the south, which rose in a series of scarred terraces from Skagway to the rocky heights of the summit. They would momentarily appear and then fade from view as the wind swirled the snow through the valley.

The answer to the problem of the railway grade lay hidden among those abrupt, precipitous cliffs. Along their sides a grade would have to be blasted and hacked – wide and solid enough to support the trains that would, in places, snake along the cliff sides a thousand feet above the valley floor. Heney still favoured the western cliffs to those on the east side of the valley. They appeared to offer the best means of elevating a heavily loaded train from sea level to the 2,865-foot White Pass summit in something less than twenty miles.

At the summit, Heney questioned Klondikers, packers, American customs men, and the North-West Mounted Police about their experiences on the White Pass trail on both sides of the summit and about their knowledge of the surrounding terrain and weather conditions.

Heney was an attractive man with an engaging manner, and he had little difficulty in drawing information from the people he questioned. But as the facts emerged, he was forced to concede that any decision to build a railway from Skagway to the interior would rest largely on faith. Disturbing questions about the whole project remained unanswered. Would it be possible to maintain a construction schedule when snow covered the grade line to a depth of twenty feet or more? What was the quality of the rock that lay hidden under the solid drifts? Then there was the matter of the grade itself. His estimated average grade of 3 per cent for the total distance could probably be managed, but there were areas on both sides of the valley where the grade might well exceed 4 or even 5 per cent. Would grades of this magnitude be acceptable? Would gravity, weather, and economics combine to render the whole project impracticable? And what about construction problems beyond the summit to Lake Bennett?

Heney questioned everyone he could find who knew the geography of the interior country beyond Lake Bennett, particularly the areas adjacent to the Yukon River. This was the only way he could learn about the mysterious interior, for he had neither the time nor the money to undertake a personal survey from Lake Bennett to the gold-fields.

The North-West Mounted Police, who had gained a fairly intimate knowledge of the Yukon River valley, gave him information about possible routes to Fort Selkirk. Their opinions were confirmed by seasoned sourdoughs on their way back to the Klondike after spending part of the winter in the warmer southern climate. With this information, he judged correctly that the engineering and construction problems north of Lake Bennett were far less formidable than those he had seen on the Skagway and White Pass trail.

Heney also had to consider the viability of a railway as an ongoing business proposition. Despite all the clatter and clamour, did the Klondike have a future? Even if it did, would a railway really be needed to support it? He found no local pessimism about the future of the Klondike. Gold fever was still rampant, and it ripped up and down the trail like an electric charge. There were rumblings about customs, the passes, the weather, the unending struggle, but when it came to the Klondike and its future, it was rainbows and riches to the men on the trail, many of whom predicted that it would become one of the

greatest gold-fields in the world, perhaps eventually surpassing the gold production of South Africa itself – an opinion that was not wholeheartedly shared
by the Canadian government.

Heney marched on towards the southern tip of Summit Lake, a ribbon of
water four and a half miles long used by the gold-seekers as a sleigh route over
the ice in winter and as a canoe route during the warm days of summer.
Beyond the pass lay open country where the wind blew the cold deep into bone
and muscle. The gold-seekers bent to it as they moved across the ice towards
the northern tip of the lake. It was obvious to Heney that, here, the railway
grade would have to be blasted out of the huge rock outcroppings that bordered the eastern lakeshore. Here, the heavy snowdrifts that blanketed the
summit were even deeper. As far as the eye could see there were massive
mounds of glacial snow that had been piled high and hardened by the relentless
winds that swept down from the north. Thousands of feet of snow sheds would
be required to keep the track open and the trains running, and during construction in the winter months, platoons of men would be required to keep the
grade clear of snow.

Heney passed by Fraser Lake where, only recently, the North-West
Mounted Police had discovered two bodies frozen to death in a tent near the
lakeshore. He pushed on to Log Cabin, a packers' rest stop fourteen miles
north of the summit. Here he learned that this site had been arbitrarily
selected by some Americans as the location of the international boundary
between Alaska and British Columbia, a claim supported by a map that had
recently been issued in the United States that showed this interpretation of the
boundary line.

Heney was surprised to discover that Log Cabin was situated on a plateau,
twenty-eight feet higher than White Pass summit. The surrounding terrain,
however, was infinitely more docile and manageable than the rocky cliffs that
characterized the pass. He noted that the land dropped away sharply to the
north towards the head of Lake Bennett – not an insurmountable problem, but
one that would call for careful consideration when conducting a detailed preconstruction survey. While the grade did not appear to be any greater than
those he had already encountered between Skagway and White Pass summit, if
the grade out of Bennett proved steeper, it could create a problem for southbound trains. This assessment was duly scribbled into his field notebook,
already filled with calculations and information on distances, grades, fills,
bridge locations, manpower, and costs.

He continued along the descending trail towards Lake Bennett. The going
was easier now. For the first time, gravity had become an advantage instead of
a curse. After a four-hour hike, the hills to the right and left opened out and

before him lay the breathtaking beauty of Lake Bennett. The snow swept down from the mountains and on to the frozen lakeshore, and mud-stained slabs of pressure ice cluttered the shoreline. Whiffs of wood smoke rose from a forest of chimneys that poked at odd angles from hundreds of smoke-stained tents spread along the southern tip of the lake's frozen shoreline. More tents and a few log buildings spilled along the banks of Portage Creek – a rough and rocky water channel that linked Lindeman Lake to Lake Bennett.

Men and horses moved along the hard-packed snow trails that had, without design, become the town's unplanned road system. Boats and barges in various stages of construction were surrounded by piles of lumber, and scattered among them were steam boxes for bending the strakes and buckets of hot tar to caulk the seams. It was a sobering sight. Bennett was a disorganized community gripped with a sense of urgency. In a few weeks, spring breakup would clear the lakes and rivers of ice, and the race to the Klondike would be on.

Some adventurers had already decided to stay at Bennett for business reasons, having envisioned the community as an important inland city and gateway to the interior. But most of the eager gold-seekers, motivated by tales of wealth for the taking, saw Bennett only as a necessary pause in their headlong rush to the Klondike. In their determination to keep moving, some of them did not bother to build boats, preferring to travel over the ice of Lake Bennett and the Yukon River to the gold-fields – some manhandling their heavily loaded sleighs, while others used dogs or horses to pull their outfits along the lake and down the frozen watercourse.

During May 1898, more than 2,400 of these eager Klondikers headed out over the ice, trusting that they would reach their goal before spring breakup. Others reasoned that the only sensible course was to wait for breakup and then travel by boat downstream on the ice-free lakes and rivers. But that year the ice did not go out until May 28. On that day alone, more than 800 boats and scows hoisted their primitive sails and cast off from the shores of Bennett. Before the 1898–99 winter freezeup, more than 7,000 craft of all descriptions, carrying 30,000 gold-seekers, were registered as they swept past the North-West Mounted Police Post at Tagish – the last boat going through on October 22, 1898.[30]

Heney walked through the maze of tents towards a rambling log building that served as barrack room, kitchen, and mess hall for the North-West Mounted Police detachment of thirteen non-commissioned officers and men. Close by stood a rough log bunkhouse operated by Messrs. McLeod and Sullivan, two entrepreneurs who had managed to stake and control the best piece of land in Bennett. Heney reserved a bed at the bunkhouse and then set about finding informed opinions about the future of the Klondike gold-field and the likely annual tonnage it would generate. He also sought information about Lake Bennett's eastern shoreline – possibly the best route for a railway leading to Carcross, twenty-eight miles to the north at the far end of the lake.

He was not surprised to learn that almost everyone who had struggled across the Chilkoot Pass or the White Pass with provisions and camp equipment wanted a more practical method of transporting men and material. While most had heard talk of a railway to Lake Bennett and even beyond, few believed that its promoters were serious about the project. Many doubted that it could be built.

There were many diverse opinions to consider, but it did not take Heney long to recognize that most of the negative responses to his questions about future transportation developments came from the packers and pack-train operators, who saw the completion of the aerial tramlines across the Chilkoot, and the construction of a railway as competitive daggers pointed directly at their throats.

The results of his reconnaissance had already provided Heney with enough information to draw five general conclusions. First, popular opinion supported the view that the Klondike would emerge as an ongoing gold producer. Second, should the Klondike live up to its expectations, it would require the support of a railway running from Skagway to Fort Selkirk, or perhaps even to Dawson City itself. Third, if the promoters of a railway failed to attract the financial support required to construct a railway to Fort Selkirk, they should at least outflank the two serious obstacles to navigation by building to a point on the Yukon River below Miles Canyon and Whitehorse Rapids where freight and passengers could be transferred to sternwheel riverboats in the summer and to horse-drawn sleighs during the winter. Fourth, Bennett would never fulfil its hopes of becoming a northern metropolis and head of inland navigation as envisaged by its many promoters; but it would serve as a valuable interim base of operations until a railway was in place as far as Whitehorse Rapids. And fifth, a railway could be constructed through the White Pass, although the unusual climatic conditions and topographical features would more than double the cost of similar work through the mountains of Washington, Oregon, or California.

Heney was convinced that a railway from the coast to the Yukon interior was the answer to the miners' freighting problems and the Klondike's future transportation needs. Although great difficulties would be encountered, he was confident that a railway through the White Pass could be built – and that he was the one to build it. All he needed was a group of strong financial backers who had faith in the Klondike and the future of the continental Northwest.

Eight

A CHANCE MEETING

ILLIAM CLOSE was disturbed. He had not heard from Wilkinson since
his departure for Canada in January, and now the expiry date for the
Exploration Company's option to take over the three railway companies, February 12, 1898, had passed without notification or comment
from any of its officials. It was now distressingly clear to Close that
Exploration's directors had never intended to take up the option, and that their
purpose all along had been simply to put the White Pass railway proposal on
hold, leaving their representative, Hamilton Smith, free in Ottawa to promote
his plan to build an all-Canadian railway to the Yukon interior.

Close reviewed the unsatisfactory progress of the White Pass railway
scheme and concluded that Wilkinson could neither raise the final £20,000
payment on his Syndicate option nor repay Close the £10,000 loan by April 9,
the due date. He now had two choices. He could either accept the loss of his
loan, exercise his prerogative to take over the rights and charters optioned to
Wilkinson by the Syndicate, and sell them for what he could get, or he could
assume control of the whole project and construct the railway as a Close
Brothers undertaking. If he chose to construct the railway, however, he could
expect little help from the Syndicate. Its directors had already made it plain
that they were in no position to build the railway, nor could they see their way
clear to finance its construction by public subscription. "Our hands are tied by
other commitments," the Syndicate's general manager had repeatedly claimed.[1]

To keep Wilkinson's option alive, Close could finance the final £20,000
option himself, but he was reluctant to do so. It would have enhanced Wilkinson's status, and recently his faith in Wilkinson had somewhat diminished.

After the start of serious negotiations in December 1897, Close, Wilkinson,
Midgely, and M. Magner, a friend and associate of Wilkinson's, together with
their respective solicitors, had spent days drafting agreements, corresponding,
and attending meetings – all directed towards advancing Wilkinson's railway

plans, yet nothing concrete had been achieved. During this period, however, Close's position had changed. No longer merely the lender, he was now the leader of the group of English businessmen interested in constructing the railway.

His emergence as the leader of the group was no accident. Close had become convinced that a railway to the Klondike could be profitable and had deftly manoeuvred to gain control of the whole project. Legally, Wilkinson still held the option. But Close held the key to financing construction of the railway through his many highly placed friends who were already heavy investors in his firm.

With a takeover in mind Close had engaged the principals of the Syndicate and Wilkinson groups, and their respective lawyers, in exhaustive meetings throughout January and early February of 1898. Everyone present, including Samuel H. Graves, who was in London, agreed that now was the time to start constructing the railway – subject to a favourable survey of the White Pass.

Sir Thomas Tancred, an engineer of international stature, agreed to conduct the survey, and he offered to complete £50,000 worth of preliminary construction work provided he received £25,000 on account. His proposal was accepted.[2]

Close quickly negotiated the transfer of control from Wilkinson and the Syndicate to Close Brothers. The Syndicate and Wilkinson would be among the shareholders of a new holding company that Close was already in the process of organizing.

Wilkinson was informed by telegram from Magner that Close Brothers was now in command. "WE AGREE HERE ON THE FOLLOWING PROPOSAL. CLOSE BROTHERS WILL SUPPLY ENOUGH MONEY TO START THE LINE AT ONCE . . . AND PROMOTE THE WHOLE ENTERPRISE TO THE PUBLIC. WILL YOUR WORK BE JEOPARDIZED IF WE MAKE THIS PUBLIC?"[3]

Wilkinson did not reply.

Magner sent a second telegram on February 18, "WHY DO YOU NOT ANSWER CABLES? UNLESS WE RECEIVE REPLY BY TOMORROW MORNING, CLOSE WILL CABLE DOMINION GOVERNMENT OF CANADA THAT WHITE PASS WILL BE BUILT IMMEDIATELY."[4]

Wilkinson telegraphed his approval. "THE KEY TO THE SITUATION IS TO COMMENCE WORK AT ONCE," he said, adding that Hamilton Smith was active in Ottawa and that the Exploration Company was vigorously pursuing its plans to build a railway along the general route of the Dalton trail. He concluded by asking for £1,000 to cover personal expenses.[5]

After taking control, Close Brothers acted immediately to consolidate their gains. On March 8, 1898, they incorporated the Pacific Contract Company, Limited to hold all the original "rights and concessions" that had been Wilkinson's and the Syndicate's. The new company was to construct and equip a railway to Fort Selkirk at a cost not exceeding $25,000 per mile, contingent on the results of Tancred's survey.[6]

Close commissioned Midgely to accompany Tancred to North America with instructions to help Graves with the legal and legislative details of the railway, the two most important being gaining a right-of-way in Alaska between Skagway and White Pass summit – still regarded as contested territory by the United States and Great Britain – and protecting the railway's federal and provincial rights and charters from political attack. Their mandate included helping Wilkinson hold Hamilton Smith at bay, as well as any other competitor in Canada and the United States who might, with the right political support, derail Close Brothers' carefully laid plans.

Tancred and Midgely left Southampton in late February and arrived in New York early March. There, they were met by Graves, who had just returned from London, and Erastus Corning Hawkins, an American civil engineer involved in Close Brothers' North American operations.

While in New York, Tancred and Hawkins contacted the leading construction supply houses, and after meetings with Graves and D. Noble Rowan, they left for Ottawa with Midgely to confer with Wilkinson. Tancred and Hawkins returned to New York for final meetings with Graves and then left for Skagway and the White Pass. Midgely remained in Ottawa to talk with government officials responsible for the regulation of railways, as well as gather information on Wilkinson's activities. He was disturbed by what he learned and reported to Close, "Wilkinson is hale fellow well met, but beyond that it does not seem to lie in his power to produce results."[7]

It was clear that bad blood was developing between them. In Wilkinson's opinion, Midgely had been sent out to monitor his actions and possibly supersede him. He took few pains to hide his resentment from his associates in England. Their reaction was immediate. "I beg of you to try and be on good terms with Midgely," pleaded his friend Magner, "for he is the key to the cash box."[8]

But Wilkinson continued to resist Midgely's intrusion, particularly when he learned that Close would not approve his request for expense money without Midgely's recommendation. Wilkinson's irritation finally compelled his solicitor in London to telegraph, "WOULD STRONGLY URGE YOU TO TRUST AND WORK WITH MIDGELY AND CLOSE."[9]

In New York Graves faced the tasks of organizing the railway companies and of preserving their rights and charters. Time was short. As soon as he arrived from England he learned that the governments of the United States, Canada, and British Columbia were all in session, and all considering bills that could vitally affect the future of Close Brothers' railway plans. "It was not an easy matter," Graves later observed, "to attend to half a dozen bills in three different legislatures which are separated by distances greater than those which separate London, St. Petersburg, and Athens."

He also learned that a bill was pending in Washington, D.C., that, if passed, would extend the land laws of the United States to Alaska. Its passage was essential, for without it not one railway tie could be legally laid or one railway spike legally driven. Because of this bill's importance, Graves left for Washington, where he found it before a joint committee of the House and Senate, several members of which he knew. "I explained to them and to personal friends in the Cabinet what our plans were and where we needed legal protection and assistance," he later reported to his shareholders.[10]

While Graves was busy in Washington, another drama of the highest importance was unfolding in Ottawa. This was a contentious bill to ratify the Canadian government's preliminary contract with Mackenzie and Mann. Its provisions, if passed into law, would signal the start of the all-Canadian route to the Yukon interior via the Stikine River valley. The bill was a serious threat to any railway operating out of Skagway because, under the terms of the contract, no other railway would be permitted to serve the Klondike through Canadian territory until Mackenzie and Mann's railway had been in operation for a period of five years.

This threatening five-year provision was not of concern to Graves alone. American government officials were also monitoring the Canadian debates on the Mackenzie and Mann contract. The bill had already been passed by the House of Commons and it had now reached the Senate. Should the Senate approve the bill, the all-Canadian route would give preference to Canadian trade, virtually eliminating Washington, Oregon, and California as major ports for the droves of American gold-seekers leaving for the Klondike. Clearly, the loss of this lucrative trade to the Canadians would be completely unacceptable to American business interests in the south and in Skagway and Dyea.

Both the American government and Close Brothers found allies in the Klondikers themselves. The Klondike miners had sent a delegation to Ottawa in the fall of 1897 to protest some of the more obstructive provisions of the Canadian mining regulations, particularly the excessive 10 per cent royalty they were obliged to pay on every ounce of gold they gleaned from the creeks. While in Victoria on its way to Ottawa, the delegation had learned of the

Canadian government's contract with Mackenzie and Mann. The delegates were shocked by the 3.75 million acres of Yukon land that were to be granted to the railway contractors and bitterly angered when they discovered that Mackenzie and Mann would be required to pay a royalty of only one per cent on gold mined on their huge government land grants. The contract, the deputation hotly contended, was tantamount to handing over control of gold-mining in the entire Yukon district to a private corporation.[11] The delegation carried its objections to the highest government officials in Ottawa, an action that subsequently helped put the brakes on the fast-developing plan.

In recognition of this opposition to their railway, Mackenzie and Mann approached Wilkinson and Midgely in Montreal early in March with a proposal to amalgamate the two schemes. They proposed that Close Brothers transfer their rights and charters to them and abandon the idea of building a railway through the White Pass. As compensation, they would give Close Brothers a share of the huge land grants they were expecting from the government. Both sides were invited to visit Clifford Sifton independently to discuss the matter. The offer, therefore, was known in the highest government circles.

Wilkinson and Midgely rejected the proposal. They declared their intention to proceed with their own railway plan and said that they would not be deterred by propositions of this nature – although they did take the precaution of passing the proposal on to Close for his consideration.[12]

Opposition to the bill continued to mount in Parliament. Sir Charles Tupper, the Conservative Leader of the Opposition, who originally advocated the construction of an all-Canadian route "to secure the trade of the Yukon for Canada," now opposed the bill.[13] He stated that the Mackenzie and Mann contract had "met with overwhelming condemnation from one end of the country to the other."[14] The controversial railway bill faltered, and on March 26, Mackenzie and Mann gave up the fight and withdrew their Senate lobby. The following Tuesday, the contentious bill that was to have created a federally sponsored all-Canadian railway through the Stikine valley died on the Senate floor.[15]

The Mackenzie and Mann controversy had raged across the country for weeks. Many Canadians had approved the all-Canadian proposal but had condemned the provisions of the contract. Others approved both the route and the contract and extravagantly bewailed the bill's defeat. The Toronto *Globe* suggested that the Senate's action "means probably a great loss of life among thousands now rushing into the Yukon over the present dangerous routes and passes. It means that neither the churches nor medical and charitable organizations can do their humane work effectively in that country." The newspaper prophesied that the defeat of the Mackenzie and Mann contract would lead to thousands of people in the Yukon being cut off from adequate means of relief, and that "one of the most tragic stories in the history of human civilization may be written on the ice and snow of that far off country, and the result may deal a blow to Canada from which it may not recover in a generation." With a few final strokes of outrage the *Globe* concluded, "the British flag will be imperilled and Canadian authority set in defiance by the struggling multitude of alien miners in that inaccessible land."[16]

Clifford Sifton was infuriated by the failure of the all-Canadian route to the Klondike. "I spent an immense amount of time and trouble," he said, "in working out a solution which would have cost the country nothing at all, and after a year or two, blundering people will find out that the course suggested was the right one."[17]

The Senate's failure to ratify the Mackenzie and Mann contract also enraged the government of British Columbia and the merchants who were eager to seize a greater share of the Klondike business through the establishment of an all-Canadian route. "If the action of the Senate leads to the railway being secured on more favourable terms it will be justifiable," wrote the *Victoria Daily Times* on March 31,1898, "but if it postpones the construction of the railway for a year it will lead to a calamity."

British Columbia's Premier Turner telegraphed Prime Minister Laurier on April 1: "THE GOVERNMENT [of British Columbia] EXCEEDINGLY REGRETS THE DIFFICULTIES IN THE WAY OF AN ALL-CANADIAN ROUTE TO THE YUKON AND HOPES THAT THE EXTREME IMPORTANCE OF THE QUESTION IN RELATION TO THE INTERESTS OF BRITISH COLUMBIA AND CANADA MAY YET RECEIVE A SATIS-FACTORY SOLUTION." Two weeks later he telegraphed again. "AN IMMEDIATE RAILWAY FROM THE OCEAN TO TESLIN LAKE IS A MATTER OF PARAMOUNT IMPORTANCE TO THE PROVINCE AT THIS JUNCTURE. WE ARE PREPARED TO ASSIST. MAY I ASK HOW FAR YOUR GOVERNMENT WILL CONTRIBUTE?" The following day, he received Laurier's telegraphed reply. "MY GOVERNMENT FULLY RECOG-NIZES THE IMPORTANCE OF THE SUBJECT TO WHICH YOU REFER. BUT IN VIEW OF THE ATTITUDE OF THE SENATE IT IS NOW IMPOSSIBLE TO SAY WHAT ACTION CAN BE TAKEN."[18]

Nationalist fervour was now running high throughout British Columbia. Many West Coast businessmen believed that without an all-Canadian route the major share of Klondike commerce would remain in American hands. This view was shared by other businessmen across Canada, who felt that Canadian entrepreneurs should control the trade generated by a gold rush in their own country. They were upset at the prospect of Canadian miners heading for the

Klondike via the Chilkoot Pass or White Pass being obliged to land at an American port and make their way across American territory before re-entering Canada. Further, United States customs would continue to retard the miners' progress, particularly if they were packing supplies and equipment that had been purchased in Canada and shipped north from a Canadian port.

Petitions were raised in Vancouver, Victoria, Nanaimo, and Comox to the Speaker of the British Columbia Legislative Assembly stating that, "it will be difficult to estimate the damage that this province will suffer in consequence of . . . the Senate's . . . rejection." The petitions urged the provincial government to take immediate steps to sponsor the Stikine River railway route, "because of its vital importance to the agriculture, manufacturing and commercial interests of the province," and that the line should be completed during 1898 and extend south to a Canadian seaport with all possible dispatch.[19]

This sudden reappearance of the Mackenzie and Mann route as a possible provincial undertaking further complicated the already confused array of competitive northern transportation schemes facing Close Brothers and Graves.

DESPITE ITS local fame as a superior inn, the walls of the St. James Hotel were uninsulated, and Skagway's winter air penetrated every corner of the building. Within the cold interior, there were oases of warmth surrounding the few Yukon wood stoves, whose black iron chimney pipes were supported by a maze of heat-blackened wires. Around a table close to one blazing stove three men sat talking and drinking Scotch – Tancred, Hawkins, and Hislop.[20] They had left Seattle on April 5, 1898, and had landed at Skagway on April 10.

The head surveyor, Sir Thomas Tancred, had been a senior contractor on the construction of the Firth of Forth Bridge and, as a consultant, he had been involved in the construction of railways in the Transvaal, Mozambique, the southern regions of the United States, Mexico, and Turkey. His international engineering achievements had earned him an imposing set of credentials and awards, including the Imperial Order of Medjidle for his work in Turkey. He was fifty-eight.

Hawkins, who had been appointed chief engineer of the group, had recently completed a large midwestern irrigation project in the United States in which Close Brothers had a substantial interest.

The third member was John Hislop, a Canadian civil engineer from Galt, Ontario. He was a graduate of McGill University and an ex-high school teacher who was Hawkins's assistant – a man fully capable of meeting Hawkins's demanding standards.

Their nightly meetings in the St. James Hotel bar had become a ritual. There, they discussed their findings about Skagway and the movement of freight. The agenda was always the same – the grade, rock formations, manpower, the availability of gravel, bridge sites, and costs – subjects that often led to serious debate.

Wilkinson had severely criticized Close's selection of Sir Thomas Tancred as the chief surveyor, stating that, "Personally I have no faith in Tancred compared to Hawkins who has grown up and lived with railways in the Rockies." Close's confidence in Tancred was, however, complete. Furthermore, he realized that a favourable report from a trusted and recognized British contractor and engineer would carry much more weight with prospective British investors than a report from an unknown American engineer.[21]

During their first few days in Skagway, Tancred and Hawkins had interviewed many of the town's leading citizens, beginning with Captain Moore, Bernard, and George Brackett.[22] The information they obtained threw Hawkins's perception of Skagway and the transportation situation into complete disarray.

The first bombshell was Captain Moore's revelation that, despite ten years of occupancy, neither he nor the Syndicate had been able to obtain title to their Skagway land. This devastating piece of news meant that a railway right-of-way through Skagway to the sea was far from secure.

The Moores' failure to obtain title was not for the want of trying. Bernard had filed notice of location with the District Land Recorder's Office in Juneau on September 13, 1888. Some eight years passed without results when, on June 29, 1896, the Moores entered into their initial agreement with Billinghurst.

Nine years after Bernard Moore's initial application, the gold-crazed army of Klondikers had assaulted the beaches at Skagway and in a paroxysm of staking had claimed the Moores' land as their own. In outraged protest, the Moores had posted printed warnings accompanied by copies of their applications to the government for title. These warnings had been ridiculed and ignored. In the opinion of many gold-seekers, the posted copies of their application for title were proof that the Moores had no more claim to the land than they had.[23]

The miners could not state, however, that the Moores' occupancy was without substance. When the stampeders swarmed across Skagway's beaches, evidence of the Moores' presence and industry was in plain sight. There were two large log houses for the two Moore families. Along the east bluff by the bay stood a wharf in the final stages of construction, and beyond were a working sawmill capable of producing 15,000 feet of lumber each day, a bunkhouse, two log cabins to shelter the men who were employed at the mill and wharf, and one large storehouse already stocked. There were also bridges, wagon roads, and logging roads leading into the surrounding forest. By the fall of 1897, the Moore properties, in which the Syndicate had a 75 per cent interest, were valued in excess of $50,000 and they were generating some $5,000 worth of business each month. Clearly, the Moore-Syndicate properties were well established and flourishing when the horde of gold-seekers arrived.[24]

Nonetheless, many of Skagway's citizens rejected the Moores' claim to the land. The protesters, led by Skagway attorney John G. Price, alleged that they were not occupying the land in good faith but had been seeking title for the benefit of Wilkinson's English Syndicate.[25]

This opposition to the Moore land claims forced the Alaskan government to re-examine the whole Skagway land situation. The Moores and the protesting Skagway citizens were ordered to appear before officers of the District Land Office, where the two sides presented evidence to support their respective claims. The protesters' evidence demonstrated that only a small part of the contested land was actually being used by the Moores and that their wharf occupied an insignificant portion of the waterfront. Therefore, the protesters argued, the Moores should be entitled to the small plots of land on which their facilities and structures stood – and nothing more. The evidence, which consisted of a melange of charges and counter-charges, opinion and fact, was duly recorded by the District Land Office, but its final judgement was deferred.

This failure to resolve the Moore land issue did little to cool the tempers of the contestants. The majority of Skagway's citizens were opposed to the extent of the Moores' claims, and their representatives left the hearings filled with cynicism, indignation, and despair. By the time Tancred, Hawkins, and the surveyors arrived in Skagway, the land issue was a major topic of conversation.

Now Tancred and Hawkins were forced to deal with the complex problem of gaining a railway right-of-way through land they had been led to believe was under their direct influence, if not under their control. It was anybody's guess what the results of the latest land hearings would be. If the decision of the District Land Office favoured the protesters, Tancred and Hawkins would be forced to negotiate with a hodge-podge of land claimants – potentially a costly undertaking if the owners of key lots continued to hold the railway builders to ransom.[26]

To provide himself with some breathing space, Hawkins approached the First Bank of Skagway and arranged with its senior officer, Mr. C.S. Moody, to secure quietly for Close Brothers' account a number of lots on which a right-of-way through the town could be developed. Hawkins cautioned Moody not to disclose the purpose of his purchases and options to anyone, for, should the reason behind Moody's activities become known, the price for the lots would go sky high. Hawkins trusted Moody and regarded him as "a thoroughly reliable person who will work heartily in our interests." If the Moores failed to obtain title to their 160 acres, or Moody failed to accumulate the necessary lots, the only remaining option was to convince the town council that the railway should be given a right-of-way along the main street, a request that would have little chance of being granted without the general approval of the store owners, businesses, and hotels along Broadway, which had become Skagway's principal avenue of commerce.[27]

The second bombshell was the state of Brackett's road. Instead of an improved pack trail through the mountains, as Tancred and Hawkins had been led to believe, the road was a fully operational transportation enterprise that could jeopardize the railway. Tancred and Hawkins, who inspected the road on horseback, determined that Brackett was already grossing between $1,200 and $2,000 a day in toll charges at a rate of one-and-a-half cents per pound, a charge that was soon to be increased by an additional half cent. Hawkins wasted no time in opening negotiations with Brackett for the purchase of his entire operation. Brackett declined to sell but offered to make a portion of the lower section of his road's right-of-way available to the railway for $206,000 – a proposal that Hawkins rejected out of hand.[28] It was not that Brackett was averse to selling his road in its entirety. On the contrary, he would gladly sell it provided he recovered his investment and earned a profit for himself and his friends.

With an alternative to Brackett's road in mind, Hawkins opened negotiations with the shareholders of the Skagway and Lake Bennett Tramway Company, which had fallen on hard times. The tramway company had started to construct a horse-drawn tramline to the summit during October 1897, but during the intervening months both its resolve and financial support had evaporated. It did, however, possess one valuable asset. Skagway's *ad hoc* town council had granted the tramway a right-of-way along the foot of the east bluff, a strip of land originally staked by the Moores but now occupied by squatters, who claimed it as their own.[29]

While Hawkins negotiated with the tramway company, Tancred sent two members of the survey team to Dyea to assess its potential as an alternative to Skagway and examine the Chilkoot trail. The two surveyors were also instructed to pay particular attention to the aerial tramlines under construction, which were being widely advertised as the most reliable route to the Yukon interior and the gold-fields.

As part of his own personal survey, Tancred examined Brackett's road as a possible rail route to the summit. The idea was discarded, however, when his survey revealed that the grade was far too steep in places to accommodate construction and subsequent railway operations. "Therefore," reported Tancred, "the road must be ruled out as a practical route for the railway."[30]

The problems seemed endless and the pressure on Tancred and Hawkins increased daily. They faced a baffling array of problems involving the governments of Britain, the United States, Canada, the State of Washington, the province of British Columbia, and the Territory of Alaska, problems rooted in politics, competition, finance, and greed. The list of hurdles seemed endless: the Skagway land claims, competition from the Chilkoot tramlines and Brackett's road, the quest for a right-of-way through Skagway, and the international boundary question that had still to be settled – a matter of extreme importance to anyone building a railway over land claimed by both Canada and the United States. And there were the unknowns that would surely surface during the construction of a railway through a rugged mountain pass a thousand miles from the closest source of supply, with a work force that would be recruited from God knows where.

Surprisingly, given the increasing number of problems and their attendant doubts, Hawkins remained enthusiastic. Hislop was optimistic but noncommittal, preferring to wait for the results of the field work before fully endorsing the project. Tancred, as always, was confident in himself but aware of the heavy responsibility he shared with Hawkins. At this stage, he was not at all sure that the railway would ever be built – and that would be an opinion Close would not want to hear.

THE ARRIVAL of Tancred and his surveyors in Skagway had given rise to much colourful speculation and outrageous rumour. One theory was that they had been sent to Skagway by Mackenzie and Mann. Another was that they were backed by a group of Canadian capitalists, who were in some way connected with the Canadian Pacific Railway. One rumour suggested that the money for the survey came from the First National Bank of Chicago, and that a coterie of American railway men were behind the scheme. Some Skagway citizens reasoned that the surveyors had been brought to Skagway by Captain Moore.

There was agreement, however, that the arrival of the "railroad schemers" heralded the construction of a railway from Skagway to Fort Selkirk in the heart of the Yukon. "Of course," complained one Skagway newspaperman, "the men here, from Sir Thomas Tancred down, are as mum as oysters."[31]

Some members of the business community deplored the railway project and complained that it would accelerate the movement of the gold-seekers out of Skagway and thus substantially reduce the town's income. Others regarded the whole scheme as a slick promotional scam, a crafty expedient oozing with deception and humbug. Some Canadian and American newspapers joined the chorus of dissenters and questioned Skagway's general endorsement of the railway and the motives of its promoters. In a front-page story, the *Oregonian* chided the citizens of Skagway for becoming too excited about the prospects of a railway through the White Pass:

> SKAGWAY, Alaska. Overshadowing all other current topics of regular interest and discussion is the prospect of a railway traversing the White Pass. The vanguard of the survey corps that arrived ... a few days ago is now in camp three miles up the trail where it is visited by many prying and inquisitive people. But the engineers are not giving out any desired information. The reticence they displayed when they landed has since been religiously preserved, and they quickly give their curious visitors to understand that they came here to work, and have neither the time nor inclination to indulge in gossip concerning their activities.
>
> In their enthusiastic rejoicing over the beacon of hope fired by the survey party's arrival, Skagway citizens never pause to consider some of the questions which ultimately must be confronted. It would not be prudent at this time to ask them whether the wished-for railway could ever clear its operating expenses, much less yield dividends to its owners. They would look and feel offended if any daring doubters were to estimate the cost of construction and compare the probable earnings with the unavoidable expenditures, and they would regard as a mortal enemy – or a lot owner from Dyea – the foolhardy person who ventured to voice a suspicion that the survey is being made at the instance of men who entertain less intention of building a railway than of obtaining and building for speculative purposes the concessions and franchises and rights of way and some other things that pertain to railroads on paper only. It would be worth as much as one's life is worth to enquire whether the already-sagging number of miners heading in via the Lynn Canal is not likely to collapse completely before a few months opens the big river to navigation and switches the human tide to St. Michael. To wonder what return freight other than gold and atmosphere could be brought from Selkirk to Skagway over the pro-

posed railroad would be equivalent to calling the Honorable Soapy Smith a liar to his teeth. Yet all these considerations must be faced when the existing spasm of exultation is spent and cool reason returns to Skagway.[32]

Tancred and Hawkins ignored this public debate and concentrated on completing their survey. Tancred's immediate concern was the route through the White Pass and across the summit to Lake Bennett. The survey was a formidable undertaking. The mountainsides and canyons were covered with deep snow and only very general estimates of the underlying terrain were possible. Further problems were caused by the quality of the maps and reports that had been furnished to the expedition, which after a short time in the field Hawkins described as "worthless and misleading."[33]

Tancred found it difficult to visualize a continuous rail line in, out, and around the splintered rockwalls and jagged spurs of granite half buried in ice and snow. Despite his advancing years, he picked his way along the eastern bank of the pass, sometimes on horseback, sometimes on foot. There he found blocks of broken granite of every size and shape and enormous boulders that hung tenaciously to the steep tree-strewn hillsides. The east bank's slope concerned everyone on the survey team. Tancred reported that "Any removal of the toe of the slope is apt to bring down avalanches of slide rock from above," a factor that could plague railway construction. Rock falls and avalanches would increase the cost of construction and operating expenses and endanger the safety of the railway and those who used it. For these reasons, he tended to reject the east side as a likely route for a railway.

He turned to the west side. There he found what he regarded as a more substantial footing for the line of rail. For the most part it was solid granite, practically free from slide rock, and infinitely more attractive on first examination than the shattered shoulders and unstable slopes that characterized the eastern side of the pass.

After a week of surveying and questioning each member of the survey crew, Tancred came to the conclusion that, although the eastern side of the pass would be best for gaining distance – thus lessening the average gradient – he remained unsure of the integrity of its slopes. On the other hand, the western side of the pass offered a stable foundation for the railway track but would require a steeper gradient. This, he advised, "would compel the employment of a special class of locomotive."

Tancred concluded that the railway could be constructed along the western slope in a shorter space of time than along the eastern slope, but that, in either case, the cost of construction would be at least double that in most other areas of Canada and the United States. No firm decision was made, and he retained serious doubts about the viability of the project. Each side of the pass presented engineering problems that outclassed anything he had experienced to date.[34]

He respected the arguments and advice offered by his associates as they sat in the hotel lobby drinking Scotch, but he knew it would be his engineering report to London that would largely determine the future of the project. He told Hawkins and Hislop that he considered the situation unattractive as it presently stood and that he was considering forwarding a negative report to London.[35]

Hawkins begged him to reconsider, as did Hislop. Hawkins was convinced that a railway could be constructed through the pass – provided the solid granite west wall was chosen. "The rock on the west side is firmly in place," he argued, "and hence it is free from the dangers of slide rock."

Tancred was inclined to agree with Hawkins but reminded him that they had not even seen the route from the summit of the pass to Bennett and on to the Yukon River, let alone the extension of the railway to Fort Selkirk. Except for what they had heard from people who had travelled through the interior, they knew virtually nothing about the topography of the route beyond the summit.

Hawkins admitted that their knowledge of the interior country was limited, "but the information we do have strongly suggests that once we cross the mountains the grades will be light with little rock work between the summit and the Yukon River." He conceded that the greatest difficulty between the summit and the Yukon River might be moss and mud, "but the frozen sub soil will render this of no great moment." As for costs, Hawkins thought that $1.6 million would be required to complete the railway from Skagway to Lake Bennett. "That includes securing all of the required depot grounds and townsites as well as fully equipping the railway with locomotives and a complete complement of rolling stock," Hawkins added.[36]

As the discussion lengthened, the contents of the bottle gradually diminished. Throughout the evening's debate, Hawkins, supported by Hislop, continued to press his position, hoping to convince Tancred that they should, as a group, endorse the project, return to Seattle, and from there telegraph a favourable decision to Chicago and London. But Tancred would not budge. He could not give his unqualified approval of the scheme. And there the matter sat.

The hour was late and they were talked out. Warm yellow light from two electric light bulbs and a kerosene lamp cast soft shadows across the tabletop. A tinkling dance hall piano could be heard in the distance. A shot rang out. By predictable hourly increments, the iniquities of the night were escalating and rolling through the town. Tancred flicked the ash off his Havana cigar, swallowed the remains of his drink, and rose from his chair. "I'm going to bed," he announced. He regarded his two companions who, out of respect, had pushed back their chairs and stood with him. "I can understand your concerns," he said. "Building a railway is one thing, but maintaining it, especially in a country like this, is another, and frankly both will tax to the utmost the best available talent in the country. Building this railway will be an immense and difficult enterprise. I shall sleep over the situation and talk with you in the morning."[37]

As they walked to the desk to pick up their keys from Davis, the desk clerk, the lobby door of the hotel opened and in came a grimy, weary Michael J. Heney. He slowly made his way through the lobby to the desk and asked Davis for a night's accommodation. He signed the register and trudged upstairs to his room, following Tancred and Hislop.

Something about this stranger attracted Hawkins's attention, and he asked Davis who he was. Davis replied that his name was Heney and that he had just returned from Lake Bennett. He added that he had been in and out since early March checking possible routes for a transportation system through the mountains to the interior of the Yukon district. "I think he has been on a scouting trip for a railway," Davis said, "but he won't be quite so enthusiastic now since seeing the passes."[38] Hawkins stared at the top of the empty stairs. Was it possible that this man Heney had information that might influence the course of their deliberations? He looked competent and assured. On a whim, he turned to Davis and asked him to invite Heney to join the three of them in the lobby for a drink and conversation.

Hawkins continued standing at the bottom of the stairs. The whole confused pattern of activities that had consumed every hour of his day and half of every night was starting to take its toll. An edginess was beginning to affect the group's attitude towards the survey and each other. Nothing was moving. After hours of discussion, nothing tangible had transpired, no major decisions had emerged. Tomorrow morning the talks would start again – the same ground covered. It was clear to Hawkins that the time had come for them to make up their minds, using the engineering data they had obtained to date. No additional information could be obtained without a full-scale survey, and that would not be possible until the summer sun had laid bare the granite cliffs.

Davis returned and informed Hawkins that Heney accepted the invitation, but pleaded for time to wash and change his clothes. Hawkins lost no time in telling Tancred and Hislop about the invitation he had made and asked them to return to the lobby where they might hear what Heney had learned about a possible rail route through the White Pass. While waiting for Heney to join them, Hawkins outlined some of the thoughts that had been on his mind since the evening conference had ended and expressed his concern about their inability to arrive at a group decision that could, with assurance, be transmitted to Graves and Close.

Tancred lit a cigar as Hawkins talked. Neither Hawkins nor Hislop smoked.

When Heney approached the group, Hawkins introduced himself and the others. Tancred offered him a Havana cigar, and Heney accepted.

Hawkins took the initiative and explained that Tancred and himself, supported by a small field staff, were in Skagway to assess the possibility of constructing a railway from Skagway to some point in the Yukon interior and the prospects for future business that could justify proceeding with the project. He revealed that the survey group was backed by a substantial London firm that was interested in undertaking the project provided there were no insurmountable engineering problems, and that present freight and passenger levels would be maintained long enough to pay for the cost of construction and provide a reasonable return on investment. He was guarded, however, revealing only the basic facts behind their undertaking. He knew nothing about Heney, other than he liked his manner.

"Our landlord," observed Tancred, "informs us that you have been running a preliminary survey over the pass. What do you think about it? Would it be feasible, with plenty of capital, to build a railway from here to Bennett in a hurry?"[39]

Heney regarded the group. He was tired. He had left Bennett at three that morning and it was now late at night. He considered the question carefully. Like Hawkins, he was guarded. He knew nothing about this group of surveyors who professed to have a connection with London's financial centre.

"Yes," he replied, "with plenty of accent on the capital."

Hawkins assumed the roll of inquisitor, courteously subjecting Heney to a series of probing questions about himself and his background. It did not take the group long to recognize that Heney possessed an unusual depth of knowledge about railways and their construction. As the probe continued, Hawkins frequently cast glances at Tancred for his reaction and consent to his line of questions, receiving from time to time an imperceptible nod of approval. Tancred remained quiet. His eyes blazed from out of a forceful face, which supported greying mutton chops and a heavy moustache. His clean-shaven chin and the set of his mouth suggested both stubbornness and determination. He would not be easily fooled.

Hawkins leaned back in his chair. No one spoke. The four sat in silence. They had been listening to Heney for a solid hour.

Heney took the initiative and broke the heavy silence. "This country needs this railroad," he said. "The entire area is clamouring for better transportation at a lower cost. And quite aside from the commercial aspects you will have the most scenic railway in the world as an added attraction." During the following fifteen minutes, Heney outlined some of his thoughts about the railway and some of the major problems that would have to be faced by whoever undertook the job. He estimated that it would require 2,000 men working double shifts, night and day in the summer, to complete construction in two years. He emphasized that the first twenty miles would be a steady climb from tidewater to the summit, with heavy rock work almost every foot of the way. "The greater part of this undertaking will require the use of heavy explosives, irrespective of which side of the pass you choose to build," he said. He confirmed that the going would be easier north of the summit because, he explained, "with one exception at Log Cabin, the line will follow a natural decline all the way to the Yukon River to a point below Whitehorse Rapids." He predicted that during the winter months the construction crews would have to handle more snow than earth. "These unusual climatic conditions, where temperatures can range from zero to sixty below for at least four months of the year, will double the cost of similar work in the United States or Canada."

Heney paused. Then he said simply, "I would like to be the man to build it."[40]

Tancred raised his arms over his head and stretched. Hawkins watched him for any sign of decision. None came, but his attitude clearly indicated that Heney had caught his interest. In fact, Heney had impressed both Hawkins and Hislop. It was not that he had told them anything they did not already know about the pass or the problems related to building a railway through it, but his manner and assurance was starting to temper their reserve and eliminate the sense of doubt that had dogged them for days.

The discussion shifted from generalities to specific questions about the route the railway should follow. The merits and deficiencies of both the west and east sides of the pass were debated but no conclusions were reached. Hawkins was the most positive. He felt that the route, while not established in any detail, offered "no insurmountable obstacles and compares favourably, except for the depth of snow at the summit, with several passes now being used by railroads in Colorado, Montana, and California." He again stated that, in his opinion, "the westerly side of the canyon along the Skagway River would probably offer the best route for the construction of the railway," an opinion that was neither endorsed nor contested by the others, although Tancred's nod suggested that he continued to support Hawkins's selection of the west side of the pass.[41] There was no unanimity, but there was tentative agreement that there were enough route options to make a workable railway a distinct possibility.

The men talked on into the night, their spirits buoyed by Heney's comments. Perhaps it was a sudden realization that throughout their previous discussions there had been a missing element – a man to recruit the work force and direct its efforts; someone to grind out the grade, blast down the rock, bridge the gaps, obtain and stable hundreds of horses, house and feed thousands of men, care for the ill and the injured, and carry out these duties efficiently, on time, and within the limits of a construction budget.

Tancred studied Hawkins's and Hislop's impassive faces. They were both waiting for him to bare his thoughts. He laid down his cigar and searched Heney's face. "Heney," he said, "we represent Close Brothers of London, England, a substantial financial house, and we would like you to consider a business proposition."[42] He then outlined the general background of the railway project and the nature of the companies that Close Brothers had acquired earlier in the year. Heney listened attentively.

Hawkins revealed that the Pacific Contract Company, Limited had been incorporated to build the railway, if the result of the present survey justified such a major step. "In the event that we do decide to build, would you be interested in becoming involved as general foreman of the Pacific Contract Company and be responsible for the employment of labourers and their supervision? This offer, of course, will be subject to the approval of Mr. Graves, who is Close Brothers' representative in Chicago."[43]

Heney promptly agreed, subject to arranging satisfactory compensation and a reasonable clarification of his duties. He had already stated during the discussion that he wanted to build the railway, although a position as foreman in charge of hiring and supervising the work force was not exactly what he had in mind. He knew that he had made a good impression, and he was also confident that he could do any railway construction job they gave him – and more.

Two hours had passed. Much had been accomplished as a result of a chance meeting in a Skagway hotel lobby with a knowledgeable stranger who had come to them out of the dark. Tancred appeared to have modified his position. Hawkins sensed the changing mood and took the plunge, suggesting that Tancred, himself, and Heney leave for Seattle that morning on the steamer *Rosalie*. They decided that Hislop would remain in Skagway and prepare for a more comprehensive survey that would start as soon as London had reached a decision.

Heney was physically exhausted when the meeting broke up and the group retired. He had been on his feet for more than twenty hours, during which he had walked forty miles over a difficult trail from Bennett to Skagway. There, in the lobby of the St. James Hotel, fate had intervened. He had crossed the paths of Hawkins and Hislop – an event that would lead to the construction of the White Pass and Yukon railway and, during the next two years, test to the limit the skills and endurance of Erastus Corning Hawkins, Michael James Heney, and thousands of other men.

Nine

LONDON GIVES THE NOD

O N APRIL 22, 1898, the pioneer Alaska Steamship Company's 136-foot steamer *Rosalie* backed away from the dock at Skagway, turned about in a ferment of foam, and headed south down Lynn Canal. Tancred, Hawkins, and Heney stood on the upper deck between two of the ship's four lifeboats and gazed at the White Pass, its disordered snow-covered ramparts appearing less formidable as they slowly faded into the distance. For the next five days the three railway builders would talk about nothing but these mangled Alaskan mountains and the most effective way of punching a railway through them.

Their meetings continued throughout the voyage to Seattle. Tancred drew on both Hawkins's and Heney's knowledge of railway construction costs and methods in his report and recommendations to London. "From a careful examination of the country from Skagway to the summit," he wrote, "and from the estimates I have made, and from reliable written offers made to me by responsible and experienced railway men, I am of the opinion that two million dollars will amply suffice to build and equip the line to Lake Bennett and afford all the necessary wharves and warehouses at Skagway, as well as additional facilities at the Canada-United States boundary and at Lake Bennett." His figures included:

Cost of Railway to Summit of White Pass	$650,000
Cost of Railway from Summit of White Pass to Lake Bennett	$460,000
Cost of Equipment, Stations, etc.	$290,000
Special Requirements for Landing and Shipping at Skagway	$170,000
Total Cost of Undertaking Skagway to Bennett	$1,570,000

To this amount Tancred added a precautionary $430,000 to cover "other possible expenditures," creating the round figure of two million dollars to build the railway and equip it for sub-arctic operations – an enormous sum at that time for so short a line.

He recommended neither the west nor the east side of the pass as the most likely route for the railway but stated, "I consider that the western bank will enable the line to be constructed in the shortest space of time." Drawing on Heney's advice, he added, "it may be taken for granted that almost every requirement for the construction of the railway will cost at least double the rates prevailing in most other portions of the United States." He estimated that the railway could be completed and operating to the summit by the middle of August 1898, and running through to Bennett by the middle of September.[1]

The results of a business survey of Skagway were more than encouraging. Hawkins was unreserved in his predictions that the Klondike would become "the greatest gold producing country now known." He wrote, "The most conservative estimates, given by people who speak from personal knowledge, place the amount of gold ready for shipment from $15,000,000 to $20,000,000, taken out as a result of last winter's work."[2]

The survey revealed that from early November 1897, to early April 1898, about 25,000 gold-seekers and 15,000 tons of freight had passed over the Chilkoot and White Pass trails. The cost of conveying this tonnage from Skagway to Bennett at the packers' winter rate of $220 a ton during the five-month period totalled $3,300,000. Tancred observed that during the summer months, this rate could be raised by fully 300 per cent.

Tancred estimated that the cost of working the railway would be four times the normal cost in the United States "if the steepest grades were adopted through the pass." He judged that to transport 25,000 passengers and 15,000 tons of freight from Skagway to Lake Bennett, at 100 tons a day, would require two trains per day for a period of five months. This, he reasoned would total 160 train-miles per day which, at his projected cost of five dollars a train-mile, would impose a mean gross railway expense of $800 a day or $120,000 for the five-month period under review. Tancred wrote, "The total cost, therefore, at which the ... freight could have been conveyed by railway, and allowing ten per cent interest for the five months on capital expended, would have amounted to £40,665 [$203,000] as against £660,000 [$3,300,000] actually paid during that period for freight. In other words, five months freightage during five of the most unfavourable months of the year, suffices to pay 160 per cent on the total cost of the railway."[3]

Tancred was by now confident about the viability of the White Pass route, and its superiority over the Chilkoot Pass and the Yukon and Stikine River routes. Having been isolated in the north, however, he was unaware of the storm that was raging over the demise of the all-Canadian route to the Yukon via the Stikine River valley. The all-Canadian route proposal simply would not die. On April 21, the *Victoria Colonist* published another of its editorials promoting the construction of a railway from Glenora to Teslin Lake, stating:

> There is no mistaking the fact that the provision of a railway from the coast to Teslin Lake meets with the hearty approval of the people of Victoria, quite irrespective of political lines.
>
> The consensus of opinion is equally general that, inasmuch as the Dominion government seems unwilling or unable to take any steps to secure the railway, the provincial government should do so, care being taken to see that some of the advantages resulting from the operation of added receipts go to the provincial treasury. An arrangement can doubtless be made whereby any company accepting a contract from the province will bind itself to pay a sum every year into the revenue that will under some circumstances more than meet the interest on any subsidy that may be given by the province.[4]

On April 22nd, the day the Tancred-Hawkins survey party left Skagway, the Board of Trade in Vancouver, British Columbia, convened a public meeting to demand the construction of a railway from a British Columbia port to the Klondike. At the outset Mayor Garden, the chairman, announced that the Board had sent a strong resolution to the provincial government at Victoria stating that, in view of the federal government's failure to endorse the all-Canadian railway scheme, the provincial government should undertake the task.

Professor Edward Odlum, an eminent theologian, scientist, educator, and businessman, then delivered what was described as "a most exhaustive speech" and exhibited a large map, which he used to detail his arguments in favour of provincial government sponsorship of an all-Canadian route to the gold-fields. *The Victoria Daily Colonist* reported that he "aroused the national enthusiasm of the audience by his apt patriotic suggestions bearing on the question."

J.C. McLagan, a local community leader, read a telegram from Prime Minister Laurier stating that the federal government could do nothing towards promoting the railway to the Yukon district "owing to the action of the Senate." McLagan launched into a rousing speech calling for the immediate construction of the Stikine railway. He was loudly applauded. He introduced a resolution that, after citing the failure of the federal government to produce the railway to Teslin Lake, stated that "it is the opinion of this mass meeting of

citizens of Vancouver that it is the duty of the British Columbia government
... to secure the immediate construction of a railway from Teslin Lake to
Glenora on the Stikine River and its early continuation to a British Columbia
port."

The resolution urged that the railway builders be provided with a subsidy
that "shall not exceed $4,000 per mile," and that the government impose tolls
on freight and passenger traffic sufficient to recoup the subsidy in the course of
time. The resolution was put to the meeting and received enthusiastic endorsement from everyone present except for a few members of the Nationalists'
Society, who opposed the granting of subsidies and urged that the construction
of the railway be undertaken by the government alone.

Acting concurrently with the Vancouver Board of Trade, the New Westminster Board of Trade conducted its own public meeting, which passed a
resolution calling for the construction of a railway through Canadian territory
to the Klondike.[5]

Unaware of the spreading furore, Tancred and Hawkins were bent on
launching the White Pass railway project as soon as their recommendations
were approved by Graves in Chicago and Close in London. Already, with
Heney's assistance, they had drawn up lists of material requirements and had
discussed plans for the recruitment of labour. Shipping forecasts were framed
to facilitate the transportation of thousands of tons of construction material
and supplies. This raised the question of ongoing purchases and the need to
establish a company-operated agency in Seattle to provide administrative and
logistic support for the builders who would be operating in another world a
thousand miles to the north. Heney tucked this requirement into the back of
his mind, planning to involve his brother, Patrick, in the establishment of a
supply house in Seattle that would be capable of bidding on and supplying
construction material for the railway.

When the *Rosalie* reached Seattle on April 26, Tancred telegraphed Graves
that he had examined the pass and that it was possible to construct a railway
through it to Lake Bennett and beyond, an opinion, he said, that was endorsed
by Hawkins and Hislop. He assured Graves that his own and Hawkins's
reports, with recommendations, would be available for discussions by the time
they reached Chicago.

Hawkins telegraphed Graves independently, seeking permission to retain
Heney in Seattle as a temporary contact man, on the understanding his future
employment needed to be approved in Chicago. Graves approved Hawkins's
request.

With this tentative authority, Heney remained in Seattle to plan a recruitment drive, line up supply houses, and locate construction equipment. These activities, he was warned by Hawkins, were not to become public. Tancred and Hawkins left for Chicago to meet with Graves. On the way they completed their reports. In the preamble to his report, Tancred stated:

> According to instructions, I proceeded, on March 23, from New York, to examine and report upon the cost and building of a Railway to Lake Bennett, its future prospects, and its extension to Fort Selkirk or other points in the Yukon district. The undertaking has a magnificent future for the following reasons:

(a) No competing railway can be constructed in time to share in the first three years' traffic from the sea to the Yukon interior, and afterwards, this railway being the shortest and most direct route from the sea, must always continue to attract the bulk of the Yukon traffic.

(b) This railway will pass for the whole of its length through country which, commencing at Skagway and proceeding to Fort Selkirk, will traverse for the whole length a mineral district, the value of which is proving itself day by day.

(c) This will be the only railway commencing at a point where ocean vessels can discharge directly on to the railway trucks, and in which, without transhipment, goods and passengers can be conveyed into the heart of the Yukon district.

(d) By means of this railway the waste of health and strength now necessarily incurred by the miner in getting his supplies into the interior will be entirely voided, and he will arrive upon his claim vigourous and strong, and no longer worn out by the privations he has now to undergo.

(e) A large passenger traffic will always be passing into the country. Many claim owners will prefer to come out for a portion of the winter, putting in the greater part of their compulsory residence upon their claims during the summer months.

(f) Owing to the frozen state of the alluvial gravel, it is impossible for claim owners to work their claims out rapidly. It is asserted by persons of experience that it will occupy 15 years at the present rate of working to exhaust the deposits already proved payable, not to speak of other discoveries which are daily being made.

(g) Passengers and freight will certainly prefer this railway route to the all-water route by way of the Bering Sea, St. Michael and the Yukon River. This railway will effect fully 24 days saving in time from Portland, Seattle and Victoria to Dawson City, and a saving of nearly 3,500 miles in distance, not to mention the perils at the mouth of the Yukon River, the shortness of time which the rivers are open and free from ice, and other dangers.

(h) The great saving which will be effected by the opening of the railway in the price of supplies and provisions will enable vast areas of auriferous ground to be profitably worked which are now lying idle. A member of the United States Geological Commission [*sic*] now studying the country says "it takes 10 cents now to represent a payable portion in Alaska and the Yukon, as against 1 cent in other parts of the United States, and all for the want of transportation for the necessities of life in these regions."

(i) The White Pass Railway is in a more favourable position for general traffic than any that could be built from any other port on the shoreline.

In addition to the two million dollars worth of estimated construction costs, he judged that an additional eight million would be required to extend the railway from Lake Bennett to Fort Selkirk, for a total cost of some ten million dollars. "The advent of the extension from Bennett," he stated, "would cause Fort Selkirk to become the distributing centre of the Upper Yukon district serving 10,000 miles of navigable waters along the Hootalinqua, Pelly and Yukon Rivers." He concluded that the White Pass "will give access not merely to the Lower Yukon River, but to Bennett, Tutshi, Hootalinqua, and the Big Salmon districts, where great developments and discoveries are now of almost daily occurrence."[6]

Hawkins's independent report was equally enthusiastic. He concluded his recommendations by stating: "I have examined the White Pass route in company with Sir Thomas Tancred, and fully coincide with him as to his report, and all the various estimates and statements contained therein."[7]

In Chicago, Graves, Tancred, and Hawkins spent several days discussing the results of the survey, covering both the technical problems and the business opportunities. To Tancred's and Hawkins's reports, Graves added a third survey prepared by C.J. Christie, a civil engineer who had been retained by an independent group of New York bankers and railway directors to examine the White Pass. Christie had conducted his survey during July 1897, nine months before Tancred, Hawkins, and their small group of survey engineers had arrived in Skagway.

At the conclusion of his survey, Christie had reported, "the White Pass is the one feasible railway route over the coast range, and the key to a vast and rich empire." But Christie had been forced to add that the rights to construct a railway through the pass and on to Canadian territory "had already been granted to an English Syndicate, the ostensible agent and promoter of whom is a Mr. Wilkinson."[8] This last piece of information effectively scuttled the New York bankers' and railway directors' plans to build a railway through the pass. But having heard of Christie's survey Graves could not resist inviting him to add his comments to the package of information he was assembling for Close Brothers' review in London.

Hawkins, who was designated Chief Engineer and General Manager of the Pacific Contract Company, asked Graves to approve the hiring of Heney and to consider the terms of his employment. "We can produce the plans and engineering," Hawkins said, "but someone has to find the labourers and put them to work, and I believe that Heney is the man for the job."

Graves accepted Hawkins's recommendation and authorized him to employ Heney as "labour contractor" for the Pacific Contract Company. He was to receive a 5 per cent commission on every dollar paid to labourers engaged in the actual construction of the railway. Because of the anticipated difficulty in enticing men to labour in a distant sub-arctic region, wages were set at the unbelievably high rate of thirty cents an hour for a ten-hour day – less one dollar a day for board, which would consist of a bunk and three meals.[9]

At the conclusion of the Chicago meetings, Hawkins returned to Seattle and Tancred sailed for England, carrying with him the results of the meetings and the conclusions they had drawn from the survey. Included was Graves's own report. It urged Close Brothers to accept the surveyors' recommendations and pleaded for a prompt, affirmative reply so that no time would be lost in establishing an organization to gather the men and material required to start construction. Arguing for Tancred's timetable, he told London that "it will be necessary to commence work at once and throw a large body of men upon the job as soon as the surveys are sufficiently advanced for that purpose." He said that labour would be fairly plentiful and steady during June, July, and August and expressed Tancred's belief "that a large quantity of granite rock could be shifted and a considerable amount of trestling and crib work completed during the summer months." Repeating Tancred's estimation, he wrote that, with an early start, the railway could be completed to the summit by August 1898.[10]

This totally unrealistic estimate demonstrated the surveyors' inability to comprehend the unforgiving nature of the North's unpredictable weather. Graves would soon learn, like the others, that the precipitous granite cliffs, the winter snows, the glacial ice, and the howling sub-arctic winds would determine the railway's construction schedule, not Close Brothers of London and its band of bold but vulnerable builders.

IN LONDON Close had been convinced by Tancred and the surveyors' reports that the construction of the railway through the White Pass was a valid undertaking. It also appeared to offer reasonable assurance of business profitability for years to come. Yet, he was reluctant to order a start. An agonizing international situation, which had been brewing for months, was threatening world peace. On April 20, President McKinley had forwarded an ultimatum to Spain demanding that it withdraw from Cuba. As this act was regarded as tantamount to a declaration of war, the Spanish government sent the United States ambassador his passport. With McKinley's call for volunteers on April 25, the Spanish-American War began in earnest. By May 1, Commodore Dewey's Asiatic Squadron of the United States Navy had achieved a notable naval victory during the Battle of Manila Bay, which forced the surrender of Manila, the capital of the Spanish-controlled Philippines. With other squadrons of the American fleet blockading Cuban ports, and Spanish and American troops preparing for land engagements on Cuban soil, the prospects for an early peace looked bleak. The flames of national fervour were being fanned to a white heat by the American press, and now Close was questioning the advisability of launching the construction of a railway that might well become mired in the sinkhole of war.

Close telegraphed his concerns to Graves in Chicago. He confessed that he was reluctant to authorize construction, but in view of the surveyors' endorsements of the railway project, he hesitated to order a complete stand-down. Finally, in order to cover all possibilities, he instructed Graves to proceed cautiously, but to confine his activities to matters that did not involve any long-term commitments or the expenditure of large sums of money. Once again, Graves found himself operating in a twilight zone. He dare not stop in case he had to start, and he dare not start in case he had to stop. He telegraphed the situation to Hawkins in Seattle. Hawkins concluded that the London-imposed restriction would be temporary. To keep the project simmering, he contacted W.D. Hofius & Company of Seattle about the possible purchase of rail and made tentative arrangements to establish an administrative and purchasing office in Seattle.

On May 2, 1898, Hawkins received instructions from Graves to devote his full attention to completing an application to Washington, D.C., for a railway right-of-way through the White Pass. Preparation of the drawings and maps took five days of tedious labour. The application, which showed the route of the projected railway on the west side of the White Pass, was completed on May 7. The documents were forwarded to Graves in Chicago, who subsequently sent them to George Needham, Close Brothers' solicitor in Washington, D.C., for filing the moment Congress extended the provisions of the Homestead Act to Alaska.

Graves had no sooner dispatched the application than he received a telegram from Close ordering him to stop further work on the railway. There were some British investors ready to place substantial sums of cash at Close Brothers' disposal, but Close wanted time to think. With war blazing around Cuba and across the Pacific Ocean, he decided that he had better subject the whole White Pass railway scheme to a second searching review. Even if the Spanish-American War ended, he still had to face the dismal fact that the Congress of the United States had yet to extend the Homestead Act to Alaska. Without its provisions in place, not a stone could be turned or an acre of ground used for the construction of a railway.

While Close hesitated, Graves waited in Chicago, riddled with suspense. His principal concern was to keep the project alive and active while Close Brothers painstakingly re-examined the uncertainties of the project and meticulously calculated the risks. Daily telegrams passed between Chicago and London in which Graves urged an immediate start. Everywhere things were moving, except in London and Washington. Graves also kept in close touch with Needham, who was maintaining a watching brief over the passage of the Homestead Act, now through Committee and before the House of Representatives.

In Skagway, Hislop continued his preliminary survey and laid plans for a major study of the pass to start as soon as he received word that construction of the railway had been authorized. In the meantime, he faced the mountains, deciphering the mysteries of their thickly wooded hills and their high granite walls. As well, he was becoming acquainted with the politics of Skagway, its community leaders, its emerging power structure, its seats of authority, and the sinister activities of its criminal gang led by "Soapy" Smith.

On May 14, 1898, the United States Congress finally extended the provisions of the Homestead Act to Alaska. Graves was ecstatic. "Now that the bill has been finally passed," he informed London, "all of our interests have been fully safeguarded by it."[11] In effect, this legislation made possible the granting of a right-of-way, land, station acreage, timber, and stone for the construction of the railway in Alaska.

Because any survey conducted in Alaska filed prior to the extension of the Homestead Act would be invalid, Needham, on Graves's instructions, refiled their preliminary survey early the same day Congress extended its provisions to Alaska. The Pacific and Arctic Railway and Navigation Company was the first Alaska railway company to file a line of survey under the provisions of the new Act – a survey that laid out a preliminary route along the west side of the pass. A few days later, Paul Mohr, a man whose name was unknown to the group, filed a line of location for a railway right-of-way on the east side of the pass. This would cause Graves many anxious moments during the difficult months ahead.[12]

THE DAY CONGRESS passed the Homestead Act, London authorized construction of the railway, after weeks of hesitation. But Close and his associates had not been idle. Throughout the period of tedious on-again, off-again assessment, they had completed an enormous amount of administrative work in connection with the railway. Even before Tancred and Hawkins had left New York for Skagway on March 23, 1898, Close Brothers had produced a draft prospectus inviting would-be shareholders to participate in the construction of a railway to the Klondike by investing in a British-based holding corporation to be known as The White Pass and Yukon Railway Company, Limited. The prime objective of the company was to utilize and exploit the charter rights and concessions that Close Brothers had acquired from the Syndicate.

Among the new company's early shareholders were Colin Macrae, Auguste de Wette, James Dugdale, Cowley Lambert, Frederick Pennington, and Edward Alfred Wigan, men whose names would subsequently grace some of the principal localities and stations along the railway's route.[13] Close, who was a founder shareholder, was joined by many of the original railway promoters, including Sir Thomas Tancred, Samuel H. Graves, Henry Coppinger Beeton, and Charles Herbert Wilkinson, who no longer played an active role in the railway's affairs but, because of his substantial shareholdings, continued to monitor its progress.

Close also attracted a distinguished array of British and Canadian railway men who would act in an advisory capacity as the project progressed. These included the Honourable Sidney Carr-Glynn, a well-known British banker and a director of the North London Railway; Joseph Price, vice-president of the Grand Trunk Railroad; Edward Hanson, a Montreal businessman; and Sir Allan Sarle, who was once general manager of the London, Brighton and South Coast Railway.

As Close Brothers' plans advanced, these investors became increasingly optimistic. American success in its war with Spain was making headlines throughout the Western world, and the wild enthusiasm for the Klondike gold rush continued unabated. There was, however, still cause for alarm. Almost every day newspapers reported new and ingenious schemes for transporting the growing army of gold-seekers and their supplies from Canadian and United States West Coast ports into the heart of the Klondike.

One company, called the Klondike Mining, Trading and Transport Company, Limited, with offices in London, had already opened a branch office in Victoria, British Columbia, and had been advertising for weeks the "Great Through Winter Route from Victoria to Dawson City."

A Canadian Pacific Railway spokesman, named Kerr, announced from Winnipeg that his company was fitting out "a number of large steamboats of about 3,000 tons each" to handle northbound traffic.[14] The business was originally to be based on Mackenzie and Mann's projected railway through the Stikine valley to Teslin Lake. And in eastern Canada, Hamilton Smith was now proposing a railway of his own through the White Pass.

Many businessmen in London were impressed by the variety of transportation schemes being organized and by the manner in which they were being promoted. They understood the problem of northern transportation and realized that sooner or later the pressure of events would force a solution. By now it was clear to Close that if he did not act, someone else would. He telegraphed Graves in Chicago with instructions to proceed with the railway with all dispatch.

Hawkins was ready in Seattle. So was Heney. They had made no firm commitments but had already alerted Seattle's supply and equipment houses. Within five days of receiving London's instructions to proceed, Heney and a hundred men, with hundreds of tons of construction materials, were dispatched to Skagway on the steamers *City of Seattle* and *Utopia*.[15] The following day, Hawkins announced at a press conference that "All of the major contracts for the construction of the White Pass railway have been awarded." The *Seattle Post-Intelligencer* reported in bold headlines, "ROLLING STOCK TO GO NORTH, SEATTLE TO BENEFIT." "The goods are to be delivered to Skagway within fifteen days," Hawkins announced at a late hour from Seattle's Rainier-Grand Hotel.

Up to this point, Hawkins had studiously avoided newspaper men. But after the supply contracts had been signed, he made known the details of the railway construction with a flood of public statements unusual for the normally reticent Hawkins. "The contracts we have let today involve thousands of dollars," he said. They included timber, ties, material for a railway roundhouse, railway stations, three locomotives, thirty-five construction rail cars, as well as construction supplies and equipment. Huge quantities of "Giant" black blasting powder and dynamite had already been dispatched, and tons more were ready on call.

"The Illinois Steel Company of Chicago, represented in Seattle by W.D. Hofius & Company, have been awarded a contract to supply all the steel rails," Hawkins announced, "and 6,000 tons are to be shipped at once. Our lumber is to be obtained from both Washington and Alaska through the Trinidad, Colorado Lumber Company." Hawkins stated that it was his present intention to secure the construction gangs in Seattle, "and we will not oblige any of our employees to enter into a contract as to the time they will remain in Alaska. They will be free to come and go as they please." He announced with some pride that the construction men would be paid the unusually high wage of thirty cents an hour.

During his press conference, Hawkins revealed that his company, which he referred to as the White Pass Railway, had encountered and solved many problems before reaching a decision to start construction. "Many complications have arisen owing to the fact that we will be operating on both American and Canadian soil, but we are now in a position to go ahead and build our road in either country." This was true, but exactly where they would build within the White Pass had yet to be resolved. Their detailed survey was still to be completed and, until this step had been taken, there was no assurance that their proposed right-of-way would be approved by the authorities in Washington, D.C.

The railway, as envisioned by Hawkins, was still much the same as Wilkinson's and the Syndicate's original concept. "Under the plan recently adopted," Hawkins told the newsmen, "it is to be built over the White Pass to a point on Lake Bennett, a distance of approximately forty miles, and from there it is the intention to push the work of construction towards Selkirk – a distance of nearly four hundred miles from Skagway." But he conceded that he was not yet in a position to say which route would be followed, "as our engineers are now at work and we will be largely governed by reports made by them."

Some of the newsmen present knew that more than one engineer had already pronounced the White Pass an impossible route for a railway. When asked to comment on these dissenting opinions, Hawkins stated unequivocally, "The people can rest assured that the road will be built through to the Yukon country as several million dollars are to be invested, and expenses will cut very little figure." Grasping the political significance of the doubters' public comments, Hawkins added, "It is acknowledged both in Canada and the United States that Seattle is the natural gateway to the goldfields, and when the railroad is built, the hardships of going over the trail will be a thing of the past, and northern movements will be found to increase in volume – all to Seattle's advantage." The usually reserved Hawkins did not stop there. "I can see nothing but prosperity ahead for both Seattle and Skagway," he went on, "and if this feeling did not exist among all of the railways' principals and investors, the railway from Skagway to the North would not be built."[16]

The tentative arrangements that Hawkins and Heney had made during the tense period of waiting for London's approval suddenly crystallized in a burst of action. Three used locomotives and a string of railway flat cars that had been purchased in Seattle were prepared for shipment to Skagway. Orders for a huge inventory of construction supplies and equipment were confirmed, including thousands of cases of tinned food, drills, scrapers, horses, feed, workmen's clothing, camp equipment, picks, shovels, and medical supplies – the latter on orders of Dr. Fenton B. Whiting of Seattle, who had been appointed chief surgeon to the Pacific Contract Company, Limited, as well as chief surgeon and administrator of a base railway hospital to be built in Skagway.[17]

Hawkins telegraphed an old friend, Frank Herbert Whiting of Denver, Colorado, and offered him the position of general superintendent. Both the salary and the challenge appealed to Whiting, and he accepted Hawkins's offer, even though he was on the point of leaving for Mexico, where he had accepted a senior mining post in one of Mexico's premier mines.[18]

Initial attempts to recruit a work force were largely unsuccessful, despite newspaper publicity generated by the railway builders. The Pacific Contract Company's recently appointed purchasing agent, George M. Rice, complained, "the workmen who we desire to employ seem to be afraid of the project, many of them believing that it's not bona-fide."[19]

The workmen could hardly be blamed for being suspicious. The whole Pacific Northwest was filled with Klondike fast-buck artists of every description, and among them were ship owners and captains who were not beyond concocting convincing tales of fortunes to be gained in the North for the price of a steamship ticket to Skagway.

Was this railway another gold-rush scam, the workers asked themselves and each other, or was it a legitimate opportunity to live for a dollar a day and clear two dollars a shift to boot? Until they were sure, they held back. To counter the negative reaction to the railway's offer of work, Heney placed advertisements in the West Coast papers setting out the railway's plans and the need for a work force that could eventually total 2,000 men. Heney's reputation as a railway builder helped the recruiting campaign, but it did not eliminate labour's lingering doubt about the legitimacy of the enterprise.

HENEY SAT UNEASILY at a desk aboard the *City of Seattle* as it rolled and pitched through Dixon Entrance north of the Queen Charlotte Islands accompanied by the *Utopia*. Once again Heney found himself isolated and afloat upon the sea – a dark and restless deep he had never learned to trust. Nevertheless, he worked steadily with Hawkins on a stack of papers and plans. In an adjacent cabin sat Frank H. Whiting, the railway's recently retained superintendent, who was busy familiarizing himself with the nature of the enterprise. Already he could imagine the problems he must face during the construction of a railway through a harsh and mountainous country he had never seen.

Early in the morning of Friday, May 27, the two ships entered Lynn Canal and steamed north towards Skagway, arriving there during the late afternoon with the railway's first cargo of construction material and its first work force of a hundred men. Skagway longshoremen immediately began to unload the hundreds of tons of construction equipment and supplies, work that continued without pause from dusk to dawn. The cool northern air condensed the breath of both men and horses as they worked the wagon loads of supplies through Skagway to a campsite that Hislop had, on Hawkins's instructions, established north of town.

Hawkins and Heney made immediate contact with Hislop, who was eager to learn of the events that had transpired in Seattle. Although letters from Hawkins had arrived regularly encouraging him to complete his survey with all possible speed, he still felt uninformed. Hawkins had also written him that the Skagway law firm of Lovell & Jennings had been appointed the railway's attorneys regarding the development of a right-of-way through Skagway.

Obtaining a right-of-way through Skagway was central to the success of the whole project. The prospect of having to use horses and wagons to transport heavy construction material – and later freight – from waterfront wharves to a railway terminal outside town was unthinkable. Close and Graves had been under the firm impression that their acquisition of the Syndicate's assets included a right-of-way along the town's east bluff. It was only after Tancred and Hawkins had arrived to conduct their initial survey that they learned this right-of-way had not only been occupied and claimed by early gold-seekers, but that the town council had already granted it to the Skagway and Lake Bennett Tramway Company. They were further shocked to learn that on January 17, 1898, nearly four months before their arrival, Skagway's *ad hoc* city council had granted a second right-of-way through town. This one gave George Brackett a franchise to build a wagon road, or a railroad, along Runnalls Street from the beach to the town's northern boundary.

ON SATURDAY, MAY 28, 1898, the day after Hawkins, Heney, and Superintendent Whiting arrived at Skagway, railway construction began.

Heney's first objective was to erect campsites to house his workers. This included raising canvas tents with wooden sides and flooring for mess halls, bunkhouses, stores, and small field hospitals. Pending the construction of a permanent railway headquarters, Hislop, on Hawkins's orders from Seattle, had rented office space in Skagway to accommodate the administrative and engineering staffs that would soon arrive.

During the builders' first full day, Heney hired every available man and horse he could find. Within forty-eight hours more than a hundred horses were at work and a hundred local men were added to the White Pass payroll. Heney let it be known throughout the valley, including Dyea, that he would employ a thousand more men if that number could be secured. The news of this announcement buzzed through Skagway, reassuring many that the long-talked-of railway was at last under way.

Not everyone, however, approved of the project. Many of the leading packers, fearing real competition, worked to hinder the enterprise, arguing that the railway would ruin the country. Others saw the railway as an opportunity to make a killing in real estate. Almost every man or woman who had a spare lot in Skagway, or along the Skagway River, wanted ten times its value because they believed that railway builders had unlimited sources of funds and would spend freely to get what they wanted. "Take them for all you can get!" became the cry of the day.[20]

Hawkins insisted that the right-of-way question be addressed as soon as they landed. A stomach disorder, however, forced him to bed, where he remained for several days. Hawkins instructed Superintendent Whiting to conduct the negotiations and to keep him informed of progress. To this end, Whiting and Hislop visited the offices of Lovell & Jennings, where they reviewed the current situation.

Whiting's first question was about the status of the east bluff right-of-way. Hawkins had informed him in Seattle that part of the railway's strategy was to regain control of the east bluff property and that Lovell & Jennings had been instructed to buy it if necessary. Jennings replied that he had approached the Skagway and Lake Bennett Tramway Company – and had offered to purchase the company's shares outright, provided the price was not excessive, which under the circumstances was unlikely. The tramway company had been launched with a good deal of publicity and public approval during October 1897, but it had failed to achieve its goals and now was virtually broke. Its two remaining assets were a bridge of limited capacity across the Skagway River and the right-of-way along Skagway's east bluff that was currently occupied by squatters. Jennings announced that he had successfully negotiated the purchase of the tramway's assets for $5,000.

The agreement, dated May 28, 1898, had been signed in Jennings's presence that morning. The terms stipulated that the railway would pay the tramway company $1,000 on signing the agreement and the remaining $4,000 on the delivery of a deed. As a concession, Jennings had agreed to allow the tramway's principals to drive two teams of horses across the bridge at any time during the year 1898, free of any tolls the railway might impose. Hawkins was pleased the right-of-way issue was resolved, but annoyed that it had presented an obstacle in the first place. He later complained that "In order to circumvent Brackett and his people we had to purchase the bridge and right-of-way belonging to a tramway company, this merely for the privilege of getting started."[21]

Superintendent Whiting's next query was about the mood of the town. What kind of support could the railway expect? In Jennings's opinion the majority of Skagway's population approved of the plan, were aware of the tangled right-of-way mess, and were already publicly expressing their disenchantment with the *ad hoc* town council. The majority of people felt, Jennings explained, that the railway should be granted a temporary right-of-way up the centre of Broadway – Skagway's main street. On Hawkins's instructions this proposal had already been formally presented to the town council by Jennings, but council members had failed to reach a consensus.

Jennings had learned from local gossip that some members of the council endorsed Hawkins's Broadway proposal but found it politically unwise to oppose the powerful group of Broadway businessmen who had vowed they would fight the railway's right-of-way plan with every legal means available to them. They had no intention of allowing anyone to tear up Skagway's main street. Trains on Broadway, they stormed at a hastily convened meeting, would drive their customers to distraction and ruin the town's growing business centre. Let the railway establish a route along the town's eastern bluff, they said, but keep it off Broadway.

When the councilmen finally emerged from their meeting late Friday night, no firm decision had been reached. Whispers soon began to circulate, however, that the railway's application had in fact been turned down. The following day the local press reported, "the council had wilfully and with malice aforethought, refused to grant a franchise that would allow the railway to operate over certain streets of the city." Those who supported the railway were appalled at this turn of events. They decided to take direct action. A pro-railway citizens' committee was quickly formed, and throughout Saturday afternoon and evening its members contacted every councilman they could find and pointed out that the railway's request was for a temporary, not permanent, right-of-way on Broadway. With construction already under way north of town, an answer to this pressing question could no longer be delayed.

Other members of the citizens' committee invaded Skagway's cafés, bars, and hotels with a petition calling for an "indignation meeting" at Blake's Theater Royal at two the following afternoon, Sunday, May 29. The object of the meeting, the petition stated, was to "summarily remove the members of the council from their official positions, and that the franchise be granted by the citizens in mass meeting assembled."

By now hundreds of Skagway citizens were outraged that the Skagway's *ad hoc* council had not done what it should have done. The word "graft" was frequently heard, as was the story that an unnamed member of the council had received a $500 bribe from the railway and that "the balance of the council will not do anything until he whacks up." Rumours circulated that Skagway's arch rival, Dyea, was offering the railway a large bonus of land and money. Many believed that the railway now had an opportunity to sell to Dyea what it had offered to Skagway as a gift. Should the railway switch its preference to Dyea, argued Skagway's shocked citizens, Skagway would become "a mere way station on the railway's route to the White Pass." To be forced to play second fiddle to Dyea, which was contemptuously described by one Skagway correspondent as "the little town whose vaulting ambition o'leaps itself," would leave Skagway's sense of superiority and pride in tatters. As news of this probability spread through the town, hundreds of Skagway's citizens rushed to sign the petition.

By Sunday morning, the railway-aided, anti-council campaign was rolling through the town with all the intensity of a hotly contested election. A band with banners marched up and down the streets exhorting the good citizens of Skagway to head for the real estate offices of Watson and Church to sign the petition and attend the indignation meeting at the Theater Royal. Soon the streets were crowded with men and women cheering the musicians who had marched so long and hard, reported the *Skagway News*, "that they were threatened with bunions." To relieve the musicians' aching feet, a wagon was provided and the band played on behind a team of plodding horses, the beating drum and blaring horns occasionally disturbing the faithful, who were listening to the Rev. Dr. Campbell's Sunday sermon.

By early afternoon hundreds of people had flocked to the Theater Royal, "filling every square inch of space," as well as the annex, which housed the theatre's popular bar. The meeting was called to order by banker C.S. Moody, who had been appointed chairman. Recording secretary Billy Saportas, a newspaper reporter in the pay of Soapy Smith, commenced by reading the names on the petition, which at last measurement was seventeen feet long. After a hundred names the crowd grew restless and, on a motion from the floor, he was told to sit down.

Superintendent Whiting took the initiative. "I'm at a loss to understand the reason for the neglect or apathy on the part of the council," he said. He made it clear that the railway had not, and would not, engage in any under-the-table activities. To ensure that there was no misunderstanding on this point, he stated that "My company does not have one dollar of boodle money for any man." All the railway wanted, he said, was a franchise to build a rail line through Skagway. "But if it's not granted right away we will look elsewhere for a tidewater terminal," he threatened, with little effort to conceal his company's warming association with Dyea.

In an effort to placate the crowd, Council President Batten rose and stated that it had been impossible to get all of the members of council together for the Friday night meeting. He could not make it, he said, on such short notice. "But we are ready and willing to grant a fair franchise at any time we can get together."

John Stanley jumped to his feet and retorted that it was not the short notice that had kept the council's president away from the Friday meeting, but rather his decision to oppose the franchise. Stanley then charged that President Batten had intentionally absented himself from the Friday night meeting, but now, after a visit from the railway people on Saturday, "it seems he has undergone a change of mind in the matter of granting a franchise."

The best address of the day was delivered by F.T. Keelar, who favoured giving everything requested by the railway company because, "on the building of the railroad depends the future growth and prosperity of the city." He closed his remarks by reading a scathing set of resolutions in which he proposed to "dethrone the members of the council for violation of the trust reposed in them."

Keelar was followed by councilmen Burns, Hornsby, and Sperry, who assured the meeting that they would support the railway's request at the next council meeting. Jennings, representing the railway, replied with a warm and conciliatory speech in which he stated that his clients had no fault to find with the council. On the contrary, he said, they were satisfied that the councilmen would do the proper thing as soon as a meeting could be called. He then moved that the citizens present request the council to grant the franchise at its earliest possible convenience. The motion was applauded and unanimously passed.

Council President Batten then announced that he would call a meeting for the following Tuesday morning and promised that "ten minutes after we have convened, the required franchise will be duly granted and signed." Before the meeting adjourned, a motion was placed before the assembled citizens testifying that "Implicit confidence is reposed in the town council, and that in their hands, the destiny of the city will be carefully nurtured and guarded." It was seconded and passed amid applause and boisterous expressions of goodwill.[22]

At last Superintendent Whiting had his right-of-way through Skagway. At least, that is what he thought.

EARLY THE NEXT MORNING, Hislop headed back into the mountains north of Skagway. Hislop had been given the title of Assistant Chief Engineer, his duties being to assist Hawkins. His immediate task was to find the best route through the mountains from Skagway to Bennett and, in Graves's words, "Find it mighty sudden!"

To establish the rail route through the pass, Hislop had ordered five separate survey parties into the field, each party bearing responsibility for a specific section of the valley. Throughout the survey, Hislop kept in constant touch with his five survey camps, often going without proper sleep for days on end. In the discharge of his duties he crossed rivers, glaciers, mountains, and snowfields "with the speed and certainty of a mountain goat," reported Graves, who respected Hislop for his thoroughness and determination.[23]

Hislop was required to satisfy himself and his principals that the White Pass was in fact the true "Gateway to the North." There were many rumours of another pass, one of the most popular being the legend of "Warm Pass." It was said that this mysterious pass was a thousand feet lower than the White Pass, and that it could be approached by easy grades to its summit. From there, it was reported, the pass descended through warm and attractive valleys to Taku Arm and the chain of lakes leading into the Yukon River. Hislop no more expected to find Warm Pass than to "pick orchids in it," but he had to seek it out and satisfy himself and his colleagues that the pass did not exist.

There were many opinions about where the pass could be found. Some claimed that it was up the East Fork of the Skagway River. Others insisted that it could be found only by following the North Fork. Some were of the opinion that its tidewater approach was "down Lynn Canal a piece." To start his investigation, Hislop climbed Mount Dewey. From a height of 5,645 feet he could see nothing bordering Lynn Canal but mountaintops and glaciers. There was no evidence of an entrance to Warm Pass. This narrowed his investigation to the East and North forks of the Skagway River. From a quick trip up the East Fork he learned that if Warm Pass existed at all it would have to be reached by crossing Denver Glacier, a crushing field of moving ice that offered an unlikely approach to the idyllic valley. So, by a process of elimination, Hislop convinced himself that if Warm Pass existed at all, it must lead on from the North Fork.

Hislop decided to conduct his investigation of the North Fork alone. "If I don't start, I won't get there," he said, and stuffing a few biscuits into his coat pocket, he headed up North Fork.

Two days later, after hiking more than fifty miles through mountain valleys, swamps, and snowfields, he gained the head of Windy Arm near the British Columbia-Yukon border. His feet were blistered and bleeding and his clothes were in tatters. He had fought his way through miles of tangled underbrush, boulders, and jagged rock. He had followed the shoreline of Windy Arm until his way was blocked by an insurmountable wall of rock, making further progress along the lakeshore impossible. From driftwood, and rope that he had fashioned from fibrous spruce roots, Hislop had constructed a raft and had launched himself onto the wind-swept waters of Windy Arm, using a tree branch for a paddle. The persistent winds that gave Windy Arm its name had swept the exhausted Hislop and his raft towards the centre of the lake. Twice he had fallen overboard and crawled back. "My greatest difficulty," he later explained, "was to keep from going to sleep during the ten-mile journey down the lake." When the wind changed, he had managed to reach shore near the north end of the Arm, where he had fallen exhausted on the beach. There he had been found by a worried survey crew that had been alerted to search for him. When he came to, his first words had been, "Well boys, I didn't find Warm Pass, and no one ever will."[24]

When Hislop returned to Skagway, he was surprised to find that the town council had still not granted the railway its temporary right-of-way along Broadway. Sixteen days had passed since the council's president had promised the petitioners that he would call a council meeting for the Tuesday following the rally at the Theater Royal. But Tuesday, June 2, had come and gone.

Supplies, material, and construction equipment were piled up along the rim of the beach, beyond high tide. The steamer *Al-Ki* had recently landed 175 tons of fifty-six-pound rail, and lumber and spikes for the railway's marine terminal to be built just south of the Moore wharf and connected to it. Contracts had been let for more than three million board feet of lumber and heavy timbers for buildings and railway trestles. An additional twenty tons of Giant black blasting powder was on its way north and a thousand bridge piles were ready for shipment from Port Blakely, Washington.[25] To add to the pressure, the huge 250-foot barge *Skookum* had arrived on Monday, June 13, under tow by the tug *Tacoma* with an additional 600 tons of steel rails.

Some construction work was under way near the beach and beyond the town's northern border, but there would be no real progress until heavy equipment could be moved through Skagway to the construction front north of town. Without a rail right-of-way through the town, the railway was at a standstill. Superintendent Whiting was outraged by the delay. Unless this continuing problem was quickly resolved, he said, serious consideration would have to be given to selecting Dyea as the railway's southern terminus, despite its limitations as an ocean-going port. To underline his threat, Whiting dispatched a group of railway workers and surveyors to Dyea with instructions to lay out a preliminary line from the town's beaches to the entrance to the White Pass north of Skagway.[26]

The Skagway councilmen had tried to keep their promise, but the Broadway entrepreneurs had mounted such a loud and continuous protest that the council had been forced to reconsider the whole matter. After hours of deliberation, they decided to call a special meeting on June 13 to place the conflicting points of view before the public.

When the meeting was brought to order, the council chamber was packed. The president opened the meeting by stating that the protests of the Broadway business interests could not be ignored, yet, under the circumstances, Broadway appeared to be the only usable thoroughfare for the railway's temporary right-of-way. He said that the only other route was the strip of land along the east bluff, "but we have been unable to deal with the people who are occupying that property and claim it as their own. Something has to be done," he said. "The railway contractor has worked his men as far as he can go, and unless they can get material to them either up Broadway or along the bluff they will be idle tomorrow."

Councilman Hornsby then presented the details of the franchise they had prepared but had been unable to put into effect because of local pressure to keep the railway off Broadway. Its two salient points were: the franchise to construct and operate a railway on Broadway would be temporary only, and that, as soon as the citizens of Skagway were in a position to give the railway undisputed and peaceable possession of a sixty-foot strip at the foot of the bluff, the track on Broadway would be abandoned by the railway and turned back to the city of Skagway. Hornsby made it plain that the council had no choice in the matter. Its main goal, he said, was to see that the railway got what was undoubtedly the wish of the people of Skagway, "namely a right-of-way through the city." He referred to the previous public meeting where the council had been instructed to give the railway the right-of-way they needed. "If the people on the bluff cannot be dealt with," he said, "and the Broadway people protest against granting even a temporary permit along that street, what is to be done? Are the railway people to be tied up and their men left idle?"

The Broadway property owners listened but remained unyielding in their demand that the railway be kept off Broadway. "Once they are on that street you'll never get them off again," shouted one. "Broadway is the best business street in the city and the railway will kill it," roared another. The hubbub grew louder.

Whiting rose from his seat and faced the crowd, who quieted as he started to speak. "We have come here to build a railway. All we need is a right-of-way through Skagway so that we can get on with the job. My understanding is that the citizens of Skagway told the council two weeks ago to provide the railway with a right-of-way. It has not happened. We now want that pledge kept at once. Either give us a right-of-way or tell us that you do not intend to do so."[27]

The time of reckoning had arrived. Give them their temporary right-of-way on Broadway, demanded the people. Give them a right-of-way but not on Broadway, protested the business owners. The situation was tense.

The Broadway protesters broke first and pleaded for time. They asked that they be given twenty-four hours to raise sufficient funds to purchase the occupied land from the squatters along the east bluff. Their request was granted on the understanding that the issue must be decided at a public meeting the following evening, Tuesday, June 14. Three committees were appointed to deal with the three separate aspects of the problem. The first committee was instructed to approach the bluff "squatters" to determine what they wanted in cash to vacate the land they were occupying. The second committee was to approach the Broadway businessmen to determine how much money they could raise to purchase the bluff property provided the squatters could be induced to sell. The third committee was to approach the railway to determine how much it was prepared to contribute towards the purchase of the bluff property that the railway insisted it already owned as a result of its purchase of the Skagway and Lake Bennett Tramway Company's assets, which included the bluff right-of-way.

The following evening the council and a large crowd of participants and spectators gathered in Meyer's Hall to hear the reports of the three committees. Dr. Bryant reported that his committee had seen all but seven of the squatters and, while some had indicated a willingness to sell, he could offer no assurance that all of them would. Mr. Lokowitz, representing the Broadway businessmen, reported that his committee had been out all day and had met with little success in raising money to purchase the east bluff property. When asked how much he had raised he declined to provide a figure, stating that "the amount of money was too small." Mr. Price reported that his committee had seen the railway people and that Superintendent Whiting had agreed to donate an amount of money equal to what it would cost the railway to lay the Broadway track and take it up again, "which Mr. Whiting estimated would be between seven and eight hundred dollars."

The meeting then asked Superintendent Whiting to comment. "We would by far prefer the bluff right-of-way if it could be given to us at once," he said. "This does not appear to be possible. But the time for talk is over. We must have immediate action." He then turned and left the hall, leaving his ultimatum ringing in the ears of the assembly.

After Whiting's dramatic departure, the advocates for both sides of the question threw themselves into a heated discussion. The Broadway businessmen gradually lost ground. Finally, the meeting passed a resolution directing the council to grant a temporary right-of-way to the railway, "on Broadway or anywhere else that would allow the road to proceed immediately with its construction work."

Later that evening, members of the council called on Whiting and asked him if he would be prepared to sign an agreement to abide by the provisions of the proposed right-of-way permit. He said he would. With this assurance, he was told that, under instructions from the people, the council would grant the permit the following morning.[28]

But Superintendent Whiting had had enough. He wanted no more meetings, no more delays. Before he went to bed that night, he contacted Heney and instructed him to set the Broadway construction plan in motion. Permit or no permit, he was determined to move. He would tolerate no more procedural delays or rearguard actions by disgruntled businessmen.

When Skagway awoke the next morning, its citizens were startled to find 200 men ripping up the centre of Broadway, guided by a neat row of construction stakes that had been driven home in the dead of night.[29]

Ten

BRACKETT'S BLUFF

ITH CONSTRUCTION now under way, Skagway's civic pride was aroused. It would be the most northerly port on the continent that connected with a railway – a rail operation that had the added distinction of being a link between the Klondike and the sea. Skagway felt good about itself; its citizens believed that its future was assured. They liked where they stood in the scheme of things and, with more than a touch of frontier boosterism, they strutted and preened on the front pages of the nation's newspapers. Skagway was now truly the "Gateway to the North," the newspapers confidently proclaimed.

Once the signal was given to begin construction of the railway up Broadway, Heney never looked back. By June 18, three days after council's last confused meeting, he had completed nearly one mile of railway grade along Skagway's main street. Heavy timbers had been hauled by horse and wagon to six bridge sites, where gangs of carpenters were already at work spanning Bishoprick Mill Creek, a rambling watercourse that intersected Broadway six times within a mile as it snaked its way to the sea.

The street was lined with spectators, some of them approving because the railway represented prosperity, a few of them cursing because they believed that it placed their businesses in jeopardy. Among the crowd of onlookers were many unemployed gold-seekers who had gone broke on their way to the Klondike. Recognizing opportunity when they saw it, they hurried off to Heney's hiring tent. Within the hour they were back wielding picks and shovels in front of Broadway's bars and gambling joints, where many of them had spent the night drowning their miseries in rotgut booze or trying to eliminate them by the turn of a card.

During the interminable right-of-way debates, barges and ships loaded with railway construction material and equipment had continued to arrive, accompanied by gangs of labourers who had been recruited in the United States and

Canada. Under the impact of this influx of men and material, the character of Skagway's waterfront began to change. Now among the stacks of Klondike-bound freight were piles of heavy bridge timbers, lumber, ties, rail, spikes, angle bars, fish plates, switches, frogs, and track iron of all types. Tins of black powder and boxes of dynamite were landed and moved to a protected storage dump north of town. Wagons were backed into the sea and loaded directly from barges that had been nudged up to the beach by a steam-powered harbour tug.

Already Heney had prepared for the construction of a temporary rail line down to the low-water mark to allow construction equipment and rolling stock to be transferred directly from barge to the track as soon as the first locomotive and flat cars arrived. There was a new sense of urgency in all this activity. If the railway was to reach White Pass summit by the middle of August and be running through to Bennett by September, as Tancred had projected in his report to London, there was no time to waste.

Hislop and his surveyors had yet to define in detail the grade from Skagway to White Pass summit, although the final direction that the line would take was gradually coming into sharper focus. Each of Hislop's five survey crews had now been in the hills and mountains for weeks, and they were on the point of exhaustion. Already one surveyor had been killed and two had been injured as a result of a snow cave-in at the summit. Heavy drifts barred the way as rodmen, chainmen, and axemen criss-crossed the valley and made their way up the rocky draws or climbed around the valley's precipitous cliffs. The nights were cold, although a warming sun turned the patches of snow to slush during high noon. In the lower levels of the valley the snow had gone. The low lands were alive with movement. Swollen creeks gushed and roared in cascades of white water nourished by millions of tons of glacial ice and snow. Surveyors crawled along the smooth granite cliffs and jagged canyon walls of the upper pass. Unlike the gold-seekers who followed a well-defined trail, the surveyors faced the unknown among the bleak and fractured gaps that shaped both sides of the pass.

Hislop had not yet solved all of the mysteries of the pass, but he had drawn one fundamental conclusion: the railway should be built on the east side of the pass, not the west side as Tancred and Hawkins had originally thought. During the St. James Hotel talks, Hawkins had argued that the west side of the canyon along the Skagway River would probably offer the best route for the construction of the railway, an opinion that had earned Tancred's approval. Now, after weeks in the field, Hislop had developed a contrary opinion with supporting figures.

Hislop's five survey parties had conducted independent surveys along both sides of the pass. All five surveys had revealed advantages along their selected routes. On the west side, the rock footing was superior but the nature of the terrain imposed too steep a grade. On the east side, the footing appeared less secure but valuable grade-reducing distance could be gained.

The final factor in the survey equation was to find a route through the jumble of natural obstacles that was capable of providing maximum gradients of four per cent or less and curves of no more than sixteen degrees. To achieve this goal, Hislop had plotted a route 19.607 miles in length along the east side of the valley from Skagway to White Pass summit. Hawkins, who had continually monitored Hislop's survey, had abandoned his original proposal that the railway be constructed on the west side of the valley and had finally accepted Hislop's surveyed line along the eastern wall of the pass.[1] There was, however, one major problem. Much to Hawkins's annoyance, Brackett's road ran along the east side of the valley for four miles north of Skagway, and the railway would likely have to cross it at several points.

Hawkins approached Brackett with a proposal to purchase all of his wagon-road assets. Brackett would not sell for less than $206,000 for all of his road's assets, the amount he needed to retire his debts and still profit. Hawkins rejected Brackett's demands, insisting that the price was "prohibitive." The only option left to him was to build a trestle across the Skagway River to carry his track from the east to the west side of the valley, build four miles of grade on the west side of the river, and then construct a second trestle to return his track to the east side of the valley at a point where it avoided Brackett's road – a costly and time-consuming detour that outwitted Brackett but left the railway vulnerable during spring breakup.[2]

By late June, the Skagway and Lake Bennett Tramway Company bridge, which the railway had acquired, was being used to move men and light material across the river, and a new 500-foot railway trestle substantial enough to carry heavily loaded freight trains was on the drawing board. The surveyors' stakes were in place and work on the bridge's approaches was already under way. As soon as the track was completed along Broadway, bridge piles, batter posts, girts, stringers, bolts, spikes, and a steam-driven pile driver would be moved to the bridge site by the railway's first work train, which was already being prepared for shipment in Seattle. It consisted of two flat cars and the railway's first locomotive, designated Engine No. 2, a Diamond Stack, type 2-6-0, built by the Brooks Locomotive Works in 1881 and purchased second-hand from the Columbia & Puget Sound Railway for $3,000.[3]

Construction camps were being erected far ahead of the grade – one of them at the top of the pass, where drillers and powdermen were already at work blasting out a 300-yard, 22-foot-deep cut through a rock barrier that blocked rail access to the summit. Hislop and Heney, on Hawkins's instructions, had also established a survey crew and a work force at the summit in preparation for a push into what they assumed to be British Columbia, an assumption that many American officials and Skagway editorial writers refused to accept.

Hislop had already sent one team of surveyors beyond White Pass summit with instructions to plot a route along the lakes and meadows that dotted the broad uplands. To the surveyors' surprise, they found their way barred by the North-West Mounted Police, who informed one of Hislop's assistants, an engineer named Edwin Hall Warner, that on instructions from the Canadian government he would not be permitted to project the preliminary railway survey line north of the summit. In his subsequent report, Warner stated, "I suppose we will have to do what they say, as they have got a Gatling gun up there that fires 600 shots a minute."

Hawkins reported this surprising confrontation to Graves, who was in Chicago. Graves, like Hawkins and Hislop, was at a loss to understand why the Canadian government would deny them the right to proceed with the con-struction of their railway through British Columbia to the Yukon. They had already been given a charter by the provincial government, and the federal government had granted a charter the previous year authorizing the railway to extend its line from the northern borders of British Columbia to Fort Selkirk. But without permission to enter British Columbia, theoretically, they could only build a railway with two ends and no middle. Graves was stunned and enraged.

After he had read Hawkins's report, he telegraphed the railway's legal counsel in Ottawa, F.H. Chrysler, and instructed him to take whatever steps were necessary to unplug this bureaucratic obstruction as quickly as possible. "If we are held up," Graves later explained to Chrysler and to government officials in Ottawa, "we will lose the summer months and be compelled to build the grade north of the summit during the fall and winter when the ground is frozen hard. Furthermore," he added, "because of the government's action we shall be delayed several months reaching Bennett with our tracks. As a result we will sustain a heavy loss of traffic. This will force us to pay packers to carry our freight from the end of steel at the summit to Bennett, instead of being able to carry the freight ourselves."[4]

Shortly after making his appeal in Ottawa, Graves was informed by Chrysler that the restrictions had been lifted and the railway was free to proceed with its work north of the summit. Graves told Hawkins that the summit problem

Skagway and the White Pass, showing the town, the first and second bridges, and the emerging grade snaking through the mountains to the summit.

(Inset) The railway's first excursion train crossing the second bridge.

Graves, Hislop, Hawkins, and Heney outside a construction-camp headquarters tent. Hislop's and Heney's dogs were a familiar sight on the grade.

Dr. Whiting's field hospitals were rough and ready, but well stocked with the best of medical supplies.

Clearing the Brackett Road of debris after a major blast was a time-consuming operation that frustrated Hawkins and tested Brackett's patience.

A construction-camp dining tent.

Horses were the major source of power along the grade. Keeping them properly shod and healthy consumed thousands of horseshoes and the talents of many veterinarians, blacksmiths, and farriers.

Rocky Point. Some said that it would never be breached.

Rocky Point breached. The Grade was notched out of a sheer cliff.

Situated thirteen miles north of Skagway, Heney was the railway's first main-line station. Michael J. Heney (standing front centre, wearing black hat) checks operations while taking a group of guests on a conducted tour. Note the top of the inclined tramway at the gap in the platform.

Foy's ingenious tramway. It delivered freight from Heney Station to White Pass City at the foot of the incline.

Guests of the railway at the end of the completed track at Rocky Point on 15 August, 1898. Note the warning tie laid across the end of the rail.

The two-man jack: one man held the drill while two men struck it with sledge hammers. After each blow, the holder turned the drill. This was the method the powdermen used to drill their blast holes. Volunteering to be the holder was an act of great faith.

Cutting the grade across the face of Slippery Rock. The men were held to the rock by ropes—
a construction technique that was repeated many times as the grade advanced to the summit.

Carving the grade through solid granite with black powder, horses, and brawn.

Workers were told to "freeze" while the camera shutter was open. Heney, with his hands in his pockets and wearing a black hat, is standing in the distant center.

August 8, 1898 was a black day on the grade. Hundreds of employees demanded their time and headed for the Atlin gold strike, leaving the railway virtually stripped of workers.

Loading black powder for a blast near the summit of White Pass.

BARLEY, AUTHOR'S COLLECTION

Driving a tunnel through this huge abutment of rock, with the south portal entering half-way up the hill, was completed in the dead of winter under the most difficult conditions.

A skyline delivered construction material to the tunnel's south portal after a working ledge had been blasted from the face of the cliff.

Bridging the gap from the Tunnel Mountain grade to the tunnel's south portal during a lull in the winter storms.

Constructing the tunnel's northern portal. The railway, unlike the packers, treated its horses with the best of care.

BRIDGE CARPENTERS AT THEIR NOON DAY MEAL, W.P.&Y.R.

Lunch time on the grade at the completed bridge and tunnel.

had been resolved and that Hislop and Heney were to start their work north of the border without delay. Once again the crews were assembled and the survey and construction work began. Once again, acting under instructions from Ottawa, the North-West Mounted Police turned them back.

During the summer of 1898, the railway builders made further attempts to complete their survey and start construction beyond the summit, but without success. "On three or four different occasions our work was suspended by officials of the North-West Mounted Police acting on instructions from Ottawa," Hawkins later reported, "and each time the instruction was revoked by action of Mr. Graves, a new and similar order would be enforced from some other department of government."[5]

This unforeseen action by the Canadian government had added a new dimension to the railway builders' growing catalogue of menacing problems. Graves was beginning to wonder if they might not be defeated by interfering politicians and bureaucrats sitting behind government desks.

The delays were not only wasting valuable summer days, when construction could proceed unaffected by ice and snow and the freezing winds of winter, but they were impeding the railway's ability to create much-needed revenue from transporting freight and passengers from Skagway to the summit and beyond.

Meanwhile, Hislop continued to refine his surveyed line between Skagway and the summit. With its massive angular abutments and boulder-strewn slopes, the twenty-mile grade presented a challenge regarded by some as unmatched in the history of railway construction. Already the end of summer was approaching. In just over ninety days, October would be upon them, bringing with it the first frosts of winter, and not a foot of rail had yet been laid.

Heney moved along the grade on horseback, accompanied much of the time by Hugh Foy, the Pacific Contract Company's foreman of construction. Aged sixty-seven, and not in the best of health, Foy had decided that the construction of the White Pass railway would be his last job away from home in Seattle. During his career, he had been heavily involved in bridge-building, railway construction, and the development of large municipal works. Wearing a bowler hat and issuing orders in a gruff voice, he was an ever-present force on the job – even rushing through the labourers' tents in the morning to see that every-one was up and ready to work. He was a fair but demanding taskmaster. And he laboured to enforce Heney's strict rule forbidding the consumption of liquor in the camps.[6]

When combined with cigars, pipes, matches, and dynamite, liquor could become a killer, and Heney demanded that his "no-smoking, no-liquor" rule

applied to everyone on the job – except himself. (A widely recognized judge of
fine liquor, Heney was never without a case or two each of Monogram rye and
Perfection Scotch, as well as a substantial stock of imported wines and a supply
of Romeo Havana cigars.) Gambling also was forbidden. This had not escaped
the attention of Soapy Smith, who intended to organize illicit gambling and the
sale of bootleg liquor along the railway grade.

To launch his illicit enterprise, Smith sent a member of his gang to set up a
games and drinking tent near the construction camp at the second river crossing. When Heney learned of the tent's existence, he ordered Smith's man off
the site, but the gambler refused to move, stating that he had as much right to
be there as Heney. In no mood to haggle, Heney called for Foy. Pointing to a
large rock above the offending tent, Heney instructed Foy in a loud voice to
"blow that rock out of there by morning, and not a single minute later, mind!"
He then walked off, leaving Smith's thug to think it over.

Early the following morning, Foy found the tent still in place, so he ordered
his powderman to load a few sticks of dynamite under the rock. Five minutes
later, Foy sent a powderman to wake up the tent's lone occupant and advise
him to move immediately or be blown to kingdom come. The gambler refused
to move. Foy took charge. Pointing to his watch, he said, "In one minute by
this watch I will give the order to touch off the fuse. It will burn for sixty
seconds. There will then be an explosion and that rock will arrive here before
you can blink your eye." Smith's man, displaying unusual determination, told
Foy to go to hell. Foy turned and shouted "FIRE!" and scurried to safety behind
a rock. Ten seconds later he was joined by the now-terrified gambler, who had
leapt out of bed and ran to Foy's protective rock in his underwear. Together,
they watched the blast and the total destruction of the tent, the games, and the
stock of liquor.

Foy went to Heney's tent and reported that the rock was down.

"Good. Where's the man?" asked Heney.

"The last time I saw him he was heading down the trail in his underclothes,
cursing," replied Foy. And that was the last time anyone seriously challenged
Heney's order that there would be no drinking or gambling on the job or in the
camps.[7]

Heney and Foy returned their attention to the construction of the railway.
One of their immediate concerns was the stability of the six Broadway bridges,
which Heney had been instructed to build to a lower-than-normal standard.
He expressed his concern to Superintendent Whiting, who replied that he
would build the bridges to a higher standard only if the railway could count on
occupying Broadway for a reasonable period of time. "If the council gets the

squatters off our bluff right-of-way," he grumbled, "we will have to move our line off Broadway, and I don't want to go to the expense of constructing pile bridges if we have to move to the bluff."[8]

Hardly a month had passed since construction began, but already Heney's influence was being felt all along the grade. His job was to recruit, control, house, and supervise the work force. His task was to see that this growing army of labourers functioned effectively and efficiently on the grade and to ensure that everything it did was in the interests of the Pacific Contract Company and the White Pass Railway. But already his drive, interest, and overall knowledge of railway-building were pushing him to act beyond this limited authority. His ability to manage men and demand their best was a natural talent that could not be confined within some vague title. He simply took charge of the work, and his authority was accepted wherever he went.

AS HAWKINS HAD foreseen on the first day he arrived in Skagway, George Brackett's wagon road, although incomplete from White Pass City to the summit, had become an invaluable supply route for the railway builders, yet its existence remained a threat to the railway. It was both a blessing and a curse. Brackett's aggressive business tactics, low freight rates, secret discounts, and special deals could seriously impede the railway's intention of eventually capturing all the freight business out of Skagway. Indeed, unless the railway could control the movement of freight, there was nothing to justify its construction. This was the railway's dilemma. It was forced to keep the road clear of debris and operating during construction while, at the same time, searching for a way to eliminate the road when the railway reached the summit.

Brackett already had shunned Hawkins's early offer to purchase the road, but his inflated selling price was really nothing but a combination of bluster and hope. He knew that with the coming of the railway he was in trouble. During the previous months he had borrowed heavily to finance the completion of his road, relying on future freight business to repay his loans and restore his lost fortunes. Now, with railway construction advancing mile by mile towards the summit, he could see his plans disintegrating.

Hawkins, sensing Brackett's desperation, persisted in his attempts to gain control of the road, but without success. Brackett would not move. In an attempt to break the deadlock, Hawkins left for Seattle where he telegraphed Graves apprising him of the situation and requesting that he leave immediately for the West Coast to meet with him and Brackett, who was due to arrive in Seattle from Skagway on June 20.

Hawkins was not the only one trying to negotiate the purchase of Brackett's road. D. Noble Rowan, who, with the Syndicate, had been the first to support the Moores financially during the early development of their Skagway homestead, had been trying to gain control of Brackett's road for months. Rowan wanted to protect the interests of his firm, the Alaskan and North Western Territories Trading Company, and to frustrate Close Brothers, who, by calling the Syndicate's loan, had captured all the railroad companies and franchises in which he had held an interest.

Because of Rowan's involvement in the Syndicate's affairs, control of the pass had always been vital to his business interests in Skagway. Acting in concert with Wilkinson and the Moores, he had repeatedly sought permission from Washington to build a road through the White Pass from Skagway to the summit. Later, he had applied for the right to charge tolls on a trail he claimed that his company – with the Moores – had completed to the summit of the pass. None of these applications had met with success. Now, in midsummer 1898, with the Brackett road apparently up for sale, he saw a new opportunity to gain the upper hand. Failing that, he could at least make Close Brothers pay through the nose for the Brackett road and, in the process, make a profit for himself. Tancred had also kept in touch with developments in Skagway and had asked that he be told should Brackett's road be offered for sale.

Brackett arrived in Seattle on schedule and visited his lawyer, John P. Hartman, to review his current position and determine the best course of action to take. Their decision was to offer the whole Brackett operation to Rowan, who had maintained close contact with Hartman for months.

"BRACKETT JUST ARRIVED FROM SKAGWAY," Hartman wired Rowan on June 20. "HAWKINS ANXIOUS TO NEGOTIATE. BRACKETT WILL ACCEPT TWO HUNDRED THOUSAND DOLLARS FOR ROAD, ALL FRANCHISES AND INTERESTS. SAME PRICE NAMED TO TANCRED. ANSWER. JOHN P. HARTMAN."[9]

Maintaining his reputation for bombast and pomposity, Rowan replied collect the following day: "RAISE PRICE TO TWO HUNDRED AND FIFTY THOUSAND TO ALL BUYERS AND REFER TO ME. MAIL ME . . . POWER TO ACT FOR YOU AND BRACKETT. I WILL PULL A SALE THROUGH. LET CLOSE BROTHERS AND CO. RUN AFTER ME WHEN THEY UNDERSTAND I HAVE IT. D. NOBLE ROWAN."[10]

No one was impressed with Rowan's pretentious reply. He offered nothing but a scheme to make a profit on the sale, influence the road's affairs, and settle his personal grudge with Close Brothers. Brackett rejected the proposal.

Tancred kept quiet, forcing Brackett and Hartman to consider alternatives that were less demanding on prospective purchasers. It appeared that their

$200,000 price tag was too high to attract the attention of serious buyers, despite Rowan's suggestion that they tack on an additional $50,000.

During their discussions, Graves arrived in Seattle. He met with Hawkins, Brackett, and Hartman at the railway's Seattle office to consider the purchase of Brackett's road. Brackett's first cautious move was to offer the road to Graves, complete with franchises, for $200,000. Graves, blessed with a lively sense of humour, declined to enter into negotiations at that level. He did, however, comment on Brackett's unfortunate predicament and offered him his sympathy and understanding – but little in the way of cash. Brackett was determined to resist Graves's disarming charm and negotiate a sale with all the skill he could muster. Bluffing his way towards a reasonable deal, he boldly stated that he did not need to sell. He claimed that he could conduct his freight business winter and summer, and that he could offer a transportation service as efficient and less expensive than the railway's. Accepting the bargaining challenge, Graves suggested that it would be virtually impossible for Brackett to compete with the railway once it reached the summit of the pass. Brackett rejected this view and insisted that he could, and would, beat the railway, and that he would do it by reducing his freight charges so that they would always be below those set by the railway. This, he insisted, would force the railway to drop its rates to compete successfully with the wagon road, a situation he felt Graves would wish to avoid.[11]

Realizing that Graves was uncomfortable with his aggressive stance, Brackett continued to press his advantage by drawing vivid pictures of his future plans for his wagon road. He expressed alarm over the constant disruptions that the railway construction was imposing on his business by constantly dumping tons of rock and debris at key points along his road. And there was the matter of the railway occupying it without let-up throughout the day and night with wagons and men. All of these matters, Brackett insisted, must be addressed if a settlement was to be achieved.

Brackett's bluff was having its effect on Graves and Hawkins. They could not help but admit that they were dealing with a determined man. His record of accomplishment spoke for itself. Despite seemingly insurmountable physical and financial difficulties, he had consistently reached his announced goals. He had built his road against enormous odds. He had raised money, influenced governments, tapped the highest political circles in the United States, gained the support of leading Canadian transportation tycoons, held off creditors, operated his toll road, and emerged as a respected citizen of Skagway.

Graves pondered. He probed for weaknesses. He suspected that Brackett's

Achilles' heel was his load of debt, which he could alleviate only by selling his road. He suggested that Brackett should present a more realistic figure. Now it was Brackett's turn to ponder. Unless he played his cards right, the railway could possibly ignore him and his road, pay for the damage and its use during the construction of the railway, and then simply abandon him when the railway was completed to the summit. But, in addition to his road, he still had two important strengths. First, the railway's surveyed line interfered with or crossed his roadway at several points. This could cause the railway serious trouble in the future. Second, he and his associates held a franchise to operate a steam railway through Skagway, a franchise Graves was most anxious to obtain.

Graves was forced to admit that it would probably become necessary for the railway to cross and recross Brackett's road "in diverse places." He also accepted that, as construction proceeded, the construction crews would proba-bly continue to "cast rock, dirt and debris across the road," as well as make use of Brackett's property and "possessory rights and right-of-way." He conceded these points and expressed his interest in acquiring the right-of-way up Run-nalls Street from tidewater to the city's northern outskirts, which Skagway's council had granted to Brackett on January 17, 1898.[12] Graves also acknowledged that the presence of Brackett's road was an invaluable aid to construction of the railway and that he wanted the right to continue using it "for the passage of material, teams, and men employed on the construction of the railway."

Brackett then suggested that a solution to the problem might be found by Graves agreeing to advance him $50,000, a sum that could lead to the railway gaining immediate control, and later, complete ownership of the wagon road. For the $50,000, Brackett would agree to settle all of his current and future claims against the railway arising out of damage caused by blasting and allow the construction and operation of the railway to proceed "without let or hin-derance." He would also agree to forfeit all past and future toll payments for the use of the road by the railway's wagons, teams, men, and material. This would give the railway unhampered access to the road during construction to the summit. For a further $10,000, Brackett said he would be prepared to give Graves an option to purchase the road outright for an additional $50,000, provided the option was exercised before July 1, 1899.

Graves agreed on the spot, on condition that the additional $10,000 included an agreement by Brackett to transfer the Runnalls Street franchise to the railway. Not wishing to retard the progress of the talks, Brackett agreed. Graves then produced a Memo of Agreement, which incorporated all of the terms discussed during their lengthy negotiations. It was signed by both parties on June 24, 1898.

The following day, a formal agreement was signed giving effect to the previous day's memo. Brackett was to receive $60,000 cash, the remaining $50,000 to be paid if and when the railway exercised its option to purchase the road outright.

Brackett had done his best, but he was uneasy about the option agreement. The way things stood, Graves was now free to use the road without further charge, and damage it without penalty. The additional $10,000 included the transfer of the Runnalls Street franchise to the railway, so what more did Graves really need? Why would he want to exercise the option? In the final analysis, Brackett had given up virtually everything for $60,000. According to the most conservative estimates, the railway would reach the summit months before the expiration of the option, and when it did, the road would become a useless piece of property.

Brackett had reason to be concerned. All he could do now was to continue operating his road. But its use in the service of the railway would relentlessly contribute to its own demise. His only hope was to keep Graves and Hawkins worried and off balance by threatening them with a competitive transportation service through the pass that would involve hundreds of teams, wagons, and, later, sleighs, operating day and night throughout the remainder of the summer and the coming winter. Graves had now become his target and the $50,000 option his goal.

Eleven

———◆———

SHOOTOUT ON JUNEAU WHARF

FTER REACHING THE agreement with Brackett, Graves and Hawkins visited Skagway, arriving on July 2, 1898, Graves to inspect the work that had been accomplished and Hawkins to take up permanent residence as chief engineer and general manager of all White Pass Railway interests in Alaska and beyond. Within hours of their arrival, Graves was visited by Soapy Smith, who now had the town's criminal element firmly in his grip.

To the dismay of many citizens, Smith had recruited a company of men, many of them new arrivals, arming and drilling them as a contingent of volunteer soldiers for the Spanish-American War, emulating Teddy Roosevelt and his Roughriders. He then offered them to President McKinley as Jefferson Randolph Smith's contribution to the war effort. His offer was referred to Secretary of War Algar, who declined to accept the volunteers in such warmly worded praise for Smith's patriotism that Smith had the letter framed and hung on his bar wall.[1]

To further enhance his prestige, Smith had organized a civic parade to celebrate the Fourth of July, which he intended to lead as a parade marshal astride a fine grey horse. At their meeting, Smith invited Graves to accompany him on horseback at the head of the parade. Smith never missed an opportunity to enhance his status in the community, and riding in the parade with the president of the railway was an opportunity he did not want to miss. But Graves was well acquainted with Smith's reputation and he had no intention of being seen in his presence, no matter how important the event.[2]

Skagway was ready for a patriotic binge. It wanted to salute the flag and mark the first anniversary of a city that the *Daily Alaskan*, in a burst of patriotic fervour, called the "Wonder of a Century." Soaring to lofty editorial heights, the paper proclaimed:

> What City in all the wide dominion of Uncle Sam's possessions had
> better cause for celebration than has Skagway? Here we can glorify and

jollify with the full assurance that in no spot in the entire Union does the bright sun of prosperity beam more effulgently and with greater radiance than here in Skagway, the metropolis of the north-west, the marvel of the last decade of the nineteenth century.[3]

Hundreds of onlookers cheered as Smith cantered at the head of the parade, waving his broad-brimmed hat at the crowd. Behind him marched the local brass band playing patriotic tunes, and then came his company of uniformed Skagway volunteers, each one armed with a rifle. Following the band and Smith's private army marched hundreds of Skagway citizens in buggies, wagons, on horseback, and on foot, each one wearing a red, white, and blue rosette with a flowing ribbon that proclaimed in large letters, COURTESY OF JEFFERSON R. SMITH. This was Smith's supreme moment. On the Fourth of July, 1898, he realized his dream. He was the uncrowned King of Skagway.

For months Smith and his gang of thieves and bunco artists had been giving Skagway a bad name, although there were some who claimed that most of the stories about him were either overblown in the telling or outright lies. "About three-fourths of the stories about Soapy have been fiction," said the *Seattle Post-Intelligencer*, and H.A. Newton was quoted in a Denver newspaper as saying, "I wish to refute the slander that Soapy Smith is one of the leading citizens . . . up in Skagway. The people there are . . . very conservative. For that reason Jeff Smith don't cut any ice at all."[4]

He may not have "cut any ice" with Newton, but to city surveyor Frank Reid and a few like-minded citizens, Smith and his gang were driving Skagway to the wall. To make their point, Reid and his friends had organized a vigilante group in January 1898, that called itself the "Committee of One Hundred and One." Frank Reid had never concealed his deep-rooted animosity towards Smith, although the two were on speaking terms and occasionally met for a drink. But talking to Soapy did little good. Because there seemed little hope that Smith would change his ways, the Committee of One Hundred and One had decided to take action to stamp out crime in Skagway and issued a public notice stating the Committee's intentions:

WARNING

A word to the wise should be sufficient. All confidence sharks, bunco men, sure-thing men and all other objectionable characters are notified to leave Skagway and the White Pass. Failure to comply with this warning will be followed by prompt action!

(Signed)
Committee of One Hundred and One.

Smith bristled and retaliated at once with an announcement of his own:

ANNOUNCEMENT

The business interests of Skagway propose to put a stop to the lawless acts of many newcomers. We hereby summon all good citizens to a meeting at which these matters will be discussed. COME ONE, COME ALL! Immediate action will be taken for relief. Let this be a warning to those cheechawcos who are disgracing our city! The meeting will be held at Sylvester Hall at 8:30 p.m. sharp.

(Signed)
Jefferson R. Smith, Chairman.

Once again, Smith appeared to stand at the forefront of law and order. Not for the first time, he was out to confuse the issue by putting himself forward as the one man who could put a stop to Skagway crime.

At the meeting, Chairman Smith delivered a fiery address, using to advantage his silk-smooth voice and his power of persuasion. "Fellow citizens," he boomed, "we deplore the present conditions here," which, he claimed, "were due to the riffraff coming in from all parts of the world." He assured his listeners that Skagway's citizens would show the crooks "who is running this town." The hall was packed, mostly with his own followers, including one newspaper reporter and an editor. "We are here to form a real committee," he said, "not a half-baked committee such as the one we have been hearing about. We are the pioneers," he concluded. "We are the people who blazed the way!"

The packed hall heartily approved Smith's concerns and ratified the formation of the "Law and Order Committee of Three Hundred and Three," with Jefferson R. Smith as permanent chairman. The Law and Order Committee then distributed throughout Skagway and up the pass a proclamation written by Chairman Smith himself:

PUBLIC WARNING

The body of men calling themselves the Committee of One Hundred and One are hereby notified that any overt act committed by them will be met promptly by the law abiding citizens of Skagway and each member and their property will be held responsible for any unlawful act on their part. The Law and Order Committee of Three Hundred and Three will see that justice is dealt out to its fullest extent and no Blackmailers or Vigilantes will be tolerated.

(Signed)
Law and Order Committee of Three Hundred and Three.

The formation of the two opposing committees had polarized Skagway citizens into two camps – those who championed the causes of Frank Reid and those who supported Smith – while doing nothing at all to reduce the level of crime. Most of the townspeople, including the leaders of the business community, remained silent but watchful. Smith's Law and Order proclamation went unchallenged for the first six months of 1898, leaving the impression that Frank Reid's Committee of One Hundred and One was not prepared to escalate the confrontation.

Smith felt secure. The encounter had, in effect, increased his hold on the city. While criminals continued to strike fear in the hearts of Skagway's citizens, Smith's apparent determination to fight them, and control them, helped him sustain a degree of respectability and power enjoyed by no one else in town. His smooth tongue and his larcenous soul helped him gain influence over Skagway's legitimate community aspirations while he directed the activities of his gang of criminals and thugs. His ability to manipulate people remained intact. He was still the uncrowned King of Skagway.

UNMINDFUL OF past confrontations between the Committee of One Hundred and One and the Committee of Three Hundred and Three that threatened the peace in Skagway, Graves faced an uneasy mix of problems that threatened the railway. The demands of the Spanish-American War were robbing the railway of desperately needed ships to move supplies, equipment, and rolling stock from Seattle to Skagway. This could seriously delay construction unless alternate shipping space could be found. And there was the border question. The whole country between the sea and Log Cabin was still claimed by both Canada and the United States, the latter holding the trump card in the form of a company of soldiers stationed at Dyea. To keep its claim alive, Canada kept three members of the North-West Mounted Police in Skagway, but they were not permitted to exercise jurisdiction in any form or even wear their uniforms. Locally, there was no law under which a properly constituted United States municipal government could be legally organized. The only local authority was a United States deputy marshal, who was in league with the town's shady dealers – and in the pay of Smith.

Amid this grim catalogue of business and political miseries, there were two bright notes: Hislop's survey between Skagway and the summit was almost complete and railway construction was well under way. Graves was determined to see for himself the quality of the work and the general progress of the undertaking. London was constantly seeking assurance about the railway's progress, and he needed information to put the English shareholders' minds at rest. On horseback, and accompanied by Hawkins and Heney, Graves set out on July 6, 1898.

The three chiefs rode up Broadway, where the grade had been completed and a skeleton ballast laid. The street was alive with activity. Land near the bay was being cleared and foundation laid for the railway's permanent depot, a two-storey building that would house a waiting room, ticket office, baggage room, and offices on the second floor for the operating departments. Wagon loads of fir ties were being flung along the right-of-way, 2,816 ties to the mile. Lengths of fifty-six-pound rail, each thirty feet long, were manhandled to the ground from the double-teamed wagons, and behind them came more wagons loaded with spikes, bolts, and bundles of fishplates – all thrown to the ground in a measured cadence that was incomprehensible to the onlookers who lined the street. They had come to watch a spectacle that symbolized Skagway's growing importance as the gateway to the North. Some doubted that the railway would ever be finished. Others regarded it as evidence of American ingenuity and raw guts. Skagway is American, they said – young, enterprising, and progressive. "Not within the present decade has any spot in the United States been transformed from a howling wilderness to a city of 8,000 in so short a time," boasted the *Skagway News*. Skagway was populated by a band of believers who regarded their town as a metropolitan miracle. It was lusty and tough; it was virtuous and fun. And now the industrial might of the nineteenth century was bursting across its doorstep and was about to blast its way north through the mountain barrier beyond.

Graves and his two companions followed the roadbed to the north end of Broadway. There they inspected an eighteen-acre block of level land that had been set aside for the railway's service yards, storage buildings, coal chutes, and a water storage tank for the locomotives and fire protection. Hundreds of stakes with coloured ribbons set out the site of a large seven-stall roundhouse, two buildings for railway car shops, a two-storey section house, and the alignment of trackage, switches, sidings, and spurs for the rolling stock.[5] Graves was impressed, particularly with Heney's energy, authority, and knowledge. He admired the way Heney handled the men and looked after their interests. It had not taken Graves long to discern what Hawkins and Hislop already knew: the construction gangs were marching to Heney's beat.

As Graves and his two companions approached the Skagway River, the hollow pounding of a steam-driven pile driver guided them to the construction site of the railway's first major bridge – the 500-foot trestle that would carry the railway across the river.

They crossed over their recently purchased Skagway and Lake Bennett

Tramway Company bridge, which lay fifty feet south of the railway crossing, and followed the emerging roadbed for two miles up the west side of the valley until they reached the site of the second trestle, already under construction. Here, the railway would cross back to the east side of the river at the start of the detour that had been forced on Hawkins before Graves and Brackett completed their recent option-to-purchase agreement in Seattle. Although the railway effectively controlled Brackett's road, it was obliged to construct the two trestles and complete the costly and time-consuming detour because construction was too far advanced to abandon.

When completed, the second crossing would be a gently curving 1,166-foot-long trestle that would lead the railway past Boulder and around the East Fork of the Skagway River and on to the precipitous cliffs of Rocky Point, where Heney already had a work force in action.

At the head end of construction, *the front*, Graves watched Heney's gangs slashing out the right-of-way as they followed the line of surveyor's stakes and rocky outcroppings that had been marked for removal with daubs of red paint. Further on, hidden from Graves's view, the work gangs were approaching Rocky Point, where a formidable granite cliff barred the way. Camps had been established at intermediate points of construction, and a special work force was busy joining them together with ten miles of wagon roads and trails.[6]

Near the second crossing, work crews were putting the finishing touches on the largest construction camp in Alaska. It housed some 500 men and hundreds of horses and mules. In its centre stood a huge dining tent that could accommodate 360 men at one sitting. Graves, who had an agreeable disinterest in an expanding waistline, sat down for lunch with Hawkins, Heney, and the men. The bill of fare, as described by a Skagway reporter who was present, consisted of T-bone steak, "of better quality than most of us in Skagway are accustomed to, fried potatoes, onions, and excellent bread, good butter and better coffee, stewed fresh apples, jellies, coffee cake, queen olives, chow-chow, and cucumber pickles. The cooking is the best," he reported, "and their service is as good as any restaurant in Skagway."

Graves was generous with his praise of Heney's attention to detail and later reported that, "in spite of the hardships to which the men were exposed, Heney took such good care of them, and fed and housed them so well, that their health was remarkably good."[7] As the months passed, however, the death toll mounted, and by the time the last spike was driven, thirty-five men had died on the grade from injuries sustained on the job, or illness brought on by exposure or too strenuous work.

Many injuries and deaths happened because of the men's rank inexperience.

Hundreds of the labourers who had been hired in Seattle and Skagway were found to be ill-fitted for manual labour. Those who were experienced had never faced the appalling difficulties of construction through hard rock in a sub-arctic environment. Many labourers, including experienced railway workers hired in Seattle, had bolted for the gold-fields the day they landed in Skagway.

Hawkins and Heney soon realized that their free transportation policy was draining the railway's treasury, and they quickly moved to plug the hole. They ruled that, other than in exceptional circumstances, no more men would be transported to Skagway at the railway's expense. They would now only hire men who had already paid their own way north, but who found themselves temporarily detained in Skagway – many of them for want of money – or men who would sign a contract agreeing to pay their own way to Skagway.

"If we had not done this," explained Hawkins, "we would have found that every man whose way we paid would have worked for only a few days and then left for the interior."[8]

They also instituted a more rigid screening process to weed out those unfit for intense physical labour, and when necessary, they trained the uninitiated who were strong and willing.

Heney established a number of "skeleton labour battalions," each one composed of skilled journeymen who were reliable and loyal to him. Around these core battalions, the work force ebbed and flowed, expanded and contracted, never stable, always on the move. "As a rule," Graves later commented, "the Skagway men we hired were immensely superior to ordinary labourers in education and intelligence." Among them were gold-smitten lawyers, doctors, artists, college graduates, schoolmasters, and French chefs. Probably no other railway in the world was built by such highly educated men as worked on the first section of the railway between Skagway and Lake Bennett. Tough-minded Superintendent of Construction, Hugh Foy, was not impressed. "We've got three work forces around here," he grumbled, "one a-comin', one a-workin', and one a-goin'." The problem of finding qualified men and keeping them on the job plagued the railway from the start of construction to the day its officials drove the last spike.[9]

Despite the shortage of skilled workers, construction quickly moved ahead. Heney told Graves that he would soon have five miles of track ready, but operations would be held up for want of locomotives and rolling stock. This equipment was ready for shipment from Seattle but could not be handled by available barges because of the locomotive's weight. The only vessel capable of accommodating the first locomotive and tender, which together weighed 39.5

tons, was the barge *Skookum*, which had not yet returned to Seattle after delivering its cargo of cattle and rails.

Shipping had temporarily become a more serious problem than labour. The United States government had purchased or chartered almost every spare vessel on the Pacific Coast to support its war with Spain. This forced Hawkins and his staff to scramble for space on anything that would float. In co-operation with local shippers, they obtained a number of dismasted sailing vessels, none of which was seaworthy for an ocean voyage but was capable of being towed between Seattle and Skagway in the sheltered Inside Passage, well protected from the open sea.

Work was further impeded by the absence of any telegraphic communications between Seattle and the railway construction front. Orders for material and administrative and operational directives were conducted by mail or carried by special courier aboard ship.

Heney now had more than 200 tons of Giant black powder and dynamite on hand, and during his lunch with Graves and Hawkins a 725-pound dynamite charge was touched off with a thunderous crack. The blast, which had been set off more than a mile away from the camp, dumped hundreds of tons of rock across the right-of-way. Graves later watched men cleaning up the rubble with picks and shovels, wheelbarrows, stone-boats, and two-handled horse-drawn scrapers pulled by mules and horses. Giant chunks of rock that had not splintered were drilled and packed with black powder to be blown to bits later when the road bed was clear of men. All blasting was carried out on a strict schedule: the first charge was set off well before breakfast, the second blasting period was during lunch, the third during the evening meal, and the last charges of the day were touched off at the end of the second shift at midnight.

It was at the site of the blast that Graves met the photographer Harry C. Barley. At Graves's insistence, Barley had been hired before construction actually began. "We need a photographer to take pictures of the work," Graves observed, "to keep our London friends informed."

Graves's concern about keeping London in touch with the progress of construction was well founded. He had already told Hawkins that he would not be at all surprised if there were some doubts about the quality of the work being performed. "Such misgivings would be natural," he said, "in view of the fact that in England, American construction is generally supposed to be cheap and flimsy in its nature, and it is well-known that the men I have selected are all trained in the American School, although Heney and Hislop are Canadians by birth and education." Graves's instructions to Barley were therefore simple and to the point. He was to illustrate the nature of the pass, the difficulties the builders faced, and the high standard of the work. Graves was no neophyte when it came to influencing directors and the shareholders who paid the bills.[10]

Graves had every reason to be satisfied with the quality and overall progress of the work. Several construction camps were now in place and operating between Skagway and White Pass summit, each one responsible for specific construction tasks at key locations along the right-of-way. Communication trails had been established to provision the lower camps, while those higher in the pass were supplied by Brackett's wagon road as far as its northern terminus at White Pass City. From there, construction freight was transported over the trail to White Pass summit by pack trains. By these routes, hundreds of men and thousands of tons of railway construction equipment and supplies were delivered to the camps and work sites. All around the camps soared the cliffs and buttresses of rock that were being blasted and hacked into a railway roadbed by men using nothing but dynamite, kegs of black powder, picks and shovels, and horses.

Each morning the construction crews left their tents on the valley floor and climbed the cliffs to their work sites, returning to their camps for rest and a hot meal at the end of their ten-hour shift. It was hard and dangerous work for which each man cleared two dollars a day after he had paid one dollar for his daily board.[11] There were murmurs of dissatisfaction, but Graves did not hear them. Neither did Hawkins. But Heney was closer to the men, and he had already identified a few of the more vocal discontented workers who could cause trouble as the work progressed.

During July the work force had gradually grown to about 1,000 men. New workers arrived with each boat as the result of Heney's recruiting drives in Seattle, San Francisco, and major cities in the eastern United States. Among the early arrivals were experienced telephone and telegraph men, who were recruited to install a telephone system to connect the construction camps with headquarters in Skagway. Already they were erecting poles and stringing wire along the semi-completed segments of the grade. Later the telephone system was used to order more supplies, equipment, and men to the construction fronts, and more than one man's life was saved through the railway's ability to summon medical aid quickly.

Graves and his two lieutenants rode south on their return journey to Skagway, moving slowly past the labouring gangs strung out along the right-of-way. Graves was a keen observer and the sights and sounds of construction were becoming familiar to him now: the shouted instructions, the rumble of a hundred wheelbarrows on the move, and the incessant grinding of the scrapers as they were dragged by steaming horses through tangled masses of roots, gravel, underbrush, and mud. The ring of the blacksmith's anvil filtered through the trees, at times competing with the metronomic beat of the double-jack drilling crews, who were driving blast holes into the granite outcroppings with nothing but sledgehammers and case-hardened steel bits. Here, the partially completed roadbed was awash with water, mud, and rotting vegetation. There, piles of stumps and forest debris had been set alight, the smoke hanging in a thin blue haze above the railway grade. Around barrels of fresh water stood clumps of men drinking from tin dippers, their hands red and blistered and their necks gleaming with sweat. Amid all the turmoil the workers lived and laboured – at night sleeping under flannel-lined rubber blankets and during the day dressed in Yellow Badger string pants and jackets sold at bargain prices by the Pacific Contract Company's well-stocked commissary.

Graves was satisfied that Hawkins, Hislop, and Heney could meet and overcome any railway construction problem, and that he could confidently report to London there was no doubt about the successful completion of the railway to Lake Bennett and beyond. The only disturbing feature was the lack of manpower. The work force remained well below requirements, although recruiting drives had increased the number of men from 1,000 to some 1,200. "But we could use double that number during these warm summer days," Graves explained, "and perhaps they will come when the harvest is over down south."[12] But they never did.

AS GRAVES and his two companions rode down Broadway on their return to Skagway, they found the town in an uproar. A young miner named John D. Stewart had been robbed of a large leather poke containing about 170 troy ounces of gold worth $2,700, and members of Smith's gang of thugs were being blamed for the crime.

Stewart had only recently arrived in Skagway from Dawson via the White Pass trail. He planned to return to Seattle with his gold on the first available boat. In the meantime, he had placed his Klondike winnings in a local Skagway bank for safekeeping. Soon after making his deposit, he had been approached by two silver-tongued citizens who persuaded him to withdraw his gold and take it to Jeff Smith's Parlors for a first-class appraisal, thus assuring that he would not be cheated in Seattle or Skagway, should he decide to sell his gold before he left. It was at this point that he met a third member of Smith's gang known as "Reverend" Bowers, who represented himself as a gold buyer from a large assaying company, with offices in Seattle and other American cities.

Stewart felt grateful to his benefactors for their advice, withdrew his gold from the bank, and, guided by his new friends, entered the snug precinct of Jeff Smith's Parlors. While being shown one of Smith's famous attractions – a stuffed eagle that was displayed at the back of the saloon – Stewart was jostled by a few members of Smith's gang and, in a wink, someone grabbed his poke. As a diversion, members of the gang began to fight among themselves. Stewart started swinging, creating a short-lived barroom brawl that left him stretched out on the floor, beaten and bloody. During the fight, most of Smith's thugs had drifted away and the man who snatched the poke had disappeared through a secret exit at the rear of the saloon.

Realizing that he had been duped, Stewart sought the advice and help of Deputy Marshal S.S. Taylor – a friend of Smith ever since Taylor had arrived in Skagway to take up his duties the previous April. Taylor asked Stewart if he could identify the man who had taken his gold. Stewart admitted that he could not describe the person who had actually wrestled the gold from his grasp. In that case, said Taylor, nothing could be done.

Stewart did not agree. Determined to take whatever action he could to recover his gold, he told some of Skagway's businessmen about his loss and asked for their help. They quickly convened a meeting attended by many of the town's influential citizens. Feeling assured that Smith's gang was responsible for stealing Stewart's gold, these businessmen decided that the time had come to deal with this civic cancer once and for all. Representatives of the meeting called on Smith and informed him that Stewart's gold must be returned within twenty-four hours and that "you and your gang must shake the dust of Skagway from your feet." Smith appeared to promise that "if there is no roar in the papers," the gold would be returned. He further promised, in the presence of a newspaper reporter, that he would use his influence to prevent such criminal acts from occurring again.[13]

But the promise was not kept, nor was the gold returned. Stewart decided to take direct action. With the assistance of a few Skagway citizens, he travelled to Dyea on Thursday July 7, and told his story to United States Commissioner, Judge C.A. Sehlbrede. Sehlbrede had little regard for Smith and decided to accompany Stewart back to Skagway the following day to determine the extent of Smith's involvement in the crime.

On the morning of July 8, before Sehlbrede's arrival, Graves, Hawkins, Hislop, and Heney were breakfasting in the railway construction engineers' mess tent when in burst the railway's purchasing agent with four Winchester repeating rifles – one for each of them. "In time of peace prepare for war," the agent declared, "and there's two hundred cartridges for starters!" Graves did not like it. Packing a rifle around Skagway was not part of his idea of the railway president's job.

Shortly after breakfast, Graves and his three lieutenants received an urgent message requesting their attendance at "a select meeting of prominent citizens" who were concerned about the loss of Stewart's gold. The "prominent citizens" had reasoned that if a miner could not travel through Skagway without being robbed, Skagway's already shady reputation would be torn to shreds, resulting in a loss of business.

Seventeen men attended the meeting, euphemistically called the "merchants committee," but, in fact, a vigilante committee and nothing less. The spokesman for the group stated that the meeting had been hastily summoned because it was felt that nothing would be achieved by a mass meeting organized by a group of worried citizens that included members of Frank Reid's Committee of One Hundred and One. No specific action was taken beyond electing a chairman and adjourning the meeting to eleven o'clock that night, at which time they would review the events of the day and determine a course of action. "Being manifestly the least qualified for such a position," Graves later reported, "I was unanimously chosen as chairman, despite my protests."[14]

Graves decided to waste no time in protecting the railway's property and personnel in the event of trouble. He sent Hawkins and Heney up the White Pass, "to prepare our camps for the hard fighting that seemed inevitable, leaving Hislop and myself in Skagway to deal with the local situation and attend the late night meeting."

By noon the whole town was aroused. Groups of men armed with rifles and hand guns roamed the streets demanding the return of Stewart's gold. Soon Smith's armed company of Skagway Volunteers, known locally as "Soapy's Lambs," appeared and started to break up the crowd that had gathered on the street corners in front of Smith's Parlors. "It was just like the London police," observed Graves. "I almost expected to hear the familiar London bobbie's warning 'Move on now, move on please'."[15]

Skagway was approaching the boiling point when Sehlbrede arrived at Jeff Smith's Parlors on Holly Street early in the afternoon. He entered and demanded to see Smith. Supported by six armed members of the Committee of One Hundred and One, Sehlbrede told Smith bluntly that he was to return Stewart's gold by four o'clock that afternoon.

Smith searched every face. No one flinched.

Sehlbrede, a small-framed man with angular features and piercing eyes, returned the gaze. "I'm giving you a deadline Smith. Four o'clock this afternoon. No later."[16]

It was one o'clock. Sehlbrede turned and left, followed by his armed supporters. Smith turned to the bar and poured himself a shot of whisky. Flushed with anger, he gulped it down and poured himself another, and another. Suddenly, without warning, he flung his glass against the wall, grabbed his Winchester rifle, and barged out onto the street. He was enraged by Sehlbrede's audacity. Smith's authority had been put to the test by a funny little man with mutton-chop whiskers who had flung an ultimatum in his face – and he had done it in front of the members of the citizens' committee. Smith's pride had been shattered, his position as town leader threatened. For the first time since arriving in Skagway he was in danger. He could read the signs as he walked along the street. Conversation among groups of men who crowded the wooden sidewalks ceased when he approached. They watched him roam from bar to bar, his face flushed, his steps unsure. Gone was his customary air of quiet assurance, his cosmopolitan manner, and with it went his confidence and his sense of command. The town was slipping from his grip.

During the course of one afternoon Soapy Smith had gone from being a civic "leader" to nothing more than a befuddled drunk filled with bar-room bravado. He cursed those who stood in his way as he stumbled along the boardwalk, and once, thinking that he had been pushed, he fired his rifle into the air. Hostility had replaced caution, and his anger, fuelled by resentment and whisky, was stripping away his carefully built illusion of leadership.

Work in the town had come to a standstill. Graves and Hislop maintained communications with Hawkins and Heney via the railway's telephone, advising them to keep a close watch for members of Smith's gang who were already escaping up the pass in an effort to avoid the showdown that was quickly coming to a climax. Many of the town's gun-toting citizens had formed themselves into a militia. The four o'clock deadline set by Sehlbrede came and went. Smith's defiance continued, and when he was told by a newspaper reporter that there would be grave trouble unless the gold was returned, Smith bellowed, "By God, trouble is what I'm looking for!"

Public indignation was rising to a fever pitch, and to give vent to their feelings some citizens called a mass meeting at Sperry's Warehouse. Smith learned of the gathering, and he and one of his henchmen attempted to attend but were prevented by Frank Reid and Charles Singfelder, who guarded the doorway. Despite the efforts of the guards, however, the meeting was broken up by a number of Smith's followers, who forced their way in.

A second meeting was called, this one to be held in Sylvester Hall, but because the space was inadequate to accommodate the huge crowd that attended, the proceedings were moved to Juneau Wharf at the Skagway waterfront. There, the gathering was called to order by J.T. Hayne, who was to "devise ways and means for ridding the city of the lawless element with which it is infested." Thomas Whitten of the Golden North Hotel was elected chairman. He, in turn, appointed a committee of four to guard the approach to the wharf and turn back any objectionable characters bent on disturbing the deliberations of the meeting. The four guards selected were J. Murphy, J.M. Tanner, a man named Landers, and Frank H. Reid.[17]

Newspaper reporter Billy Saportas took a quick look at the crowd gathered on Juneau Wharf and hurried to Jeff Smith's Parlors to tell Smith of the mood of the crowd and the purpose of the meeting.

Smith, drunk and defiant, tossed off the remains of his drink, and, grabbing his Winchester, he headed for the wharf. Several of his henchmen followed, but Smith ordered them back, declaring that he would handle this alone.

Graves and Superintendent Whiting, who were inspecting the unloading of 1,500 tons of rails, timber, and ties, noticed the crowd assembled on the adjoining Juneau Wharf but paid little attention to it.

Suddenly, Whiting exclaimed "By the Lord, here comes Soapy! Now look out."

"Nonsense," Graves replied as they moved closer to the entrance to Juneau Wharf, "he's only bluffing."

Smith resolutely marched on, his eyes fixed on Reid and Murphy, who were positioned about fifty yards along the wharf protecting the meeting that was in session some eighty yards further on. Smith, armed with two revolvers, a belt of cartridges, and his Winchester rifle, passed so close to Graves that he could have reached out and touched him. Graves stood laughing at the ludicrous scene until he noticed that Smith was being followed at a discreet distance by fourteen gang members, who had disobeyed Smith's orders and had turned out to protect their chief. Graves watched Smith advance with measured steps towards the guards with his rifle nestled against his chest. Smith paused and shouted, "Now all you people chase yourselves home to bed."

No one moved.

Smith continued walking towards Reid and Murphy, his rifle at the ready. His judgement flawed by rage and whisky, he walked up to Reid and, with an oath, asked what he was doing there, at the same time striking out with his rifle barrel. Reid grabbed for Smith's rifle and pushed it towards the ground, drawing his own revolver at the same time. As the rifle descended Smith pulled the trigger. A shot rang out and a bullet passed through Reid's groin, emerging through the lower part of his right hip. At the same moment Reid fired three shots from his revolver in rapid succession, the first one misfiring, the second piercing Smith's heart, and the third entering his left leg above the knee. As Smith fell, he fired a second shot, striking Reid's right leg. Both men fell to the ground, Smith dead, Reid mortally wounded. The shots echoed across the valley and gradually faded away.

The onlookers were stunned. There was a moment's hesitation. And then a cry rang out, "Jeff's dead," as Smith's men sprang forward with a ferocious yell towards the three remaining guards and the assembled citizens, drawing their revolvers as they came. What Graves first regarded as an amusing piece of frontier humour had become a catastrophe.

The crowd that had stood paralysed during the shootout leapt forward with a blood-thirsty yell, stalling Smith's men in their tracks. They quickly turned tail and ran past Graves and Superintendent Whiting, who were forced to jump aside to avoid being trampled. After them ran the charging crowd in hot pursuit, leaping over the dead Smith and wounded Reid in their mad rush.[18]

Reid was quickly taken to Dr. Moore's office, where all of Skagway's leading medical men gathered to tender their services to the stricken man. After an initial examination of his wounds, they formed a medical council to act in a consultative capacity during the early stages of treatment. Although his wounds were serious, it was first thought that his chances of recovery were favourable. Smith's bullet had entered Reid's right side two inches above his groin, making its exit an inch to the right of his spine. Its passage had resulted in a compound fracture of the pelvic bone, several fragments of which were removed during the examination. The still-conscious Reid asked the doctors for a cigar, which he calmly smoked while they carefully removed the shattered fragments of his pelvis without the benefit of anaesthetic.

Smith's remains were taken to E.R. Peoples' Undertaking Parlor, where a post-mortem was conducted by Dr. J.C. Cornelius, who found that he "came to his death from the effect of gun shot wounds, one of which entered the left side passing through the heart and both lungs, lodging in the chest wall on the right side."[19]

As soon as the news of Smith's death reached the remaining members of his gang, they bolted in every direction, hoping to avoid capture. Before, they had boasted of their strength under the leadership of Smith; now that he was dead, they were frightened, desperate men scurrying in every direction, seeking ways to escape. One hundred special duty marshals, who had been hastily sworn in by Captain J.C. Turner, U.S. Army, chased after them. Turner had been appointed just hours earlier by Sehlbrede to replace Marshal Taylor, the gamblers' friend, who had fled Skagway and was hiding in the hills.

Seeing the members of Smith's gang fleeing towards the pass, Graves rushed to the railway's office tent and telephoned Heney at Camp 3 and Hawkins at Camp 5 and described what had happened. He warned them to "hold the peace and let no one go by without a written order signed by either Hislop or me." He also instructed them to keep their men ready to "help clear up the town if we call for assistance." Armed guards were posted on all wharves with orders to shoot on sight anyone who tried to escape by boat. Patrols north and south of the town cut off the gang by land and sea. Some tried to escape up the pass but were captured by Heney and Hawkins. The rest were ferreted out by an organized search of the town. Soon thirty-one of the more prominent members of Smith's gang had been rounded up and jailed. Several hangers-on were released with a warning to get out of town, and keep out!

The jail, which was nothing but a rough-board shanty, could barely accommodate all the prisoners. They were huddled together like sheep, Graves later reported, "while the infuriated mob clamoured for their blood." To ensure their safety, Graves detailed a number of railway men to guard the shanty and protect the now thoroughly terrified prisoners from the howling mob that wanted to lynch them.

By Wednesday July 13, five days after the shootout, the town began to quiet down. Before complete calm had returned, however, Graves took one of the prisoners, who had been demanding his rights, and threatened to turn him loose to the mob unless he signed a prepared document requesting the protection of the committee and granting the committee the right to keep the money that Graves had taken from him during his interrogation.

"I have rights!" shouted the prisoner. "I'm damned if I'll sign."

"Sign, or step outside," barked Graves. "We can't bother with you any longer."

One by one the prisoners were given the same option. Each of them signed Graves's document. Graves later admitted that his committee did not have "a shadow of law to warrant their imprisonment, and still less for taking the money found on them."

Some of the recovered money went to compensate Stewart for gold dust missing from his stolen poke, which had been found hidden among Smith's belongings, and the rest of it was set aside to pay for legal expenses and the cost of deporting some of the lesser members of Smith's gang of thugs.[20]

By July 14, six days after the shootout, fourteen of the more notorious members of the gang had been herded aboard the steamer *Athenian* in handcuffs to be transported to Sitka for trial. After indictment by a grand jury, five of them, Reverend Bowers, "Slim" Jim Foster, George Wilder, Old Man Tripp, and Ex-Marshal Taylor, were tried and received sentences that ranged from one to ten years in a federal prison. Others were transported to Seattle, where they were arrested for crimes they had committed within the United States before they had established their underworld outposts in Skagway and along the gold-rush trails.

Few Skagway citizens attended Smith's funeral, which was conducted by the Reverend John A. Sinclair. From Proverbs 13:15 he read, "Good understanding giveth favour, but the way of transgressors is hard." To which Smith might have added his favourite quip, "to quit." The Reverend Mr. Sinclair intoned:

> We lament that in the career of one who has lived among us there is so little that we can look back upon today as unmistakably good or heroic. Not knowing the heart we cannot judge . . . but he has paid the penalty of his mistaken and misguided judgement. He has been laid low in ignominious death by the hand of a fellow citizen in self defence, and in heroic protection of the lives of his fellow men. He was ushered into eternity in an instant, while in a mood in which the most daring and sceptical would prefer not to die. His remains lie there today cold and still in solitary death, no worthy mourner near his bier, no tears of sorrow shed by his fellow citizens. In an awful sense he lies unwept, unhonoured and unsung.[21]

Graves left Skagway on the same ship as Smith's shackled cohorts and observed them being turned over to the local authorities during a brief stop at Juneau.

By the time Graves arrived in Victoria, Frank Reid was dead. The *Skagway News* reported that he had "quietly and peacefully breathed his last at the Bishop Rowe Hospital at the hour of noon on Wednesday, July 20." Skagway was shocked, for Reid had become a martyr, a man who died for the citizens of Skagway. "His death," mourned the *News*, "has caused a mantle of sadness and pallor of gloom to spread over Skagway, such as has never been known in the history of the promising young city." He was buried with all the honours that Skagway could confer on their "brave soldier and hero," who during the Civil War "donned the blue and went into battle for his country." Every flag in the city was flown at half mast, every business was closed from noon until six in the evening, and almost every citizen of Skagway paid his respects.

"Skagway's first public funeral was the greatest popular demonstration that Alaska has ever known," reported the *News*. "What the burial of General Grant was to New York and the nation, the public funeral of Frank Reid was to the people of Skagway and Alaska." The service was held in the Union Church, but it could not begin to accommodate the number of people who came to pay their respects. The Reverend Mr. Sinclair was obliged to deliver his funeral oration from the church steps. During his sermon he said:

> Words cannot express our sense of new liberty and new hope bequeathed to us by brave Frank Reid. We mourn today the loss of a heroic fellow citizen ... who gave his life for us. Though in imminent danger ... after he was wounded, his customary profanity was not in the slightest modified. But gradually his interest in the ministers of the gospel increased. At last, purely of his own accord, he desired us to pray for him, not that his life should be spared, but that God would prepare him and take him home. Let me say in this connection: I ordinarily have little confidence in death-bed conversions ... but I have never seen ... one so striking ... as that of Mr. Reid's. We would have rewarded Reid with longer life, our praises, and fickle honours. But what are these compared to what Reid himself expressed with rapturous delight ... a life gone wrong, but gone right again – right for evermore.

After singing Reid's favourite hymn, "Nearer My God To Thee," the cortège, the largest ever seen in Skagway, moved to the cemetery. There, the Reverend Mister Wooden conducted the Episcopal funeral service. Then the veterans of the Grand Army of the Republic performed their funeral rites over the open grave, closing by firing a salute over "Frank Reid's eternal abode."[22]

Hawkins, Heney, and Hislop were there, along with other railway men who had left their work to attend Reid's funeral. The events of the past two weeks brought on by the shootout, the roundup of the gang, and finally Reid's death, had disrupted lives, businesses, and work throughout Skagway and Dyea and along the Chilkoot and White Pass trails. Now it was time to return to railway construction with a singleness of purpose. Skagway was now free of the social turmoil that had erupted the eventful night when Jefferson R. Smith and Frank H. Reid, in one moment of violent and irrational bravado, had slaughtered each other on Skagway's Juneau Wharf.

Now they had been buried within a few feet of each other. Smith's grave was marked with a plain wooden board. But for Frank H. Reid, the citizens would soon erect an imposing stone monument bearing the inscription: "HE GAVE HIS LIFE FOR THE HONOR OF SKAGWAY."[23]

Twelve

THE FIRST TRAIN

O N WEDNESDAY, JULY 20, 1898, the day that Frank Reid died, the railway's first locomotive was fired up, and without ceremony, it was sent puffing up Broadway towards the construction front hauling two flat cars loaded with timbers and railway iron. There were no cheers to be heard. A few businessmen and four young boys gathered around the chuffing locomotive to give her a sendoff, but Alaska's first train failed to draw a crowd or raise a single hat in salute. Perhaps many of Skagway's citizens had not been away long enough from urban life to be impressed by a rumbling locomotive venting black smoke, cinders, and steam. Possibly the town was simply too drained emotionally by the alarming events of the past week to take any notice of a mundane locomotive, even if it was a symbol of their town's future as a railway terminus and its growing international reputation as the gateway to the Klondike. A few horses fretted as the engine chuffed by, and its staccato whistle blasts set off a chorus of barks and wails from Skagway's roaming dogs, but as an historical event it laid an egg.[1]

In Seattle that day two additional locomotives were being loaded into the Pacific Clipper Line's barges *Ajax* and *Bjax*, while the tug *Iowa* stood by to take them in tow. Ten flat cars already had been winched aboard the barge *Skookum* with an additional cargo of fifty-six-pound rail, track iron, and bridge piling. The dismasted barque *Shirley* loaded with 600,000 board feet of lumber was on her way north, towed by the tug *Tacoma*. The barge *Colorado* was being hurriedly loaded with a cargo of lumber, rails, and machinery, all destined for the construction front.

In Nanaimo on Vancouver Island, a 400-ton cargo of high-grade locomotive steam coal was being hoisted aboard a converted sailing ship. A 180-ton cargo of blasting powder was on its way north from San Francisco. A miscellany of other cargo followed: tents, rubber-lined blankets, wet-weather gear, and meat out of Vancouver; boots, socks, hospital equipment, and medical supplies from

Victoria; office desks, chairs, and thousands of cases of tinned food from Seattle, Tacoma, and San Francisco; dynamite and fuses from Portland; flanged wheels, axles, grease, and brake shoes; toothpicks, Braid's coffee, and pickles; chewing tobacco, tin mugs, and Tetley tea – each item purchased, paid for, and shipped by the railway's base office in Seattle. The list seemed endless; the demands incessant.

At Skagway the construction materials were manhandled across one or another of the town's four wharves to supply dumps and warehouses or transported directly to the construction front, where they were used by the builders within days of their arrival. In only two months of active life the Pacific Contract Company had become a hard-muscled frontier enterprise with a voracious demand for labour, machinery, and supplies. Seven miles of roadbed had been graded to Rocky Point and more than five miles of rail had been laid.

"We are lost in wonder at the extremely rapid progress being made," reported the *Skagway News*. "In fact there is no case on the records of this country where such fast time has been made under such adverse circumstances."[2] But it was still not fast enough for Hawkins, Heney, and Hislop. Winter was coming, and unless more men could be found, the builders would be trapped in the pass in freezing sub-zero weather, battling rock-hard snowdrifts up to thirty feet deep. Hawkins and Heney were desperate. They called for an additional 1,500 workers to augment the 1,500 who were now on the payroll. The cry for men went out to labour recruiting offices in the principal cities of the United States and Canada, but while they pleaded for a flood only a trickle emerged. Already the construction timetable was slipping. There were now serious doubts whether the builders could reach the summit by September, or even by year's end, despite the optimistic progress reports that appeared in newspapers and trade journals throughout the United States and Canada.

Except for the packers, Skagway residents were now solidly behind the railway. Already the town was counting the benefits. The day the first train ran up Broadway, the railway paid out $50,000 in wages for labour performed during the month of June.[3] "The amount to be paid out next month for labour performed in July will be upwards of $100,000," wrote the *Skagway News*, "and a large part of this money is placed in immediate circulation." Skagway Postmaster Meem reported that his money-order business had grown substantially, a laudable increase he attributed to the White Pass railway's construction wages.

"Today, Skagway is the largest, best and most-prosperous city in Alaska," boasted the *Skagway News*. "Is it any wonder that people are coming to Skagway from Dyea, Juneau and Wrangell? They realize that as soon as the railroad is completed it will be the one and only route to and from the gold fields of the interior."

The gold-fields still were the central theme of northern life, the dream that fuelled all enterprise. On July 21, forty-five Klondikers arrived in Skagway carrying an estimated $375,000 in nuggets and fine gold. They had it stashed in hand satchels, rolled up in blankets, stuffed in canvas bags and old tin boxes. One man, a Frenchman named Gerrow, had a box so full of gold, it took two men to lift it. Skagway had every reason to feel confident about its future. Soapy Smith was dead, the gold was flowing, and business was brisk.

THE DAY FOLLOWING the first run of the work train, less than two months since the start of construction, the first passenger train, consisting of two flat cars fitted with rows of wooden benches, rumbled out of Skagway. Aboard, dressed in their finery, were many of Skagway's leading citizens and guests, who had been offered a complimentary ride to the construction front by Hawkins. Unlike the previous day's work train, the first passenger train attracted considerable attention as it steamed up Broadway with its load of dignitaries. It chugged past Camp 1 and crossed over the recently constructed railway trestle to the west side of the Skagway River. After a short run it passed Camp 2, a large base installation and supply point. At Mile 5 it steamed past the abandoned site of Camp 3, which had been moved two miles up the grade to Rocky Point at Mile 7. Reducing speed, the train slowly crossed back to the east side of the river via the gently curving 1,666-foot railway trestle that was now virtually complete. All along the right-of-way, crews were refining the grade, clearing the rock cuts, constructing retaining walls, aligning the track, and hauling materials to the construction front.

Good-natured shouting and hat-waving accompanied the train's progress as it slowly passed by the lines of workmen, who took advantage of the occasion to enjoy a moment's respite. The train rolled on past Boulder, where the railway grade started its long and arduous climb towards the summit. The excursion slowly approached the East Fork of the Skagway River, where a large work force still laboured to complete a bridge across the raging torrent. As the train inched across the incompleted bridge, the workmen clung to the outside timbers with one hand and waved their hats in greeting with the other, their recklessness causing the women in the party to shudder.

The train continued north, parallelling a succession of heavily wooded bluffs.

These were interspersed with granite abutments and craggy masses of rock, which had once formed a series of barriers across the railway's right-of-way but now lay broken by the shattering power of dynamite and black powder. Suddenly, with a blast of its whistle, the locomotive came to a halt facing the remains of a giant perpendicular cliff. They had reached Rocky Point and the end of steel.

After a tour of the work at Rocky Point, conducted by Heney, the train was carefully backed down the grade and across the East Fork bridge, where it was brought to a halt. The passengers alighted and were taken to Camp 3 for lunch and a visit with the hospital patients, but not before Dr. Whiting had provided the entire party with a stiff remedy to counter "the dryness of the atmosphere at these altitudes." The meal, which was to be the forerunner of many memorable celebrations on the railway, was reported to be hearty and wholesome, and graced with many luxuries including caviar and chutney. Their meal over, the first White Pass railway passengers departed for Skagway.

Far below, men, horses, and wagons were strung out along Brackett's road. To the south lay the blue waters of Skagway Bay and the snow-capped mountains that gave it its shape. To the north was Rocky Point, a sheer mountain bastion, seven miles north of Skagway. This immense perpendicular spur of granite swept down 800 feet to the valley floor, effectively blocking further progress. It offered no choices: either find a way around it or quit. It had always been recognized as a colossal barrier, even during the earliest surveys, but Hawkins, Hislop, and Heney were confident they could force their way around this formidable obstacle with dynamite, black powder, and brawn.

They first had to establish a construction line that would cross the face of the cliff 700 feet above the floor of the valley. Then they had to blast out a sixteen-foot-wide shelf to carry the roadbed and track around this massive obstruction. Several engineers who were heading for the Klondike openly ridiculed the builders' boast that they could cut a roadbed across the upper reaches of this seemingly impregnable mass of rock.[4]

Heney's initial task at Rocky Point was to prepare and detonate a series of blasts, which would clear an approach to the main obstacle, a huge buttress of rock 120 feet high, seventy feet wide, and twenty feet thick – a 20,000-ton granite plug that some said would stop the railway builders cold. Heney's plan was to honeycomb the obstruction with blast chambers, charge them with black powder, and blow the upper face off the cliff. This, he claimed, would provide him with a narrow ledge, a rough-hewn toehold from which he would mount his final attack, creating a railway roadbed notched in the side of the mountain spur.

Four hundred men were already based on Camp 3. Almost a third of them – rock men and powder men – were given the task of drilling blast holes and powder chambers deep into the granite layers of Rocky Point. The remaining 275 men were sent north of Rocky Point to blast their way along the mountainsides, following the surveyed line. Leap-frogging workers around major obstacles was part of Hawkins's construction strategy, a procedure thoroughly endorsed by Heney. Because of this method little time was lost. As soon as a breakthrough was achieved at a particularly difficult point on the line, the initial cuts and work trails beyond had already been completed, making a rough but immediate linkup possible.

To start the Rocky Point cut, the drillers and rock men were swung down the side of the cliff on ropes, a gymnastic practice that would characterize much of the rock work between Skagway and the summit. After chipping out narrow ledges on which to stand, they attacked the sheer cliff with drills and two-man and three-man jacks. Gradually they enlarged their footholds and began to develop the blasting plan designed by Hawkins and Heney. The explosive they selected was black powder because of its ability to heave rather than shatter the rock. Black powder, the slowest burning of all commercial explosives, provided a greater degree of control than did dynamite, and, at this stage, control was vital to safety as each blast would dump thousands of tons of rock and debris down the mountainside, much of it falling on Brackett's road. It was a dangerous business. Shaping the rock to the railway's profile not only imperilled the men who dangled like spiders on their lifelines, it also threatened the defenceless packers and gold-seekers who were struggling along the floor of the valley between Skagway and the summit.

For days on end, Heney's crews drilled and blasted the cliff, pulverizing the rock with a series of black-powder charges that Heney claimed rivalled the noise of Admiral Dewey's bombardment of Manila. The constant boom of the blasts, the smell of blasting powder, and the swirling clouds of dust irritated the eyes and ears and noses of the packers and gold seekers who toiled along the valley floor.[5] "Sometimes more than 100,000 tons of granite were dislodged by a single battery blast," Graves later reported to the company's English shareholders. One charge blasted off a huge slice of rock that fell with a deafening roar into the Skagway River, changing its course. The expense was enormous; powder and dynamite cost more than $600 per ton delivered from Seattle to the site. Rocky Point alone consumed more than 250 tons of explosives, and it was only the first of a string of obstacles that faced Hawkins and Heney and their inexperienced workers.

Construction costs were further increased when it was found that often there was insufficient space to use horses along the cuts. Even when the grade had been sufficiently widened to make the use of horses possible, they could rarely negotiate the gradient to reach work sites high up the precipitous cliffs. This meant that every cubic foot of rock blasted down in restricted construction areas had to be levered over the side of the cuts by manpower alone. Under normal circumstances, blasted rock would be hauled by teams to areas behind or ahead of the obstruction where fill material was required. But lack of space and horses made this routine practice impossible. This costly waste of heavy rock fill exasperated Hawkins. "After we have dumped all of this rock over the side by hand," he said, "we must later go out and find new material to replace the rock fill we have been forced to throw away." And because the railway south of the summit was a "veritable shelf in the mountains," fine gravel for track ballast had to be hauled hundreds of feet up the grade from the riverbed.[6]

Because the Rocky Point operation was so hazardous to life and limb, Dr. Whiting and his medical team had already established a first-aid hospital at Camp 3 for the injured. Far below on a windswept ridge, a number of earthen mounds already marked the graves of several gold-seekers who had died on the trail; soon new mounds would appear, covering the broken bodies of the railway construction men who died of injuries or illnesses while working on the White Pass grade.

One of the first accidents at Rocky Point was suffered by Barley, the company's photographer, who had already gained a reputation for bringing work to a full stop wherever he appeared. His huge box camera, tripod, and heavy case of glass negatives were a familiar sight along the grade, but his demand that all work "freeze" while he peered through his lens infuriated the foremen, who were responsible for keeping the job moving.

On this occasion Barley had arrived to photograph one of Heney's more spectacular Rocky Point detonations. "Put me close enough to the blast and I'll stuff the echo," he would boast, but this time he got too close. The charge went off and seconds later a huge boulder demolished his camera and a smaller rock struck him in the leg. When he was picked up conscious but speechless, he pointed in disgust to the remains of his camera and the crumpled legs of the tripod. He was rushed off to Dr. Whiting's field hospital where, unable to walk for a week, he spent his time developing and printing his pictures.

Barley was a terror to those who were sent to help him. Only three days earlier, he had come close to being seriously injured while trying to climb a precipice with his camera equipment. His assistant had turned back from the expedition in horror, stating that he wanted nothing more to do with Barley's incurable devotion to high cliffs and exploding rock – a decision that probably saved the assistant's life. Had he remained with Barley, he would have been standing beside him during the great Rocky Point blast. Fortunately, a volunteer replacement could not be found, so Barley had been forced to "shoot the blast and stuff the echo" alone.[7]

As occasionally happened, one particular charge during the Rocky Point operation failed to detonate. For reasons known only to himself, an inexperienced workman decided to poke an iron rod down the offending borehole, presumably to stir it into action. It obliged by suddenly going off, driving the rod up between the legs of the startled workman. Shaken but conscious, he rejoiced to find that, other than his dignity, he had survived the blast with his proudest possessions still intact.

Blasting accidents often tested Dr. Whiting's medical skills and ingenuity to the limit. Once, when needing help with an emergency operation, he sent for a doctor he had found working as a labourer on the grade. After assisting in the operation, the hastily recruited doctor was shunted back to the grade, where he took up his shovel and continued work.

More than 1,500 men were now working two ten-hour shifts, chipping, drilling, and shattering the rock, shaping it to the railway's needs, the raw power of explosives their primary tool. Rolls of Thermaline igniter cord, safety fuses, and crimping tools were scattered in the debris. Along the grade were piles of fibreboard boxes, each one containing two twenty-five pound bags of Giant or Judson blasting powder, a black free-flowing substance that had been glazed with graphite to prevent it from caking in wet weather. When it became damp, it was usually dried in warming kettles with reasonable safety. But some powdermen, through bravado or inexperience, simply dumped their damp powder into iron wheelbarrows set over an open fire. This dangerous practice became less popular after one wheelbarrow-load of damp powder exploded, killing two men, the force of the blast hurling their shattered bodies off the grade into the depths of the canyon.[8]

The casualties mounted. One man, a quarter of a mile from a blast, was struck in the head by a piece of flying rock. He was carried unconscious to Dr. Whiting, who removed several pieces of shattered bone. Deep in the cavity, Whiting observed something black. He carefully removed the foreign object only to find that it was a piece of the man's black felt hat. After two months the man recovered, the only evidence of his ordeal being an ugly scar. "The loss of a portion of his brain does not appear to have affected him in the least," said a fellow worker.

Blasting out the sixteen-foot mountain notch along the eastern wall of the White Pass was dangerous, challenging, and repetitive. Week after week the men drilled the boreholes, loaded them with powder or dynamite, and detonated. Down would come thousands of tons of granite, hurling rock and rubble across the trail and the wagon road at the bottom of the gulch. Then, through the dust and fury would come an army of construction workers scrambling down the cliffs and mountainsides to clear the trail and wagon road of debris, repair Brackett's damaged bridges, and restore the way to common use. Their task done, they would climb back to the grade to drill, load, and detonate once again.

By July 25, 1898, the directors of the Pacific and Arctic Railway and Navigation Company had officially adopted Hislop's railway survey of the White Pass. This catch-up of documentation would be repeated in many forms during the months ahead, for the builders worked at such a fast pace that, almost without exception, the preparation and filing of government papers, maps, and profiles lagged well behind Hawkins's and Heney's frantic construction schedules. Do it now and damn the papers was the order of the day. Time was short. In a week or two the nights would start drawing in, shortening the workday, and by late August the first chills of winter would be stabbing at the upper reaches of the pass.

Fifteen miles of the route had now been graded, but as winter approached, the builders had to concede that the railway might not reach the summit by September, and that they would be forced to suspend construction work when the full fury of winter struck the grade. Mr. H.D. Helmcken, the railway's Victoria legal adviser, said, after inspecting the railway's progress, "Weather conditions may be expected to terminate the work for the season by October 1." Hawkins kept his options open, avoiding a firm commitment regarding winter construction. "We have been told that it will be impossible to work the men from the middle of December to the middle of March," he told a Seattle reporter, "but the work will be pushed forward as long as the weather will permit."

Throughout June and July, Hawkins and Heney had been operating two ten-hour shifts in a vain attempt to beat the winter and reach the summit by the announced September deadline. Accompanied by construction superintendent Hugh Foy and Walter Sweet, who looked after the saddle horses, Heney ranged the grade from dawn to midnight. From time to time they would dismount and instruct Sweet to take the horses ahead a mile or so while they made a detailed inspection of the work. Both Heney and Foy were sticklers for discipline, particularly during blasting operations. "You weren't allowed to smoke when there was powder or dynamite around," Sweet recalled, "and if Heney caught you he would knock the pipe right out of your mouth."[9]

By late July, the railway's work force was strung out in labour gangs all along the route, "building the grade in patches," reported Helmcken, who observed that the railway right-of-way was "well-graded, well-ballasted, and well-made."[10]

But not without the cost of more lives. One day in August, two men were drilling blast holes in a 100-ton block of granite that hung out from the cliff like the sword of Damocles at Mile 10.2. Without warning, it began to slide, tumbling across the grade, smashing everything in its way. The two drillers died instantly, buried beneath the rock that came to rest in a gully below the right-of-way.

Work gangs cleared the rubble and shattered granite. The rock could not be moved without blasting it to pieces, but blasting would disturb the remains of the two drillers. They had no alternative but to leave them beneath the rock – undisturbed. Later, Heney had a black wooden cross erected at the site – a simple cross that became a memorial to all who died on the grade. The site is still known as "Black Cross Rock."[11]

ON JULY 28, 1898, disaster struck Skagway. A fire that had started in a trash heap swept through the town's northern district destroying twenty houses and cabins and several business establishments. Pells Brothers Packers' horse tent and cabin, together with the company's harnesses, blankets, supplies, and household effects went up in smoke. Seeing the smoke and flames, hundreds of citizens ran to the fire, which was spreading north towards the railway's explosive dump where 300 tons of dynamite and black powder were stored. The roar of the flames, the shouts of frantic men, the neighing of horses, the staccato crack of exploding small arms ammunition, and the possibility of the flames reaching the powder dump propelled the town into sudden action. Packers rushed to rescue Pells Brothers' horses and mules, which they led through the smoke to an island in the Skagway River. Others struggled to move tons of stored freight to places of safety, and all the while the sparks and cinders from the flaming buildings, tents, sacks of feed, and bales of hay were swept closer to the railway's explosives dump by a stiff offshore wind.

After a hurried meeting at the railway's Skagway office, Hislop telephoned the construction camps north of town and ordered them to shut down construction and immediately dispatch every available man to Skagway to help fight the fire. Construction supplies were unceremoniously tossed off the work train. Workers threw down their picks and shovels and piled onto the now empty flat cars. The train rocked down the track, picking up men as it went and blowing its whistle to let townspeople know that reinforcements were on their way. As the work train speeded south, a second train was assembled in Skagway ready to be dispatched to the construction sites to pick up men who had been working too far away to answer the first call.

Soon the railway had delivered 400 men to the scene of the fire. Two hundred of them were immediately dispatched to the explosives dump to tackle the clouds of wind-borne sparks with wet burlap bags and buckets of water. The remaining 200 formed bucket brigades to haul water from the Skagway River and to draw water from the town's recently completed waterworks.

As the hours passed, the situation became desperate. Sparks had kindled bush north of town, creating two separate fire storms that threatened to envelop the railway's dynamite and powder shacks. Many citizens had given up hope of saving the town. Captain Roberts of the coastal vessel *Farallon* reported that hundreds of citizens were panic-stricken, "rushing hither and thither, fighting the fire in an aimless sort of way." A messenger, who had boarded the *Farallon* just before she left for Seattle, was sure that the city of Skagway was doomed. As Captain Roberts sailed out of the harbour that evening, he recorded that the red glare from the burning houses, cabins, and barns could be seen for miles. The all-frame buildings were like tinder, the flames leaping from structure to structure.

The volunteer fire brigade, augmented by the contingent of men from the railway, fought on into the night. "Too much credit cannot be given to the railway men who acted decisively as soon as the dangerous nature of the fire was made known," wrote the editor of the *Skagway News*. Indeed, they earned their pay that day, many of them braving the fire to carry boxes of dynamite and kegs of powder away from the path of the fire. One man, William Shay, fought so vigorously that he was overcome by smoke and fell to the ground unconscious. "The boys took him up bodily and threw him into the river," reported the *Skagway News*, "where he soon revived."

Little could be done to save buildings already on fire. Many horses were incinerated in their own barns; others tethered in their stalls and surrounded by smouldering hay died of smoke inhalation. Although not in the flames, some buildings were so hot to the touch that they blistered the firefighters' hands. But many of the threatened structures were saved by the superhuman efforts of the bucket brigades. By night, the danger was over. The flames were under control, and the railway's explosives dump had been saved, although all who were present agreed that it had been touch and go whether Skagway would survive the day or be blown off the face of the earth.[12]

SIX DAYS AFTER the fire, Hawkins felt sufficiently confident to announce that the railway would be transporting freight and passengers from Skagway to White Pass summit by September 20, and that the trip would take no more than two hours. There was some justification for Hawkins's prediction. By the end of the first week in August, sixteen and a half miles of grade had been completed and eight miles of track were operational. While construction beyond the summit was still blocked, four survey parties were in the field examining possible routes that the railway might follow from the summit to the town of Closeleigh, the Yukon River transportation centre that would later become known as Whitehorse. Two other parties were examining possible routes from Closeleigh to Fort Selkirk. "We have two routes to Fort Selkirk under consideration," Hawkins announced, "and one of them will soon be chosen." Surprisingly, during late July and early August, there had also been an unexpected rise in the number of men employed on the grade, and by late August more than 2,000 men were registered on the railway's payroll.[13]

Then, only twelve days after the Skagway fire, disaster struck the railroad.

On August 9, Hislop and Heney were resting at Log Cabin after completing a broad reconnaissance of the interior country that had taken them along the shores of Lake Bennett and Windy Arm, covering eighty miles in thirty-five hours. They were awakened by a noisy influx of railway workers who had quit their jobs, many of them still carrying the railway's picks and shovels. Heney demanded to know where they were going with the railway's property and why they had left the grades and their jobs. The workers answered that they were going to Atlin, in northern British Columbia, where a rich new gold-field had recently been discovered. It was bigger than the Klondike, they had been told, and the quicker they could get there the better their chances of becoming wealthy, which was more than they could say for working on the railroad. They were the first to leave the grade, but hundreds more railway men had quit their jobs, they said, and were now heading for Log Cabin. From there they would make their way to Atlin – although none of the workers seemed at all sure of the exact location of the new Atlin strike.

Hislop and Heney were alarmed by the size of the exodus, and by the toll the departure of so many men would have on the railway's tight construction schedule. They left immediately for Bennett, where hundreds more of their workers had gathered – all of them talking of the riches waiting to be gleaned from the Atlin gold fields.

At Bennett, Hislop and Heney learned that on August 7, three miners had stopped at White Pass City where they had exhibited some fourteen pounds of nuggets and gold dust, which they claimed to have washed from Atlin Lake's gold-bearing creeks. News of the miners' gold flashed through the construction camps, spreading like wildfire all along the railway grade from Skagway to the summit. *"Gold!"* the workers shouted, and within hours the stampede was on. The old familiar restless insanity triggered by the shout of gold drove sleep from everyone's mind, and by the morning of August 8 more than 800 men were lined up at the railway's pay tents demanding their wages. Some, in their hurry, had already left for Atlin without bothering to collect their pay or even attempting to find out exactly where Atlin was. The railway workers were joined by hundreds of Klondike-bound gold-seekers who had quickly switched direction to follow the new stampede.

"It made no sense," newspaperman Cy Warman wrote, "but many scrambled to Atlin without a dollar or a doughnut." Others left without a proper outfit, expecting to acquire one along the way, only to be fleeced by the slickers at Bennett, who were ready to sell anything from bedrolls to boats at exhorbitant prices. On they went, pouring into the maw of the North. "Men working in a mining region are like a herd of steers feeding in a narrow field," Warman warned. "They are due to stampede at any moment." Unfortunately for the railway, Warman's assessment was all too true. Every time a travel-stained miner came through the construction camps, he would be eagerly questioned by the graders. If he painted a rosy picture of gold for the taking at some obscure creek deep in the interior, a half dozen, a score, or fifty men would be missing from the grade by the following morning.[14]

Hawkins was obliged to admit, "when a man believes that he can realize a fortune in a few days, it takes considerable cash in hand to hold him down to a steady job." It was a serious blow to the railway. There was no local labour pool available from which the work force could be rebuilt. The nip of fall weather would soon be upon them and the railway's labour ranks were severely depleted. Hawkins, who was in Seattle when the work force stampeded, arrived in Skagway depressed and deeply concerned. "I am sorry so many men have left," he lamented, "for their departure has crippled us keenly." The buoyant and energetic thrust of the project had evaporated overnight. Hawkins felt let down. "Not only did they leave by the hundreds, taking with them our picks and shovels," he said, "but they took anything else they could lay their hands on."[15]

A quick survey of the damage revealed that thousands of dollars worth of the railway's property had been stolen, and that the total work force had been reduced to less than 700 men. Most of those who did remain were green hands and unskilled, and this severely handicapped the company's capacity to complete the difficult rock work left abandoned by the frantic exodus to Atlin.

After the initial shock had passed, Hawkins and Heney intensified their campaign to replace and, if possible, increase the work force. But the task seemed hopeless. Of 250 new recruits, who had arrived in Skagway ten days after the Atlin stampede, only eight were induced to stay on the job. The rest followed the rush to Atlin.

Hawkins announced that it was the railway's intention to put 2,500 men to work, and that men had already been secured in San Francisco and in the eastern states. He emphasized that any newly hired man would not be used to replace those who had quit. The new men would be in addition to the force that existed before the rush to Atlin, he said. But he admitted that "if those who went to Atlin do not return, we will still be short and we will have to find more men to fill the gap."[16]

But the 2,500-man goal was never reached. Only a few hundred new workers joined the railway, and only a few who had left for Atlin eventually returned to the railway tired, broke, and disillusioned.

It was now becoming clear to Hawkins that there was little chance that the railway would reach the summit by September 20, as he had so recently announced. The rail-laying gangs were still trapped south of Rocky Point, although the rock work there was now virtually complete and the grade across its face was starting to take shape. With luck they would be in a position to complete the grade and lay steel around Rocky Point by the middle of August and link up with the mile of grade beyond, now in its final stages of construction.

As the work advanced, the cry for more men continued. But the problem seemed to defy solution. A hundred men would sign on and concurrently a hundred would collect their time and leave. Current recruiting campaigns were, however, meeting with some success. Twelve hundred or so were now labouring between Skagway and the summit, but this was still far short of the number Heney had stated they would need to punch the railway through to the Yukon River by the midsummer of 1900.

"I estimate it will require two thousand men, working double shifts, night and day, winter and summer, to complete the job in two years," he had said during the St. James Hotel meeting, but he had underestimated the country, the weather, and the availability of manpower in a far-off frontier land where men were distracted by the mood of the moment and the ever-present glitter of the gold-fields so close at hand. Now, with the full blast of sub-arctic blizzards less than three months away, the railway builders were forced to concede that hundreds of labouring jobs would never be filled and that their plan to continue construction throughout the winter months might not be realized.

Heney now had eight work camps in full operation between Skagway and the summit, each camp responsible for a specific construction project or a designated section of the grade. Camp 6 at the summit was still blocked at the provisional boundary by the North-West Mounted Police. Hawkins's reaction to this continuing rebuff had been swift and positive. He again wrote and telegraphed Graves to induce Ottawa to unplug the border blockade. At the same time, he ordered his summit construction force to reverse direction and reinforce a large contingent of labourers who were blasting their way south from White Pass summit towards Rocky Point.

Graves, recognizing the problems facing the railway, now publicly admitted for the first time that there might be a delay in reaching the summit by September. "It will not be possible to work during the winter on account of the shortness of the days and the severity of the weather in that northern latitude," he explained in a letter to *The Railway and Shipping World*.[17]

But Graves had not taken into full account the management abilities of Hawkins, his chief engineeer and general manager, or Michael J. Heney, the railway's labour contractor whose growing influence along the right-of-way had far outstripped his limited authority. Neither Hawkins nor Hislop could ignore the fact that their labour contractor was emerging as a commanding personality on the project, earning their respect as well as the respect of most of the men – but not all. Some of the labourers resented his unremitting drive, his capacity to work for hours on end without sleep, and his insistence on a full day's work for a full day's pay.

As a result of Heney's growing reputation, the word "Labour" was, by common usage and consent, unofficially dropped from his title and he became generally known as "Contractor" Heney, although he held no contract to build the railway. "He was employed," Hawkins later reported, "as general foreman or superintendent ... responsible for the employment of labourers and the superintending of same."[18] This responsibility would hardly elicit a mention on any other construction project. Yet, when Graves was describing the organization of the Pacific Contract Company to the shareholders in London, he took time to explain Heney's role as labour contractor in the company's managerial structure. Heney's status was changing, and from the midsummer of 1898 it was generally accepted that he had become part of the senior construction directing staff: Hawkins, Hislop, and Heney, the brilliant trio of railway builders who became known through the North as "The Three H's."[19]

Within a week of the Atlin stampede, the White Pass and Yukon Railway opened for limited business between Skagway and Rocky Point. A huge quantity of customers' freight moved by train to the end of steel near White Pass City, where it was transferred to pack trains for onward shipment across the summit to Bennett. Passengers, who were prepared to brave the elements and sit on wooden benches bolted to a railway flat car, were also carried to Rocky Point – for twenty-five cents per mile. Tappan Adney, who was writing for the *London Chronicle*, observed that the fare from Skagway to the summit at that rate would be five dollars, "making it probably the most expensive railroad travel in the world." The *Seattle Post-Intelligencer* reported that the receipts from business already transacted were highly satisfactory. "This is evidence that the investors in the railroad are taking time by the forelock to realize [a profit] as soon as possible on their investment."[20]

The White Pass and Yukon Railway was starting to roll. During late August, three more locomotives were shipped to Skagway from Seattle along with ten more flat cars and three passenger coaches – all ready for immediate service. Additional flat cars and boxcars under construction at Seattle were due to be shipped north in early September for final assembly in the railway's recently completed carpenter shop in Skagway. A large seven-stall locomotive roundhouse was now complete, and the ground was being prepared for other buildings to house the maintenance and repair of the railway's growing inventory of rolling stock.

As the end of September approached, seventeen miles of grade had been completed and twelve and a half miles of railway were in operation, but construction continued to fall behind schedule. There were still not enough men at work, although their ranks had been augmented by some 500 new recruits and a trickle of Atlin stampeders, who had returned to the railway disillusioned and broke.

Because of the Atlin debacle and unforeseen construction problems, costs were mounting beyond expectations and London was becoming alarmed. Some of the English investors were openly critical of the huge expenses generated by the high standards of construction Hawkins and Graves had adopted. Knowing nothing about the country or working conditions, these discontented shareholders urged that costs be held to a minimum by abandoning the railway and building instead a light tramway. They also suggested that Graves could further reduce costs by "not being too particular about gradients." This unsolicited advice infuriated Graves, and he informed his critics that he would continue to build a railway with the lowest possible gradients, "and a solid roadbed over which heavy engines can haul heavy loads up the hill in summer, and accommodate modern appliances for snow fighting in winter."[21]

While Graves did not accept the opinions of the aroused English investors, he could not deny that the mounting costs were a matter of concern. It was now known that some sections of the railway were costing as much as $120,000 per mile – an exorbitant sum for construction of a narrow-gauge railway. The least cost per mile to date was $10,000 for the three miles immediately north of Skagway. The overall expense figures could no longer conceal the fact that the average cost per mile from Skagway to Heney Station had reached $60,000.[22]

In defence of his position, and in support of Graves, Hawkins observed that, under the circumstances, unusual expenses were to be expected. "Our coal alone costs us eight times that which is consumed by most roads in the States," he said, "and the loss, damage and destruction of our goods handled by pack animals has added substantially to the expense of building the road." He cited the costs of provisioning and feeding the work force, and purchasing and delivering supplies to the camps strung out along the pass and the proposed Fort Selkirk extension.

"One of our major problems," Hawkins explained, "is that in some places we can devote only as little as 25 per cent of our time to constructing the railway. The remaining 75 per cent is spent clearing away the debris from the blasts scattered along Brackett's wagon road."[23] And keeping Brackett's wagon road open was vital to the railway, not only because it was needed as a supply trail, but because the railway's rivals were continuing with the construction of their aerial tramway up and over the Chilkoot Pass, an ingenious system designed to wrest control of transportation from Brackett and the Skagway packers, as well as the railway, and place it in the hands of the champions of Dyea and the Chilkoot Pass. Keeping Brackett's road clear and operational was the railway's immediate answer to the Chilkoot aerial tramway's growing challenge.

Another unusual cost to the railway was the construction of bridges, which could be built only after the canyons and crevasses had been reached by the track. These high and remote fissures, clefts, and rifts were utterly inaccessible to horses, which under normal circumstances would have hauled the material to the bridge sites long before they were reached by the grade.

The mounting construction costs were the immediate concern of Robert Brydone-Jack, a Canadian civil engineer who had been retained by the Railway Share and Trust Company Limited, a London firm that acted as trustee for the railway's shareholders. This company's responsibilities were to audit and oversee the expenditure of funds, to release funds to the Pacific Contract Company on receipt of construction expenditure vouchers submitted by Hawkins, and to ensure that the railway was being constructed in accordance with the terms of the contract. Brydone-Jack's job was to act as the trustee's on-site watchdog.

He had arrived in Skagway to take up his duties on August 25, 1898. Hawkins, who was by nature a proud and sensitive man, resented the idea of being watched by the trustee's consulting engineer and he made no attempt to conceal his indignation over Brydone-Jack's intrusion into the railway's affairs. Hislop and Heney, however, adopted a less combative attitude. They regarded Brydone-Jack's arrival as a welcome diversion that offered amusing opportunities to test his knowledge, stamina, and sense of humour. Graves was concerned over possible clashes between Brydone-Jack and his three tough-minded railway builders, who regarded the trustee's engineer as a useless and time-consuming appendage to their hard-driving construction team. "When Mr. Brydone-Jack presented his credentials," Graves later observed, "I hoped, rather than expected, relations to be cordial."[24]

Brydone-Jack immediately conducted a cursory examination of the work and its general progress. By early September he had sent his first dispatch to London informing the Trust Company that he had not yet had an opportunity to inspect the grade in detail or to speak to Hawkins, "but I intend to start over the line with him and obtain all possible information in accordance with your instruction." He observed that the wharf at Skagway was not being fully used, "owing, I believe, to trouble with the owner, Captain Moore." This was the first official indication of difficulties between the railway and Captain Moore, who with his son Bernard still represented Wilkinson's Syndicate in Skagway – the group that held the controlling interest in Moores' wharf and their contested Skagway lands.

Brydone-Jack's first meeting with Hawkins was amicable, although he expressed his concern over the high cost of rock removal. After completing his first full inspection, however, he reported that he was "surprised to find a remarkably well-surfaced and graded road, no expense having been spared to obtain a solid roadbed." He further stated that the amount of trestling and bridging was unusually small for mountain work of such a rough character, but "where they are required, a well-built trestle will be found." He was impressed with the quality of the bridge timbers and track ties used in the construction. The weight of the rails caught his eye and he reported that they were "unusually heavy for a road of three foot gauge weighing fifty-six pounds to the yard."[25]

The Railway Share and Trust Company had been judicious in its selection of

Brydone-Jack. He was a graduate of the Royal Military College at Kingston, Ontario, and although only thirty-six years old, he had already gained an enviable reputation as an efficient engineer on many public and government construction projects, ranging from the installation and management of civic waterworks to railway construction through British Columbia's Crow's Nest Pass.[26]

London could not have been encouraged by Brydone-Jack's reports. Cooling weather and a steadily declining work force were seriously impeding progress. Despite a continual search for workers, the Pacific Contract Company's payroll never exceeded 2,000 men throughout August. At the summit, the North-West Mounted Police still denied the railway the right to send its construction crews across the provisional boundary, although survey crews had been permitted to cross.

Signs of approaching winter were by now well established. The nights were drawing in, reducing activities on the grade to one ten-hour shift each day. Each morning the puddles were covered with thin layers of ice, which disappeared by noon, only to return again in the chill of the night. The trees were ablaze with colour, and fresh dustings of snow lay on the mountain peaks. The shadows lengthened, and the land grew cold.

Although the rate of construction was slowing, the railway's operations continued to expand. Freight tonnage and passengers were increasing daily between Skagway and the end of steel, where a railway station and freight-handling facilities had been erected. They named the new station "Heney," which was further evidence of Heney's growing reputation. Hugh Foy constructed a winch-powered tramway that transported freight in specially built, wheeled gondolas down a sharp 300-foot incline from Heney Station to White Pass City. From there, independent packers hauled the freight to the summit and beyond.

The Atlin gold-fields, once a curse that depleted the railway's work force, were now emerging as an additional northern destination point for men, material, and supplies. Already the railway was slashing a trail from Log Cabin to Atlin in an attempt to control the movement of freight to the new gold-fields. Superintendent, F.H. Whiting, claimed that Atlin would become one of the best gold districts in the entire Northwest. In a letter to the company's Victoria lawyer, H.D. Helmcken, Whiting stated that the area was largely unprospected and that the new bonanza would be the scene of huge gold developments in the coming spring. "And furthermore," he observed, "the gold from Atlin is of a higher character and worth more per grain than the gold from Dawson City."[27]

Thirteen

BLASTING THE GRADE

IN LATE SEPTEMBER 1898, the railway company finally received authority from Ottawa to enter northern British Columbia and build the railway to Lake Bennett and on to Fort Selkirk, the final destination.[1] Not everyone was happy. Many American officials and citizens still insisted that the boundary between Canada and Alaska should be established at Lake Bennett, and that Canada had no business authorizing the use of territory to which, in their opinion, it had no clear title. "It will be Canadian territory," cautioned the *Seattle Post-Intelligencer*, "when the settlement of the boundary question shall determine whether the arbitrary removal, by the Canadians, of the boundary line at Bennett to the summit was a legitimate action."[2]

Breaking ground in what was commonly referred to as "British Territory" was marked by an informal ceremony on October 4, 1898. The first sod was turned in a meadow five miles beyond the summit, where a grading camp had been established. The honours went to Captain F.L. Cartwright of the North-West Mounted Police, who commanded the Log Cabin detachment, and Judge C'Aime Dugas of Montreal, who was enroute to Dawson City to take up his duties as a judge of the Yukon district. Captain Cartwright cut the first sod and Judge Dugas drove a spike into a railway tie that had been placed on the surveyed grade.

Other guests invited to the hastily organized ceremony included Superintendent Teal of the Dyea-Klondike Transportation Company's aerial tramway; Mr. Peale, Canadian Customs officer at Log Cabin; Mr. Aime Longpré of Montreal; the Honourable C.G. Hartman of Toronto, an influential member of the legal profession who acted for the railway; Major Cooper of London, who was bound for Dawson to represent British business interests; and correspondents from Associated Press and the *Daily Alaskan*. Senior railway officials present included Hislop, Heney, and the engineers in charge of construction

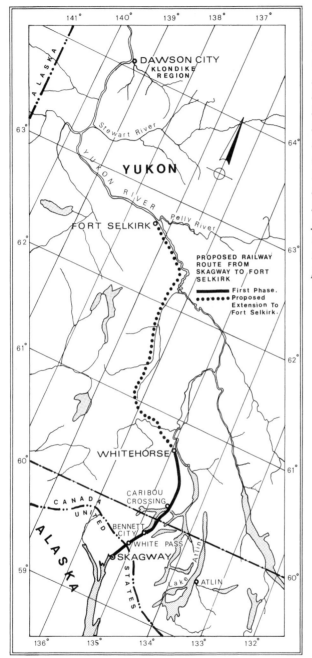

THE RAILWAY'S
ORIGINAL ROUTE
*At first, the railway
builders planned to
lay rails to Fort
Selkirk and believed
that they might one
day be extended to
Dawson. But,
eventually, White-
horse became the
final northern
terminus. Riverboats
took freight and
passengers to
Dawson.*

along the Summit-Fraser Lake section. The railway's photographer, H.C. Barley, came to record the historic occasion.

The guests had taken the early morning train from Skagway to the end of steel at Heney Station, where they were met by Hislop and Heney (Hawkins was in Chicago on business with Graves). They were escorted to Dr. Whiting's hospital tent near White Pass City, where they were offered a wide choice of spirits to help combat the chill of the morning and fortify themselves before tackling the ordeal of the trail. Warmed and refreshed, the party mounted saddle horses and rode up the trail from White Pass City to the summit, a distance of four miles, and then a short distance beyond to Summit Lake. There, boatmen in Peterborough canoes paddled them four and a half miles to the north end of the lake. After a further half-mile walk, they finally reached the grading camp and the site of the ceremony – at half-past four in the afternoon.

The surrounding mountains formed an inspiring backdrop to the simple but impressive ceremony that marked the start of grading operations in Canada. As soon as the ceremonial sod was turned, a gang of men moved forward with picks, shovels, scrapers, and teams to begin grading the land for the rails that were to come.

The guests, accompanied by the railway officials, repaired to a specially erected dining tent, where several bottles of Pommery and Four Crown Scotch were demolished. After a sumptuous meal, Judge Dugas rose to his feet and addressed the gathering, honouring Hislop, Heney, and the absent Hawkins during the course of his remarks. There followed several toasts, the first one offered by the Honourable C.G. Hartman to "Her Most Gracious Majesty the Queen." The dinner ended with the guests thanking the railway by singing "For They Are Jolly Good Fellows."

Judge Dugas and his party hastened on to Log Cabin by canoe down Fraser Lake while Hislop, Heney, and the rest of the guests started south on horseback, spending the night at White Pass City and returning to Skagway the following day.[3]

The day after the sod-turning ceremony, Summit and Fraser lakes were glazed with ice and the ground was frozen solid. Following the sudden drop in temperature, a short, violent storm covered the earth with five inches of snow. With it came the north wind, which gusted across the land biting the ears, noses, and fingers of the graders and blowing the fallen snow into ribbons of white crystals that swirled and snaked across the surface of the land to drift into the gullies and hollows along the right-of-way.

Winter had returned, and with its arrival many workers left. They headed down the pass to Skagway and took passage on any ship they could find that would take them to warmer southern ports.

"A number of men who have been working on the White Pass railway came down on the *Cottage City* unable to withstand the severe cold weather," reported the *Victoria Colonist*. "It takes a pretty hardy man to work in the open with the thermometer fifteen degrees below zero." Those who remained and those who would join them as the winter progressed were made of sterner stuff, for they would work in temperatures that would plunge to thirty and forty below and battle snowdrifts thirty feet deep.

BY THE END of October, construction between Skagway and the summit was above the timberline, where the graders and track-laying crews were exposed to the full fury of the winter winds. By mid-November it became so cold it was no longer possible to work in the exposed summit area.

The projected September date of completion to the summit had long since come and gone. In less than three months, the builders would enter the new year still far short of their goal. The grade was being shaped and refined, but three major obstacles remained between Heney Station and the summit before the rails could cross into British Columbia.

The first obstacle was the smooth face of Slippery Rock, a huge slab of granite that bellied out from the face of Tunnel Mountain three miles beyond Heney Station. Here the builders were confronted with a fifty- to sixty-degree slope that formed the southeastern corner of the mountain. They had started work on Slippery Rock during the warm summer weather of August by suspending men on ropes and lowering them to the grade site. "It was a strange sight," wrote a reporter for *Alaska Magazine*, "to see the workmen hanging from a stout life-line half way up the precipitous mountainside, where there was scarcely footing for an eagle." From there, Foreman Fisk and his men had started the tedious task of cutting a narrow foothold along the side of the huge granite bulge. Day and night the rock was alive with drillers and powder-men, who blasted and slashed their way across its face, creating an irregular gash that became known as Fisk's Cut. There was no room for horses. Every boulder or shattered granite slab was pried, levered, and jimmied off the cut to tumble down the mountainside, some pieces cartwheeling a thousand feet into the valley below. It was back-breaking work, which became more precarious as the winter frosts knifed into the workers' limbs, reducing their efficiency and lowering their morale. Every morning, the work gangs would leave their camp near White Pass City, climb to the grade, shovel off the snow, drill and blast the rock, hand pick and discharge the rubble, and return to their camps cold and exhausted in the late afternoon gloom that precedes the darkness of the northern winter night.

Beyond Slippery Rock, at Mile 15.7, the builders faced the second of the three obstacles – an enormous rock face that led to a deep 150-foot-wide chasm. On the far side, facing this rock-strewn abyss, was a sheer granite buttress resting on a mountain spur that fanned out into the valley more than 900 feet below. The builders' task was to drive a tunnel into the sheer eastern wall of the buttress and bridge the 150-foot void in a place where neither man nor beast could stand.

To reach the chasm, the builders cut their way along the nearly vertical sides of Tunnel Mountain, creating a rough grade fourteen feet wide at the base. The dangerous and difficult work was a repeat of that at Slippery Rock. The men dangled by ropes against the side of the mountain as they drilled their blast holes, set their charges, and levered the broken rock off the grade, leaving a clean white gash in the weathered granite and a littered fan of rubble below.

At the tunnel site, Heney and the construction engineers faced a chasm that could not be bridged until the grade had been completed and the rails laid from Heney Station and Slippery Rock. There was no way to deliver the heavy timbers, bridging materials, and hardware other than by the railway itself, a predicament common to almost all bridge sites between Skagway and the summit. And, as no connecting grade yet existed between Heney Station, Slippery Rock, and the tunnel site, every piece of equipment had to be carried up a series of narrow, tortuous trails from a base construction camp near White Pass City, more than a thousand feet below – a journey that took two to three hours at times. Shovels, jacks, sledges, drills, axes, ropes, and cables were backpacked up the steep rocky trail that was slick with mud when it rained and buried under ice and snow after the winter storms arrived.

By early November, nearly ten miles of trails and wagon roads had been constructed to service the Tunnel Mountain grading, bridging, and tunnelling operations. Powder, dynamite, detonators, and light lumber were delivered to the site by the packers, whose rates shocked Hawkins and confounded Graves. Up the mountain went tents, food, fuel, and water to support the small group of drillers precariously camped on a rocky plateau above the site. On a blasted-out toehold near the lip of the chasm, they set up a blacksmith's shop complete with forge, anvils, tools, bellows, and coal. Without blacksmiths, the drills could not be sharpened, nor repairs made to the machinery, including the four Ingersoll steam drills, which were used night and day for almost three months during construction of the 250-foot tunnel.

Once established on their narrow working ledge, the builders faced the ravine that separated them from the cliff through which the tunnel would be blasted. There, with the aid of ropes, suspended platforms, and ladders, the drillers and powdermen drove a preliminary adit directly into the cliff to gain space for themselves, their equipment, and the coal-fired boiler that drove the four Ingersoll steam drills.

How to drive a tunnel into a perpendicular rock face that had no foothold was one of Hawkins and Heney's most pressing concerns in terms of time and costs. "On account of the deep ravine on the east approach of the tunnel it was almost inaccessible, and only with the greatest difficulty and expense was the necessary machinery put in place to perform the work," Hawkins later reported to London.

While gangs worked their way north from Slippery Rock towards the tunnel site and enlarged the initial probe into the tunnel's eastern portal, a second contingent of two separate gangs worked in from the upper or summit side of the buttress. The first gang, made up of rock men and graders, was given orders to blast the grade to Mile 19 – three miles of rock work along a steep mountainside that Hawkins described as "utterly inaccessible, except when the men were suspended by ropes."[4] The second gang was ordered to start tunnelling towards the centre of the buttress where they would meet the rock men drilling their way in from the eastern portal.

Heney then constructed a rough wagon road running to the site from the construction base near White Pass City. This road enabled him to transport men, horses, scrapers, and stone-boats to aid in the removal of rubble from the western tunnel portal and grade – an advantage denied the gangs grading and tunnelling in from the east.

At Mile 19, the builders faced the third obstacle south of the summit: a rugged canyon, 1,200 feet wide at its mouth and too deep to be crossed by either an ordinary trestle or a standard railway timber span. To avoid months of delay waiting for the erection of a metal cantilever bridge, a decision was made to construct a switchback to convey the trains from one side of the canyon to the other. This involved laying a track along both the east and west sides of the canyon, which joined at the far end at a switch and runoff track. A turntable was built to turn the locomotives around so that they faced the right direction after negotiating this irksome detour that, when completed, looked like a huge pair of extended dividers.

Work on the switchback had started during late October, long before the grade reached the site. Once again, Heney had to rely on packers to deliver materials, tools, and supplies to this construction front.

There were now 1,200 men strung out along the surveyed route, 200 of them working in Canada and 1,000 in Alaska, working on either Slippery Rock, the tunnel, the switchback, or blasting out the intervening grades that would link them all together.

North of the tunnel site, the graders cut across Inspiration Point, a prominent moss-covered bench of granite that provided an unrivalled view of Skagway and Lynn Canal. Eight hundred feet below lay Dead Horse Gulch, its mounds of broken horseflesh now hidden beneath a mantle of pure white snow.

The dynamite and powder blasts cracked the air and rumbled through the valley, leaving gaping wounds in the granite cliffs and tons of rubble scattered down the mountainside. There was constant movement on the mountains – the slow plodding of cold and weary men and the exhausted, measured pace of horses and mules.

Heney was in his element. Daily he faced the awesome challenge of building the railway around the cliffs and defiles to the summit of White Pass and beyond. In this he performed brilliantly. But while Heney's stature grew as the work advanced, Hawkins never released his personal grip on the affairs of the Pacific Contract Company or the railway. Yet, at times, Hawkins was forced to remain in Seattle for weeks on end where, in consultation with Graves, he directed many of the railway's political, financial, and legal affairs. He organized freight sales and the appointment of the senior staff member who would solicit freight and passenger traffic for the completed section of the railway. As well, he had the tedious task of preparing maps and documents supporting a multitude of filings with the governments of Alaska, British Columbia, the State of Washington, Ottawa, and Washington, D.C. – most of them dealing with property for stations, terminals, and the railway's right-of-way.

Hawkins was inundated with work – often more than his indifferent health could stand. It is little wonder, therefore, that as soon as Heney had proved his worth as a competent railway builder, Hawkins leaned heavily on him. He recognized Heney's growing influence and accomplishments, and he had the grace to inform the English shareholders of Heney's extensive contribution to the construction of the railway.[5] There was no question of Heney's widening responsibilities and his ability to drive men, beasts, and machines to the limit of their endurance. He was now effectively in charge of the construction details of building a railway through the rugged and hostile terrain of the White Pass, creating what was described honestly, if ungrammatically, in the *American Review of Reviews* as "one of the most unique railroads on the planet."

HIGH ABOVE White Pass City the grinding clatter of the drills sounded night and day throughout November as the tunnel crews drove through the buttress from the east and west portals. After each blast, water coursed down from underground streams, quickly freezing into blackened icicles impregnated with rock chips, dust, and mud. Water on the tunnel floor froze, creating hazardous footing for the men working from the east and for the men and horses driving in from the west. At this stage, few men left the job. Many had only one thought in mind: build a stake and head for the Klondike or Atlin with the coming of spring. Meanwhile, they were in the North, close to the gold, enjoying reasonably comfortable quarters and meals, and making good wages. With overtime, some were clearing anywhere from $60 to $120 each month, with foremen earning between $250 and $500.[6]

Throughout November 1898, progress was slow and unsatisfactory. At times the darkness, snowstorms, and high winds shut down construction south of the summit. Some 1,400 men were now working along the grade, and most of them were doing nothing but shovelling snow off the roadbed. "This is a dead loss to us," Hawkins reported to Graves, "and does not show anything on the Construction Account, yet it is positively necessary." Committed to reach the summit "at the earliest possible date," Hawkins now knew that he had to beat the snow problem or fail.[7] Unless the completed section of track from Skagway could be kept clear, trains would be unable to transport customers' freight to Heney Station on a scheduled basis or deliver the construction equipment and supplies required at the front. Even after forcing work trains through the snow to the end of steel, the problem of packing construction materials up and along the frozen supply trails and over the scattered sections of fragmented grade still remained. To keep construction moving at the summit and beyond, it was now necessary to employ additional battalions of labourers to shovel snow off the surveyed line, which often lay buried under huge drifts.

During late November and early December, Heney had succeeded in laying steel beyond Slippery Rock and around the crags of Tunnel Mountain to the chasm obstructing the approach to the tunnel. Now the east portal had been opened, the gap could be bridged – provided the track between Skagway and the lip of the chasm could be kept clear of snow and the bridge materials delivered. But keeping the track open was often beyond the capacity of either men or machines. Construction was still suspended at the summit because of weather, but during lulls in the storms, train loads of bridge timbers, equipment, and machinery – including a steam winch – were hauled to the tunnel site over the railway, which was kept open by hundreds of shovellers, a double-flanged snowplough, and two powerful locomotives. But often, the plough and locomotives were so deep in snow that they could neither push ahead through the drifts nor pull back to safety. "This morning we had three engines and a snow plow at work on the railway and at last report they had not reached Glacier," Hawkins wrote when reporting how his locomotives, on occasion, simply disappeared for a time among the acres of snow that immobilized his railway for days on end.[8]

The workers laboured on along the weathered cliffs, many of them approaching their tasks with dread. Benumbed by the cold, they were relieved at intervals by fresh men, who, in turn, would be relieved after an hour's exposure to the weather. They worked with death at their elbows. One false step could mean a fatal plunge hundreds of feet down the mountainside.

At the tunnel construction site, the bridge builders were given no respite from the weather. Progress was slow. But until the tunnel gorge was bridged, neither track nor bridges could be constructed north of Tunnel Mountain. The railway was now more than three months behind schedule and there were few prospects for improvement before spring breakup.

Protected from the weather, the tunnel men drilled and blasted without interruption night and day, gradually reducing the interior rock plug that separated the east and west tunnel crews. Outside, the bridge men faced the full fury of the elements. Their job was to erect the east-portal access bridge, complete with rails, and have it ready by the time the tunnel was clear through the Tunnel Mountain abutment.

Many days the weather was so severe, the tunnel bridge crew accomplished little. Because of the winds and snow during one day in late December, they spent one eight-hour shift erecting a single timber, and on the day following they succeeded in raising only two more. The cold was intense, and the swirling snow blotted out the far side of the chasm. The loudest shouts could not be heard above the howling winds.

NORTH OF THE SUMMIT, amid the overhanging granite ridges along the shore of Summit Lake, the right-of-way lay concealed beneath massive snowdrifts, their edges honed razor sharp by the relentless pounding of the winds. Heney was forced by the storms to abandon all work along the shores of Summit and

Fraser lakes. The summit rock was buried under more than thirty feet of snow, and the grade leading to it had disappeared from sight.[9]

With the exception of drillers and rock men working in from both ends of the tunnel and the heavy-duty carpenters constructing the bridge to the tunnel's eastern portal, Heney had moved his men into British Columbia and set them to work between Log Cabin and Lake Bennett, where the snow was not as deep and his men less exposed to the piercing winds. Three hundred men were left south of the summit to keep the rail open between the dock at Skagway and the construction sites at the end of steel.

The construction teams were now working under the triple pressures of time, winter, and difficult terrain. That they were able to complete their demanding tasks under these appalling and at times terrifying conditions was a credit to the workers' determination, the skill of the construction foremen, and the outstanding quality of Heney's tough-minded leadership. The men worked hard because they needed the money. The railway was the only substantial payroll in the district, and each man knew that despite the general shortage of labour, non-performing workers were quickly identified and fired.[10]

Heney was constantly on the move, often accompanied by Hislop. Together they would snowshoe from camp to camp, project to project, encouraging, ordering, inspecting, often putting in sixteen-hour days, sometimes getting by on four hours' sleep or less in one of the camps high in the mountains or along the Canadian grade beyond the summit. Both Heney and Hislop were in magnificent physical condition, as Graves noted when he reported that "they performed like mountain goats on the trail." After many months together, each had accepted the other as his equal in speed and stamina.

Mr. Brooks, the Company's paymaster, tried valiantly to keep up with Hislop during their pay trips to the construction front. After returning from one particularly difficult trip, Brooks gasped, "Mr. Hislop can set a pace that will make a boss packer hustle in the first mile, struggle in the second and faint in the third." During that trip one old powderman was heard to remark, "I'll be blowed up, if that isn't Hislop in his seven-league boots. He passed here heading north this morning and he will have supper in Skagway tonight. But Brooks won't. He'll be lucky if he gets around next payday after making a pay trip with such a pacer."[11]

Heney's reputation was no less remarkable.

At times, Brydone-Jack accompanied Heney and Hislop on their expeditions into the mountains and along the grade. He prided himself in never having met a man who could stay with him on the trail. Brydone-Jack's engineering knowledge and personal tact had already earned him the respect of the railway's senior officials, even though he had been sent to report on the quality of their work and their control of costs. They trusted his professional credentials and his engaging personality did the rest. It was not long before Hislop and Heney invited him to share their tent, an invitation he quickly accepted. Their compatability worked to the advantage of the railway and everyone involved in its construction. "As the winter progressed," Graves later wrote, "the sympathy between the three men living and working and sharing dangers and hardships became deeper and deeper until they were more united than most brothers."[12]

THE RAILWAY'S freight business during the summer of 1898 had been reasonably good, although its ability to defeat its Chilkoot Pass aerial tramline competition before the onslaught of winter had remained in doubt. The railway was, with difficulty, now operating two scheduled freight and passenger trains a day between Skagway and Heney Station, but it was clear that its rails would not reach White Pass summit until December or January, a good three months later than its initial target date. To counter any public doubts about the railway's future, Hawkins had publicly claimed on his return to Skagway from Seattle on October 10 that the summer of 1899 would see the start of a great northern tourist industry that would attract people from all over the world. "In time," he prophesied, "summer tourists will be as familiar with the scenic grandeur along the White Pass railway as they are with the fame of the Matterhorn and the vaunted beauty of the Alps." He announced that the railway had appointed a passenger agent who "is already on the road arranging excursions for the coming summer season."

He did admit, however, that the lack of sufficient manpower continued to be one of the railway's most pressing problems. "It is my desire to have at least 2,500 men at work all this winter, but it has been impossible to secure any such number." Certainly, he could have had the men he needed if Chinese labour had been recruited from the Oriental labour pools in the United States and Canada. But times had changed since the completion of the transcontinental railway systems – where they had been employed in great numbers – and they were no longer welcome on the great construction projects. The Occidental workers regarded them as the "Yellow Peril" that threatened the stability of the work force and the home.

Heney had employed Chinese labour on some of his early railway contracts, and some men on his present work force did not let him forget it. "Heney, the Chinese herder," they scrawled on the railway depot walls. "Heney will have a pig tail by the time he gets to Bennett," and other uncomplimentary remarks about his off-duty behaviour were heard from time to time. By the end of the nineteenth century, the Chinese in North America were virtual outcasts. They were later branded by a Canadian government Royal Commission on Chinese and Japanese immigrants as "unfit for full citizenship ... obnoxious to a free community and dangerous to the state." Faced with this hostility to the Chinese, Heney and Hawkins were forced to accept society's attitude and ban their employment on the grade.

To solve the work force problem, Hawkins had engaged labour agencies from San Francisco to St. Paul to seek qualified men and induce them to work on the construction of the White Pass railway – but without success. "The fact is the men are suspicious of this northern work," Hawkins said. "They seem to think that it is too much like a winter expedition to the north pole."[13]

"How many men have you at work on the line now?" Hawkins was asked by the *Skagway News*.

"There are about 1,100."

"Will the decreased force of workmen make it impossible to complete the line to Log Cabin in February, 1899, as contemplated?"

"No, not necessarily. After we have the line completed to the summit it will be easy work from that point to Log Cabin. From the summit north there is no heavy work, and we can push tracks along very rapidly."[14]

Hawkins's remarks were optimistic, but others did not share his confidence. Helmcken had already told the Victoria newspapers that weather conditions would probably terminate construction work by November 1. As early as August, Graves had informed *The Railway and Shipping World* by letter that it would probably not be possible to work during the winter because of the shortness of the days and the severity of the weather in the northern latitudes. These contradictory statements stemmed from the builders' inability to assess the difficulty of winter construction and the results of their incessant search for workers. No one knew for sure whether construction could continue through the winter months or not. Hawkins only added to the confusion with his optimistic announcement that the railway could possibly reach Log Cabin – some eight miles beyond the summit – by February 1899. This prediction was probably nothing but wishful thinking – a rare lapse into fantasy for the railway's normally fastidious general manager and chief engineer.

These were tough months for Hawkins. The railway's freight business was increasing week by week, but Brackett's wagon road remained a formidable competitor. Hawkins needed income from freight to help pay for the railway's enormous construction costs, and until he could deliver freight to the summit without having to transfer it to pack trains at White Pass City, his railway would always be at a disadvantage. To make matters worse, Dyea's unrelenting campaign against Skagway showed no signs of abating. The Chilkoot aerial tramway companies, supported by Dyea's businessmen, were doing everything in their power to convince West Coast suppliers and shippers that the Chilkoot Pass's aerial tramway system was the safest, fastest, and least-expensive way of moving goods from tidewater to the interior. Their aggressive advertising campaigns throughout the summer and autumn of 1898 had attracted more freight business than the tramway could properly handle. Under these circumstances, Hawkins's enthusiastic predictions about reaching Log Cabin by February 1899, were understandable – even if his optimism was, of necessity, somewhat forced.

Echoing Hawkins's predictions, the *Seattle Post-Intelligencer* reported that the railway track would cross the summit "within the course of the next few weeks." It called attention to the railway's ongoing efforts to secure several thousand labourers to work on the road. "White men only, of course, are wanted," it said, reflecting the railway's early hiring policy, and the outrageous insensitivity of the times.

Fourteen

WINTER IN THE WHITE PASS

AWKINS, HISLOP, AND HENEY had agreed during late November that the extreme cold, heavy winds, and snow would force a slowdown in construction during the winter months. Brydone-Jack had reported this decision to London on November 17, stating that low production and high costs necessitated the cutback in the construction schedule. "This I think is the best course to pursue," he wrote, "as the completion of the work during the winter will exact very heavy expenditures which may be avoided by waiting for a more favourable season."[1]

London was extremely concerned about the immense flow of cash to the railway and was starting to resist the constant calls for capital. The directors were now urging Graves to finance more of the construction out of freight earnings and to reduce capital and operating expenditures to a minimum. While the London directors did not appreciate the railway's construction problems, their position was understandable. Income from freight had not reached the level expected. Further, by mid-November the railway had spent nearly $1,200,000 on construction, and all it had to show for it was thirteen miles of operational track and a discontinuous grade between Skagway and the summit that was still solidly blocked in key places by overhanging cliffs and precipitous canyons.

The day that Brydone-Jack reported the winter cutbacks to London, the railway's Skagway offices caught fire and burned to the ground. All of the company's files, engineering field notes, and drawings were destroyed, along with $2,800 in cash. The railway's files on the Canadian government's obstructive actions at White Pass summit during the previous June and July went up in smoke – a loss that seriously hampered Graves's plans to sue the government for the extra construction costs incurred because of its delaying tactics.[2]

In response to Hislop's desperate calls, the railway's purchasing department in Seattle quickly shipped office equipment to Skagway. Within a matter of days a temporary building was erected, and the engineering and administrative staffs started the long and involved task of replacing files, engineering notes, and drawings, reproducing some of them from copies in the railway's Seattle office.

In an effort to bolster the dwindling work force, Hawkins reduced the working hours each day from ten or more to nine and raised the wages from thirty cents to thirty-five cents an hour. As a result, the number of workers on the payroll actually increased, an achievement Hawkins credited to the higher wages and the workers' disinclination to travel the gold trails to Dawson City or Atlin during the winter months. Many workers conceded that the Pacific Contract Company offered a man high wages, a reasonably steady job, and good food and accommodation – although not everyone approved of living conditions in Heney's construction camps.

"After reaching the top of a zig-zag path," wrote Clarence D. Baker, a newly recruited labourer, "we saw before us the summit camp with a dozen or more large tents which are pitched on the ground – no floors – with one camp stove in each end . . . so we haven't all the 'modern conveniences' we were led to expect." He said that every steamer arriving in Skagway was loaded with men, "and if they knew what they were doing they would wait . . . till after winter for it's a mighty cold place just now."[3]

He was right. But during the latter part of November, the number of men in the work force suddenly increased. The town's four operating wharves were covered with hundreds of tons of construction equipment and supplies, with more arriving on each ship. Mounds of goods and merchandise filled the freight handlers' warehouses – all of it destined for businesses in Skagway, Bennett, Whitehorse, Dawson City, and Atlin. And there was machinery and equipment for the industrial and riverboat ventures that were springing up along the interior waterways.

Each day during November and December, the tempo of Skagway's water-front activities increased, and an endless stream of gold-seekers struggled up the White Pass trail to the summit, each man or woman freighting in a year's supply of food and equipment. Many of them paused only briefly at Lake Bennett before setting out over the frozen lake and down the ice-bound Yukon River to the Klondike more than 500 frozen miles to the north.

Hawkins and his senior construction team, which now included Brydone-Jack, were faced with more freight tonnage than they could handle – just at the time when they had, as a matter of policy, reduced the construction schedule to a bare minimum. There was only one thing to do: reverse the decision to slow the work during the winter months. This they did without delay, leaving Brydone-Jack with the task of informing London that there had been a sudden and dramatic change in the railway's construction schedule.

"The demands for freight are so high" he wrote on December 3, "that the railway has been forced to reverse its 17 November decision to retard construction due to the extreme cold. . . . It is more desirable that the work of the track laying to the summit be kept up and not left waiting for a more favourable season, as the extra cost will be more than balanced by the amount earned by the additional freight."[4]

BRACKETT WAS ALSO benefiting from the upsurge in freight shipments through the White Pass during late November, but he was realistic enough to know that there was no long-range future for his wagon road. He had reluctantly accepted the railway's ultimate supremacy and knew that, in a few months at best, his road would be forced out of business by the relative efficiency and power of modern steam locomotives. He was still heavily in debt and short of operating capital. Unless he could force the railway to exercise its $50,000 option to purchase his road outright, as set out in his Agreement with Graves, he would not only lose the cash from the sale, but the value of his road would diminish month by month until it was worthless. If he was to avoid bankruptcy, now was the time to strike. Brackett left Skagway for Seattle and a meeting with Graves, who had recently arrived from Chicago, and Hawkins, who had just returned from the North.

As was his style, Brackett took the initiative. He announced that he was preparing to operate teams and sleds over the wagon road throughout the winter months, and claimed that he would provide a reliable transportation system that would compete in speed and costs with any combination of services and rates devised by the railway. He admitted that both he and the railway could handle the freight through their own facilities as far as White Pass City, but as he pointed out, the railway terminated at Heney Station, high on the cliffs above the floor of the valley, and every pound of the railway's freight had to be jostled down Foy's inclined tramway to White Pass City where it was transferred to pack trains for onward shipment. Pressing home his point, he insisted that his winter sleigh service to the summit would eliminate this need to transfer freight at White Pass City. "You will have to accept the fact that I can operate sleighs to the summit, and move freight as cheaply as you can on the railway."

Graves thought not, and said so.

Brackett retaliated by stating that he was completing plans that would continually force the railway to drop its rates. "You will always have to make new rates in order to meet mine," he said, "and it will be a difficult matter for you to make any money unless you are prepared to compromise."[5]

Under Brackett's aggressive management, the wagon road was a continuing threat to the railway. As well, there was always the possibility of the road falling into the hands of a third party if the railway did not act – an eventuality that could involve the railway in litigation. Further, if Brackett continued to capture a large share of the business, it made sense for the railway to purchase the road and operate it for its own benefit until the rails reached the summit and then, at an appropriate time, shut it down. Brackett's resolute stance had the desired effect.

After considering the matter that evening, Graves, Hawkins, and their lawyer met with Brackett the following morning and agreed to purchase the road. On Wednesday, November 9, 1898, they signed an Agreement which, subject to final payments, transferred ownership of all of the assets of the Brackett wagon road to the railway.

The Agreement stipulated that Brackett would receive five dollars per ton on all freight transported over the railway until $50,000 had been paid, the only exception being railway earnings derived from the transportation of lumber, machinery, steamboat materials, and corrugated iron. The purchase price would be paid in $1,000 increments drawn from a trust fund into which the five dollar-per-ton charge would be deposited.

It was agreed that Brackett would continue to manage and operate the wagon road, but under Hawkins' direction, and that the net earnings, after deducting maintenance and operating charges, would be credited to the purchase price of the road as if paid by the railway.[6] The Agreement was to take effect on December 1, 1898.

Brackett wrote to Sir William Van Horne in Montreal, "I have forced a compromise with the railroad company that will make the situation vastly different. . . . Today I closed a trade whereby they are to pay me $5.00 per ton on all freight except lumber that shall go over their road until such time as they have paid me $50,000, when I agreed to transfer to them the wagon road. I feel that I have made the best terms possible under the circumstances, and shall now be able to repay you quite an amount, if not all, of the money you so kindly advanced."[7]

WITH THE WAGON ROAD now under his control, Graves departed for London where, on December 5, 1898, he addressed the first general meeting of the White Pass and Yukon Railway, Limited's directors and shareholders.

It was a *statutory* meeting, which by law the company was obliged to hold within four months of its date of registration. Chairman Carr-Glynn, with tongue in cheek, observed during his opening remarks:

> This meeting is one of those curious inconsistencies which confounds the lay mind. Although we are obliged to hold it and, having done so, we might conclude that it would be our duty to transact business, we are not by law allowed to do so. We have therefore no business to bring before you, and no resolutions can be passed. I am bound to believe, therefore, that the only reason for holding these statutory meetings is so that we may be given the pleasure of introducing the shareholders to the directors and the directors to the shareholders.

Carr-Glynn then introduced Graves and asked him to provide the meeting with an account of "all that has been done and our prospects for the future."

Graves gave the gathering an informative and entertaining report on the railway's progress, starting with his arrival in New York in March 1898, to take charge of the project. He related in detail the main events up to November, when he acquired the Brackett road. He stressed his disappointment over the railway's failure to meet its publicly announced construction target dates, and he was forced to admit that after the Atlin stampede their labour recruitment campaigns had achieved only minimal success. As a result, the work force had hovered around a thousand men during the months of October and November, "and in spite of all our efforts since, we have been unable to increase it materially above the latter figure." As a result, he informed his audience, "we are only now approaching the summit, when we had hoped to have long since reached Lake Bennett."

Graves had been warned prior to the meeting that some directors and shareholders would be present who were openly critical of the huge sums of money being spent on the construction of the railway to a standard far higher than they thought necessary. When these dissidents had been invited to invest in the project, they had understood it to be a simple tramway to the top of a mountain pass that could be abandoned after it had made a profit and had served its purpose. Graves met this problem head on by stating:

> Had our object been to build the cheapest possible line we could have got to the summit at considerable less expense. But it would have been

false economy as the capacity of the line would have been greatly diminished, and the expense of operating and maintenance greatly increased. The cheapest way to reach the summit would have been by adopting very steep gradients. But such a line could not carry nearly so much traffic, the cost of carriage would be enormous while the strain on rolling stock and track ... would add considerably to maintenance charges and the risk of accidents.

Graves pressed home his arguments with telling effect. His manner and knowledge were convincing, his presentation impressive. He explained with illustrations that the railway's maximum gradient would be less than four feet in one hundred, and that no curve exceeded sixteen degrees.

These figures excite universal surprise and admiration among men familiar with American mountain railway work. We have preferred economy and safety of operation to economy of construction. By considerably increasing the cost of construction we have succeeded in making several large level sidings, and thus we have, in effect, cut our hill into a number of smaller hills separated by level places where trains can pass. Being able to pass at several places between Skagway and the summit means that a number of trains can operate at once, thereby greatly increasing the capacity of the line. One does not need be an expert to see the effect of this on the safety and economy of operation and the capacity of the line for heavy traffic.

The meeting broke into cheers. The doubters were silenced.

Graves then addressed the delay in reaching the summit, citing the Contract Company's inability to fill the ranks of the work force, the severe weather conditions that were much worse than expected, and the devastation that resulted from the Atlin stampede. These were the reasons, he explained, why the railway failed to reach the summit as planned. "Disappointing as all this may be for the moment," said Graves, sugar-coating the delays, "it is a small price to pay for the discovery of the Atlin Gold fields within a few miles of our line."

Graves turned to his senior lieutenants in the field, mentioning Hislop and Heney in the course of his remarks. But it was Hawkins on whom he dealt at length:

Of Mr. Hawkins, his work speaks for itself. He has not only great engineering skill and originality, but he is full of resource and resolution in meeting and overcoming difficulties. He is absolutely fearless and honest, can neither be intimidated nor bought, and puts his employers' interest above his own. In fact, his only fault is the recklessness with which he overworks himself. I have often told him that he would be ashamed to treat an employee or a horse in the way he habitually treats himself, and his only reply is "that's different." I suppose it is too late to reform him. But I can say that the great success which has attended our work is due to Mr. Hawkins more than any other man.

What lay ahead for the White Pass and Yukon Railway? What were the prospects for the Yukon country on which its future prosperity must depend? Graves answered these questions:

> A year or more ago, the extraordinary richness of . . . the Klondike drew the attention of the whole world. A rush to the Klondike ensued. Cab drivers, barbers, the unsuccessful in all walks of life, seemed to think that if they could only reach the Klondike they would shovel gold dust into sacks, and that their wealth would only be limited by the number of sacks they could procure.

Graves emphasized that only the very rich Klondike claims could be worked at the present time because of the Yukon district's high cost of living and the inflated price of labour. "Under these conditions," he said, "probably not five per cent of the proved gold-bearing ground can be worked at a profit." Graves predicted that as a consequence of railway communications with the outside world, it would be possible to work up to 75 per cent of the known Klondike claims.

Graves saw that the Yukon could become a spectacular northern mining area producing untold wealth, and so he took issue with the popular view that quartz mining would never be a part of the Yukon district's future. "No assumption would be more absurd," he stated. "Gold quartz has been found cropping out in innumerable localities. A man must be fitfully blind who refuses to see that within the next few years gold quartz will be mined . . . at many places in the Yukon."

Not all of Graves's predictions were realized, notably his prophecy about gold quartz, but there is no question that he had unbounded faith in the future of the Yukon district, and that he felt perfectly justified in sinking millions of dollars into the construction of a railway that would not only support his prophecies of northern growth and expansion but would earn for its investors a handsome profit in a relatively short time. He was a believer. He was a man who was bullish on the North and his enthusiasm never failed: "The White Pass and Yukon Railway is the key that is about to unlock the door to this rich country, and the key is now on the point of being turned in the lock."

The English shareholders were thoroughly convinced that the railway's progress was assured and that their investment was secure. Graves left for Europe where he indulged in a one-month gentleman's holiday in a luxurious Swiss resort.[8]

WHEN GRAVES addressed the annual general meeting in London, he had no idea that trouble was once again brewing in Skagway. On Wednesday, November 30, the main street of the town had been plastered with circulars declaring that the railway workers were preparing to go on strike. The contentious circulars were distributed by a heavy-set man with a sandy moustache, who appeared to be a railway construction worker. But no one could place him. He was a mystery; a stranger to those who watched him move from place to place tacking up his blue and white dodgers.

> NOTICE – To Whom It May Concern: All railroad and other working men who may be seeking employment, are hereby notified that a strike has been declared against the Pacific and Arctic Railway and Navigation Company. The cause of the strike is an order for reduction of wages of employees, and until the matter is settled satisfactorily to those concerned, new men are warned against accepting positions with the above corporation. (Signed,) The Committee.

The moustached stranger announced that the strike would start on Thursday, December 1, when 300 men from the construction camps would stop work.

The *Skagway News* was mystified. "Evidently the Committee was premature, as there was no strike and no symptoms of one," it reported on Friday, December 2.

When Heney was asked if there was a strike, he said, "Yes, nearly a thousand men are striking rails and spikes up the line, but that is all the strike I know of."

Referring to Hawkins's recent order reducing the hours of labour during the cold winter months, Heney added, "The facts are that the working day has been reduced from ten to nine hours daily and the wages have been raised from thirty to thirty-five cents per hour. A man can therefore make more by fifteen cents in nine hours, than they formerly made in ten."[9]

The furore was soon over. No strike occurred. In public, the matter was treated lightly by Heney. But in the construction camps, something was brewing. On December 13, fifty men came into Skagway from the camps. They claimed that they had quit work because they understood that their workday was to be reduced another hour, giving them only an eight-hour day. This did not suit them, they said, so they stopped work and came to town.[10]

This walkout failed to excite the remainder of the work force. No order had been issued reducing the workday a further hour. But something was wrong. Misinformation was being whispered along the grade by persons unknown, and the only evidence of their existence was dozens of posted dodgers lettered in blue and a stranger with a sandy moustache.

Hawkins hired a Pinkerton man to roam the grade and find the troublemakers. Work returned to normal. Talk of strikes and walkouts and hours of work, while secretly discussed, no longer circulated among the rank and file. The men faced the mountains and the broad uplands beyond, their noses and ears blanched a waxy white under the onslaught of the winter winds. The unceasing struggle to gain the summit continued – at some sites work proceeded day and night. The grade bosses watched for signs of trouble. So did Heney. And so did the small group of workers who called themselves "The Committee."

THROUGHOUT THE dark winter months of November and December 1898, snowstorms shrieked through the ragged cuts and canyons of the White Pass, sweeping down through the coastal forest and across Skagway's rooftops, finally dissipating their fury against the surrounding mountains.

Above the timberline snow swirled across the railway grade, filling the hollows and, at times, obliterating the mountain peaks and the work camps in the valley below. The sharp winds pierced the workers' parkas, froze their fingers, and forced them to seek shelter amid the boulders and broken rock that littered the unfinished grade. The ground was white and as solid as cement. More often than not, the summit was hidden in heavy clouds or wiped out of view by the wind-borne snows. Work along Fraser Lake was abandoned as it was found impossible to complete the most elementary tasks when the frigid temperatures were accompanied by howling winds and drifting snow. To keep the work moving, Heney established additional camps in sheltered areas near Lake Bennett and continued grading along the surveyed route, leaving the open areas to the spring of 1899.

Hawkins, Hislop, and Heney continued to recruit and mobilize their platoons of workers and send them into the mountains. Each morning the heavily clothed workers left the comfort and safety of their camps, their ears muffled and their legs wrapped in sacking, to trudge eight hundred, a thousand, twelve hundred feet up the mountain side to the grade – each man carrying a lunch package of sandwiches, for there was no time to return to camp for a hot meal. Those who were fortunate enough to be working close to a cookhouse could slide down the hillside on their shovels to gain extra eating time, rest, and a few precious minutes of warmth. On the grade, all too often the labour gangs could accomplish little or nothing at all. Before work could begin, they had to shovel snow off the grade, an operation that sometimes took the entire day. When they returned the following morning, they would often find that the winds had drifted the snow during the night, and they would be forced to shovel again.

On New Year's Day of 1899, Heney and Brydone-Jack left Skagway on the steamer *Rosalie* to visit Vancouver, Seattle, and Victoria. Heney went to purchase supplies and Brydone-Jack went to attend the opening of the railway company's freight and passenger office on Trounce Avenue, Victoria, and to assess the value of future business for the English shareholders.

During a newspaper interview in Victoria, Heney confessed that his major problem was a shortage of manpower. "Nowhere in the world are men earning as high a wage for the same class of labour than we are paying," Heney said. "Last summer when the days were longest an ordinary labourer cleared as much as $120 a month." When asked why men were not responding to his invitation to high wages and adventure, Heney said that "there have been so many fake propositions floated on the world with the name Alaska associated with them that I do not wonder at the indifference shown."

Heney confirmed that Fort Selkirk was still the railway's initial destination and added, "I would not be far astray in saying, however, that a thousand miles of road will be built and no less than $4,000,000 will be spent in the purchase of supplies during the next three to four years." Both Heney and Brydone-Jack expressed the opinion that Vancouver and Victoria could provide all of these supplies, but that neither of the cities had taken a positive interest in catering to the needs of the railway. "We are both Canadians," said Heney, "but we cannot let our patriotism stand in the way of business."[11]

On the construction front occasional lulls in the storms permitted a general acceleration of the work along active sections of the grade. Preliminary construction work on the switchback's two main bridges at Mile 19 were well under way, using materials that had been hauled to the site by horse and sleigh over a rough-access snow road. The bridge's main timbers, however, would have to await the arrival of the track, which, in turn, could not advance until the grade between the switchback and the tunnel had been completed and the tunnel itself had been finished.

January 15 dawned bright but cold. John Hislop felt confident that a promised excursion for senior Alaska government officials and members of the legal fraternity could be safely conducted to the construction front. After an early start and a brief stop to drink a cup of Dr. Whiting's traditional fortifying spirit in his tent near White Pass City, the railway's guests continued by train to the east portal of the tunnel. They then clambered around the rocky crags and over the buttress to the west portal of the tunnel.

"It was a sight that only a few had the good fortune to witness outside of the thousands of workmen who have laboured on the great enterprise," exclaimed Judge C.S. Johnson's wife, who with great enthusiasm had pitched two shovelfuls of snow off the grade and assisted in sharpening a drill at the blacksmith's shop. Playfully regarding herself as a railway worker, she claimed the right to be put on the company's payroll, threatening legal action to enforce her demand. In defence, the company acknowledged its debt but "disputed the value of the labour performed."[12]

By January 23, 1899, the work force had grown to 1,800 men, more than half of them employed shovelling snow. Additional men were assigned to speed up work on the tunnel. On the morning of January 29, the powdermen blasted down the last remaining wall of rock that separated the east and west portals. By evening, the two crews had broken through the rubble to meet among the tunnel's eerie shadows cast by half a hundred carbide lamps. Inside it was comparatively warm, but outside a snowstorm raged, creating brutal working conditions for the bridge builders, who were urged on by the imposing presence of Sam Murchison, Heney's walking boss, Hugh Foy, the general foreman, and F.B. Flood, engineer and superintendent of the railway's summit division.

Work along the Tunnel Mountain section of grade, including the east portal bridge, was pushed ahead "under almost incredible conditions," reported Hawkins during the first week in February. "For three days it had again been storming so hard that it is almost impossible to remain out of doors or do any work in the upper part of the canyon."[13]

The bridge builders, hunched against the wind, moved ever closer to the tunnel's eastern portal, and during the night of February 2, the chasm was successfully bridged. The track men, who had already laid their rails half way across the bridge, pushed on into the tunnel. By the next morning, the track was through the tunnel and linked to the grade that had already been notched out of the cliffs between the tunnel and switchback. Hawkins reported that nothing remained to be done "but to lay the track from the tunnel to the summit and put in three or four bridges." But building the bridges had become the bane of Hawkins's life because "every bridge which we have had to erect had caused a delay as the track could not proceed until the bridge had been finished."[14]

Heney arrived back in Skagway and regrouped his forces to support Hawkins's drive. His gangs laid track to within two miles of the summit cut. But the effort was costly. "Laying the track to the summit is proving very expensive on account of the adverse weather," Brydone-Jack reported to London, "but Mr. Hawkins thinks, and I perfectly agree with him, it will be necessary for the welfare of the railroad to push on." Forcing the work under adverse conditions and achieving the rapid dispatch of freight from Skagway to Lake Bennett would, in Brydone-Jack's view, bring valuable advertising to the railway and earn "net profits from the traffic obtained."

Brydone-Jack cited the results of a survey he had completed to support his predictions of high profit from large volumes of freight. His conservative estimate suggested that some 8,000 tons of freight would be shipped north through Skagway during February, March, and April, 1899, "on which the gross receipts to the railway will be $58 per ton or $464,000." He estimated that the railway's operating expenses for this period would be $84,000 – an amount that would cover snow removal, freight handling, coal, and the cost of administration – and projected that the railway could make a net profit of $380,000 for the three-month period. But he added that this profit should not be distributed to the shareholders, "as Mr. Hawkins intends using the income from the traffic department for the purposes of construction." This policy was eventually adopted as the basic method of financing the completion of the railway.[15]

The projected profit, however, would be earned only if the competition from the Chilkoot tramline could be held in check, and this was by no means assured. The three aerial tramlines, which now operated under the name of The Chilkoot Pass Route, had been advertising throughout December that its system was complete and would be open for business on New Year's Day, 1899. "Having handled three-fourths of the traffic over this route last season," the advertisements proclaimed, "the tramline will be in a better position than ever to give prompt, safe and efficient service during the season of 1899."[16]

Not to be outdone, Hawkins authorized railway advertisements in the West Coast papers announcing in bold type that the dangers, difficulties, and delays suffered in reaching the Klondike and the new Atlin gold-fields "were now overcome." The advertisements boasted that the railway could convey gold-seekers "from Skagway, Alaska, to the summit of White Pass in a comfortable railway train," and that the White Pass and Yukon Railway was now prepared to move all manner of freight across the mountain barrier "and guarantee delivery at the lakes."[17]

Of course, neither the railway nor the tramline was capable of living up to its boasts. Both were far short of completing their transportation systems, and neither one had reached its respective summit.

On February 3, L.H. Gray, the railway's general traffic manager, arrived in Dyea to inspect the Chilkoot Pass tramlines. He landed at the aerial tramline's unfinished dock, where he was obliged to wait four hours for the tide to go out before he could safely step onto Dyea's muddy beach and walk to shore. "I found the town almost deserted," he reported to Hawkins, and added that "only five tons of local freight had been landed on the dock by steamers from Puget Sound ports during the past week." He found the trail across the Chilkoot Pass generally rough and rocky. In places the snow lay forty to a hundred feet deep, and the way between Chilkoot summit and Crater Lake was virtually impassable.

Gray found that the three combined tramlines were in hopeless condition: parts of the line were unfinished and the completed sections were not yet in running order. From Sheep Camp to the Scales the tramline was in deplorable shape, its wire lying frozen and twisted on the ground, and from the Scales to the summit its cables and towers were completely covered with snow. "I noticed twelve men digging the wires from beneath a twenty-five to forty-foot snow trench," reported Gray, "and under this snow the wire was buried from four to six feet in solid ice." The weather had forced the tramline to miss its previously announced New Year's Day opening date, and now its general manager, Hugh C. Wallace, was assuring prospective shippers that he would have his transportation system ready for business by February 15, a boast Gray rejected as highly improbable. "I cannot see how it is possible for the Chilkoot tramline to protect any of their low quotations during the next six weeks," he said.

Both the railway and the tramline now had agents operating in the major West Coast ports, who were soliciting through-freight shipments from the head of Lynn Canal to the lakes. A successful aerial freighting system across the Chilkoot Pass could seriously threaten the railway's projected business. Hawkins, who had been troubled by the tramline's boasts, took heart from Gray's assurances that it was doomed to fail. "They will no doubt be able to induce a few poor misguided unfortunates to ship over their lines," concluded Gray, "but to deliver the commodity in large quantities is absolutely impossible."[18]

Initially, Hawkins received Gray's report with considerable relief. "After all our struggles this winter," he commented, "it would have been quite a mortification to me to have had the tramline in operation over the Chilkoot Pass before we reach the summit of White Pass with our railroad."[19]

Gray's report was the only bright spot on Hawkins's horizon, but even this momentary glimmer of encouragement subsequently proved to be less accurate than either he or Gray had hoped. Wallace refused to quit digging his lines and towers out of the snow, and his agents continued to book freight. Many West Coast shippers believed the tramway's claim that the only reliable route into the interior was via its bonded Chilkoot Pass route, and that it could move freight faster, cheaper, and safer than any other system — including the railway.

Who in the south could tell which route was the better? Who could tell who was telling the truth? Both companies were making extravagant claims in order to attract the most freight. Both hoped to make great profits for themselves and, at the same time, bankrupt their competition. The battle lines were being drawn. Slowly, inexorably, the two rival transportation systems were clawing their way north, both proclaiming that with the coming of spring they would deliver freight to their respective summits – the railway on the ground and the tramline through the air.

Hawkins's optimism on hearing Gray's report on the Chilkoot tramline was fast waning. The winter weather, the distressingly slow progress on the construction front, and Wallace's damnable persistence with his tramline made him despair. "I have never been so disheartened and discouraged with anything in my life," he wrote to Graves with uncharacteristic candour and emotion. "But," he quickly added, "I will keep right at it."[20]

Hawkins had good reason to be concerned. More men were shovelling snow off the railway grade than were working on construction. Throughout the last week in January and the first week in February it had been impossible to keep the construction sites north of the tunnel clear of snow. For days on end the bridge foundations, which had been built during the summer months, were buried under rock-hard drifts. Only during lulls in the storms could the work crews locate and uncover the hidden foundations and allow the bridge builders to erect their heavy timbers.

In Skagway business was brisk. Seven cargo ships, each loaded with freight and passengers destined for Dawson and Atlin, had just arrived. Prices soared as Skagway entrepreneurs took advantage of the newcomers. By the first week in February, hotels had doubled their rates, and one shocked gold-seeker wailed that drinks were being sold at the sky-high price of twenty-five cents a shot or five shots for a dollar. "A great many people are leaving Skagway to avoid the extortionate charge for living," reported the *Victoria Colonist*.

Freight was piling up at Skagway. The railway was moving three to five boxcar loads of freight each day from Skagway to Heney Station, as well as two or three flat cars loaded with rails to the work sites beyond the tunnel. But the snow was taking its toll on men and equipment. On February 11, Division Superintendent Whiting told Hawkins that a train with four boxcars of freight had been dispatched north led by a snowplough "that required three engines to push it around the point this side of Heney Station." Later he reported that "the locomotives are leaking badly and are in bad shape from the hard service they have had."

Slowly the rails advanced north of the tunnel to the switchback at Mile 19, and by February 13, Heney had succeeded in laying the steel rails to within a mile of the summit. But, unable to keep the grade clear, he had been forced in places to lay his tracks on top of graded snow, an expedient that would be corrected in the spring when the snow had melted and the weather improved.[21]

BRYDONE-JACK'S ENTHUSIASM mounted as the rails approached the summit. Heney and Hislop were no less excited and had arranged to inspect all construction activities, especially those at the summit. Brydone-Jack proposed that he accompany them on their week-long trip, which would involve heavy snowshoeing along the grade and over the trails. Hislop and Heney readily agreed, and on February 4, 1899, the three set off from Heney Station.

The snow was deep and the weather was bitterly cold. At times the wind was so fierce that it stopped them in their tracks. But they bent to it and pushed on – occasionally pausing to make notes or reach a decision.

Brydone-Jack watched his two friends, taking careful note of their stamina and their ability to maintain the strenuous pace they had set. For months he had been waiting for an opportunity to demonstrate his superior trail skills and settle the matter of who was best once and for all. Not a word had ever been spoken about their respective staying powers, their prowess on the trail. Heney and Hislop knew where they stood. As trailmen they were dead even. On the other hand, Brydone-Jack's abilities on the trail had yet to be proved. They snowshoed on. As the hours passed, each became aware that a contest was brewing. Brydone-Jack was pressing, and it was clear that by the time they returned to Skagway, Brydone-Jack would have won or lost this competition.

Few men could have stayed with Heney and Hislop that day. Brydone-Jack was one of the few, but he had not been hardened to the trail. By lunch it was clear he was on the defensive. But he doggedly snowshoed on, determined not to give in. In vain Heney and Hislop urged him to slow down, but the more they protested the more he persisted in pacing the expedition. When they reached the summit that evening, Brydone-Jack was exhausted. It was bitterly cold and the flapping tent gave them little protection from the sharp arctic wind. By morning Brydone-Jack was running a fever but still objected strenuously when Heney and Hislop urged him to catch the work train on the grade below the summit and check into the hospital at Skagway. During the following three days, Brydone-Jack's fever increased. On the fourth day, Heney and Hislop decided to overrule Brydone-Jack's objections and move him at once to hospital. They carried him in his blankets a mile and a half down the pass to the end of steel. There, they commandeered a locomotive and ordered that it make a direct run down the grade to the hospital at Skagway.

Heney was worried. He suspected pneumonia. "Better run some," Hislop shouted at the locomotive engineer, who needed no urging after being told of Brydone-Jack's condition. Graves later reported to London, "The way that engine ran the hill that day is spoken of still as an intervention of providence." The train "jumped and rolled" around the curves of the unfinished track "in a way that no engine has ever done before."

But it was all to no avail. In spite of every care, Brydone-Jack died the following day, February 13, 1899, the cause cited as "apoplexy brought about by an attack of the grippe."

Hawkins, who was to leave Skagway for Seattle that day, was detained by Brydone-Jack's death. He wrote to Hussey, his Seattle office manager, asking that Graves be informed. "Mr. Brydone-Jack was so favourably known here and was such a friend to all with whom he came in contact that it is thought advisable to have a short funeral ceremony in the church before shipping the body south."[22]

Heney and Hislop were shocked and had great difficulty accepting Brydone-Jack's death, as did many White Pass employees who knew and admired him. To signal their esteem for him, they ordered the railway's offices closed and all of the locomotives draped in black.

Hundreds of people attended the short funeral service held in the Union Church on February 16, where the Reverend Mister Sinclair officiated. The hearse, drawn by two horses, left E.R. Peoples' Undertaking Parlor and passed through a double line of 200 railway employees along 5th Avenue. Behind the hearse walked the pallbearers – Hawkins, Hislop, Gray, Heney, Dr. Whiting, Superintendent Whiting, and Hugh Foy.

After the service, Hawkins and Brydone-Jack's cousin, James A. Black, accompanied the body aboard the steamer *Rosalie*, which left for Vancouver at noon that day.

"He was one of the most practical engineers going," said a shaken Heney, "and as a construction engineer he was at the head of his profession."[23]

Traffic Manager Gray offered the observation that Brydone-Jack's death "was the greatest loss that the White Pass and Yukon Route had ever had. It has cast a gloom over us all," he said, and then added prophetically, "we all wonder who will be next."[24]

Fifteen

CRISES OF MEN AND MONEY

O N FEBRUARY 18, 1899, with the thermometer registering twenty below, the exhausted construction crews faced the final mile and hammered their way to the summit, their hastily laid track temporarily ballasted with snow.

A boxcar loaded with freight had been attached to the work train – the first commercial freight to be transported by rail from Skagway to the summit of the pass. The freight was Hawkins's idea. On February 15 he had written to Superintendent Whiting, "it is most important that I cable London that we have reached the summit and have shipped freight to that point . . . an official notice that will be repeated in the papers all over the world."[1]

Late that evening, Heney, after making a brief address, ceremoniously drove home the last spike on Alaska's soil and the first spike on the soil of British Columbia. Pacific Contract Company engineers, track foreman Hugh Foy, and some 200 workers gathered in the freezing cold and dark to witness this historic occasion. Slowly the locomotive chuffed past the two freshly driven spikes and, with a squeal of brakes, came to a halt.[2]

Hawkins was not there. He had not yet returned from his journey to Vancouver with Brydone-Jack's body. Neither was he present on February 20, when the first official passenger train reached the summit of the White Pass, a date the *Daily Alaskan* proclaimed to be "The Proudest Day in Alaska's History."

The paper was impressed with both the event and the day and said so. "Good Dame Nature, arrayed in all her virgin white under a bright and cloudless sky, smiled on the White Pass yesterday, in honor of the arrival of the first train ever to set out from Skagway over the now famous White Pass Railway."

The paper was supremely satisfied. "We are 2,900 feet closer to Heaven," it declared. And when the train chugged to the end of the rails, belching smoke and venting steam, the paper rhapsodized that on its arrival, "the eagle cooed and the land purred."

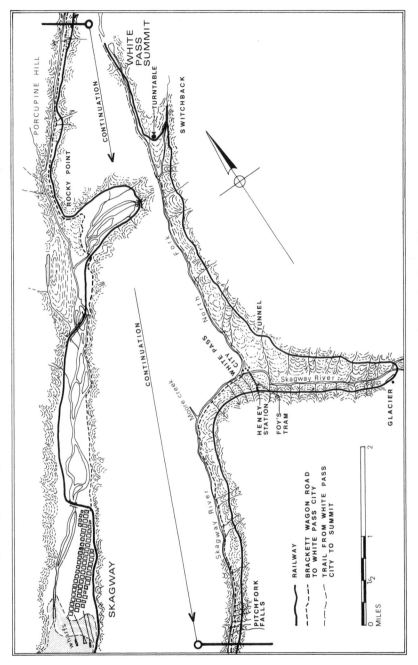

SKAGWAY TO WHITE PASS SUMMIT

Just north of Skagway, the railway crossed the first of two bridges to avoid trespassing on Brackett's wagon road. Both rights of way clashed between Rocky Point and Pitchfork Falls, and White Pass City was served by both the railway and the wagon road until the railway was finished. Railway construction between Heney Station and the summit involved very heavy rock work, particularly between the tunnel and the switchback.

One hundred guests had been invited to travel on this train and to attend a commemorative lunch at the summit of the pass. It was four degrees below zero and an unpleasant north wind was blowing through Skagway when they boarded the passenger coaches at the newly completed railway depot building at ten in the morning. As the train slowly climbed to the summit, the cold intensified, but there were no complaints. The train's two coaches were well heated with coal stoves, and the guests were bundled up in fur coats and parkas. Barley was unable to attend, so Eric A. Hegg was hired to photograph the day's events. The *Daily Alaskan*'s reporter observed that "there were enough Kodaks on board to start a camera club." The views of the White Pass proved to be a "never ending source of delight," but because the windows kept frosting, the guests were kept busy "scratching them clear so that they could secure a good view of the passing scene."

The train reached the summit at half past one, after making numerous photographic stops. For the last half mile the guests saw little as their train passed through walls of snow from six to twenty feet high. The train chuffed slowly through this colossal white channel, kept open by more than 300 men shovelling in shifts day and night.

At the summit, the unofficial boundary had been marked with two flagpoles fifty feet apart, one flying the Stars and Stripes and the other the Union Jack. A small community had grown at the summit, consisting of the railway's extensive construction camp, several privately operated grub tents, and one substantial structure known as the "U.S. Hotel." Here, amid the piles of rail, ties, lumber, blacksmith's coal, and frozen garbage, a weary traveller could find rest and sustenance for himself and his dog, his horse, or his mule.

Hugh Foy greeted the guests and directed them to two tents – one with a blazing heater and decanters of sherry for the ladies, and one stocked with cigars and hard liquor for the men. There, the sightseers were thoroughly warmed by the fire and by generous draughts of bottled spirits, and then escorted to the dining tent, where they were served a lavish meal that included caviar and champagne.

In his after-lunch speech, Heney described many of the difficulties and dangers that his men had faced while blasting their way to the summit, and he spoke warmly of how construction problems and complications had been met and overcome by the indomitable will of the construction chief, Mr. Hawkins. The Reverend Mister Sinclair then rose and spoke highly of Heney, touching on the many kindnesses he had seen him perform in both his business and private life. He talked of Heney's competence as a railway contractor and as a man who did not know the meaning of defeat.

After short speeches by representatives of the Canadian government, the government of British Columbia, the North-West Mounted Police, and John Hislop, Mr. Sinclair suggested a moment of silence for Robert Brydone-Jack, "who would have graced this banquet with his handsome presence, his mellow voice, and his merry words."

The train left the summit on its return trip to Skagway at four, but not before Hegg had taken a group photograph of the guests in front of the locomotive. At the Skagway depot, the railway officials were given three rousing cheers and a tiger for having reached the summit, and for continuing their push to the lakes beyond.

"As a function," observed the *Daily Alaskan*, "it was extremely simple. As an historic commemoration it was simply great."[3]

IN NONE OF the speeches that day did anyone mention that the railway had reached the summit five months late. Clearly, Tancred and Hawkins had misjudged the magnitude of the job and the harshness of the weather, which had delayed construction and the start of freight and passenger services. Now the railway could not fund construction from its own earnings to the extent its London investors had projected. As a result, Close Brothers had been forced to raise new capital. By February 1899, the delay and the loss of earnings were precipitating a financial crisis that threatened to delay construction further or, even worse, bring the entire project to a halt.

The railway's inability to attract a stable and qualified work force was another source of continuing worry. Of the hundreds of men that were hired in Skagway, few had any railway construction experience, and many of them had never before completed a day's physical labour in their lives. Now, some recent hirelings were grumbling about their pay and working conditions.

The growing discontent among the men was more than balanced by Hawkins's growing impatience. "I am astonished and disappointed at the lack of progress and the apparent indifference with which your men are performing their work," he wrote to F.B. Flood, one of his operating railway divisional engineers. "Instead of pushing the work through in the shortest possible time it looks as if there is a systematic attempt to put in the greatest number of hours in shovelling snow, blasting out fog, and doing other unnecessary work." He concluded his knuckle-rapping letter by warning Flood that he planned to spend a day with him, "or as many as are necessary," to put things right.[4]

Hawkins was also having problems operating the recently acquired Brackett wagon road. John Hislop was responsible to the railway for the wagon road's efficient operation, and Al Brackett, one of George Brackett's sons, had been retained to collect the tolls and administer its day-to-day affairs. Now, young Brackett, his toll collectors, and the railway were daily confronted by irate packers, who insisted that neither Brackett nor the railway had any right to charge a toll to use the wagon road. They claimed that George Brackett had fraudulently obtained authority to charge tolls from the United States Secretary of the Interior by reporting that he had completed a road from Skagway to the summit of White Pass, and that a wagon loaded with 2,000 pounds of freight could be hauled over it by a normal team of horses.[5] The packers argued that this was nonsense, insisting that Brackett's road ended just beyond White Pass City, some three miles short of the summit, and that the final three miles was nothing but a trail that no team and wagon could manoeuvre – only pack trains of horses and mules. They also claimed that they had constructed these final miles to the summit themselves months before Brackett arrived in Skagway and that they had paid for this work themselves and through public subscription. In their opinion, the last three miles were not part of Brackett's road, and he had no right to charge a toll for its use.

George Brackett angrily rejected the packers' claim. He acknowledged that the trail existed before he arrived, but he insisted that he had improved it at great cost, and that the original trail could not have handled the freight traffic he had generated by constructing his wagon road to the Ford – a point just beyond White Pass City. It was just below the Ford, the entrance to the packers' original trail, that Brackett had erected his "Upper Gate." It was this toll gate, with its fence stretching from one side of the narrow canyon to the other, that infuriated the packers. They could outflank most of Brackett's road during the winter months by following the frozen Skagway River. But here in the narrow canyon above White Pass City they were hemmed in and forced towards Brackett's hated gate like a herd of cattle. It was here that Brackett extracted his toll.

On January 23, 1899, packer Gus Davidson decided to stop talking and take action. At one in the afternoon he reached the "Upper Gate" with sixteen head of cattle. Gus Holmquist, the gatekeeper, demanded a dollar a head for the cattle, a dollar for Davidson's horse, and twenty-five cents for his dog.

"Not one cent of toll do you get from me," roared Davidson.

"But I am the agent of this wagon road and I am here to collect a toll and I will have it," replied Holmquist.

Without further comment, Davidson produced an axe, demolished the gate, and drove his cattle through. A witness said it was "like the case of a six shooter beating a straight flush." Davidson was arrested and charged but was subsequently discharged by Commissioner Sehlbrede on the grounds that Brackett had failed to comply strictly with all of the provisions of the law under which he was granted the right to construct and operate a toll road.

After taking steps to conform to the provisions of the law, and posting public notices to that effect, Brackett re-erected his "Upper Gate" and once again started collecting tolls from packers and prospectors.[6] But ten days later, on February 3, the now notorious "Upper Gate" was attacked again by a group of angry packers, who were determined to end the collection of tolls and turn Brackett's road into a public highway.

Packer J.H Brooks, accompanied by five men with a pack train of thirty horses loaded with feed and merchandise, approached the gate and faced Gus Holmquist, the gatekeeper, and toll collector Elmer Kane.

"Do you have a toll receipt Mr. Brooks?" Holmquist asked.

"No," Brooks replied.

"Do you want to pay a toll?"

Brooks ignored the question and asked if there were any United States marshals present.

"There are no marshals here," replied Holmquist.

"Then I demand that you open up the gate," shouted Brooks. "I will pay no toll!"

Kane stood directly in front of the gate during the heated exchange between Brooks and Holmquist. Jack Farr, one of Brooks's packers, stood nearby with an axe in his hand. When Brooks stopped talking, Farr leaped forward to chop the gate away. Kane jumped between Farr and the gate and Farr swung his axe to fend him off. They fell to the ground and fought for some three minutes. The onlookers appealed to Farr not to injure Kane, but they did not attempt to separate them. Wild with anger, Kane lunged for the axe, which plunged down, gashing open Kane's forehead.

During the fight, a second packer attacked the gate with his axe. Holmquist sprung forward to restrain him, but a third packer pulled a revolver and aimed it at Holmquist.

"Let the man chop," ordered the revolver-wielding packer.

Accepting defeat, Holmquist retired from the fray to help Kane. Brooks and his packers passed through the demolished gate and continued their journey, leaving the toll collectors raging.[7]

Warrants for the arrest of all parties involved in the fracas were issued the following day. Court appearances followed in Skagway, Sitka, and Juneau, which led to tangled, frustrating, and time-consuming legal arguments. Hawkins was near the breaking point. "We are having continuous fights [between] the Packers and the Brackett people," he lamented in a letter to Graves. "We are, of course, supporting Brackett ... who was arrested for maintaining the Toll Gate across the Road, the Packers claiming this to be a public highway."[8]

But the law came down on the side of the railway. On February 20, Judge C.S. Johnson issued an order restraining Brooks and others from passing their animals and freight over the road without paying the schedule of authorized tolls. This order was ignored by the offending packers. So Brackett, on the railway's advice, applied to the court to have the defendants show cause why they should not be punished for contempt. After a change of venue to Juneau, the court fined Brooks $500 and his accomplice, Mahoney, $250. There the matter rested, but little could be done to allay the resentment and ill-feeling between the hostile packers and the Bracketts.

Hawkins was being tested physically and mentally to the limit of his endurance. In addition to his normal duties, he had been asked to take Brydone-Jack's place as the Trustee's watchdog. This request indicated the faith the Trustees had in Hawkins as, for all practical purposes, he would now be reporting on his own performance. "It was a graceful act on the part of the Trustees," Graves observed, "and a very wise one as well." But these additional duties took their toll. "I have neither time to get my hair cut nor my shoes shined," he wrote to the railway's Seattle-based office manager in February 1899. He had cause to be worried. In addition to his other problems, the Atlin gold fields were causing problems again. Without notice to the American public, the government of British Columbia amended its Placer Mining Act in January 1899. This legislation, in effect, barred American miners from the Atlin mining district, allowing only British subjects to hold placer claims. As soon as it became known that it was useless to continue mining in the Atlin gold fields, the Americans there threw up their hands, sold their outfits, and left the country.[9]

This development was a devastating blow to Hawkins, who had come to rely on American Atlin-bound freight to help finance the construction of the railway. Ironically, the area that had robbed him of workers the previous summer had become a prime source of business. And now this lucrative new market was virtually destroyed by the provincial government's action.

The Act, which became known as the Exclusion Act, created havoc among American businessmen, especially those in Skagway, who regarded their port as the gateway to Atlin as well as the gateway to the Klondike. John Hislop, who had recently been elected mayor of Skagway, wrote to the Governor of Alaska, pleading for relief from the Exclusion Act, stating:

There are thousands of men, Americans, waiting at this point for a chance to move into the Atlin country in the spring. It is the American element that has opened this territory and this bill will ruin many a poor man who has invested his last dollar in this venture. We beg you to do all in your power to immediately place our position before the proper legislative bodies with all the force and influence your honorable office commands, and impress on those bodies the necessity of immediate action in appealing this injurious measure.

This town will be crippled beyond measure if this bill is allowed to stand . . . its mere existence is a menace to prosperity in this district.

John Hislop, President
City Council of Skagway[10]

Hawkins had every reason to be alarmed by the British Columbia government's action. This latest Atlin shock happened just as London was looking for increased railway earnings to help finance future construction, reducing the constant drain on Close Brothers' construction account. To ease London's concerns, Hawkins had assured Graves that the railway would earn a great deal of income through the winter of 1898-99 from the freight tonnage to Atlin. Hawkins had been confident that this business would increase that spring when hundreds of American miners would return to Atlin to work the claims they had staked the previous fall. Now Hawkins had to inform Graves that, by the stroke of a pen in Victoria, the prospects of increased freight earnings had vanished.

"The passage of the Exclusion Act," he wrote, "is going to very materially cripple our income and finances from now until such time as it is repealed or gradually evaded. It means taking from us sixty-five per cent at least of our business for the next four months, hence the cable which I sent to you in London stating that the income of the railroad would pay for the extra construction work will have to be modified.

"We will need considerable money for the next three months. Unless this is provided in some way exclusive of depending upon the earnings of the Road I shall have to materially reduce the force, and you know that it is of the utmost necessity that we reach Lake Bennett by the first of July."[11]

Close Brothers' investment was escalating at a far greater rate than had been anticipated. The railway company had already expended some million and a half dollars in surveys and construction since April, 1898, and it was currently paying out between $60,000 and $90,000 a month in labour.[12]

In an attempt to slash expenses, Hawkins dispatched cost-cutting letters to everyone in the organization who had authority to spend cash. He wrote to the railway's freight agent in Seattle, "our business has been so reduced on account of the Exclusion Bill that it is not worth our while to advertise. Our business has been cut 60 to 70 per cent and we were depending principally on the Atlin business for this winter's traffic."[13]

Meanwhile, a stiff letter to Heney left no doubt about Hawkins's dissatisfaction with the Pacific Contract Company's rate of pay.

"I am informed today," Hawkins wrote, "that the wages being paid . . . are thirty-five cents per hour and ten hours allowed as a day.

"I trust this is not the case. If such a rate is being paid we must at once change it back to the thirty cents rate. This is in accordance with a conversation I had with you several days ago in which I wished, as soon as possible, to make the working day ten hours at thirty cents."[14]

Heney immediately reduced the rate to thirty cents per hour, although he had not been responsible for the troublesome inconsistency. Most of the 1,400 workers on the payroll accepted the lower rate without question, having been hired on that basis. But some of the new arrivals, who had been promised the higher rate, began a protest that spread through the work force from Skagway to the camps beyond the summit.

NOW THAT THE railway operated from Skagway to White Pass summit, it was no longer necessary to use Foy's inclined railway between Heney Station and White Pass City or to pack the freight by horse or mule from there to the summit. This detour had at last been eliminated – a change that presaged the end of White Pass City as a packer's base and transportation centre and the eventual demise of the packers' business.

With three to five loaded boxcars arriving at the summit daily, Hawkins was now faced with the problem of moving this revenue-earning commercial freight from the end of steel to Log Cabin and Lake Bennett. A sleigh road had been built, partly by the packers and partly by the railway builders, by sending team after team of horses through the snowdrifts. Marked by stakes and saplings on both sides, this hard-packed snow road could be followed in the darkest night and the severest storms. Hawkins described it as "very nearly level and much better than an ordinary country road in winter."[15]

Heney, with Hawkins's agreement and approval, formed the Red Line Transportation Company, which contracted with the railway to deliver commercial freight to Log Cabin and Lake Bennett and the railway's construction supplies to the camps.

"We have gotten our packing business from the end of our line down to a very satisfactory basis," wrote Hawkins to Graves. "It is done by M.J. Heney . . . who distributes the freight to responsible packers, of course under our direction, and we only have one outfit to deal with."[16]

Heney had placed William Robinson in charge of the Red Line's daily operations. Known locally as "Stikine" Bill, he indulged in creative profanity and Black Strap chewing tobacco, which he could spit with unerring accuracy. He was six-foot-three, weighed over 300 pounds, and gave the impression that the seams of his clothes were about to split. Robinson had joined Heney's work force in the fall of 1898. He had worked for Mackenzie and Mann's proposed railway through the Stikine River valley until it collapsed, hence his nickname "Stikine" Bill. Robinson proved to be a veteran railway builder who, it was claimed, could talk to horses.

Every morning at ten, weather permitting, two to three locomotives pulling three to five heavily laden boxcars reached White Pass summit. Stikine Bill's fleet of wide-runner, four-horse transport sleighs, each capable of hauling half a ton of freight, swung into action. Men drawn from the construction gangs manhandled the freight from boxcars to sleighs and to sub-contracted pack trains of horses and mules. Checkers, with fists full of papers, directed the flow of traffic. Smoke and steam swirled among the piles of boxes and bags and hot cinders dropped by the locomotives bored holes in the dirty, hard-packed snow.

The flow of freight from Skagway north was never ending, and as the daily tonnage rose, Heney was forced to enlarge the Red Line's fleet of sleighs and extend his packers' contracts.

Tons of freight had accumulated at the summit, and Heney stored it in a large warehouse tent. A few days later, warehouseman Ennis complained that it was full to the ridge pole and that more than seven tons of merchandise were stacked in the snow outside. The job of moving this quantity of freight, often in the middle of storms, was taking its toll. "Storms are raging through the pass, weather extreme in every way," Hawkins informed the Seattle office during early February. "Men are out shovelling all along the line trying to control the drifting snow."[17]

Delays were inevitable, and men and metal cracked under the strain. Superintendent Whiting's temper rose with each new snowfall, each new demand. In answer to a testy complaint from F.H. Gray, the railway's general traffic manager, Whiting wrote, "I notice your memos and verbal complaints about the freight not getting to the summit. I will advise you Sir, that when the operating department is provided with a rotary snow plow, and with engines that have not been condemned to the scrap pile, we will try in ordinary weather to meet all the requirements of the traffic department. Until that time it is exceedingly doubtful during these stormy periods, whether we can operate beyond Glacier."[18]

Whiting's job had become very stressful. On February 23, he reported that six boxcar loads of freight, pulled by three locomotives, had attempted to reach the summit. At Glacier Station, fourteen miles north of Skagway, the snow was so deep the train crew had been forced to drop off three cars. After reaching the summit, the three locomotives returned to Glacier to pick up the three dropped cars. Once again the crew faced the steep grade, but at the first siding north of Glacier, they were forced to drop off one car. The two remaining cars finally reached the summit at midnight. "The track is in fearful condition," Whiting reported, "and the snow drifts like fine sand over the track."[19]

The locomotives were being battered and overworked during their daily trips to the summit. So were the train crews. Tensions erupted between Superintendent Whiting's railway operating department and Gray's freight sales operations in Seattle and Victoria when it became known that Gray was guaranteeing customers specific delivery dates at destination – promises it was almost impossible for the train crews to meet.

Hawkins was aware of the drop in morale among the operating, engineering, and administrative staffs. They had been working too long each day, seven days a week, for months. The construction crews were allowed to book off work almost any time they wished, or work overtime shovelling snow if they wanted more money in their pay packets. The office staffs, however, did not have this choice, and the long hours and the weight of events were wearing them down. "From this day until further notice," Hawkins ordered on February 11, "all offices will be closed on Sundays. No work will be allowed on that day except when necessary." He also reduced the office day to ten hours, from eight in the morning to six at night, with time off for lunch. But, he added, "In case of arrival and departure of vessels it may be necessary to ignore this rule. Employees will ... regard the interests of the company in this matter." The order applied to the offices of the Pacific Contract Company and to the Pacific and Arctic Railway and Navigation Company.

"A commendable order," wrote the *Daily Alaskan*, "and one that will be appreciated by the community."[20] But for Hugh Foy the order came too late. Sensing a gradual deterioration in Foy's health, Heney had been urging him to take a vacation, but he had refused to leave the work until the railway reached the summit. On that day, he told Heney, he would arrange to take some time off. After the summit celebrations, he prepared to start his vacation on February 28 and leave for Seattle on the steamer *Rosalie* on March 2.

On February 24, four days after the summit ceremony, the upper pass was struck by a blinding snowstorm, trapping two locomotives and their crews between Glacier and the summit. Foy and a large party of shovellers tramped the grade, battling snowdrifts and ice-encrusted ridges until they found the stranded locomotives. They worked all night to free the engines from the grip of the storm. By morning, Foy was exhausted and flushed with a high fever. The next day it was clear he had pneumonia. He died early in the morning of February 28, the day he was to have begun his vacation.

On the morning of March 2, senior officials and construction workers gathered at the Reverend Mister Sinclair's new church edifice, known as Victoria Hall, for a funeral service. Foy's remains were then placed on the steamer *Rosalie* – ironically, the same ship and the very trip he had arranged to sail to begin his vacation.

WHILE THE MEN on the railway were fighting snowstorms, Hawkins and Graves were in Seattle battling with the vexing problems of financing construction through to Lake Bennett. After much deliberation, they cabled London that, as of March 1, they would require $350,000 to complete the railway to Bennett. Of this amount, $150,000 could come from railway freight earnings, leaving $200,000 to be raised by Close Brothers' offices in London and Chicago.

Graves agreed to forward $50,000 to Hawkins on March 7, and a second $50,000 on March 16. Hawkins could expect final increments totalling $100,000 as the rails approached Bennett. The remaining $150,000 required to complete the line to Bennett had to come from the railway's freight earnings.[21] Hawkins was unsure this could be done. Conditions had changed since Brydone-Jack's optimistic predictions in January that the railway would earn a net profit of $350,000 during February, March, and April – an estimate that had been enthusiastically received in London.

There had been, however, a few promising developments. Vast amounts of freight destined for the Klondike and some destined for Atlin were stockpiled in Skagway, the railway had reached the summit, and transportation from the summit to Bennett was firmly in Heney's capable hands.

Graves left Seattle for Chicago reasonably content. Under the circumstances he could not have asked for more of Hawkins, although he would have been happier if the railway was able to finance more of its own construction out of freight earnings and make fewer calls on London and Chicago for funds. Hawkins remained in Seattle to complete his plans for the final push to Lake Bennett. He, too, felt confident. Soon, warmth would return to the North, and then his construction workers could start laying rail through the rocky uplands north of the summit and blast their way into Bennett by July 1, 1899, a date he had promised Graves.

A week later his confidence was shattered. On March 5, a boat from the North brought mail describing the appalling conditions in Skagway and all along the line. As he read the report, his serenity vanished, his anger rose, and his sense of helplessness came close to breaking his spirit. Later boats brought more reports, which detailed how unbelievably severe storms had shut down most of the railway's operations and announced that freight services to the summit were now completely blocked by snow. Worse, construction was at a virtual standstill because of a strike over the reduction in wages.[22]

Hawkins telegraphed Graves with news of the strike. The careful plans they had so recently made were now inoperable. Nothing could be done about the storms, and for the moment little could be done about the strike, which was being led by a small number of men described by one Skagway newspaper as a group of "anarchists."[23]

Hawkins and his Seattle staff concluded that, despite the weather and the strike, modest earnings might be realized if Whiting re-established the rail freight run to Heney Station and on to the summit via the Brackett road, utilizing the services of the Red Line Transportation Company from White Pass City to Bennett. Hawkins need not have worried. Hislop and Whiting were already attempting to reach Heney Station with boxcars of freight. Fortunately, Whiting's train crews and shopmen were on duty. Only the construction workers had thrown down their tools and walked off the job.

THE FIRST PUBLIC REPORT of the strike appeared in the *Skagway-Atlin Budget* on February 28. The newspaper had rushed the story into print by publishing an "extra" carrying the headline "RAILROAD STRIKE – A Remonstrance From Employees Against A Reduction." Overnight "The Committee" had reappeared, and a series of resolutions condemning Hawkins's wage reduction had been signed by more than 900 men.

The first resolution laid out the workers' main complaints, "Thirty cents an hour is not requisite compensation for laborers in this latitude." A second resolution stated, "The hardships undergone in such an inhospitable climate could never be sufficiently remunerated." The Committee's supporting statement read, "the conditions, at and beyond the summit, and the lack of Sunday work, makes the results too small for anyone to practically risk their lives in the employ of the company."

The strikers appointed a committee of three – C.D. Baker, J. McNeil, and F.W. Beasley – to negotiate their demands with Heney. A protracted meeting produced no results. The battle lines were drawn. Heney claimed that he was merely returning to the standard wage and could not possibly pay thirty-five cents an hour for ten hours' work. The Committee sent word up the line notifying the workers that negotiations had failed. "Stuff's off. Heney said he'll be d...d if he will."[24]

The men left their jobs in droves, and by March 2, more than 1,200 men were on strike. They arrived in Skagway from the work camps, headed for the paymaster's office, received their time checks, and then demanded their pay in full to date – a demand that the company could not meet on such short notice.

More than a thousand men had surged into town with no food, no blankets, little money, and no place to stay. The Reverend Mister Sinclair approached Hislop with the suggestion that the church's new parish hall be used to house the strikers. "Their strike committee has asked for the privilege of sleeping on the floor," he said.

The request placed Hislop in a difficult position. Not only was he a director of the church, a financial contributor to the construction of the new parish hall, but he was also a recognized senior official of the railway. To agree to the request could conceivably be construed as support for the strike.

Hislop considered the matter. "I want you to do what you think is best Mr. Sinclair," he said. "I have full confidence in your judgement. Personally, I have no objection to the strikers using the hall."[25]

The town was divided over the strike. Most of Skagway's citizens supported the railway, but a number of Skagway and Dyea businessmen, saloon-keepers, Chilkoot tramline operators, and packers gave their support to the strikers. They had their reasons: "Those who support the strikers have no more interest in the men's welfare than Satan or the Sultan's," was the way one journalist put it. Indeed, the strike played right into the hands of the packers and the operators of the Chilkoot tramlines. The longer the completion of the railway could be delayed, the longer the packers' high rates would remain undisturbed. A strike-bound railway meant that thousands of tons of northbound freight would pile up on the docks of Skagway and Dyea, providing work for the Dyea tramlines and packers for months to come.

On March 3, Whiting was interviewed by Deputy United States Marshal Tanner, who claimed that the strikers were not being paid the wages they were owed. These wages, the marshal claimed, should be paid "promptly." Whiting hotly denied that the company was reneging on the paying of wages. "The company in fact has never refused payment to any man, after proper approvals have gone through the regular channels," he stormed. "When the payday comes they shall be promptly paid at the full rate in vogue while the work was being done."

Superintendent Whiting then pointed an accusing finger at Deputy Marshal Tanner. "A number of our men want to work and are willing to work," he exclaimed, "but they are being prevented from doing so by the strikers because you are not fulfilling your duties as a United States Deputy Marshal."[26]

By March 7, most of the strikers had spent what money they had left. The strike was now in its second week. To the amazement of the townspeople and to the chagrin of the strikers, neither the Pacific Contract Company nor the railway had made any effort to end it.

In one way the strike was a blessing to the railway. The storms and cold weather continued to restrict rail operations, freight revenues were negligible, costs continued to rise, construction was at a virtual standstill, and, instead of building a railway, most workers had been shovelling snow. As a result, during February, the railway had faced an exasperating dilemma. Costs could be cut by reducing the number of construction workers, but it would be virtually impossible to replace them when they were needed in April, at which time, with improving weather, the long-awaited push to Bennett would begin. So, to ensure the availability of a large and experienced force of construction workers in the spring, it had been decided to keep them employed and suffer the cost of their wages during March.

The strikers themselves, however, had resolved the dilemma. They had quit work on their own initiative, thereby reducing the cost of labour. But, at the same time, most of them remained in the area ready to be rehired when the wage issue was settled and spring returned. This, in effect, provided the railway with the labour pool it desired without the cost of maintaining it. So it was not surprising that the railway appeared to be unconcerned about the strike.

The same could not be said for the strikers. Led by a small but militant committee, the workers met daily in the church hall, which now carried a large banner spelling out STRIKE HEADQUARTERS in bold block letters, much to Sinclair's disapproval.

At the hall, where he had gone to discuss the unauthorized mounting of the sign, he found a meeting in progress. "Wild statements and misrepresentations were being made by a couple of agitators," he said, "who were disparaging the company and the officials."

Sinclair worked his way to the platform and demanded to be heard. He refuted the charges that had just been made by the strike leaders. "I succeeded in discrediting their garrulous spokesman," he wrote, "and I was amazed that the men gave me such a respectful hearing as I am emphatically opposed to them in the main."

Later, in an effort to discredit the company, the strike committee circulated a pamphlet listing the names of workers who had been killed while working on the grade. "Their deaths," said the pamphlet, "were due to the callous indifference of the company."

Sinclair was determined to verify this disturbing statement. He checked with the deputy marshal's office and with the local undertaker to find out how many men had been killed and under what circumstances. Armed with the facts, Sinclair returned to the hall where the strikers were living, mounted the platform, and confessed that some railway officials had called him to account for allowing the strikers to use the church's facilities. "But now, because I am insisting that you stick to the facts, I am being accused by your strike leaders of favouring the railway."

Then, waving the committee's pamphlet in the air, Sinclair acknowledged the deaths of the men listed, "but not all of them," he said, "died on the grade as the result of accidents. But of those who did there is no evidence of any callous indifference on the part of railway officials or foremen. These were accidental deaths," he went on, "and it is a matter of record that each accident was personally investigated by the United States Commissioner." Sinclair declared that there was not one single shred of evidence to support a charge of callous indifference on the part of any person representing the contract company or the railway.

Sinclair was immediately challenged by a strike leader named Hukell. He insisted that twelve men had been buried under a rock slide and that the company had refused to detail a work crew to recover the bodies.

Pointing a finger at Hukell, Sinclair replied, "I was present when the United States Commissioner, not the railway officials, decided that it was useless to attempt to unearth the bodies. It was recorded as an absolute fact that there were two men involved and not twelve as you claim."

John Gordon, a striker, rose and verified Sinclair's statement. "I was there and can testify that there were two men killed. It was purely an accident and not the result of negligence."

Sinclair then named the two victims and invited Hukell to name the remaining ten. He was unable to do so and was forced to admit that he was relying on hearsay evidence.

Hukell seized the initiative again and hurled another charge at Sinclair. "Do you know that Heney ordered his foreman to discharge any man who refused to take off his topcoat to work when the temperature was thirty below?"

"There is not one element of truth in that statement, and you know it," Sinclair shot back. Turning to the strikers, he asked, "Are there any men here who saw Heney rescue an injured man at the summit at the risk of his own life?" A chorus of approvals came from the floor. "Yes," many shouted, they had seen Heney bring the man in. Hukell's last grand play to regain his authority was to challenge Sinclair to admit that, because God was the source of all good, God should get the credit for saving the man's life.

Sinclair faced the strikers and said, "Now in all fairness, if Mr. Hukell gives God the credit for Heney's good deeds, then surely he should credit the Devil for any evil things that Heney has done. It wasn't Heney who did bad things, it was the Devil!"

The meeting broke into laughter. Sinclair was winning the day. He continued to attack Hukell's extravagant statements about accidents and the number of workmen killed on the grade, and revealed that one of Hukell's purported victims had actually been killed in a fight over a woman in Skagway. Another had been stabbed to death in a drunken brawl.[27]

Hukell's influence had been irreparably damaged. The meeting broke up as the strikers left in disgust over Hukell's emotional charges and his inaccurate and inflammable statements.

"A few words of friendly advice to the strikers will not be out of order now," wrote the *Daily Alaskan*. "Throw off the yoke that has been saddled on you by outsiders with an axe to grind, confine yourself to making an open and honorable fight with your adversary, the railroad; and, above all, secure leaders who are possessed of diplomacy and ability sufficient to command respect, not only of yourselves, but of every representative citizen of Skagway."[28]

CONSTRUCTION WAS DOWN to a minimum because of the strike, and snowstorms were making it almost impossible to transport freight to the summit and on to Bennett. Superintendent Whiting reluctantly reported this to Hawkins, who was still in Seattle.

The day after Hawkins received Whiting's pessimistic report, a second jolting letter arrived from Earl E. Siegley, the Pacific Contract Company's accountant and a Heney confidant. In it Siegley made a totally unexpected demand for $100,000 to cover increased construction and snow-removal costs and to meet the strikers' demands that their outstanding wages be paid without delay. Hawkins was horrified. This figure was double the amount he had forecast for March expenditures during his recent budget meeting with Graves.[29]

Hawkins was in no position to question Siegley's figure of $100,000 or the facts on which it was based. Ten days to two weeks would pass if he sought confirmation by mail. So, he accepted Siegley's figure and included the request for the additional funds in a gloomy telegram to Graves in Chicago on March 12.

> I DO NOT KNOW OF WORST STORMS AT SUMMIT OF WHITE PASS. COMPLETE SNOW BLOCKADE SINCE MARCH 1. WE ARE LIMITING OUR OPERATIONS TO HENEY STATION. STRIKE CONTINUES WITH COMPLICATIONS. WILL HAVE TO MAKE IMMEDIATE PAYMENT TO MEN ON STRIKE AND NECESSARY TO TAKE UP RAILROAD EMPLOYEES PAYCHECKS. WANT IMMEDIATE $100,000 IN EXCESS OF THE $50,000 EXPECT TO RECEIVE ON 16 MARCH. THINK ADVISABLE TO DISCONTINUE CONSTRUCTION OWING TO THE SEVERITY OF THE WEATHER.
>
> E.C. HAWKINS.[30]

Graves received Hawkins's cable on March 13 and went into immediate shock. He wrote by return mail:

> Your telegram to hand this A.M. has paralysed me. Having to provide the whole of the original $100,000 estimated for March without any help from earnings was bad enough, but to be called for another $100,000 on top of it . . . at a time when the railway is earning nothing, shut up by a snow blockade, a strike on and no more Engineer Certificates in sight is a "knock out" blow.

Graves reminded Hawkins in the strongest terms that "London has thrown up its hands" and was insisting that the railway be completed to Bennett out of freight earnings.

> It looks as if you and I will have to complete the railway personally in our shirt sleeves, with picks and wheelbarrows. I don't see how else it is to be done. If I can scare up this $100,000 for you, it looks as if it would be all gone in a few days and more wanted. It is like pouring water through a sieve. What is to be the end of it?

Not satisfied with this outburst, Graves added a postscript to make his feelings absolutely clear.

> It is perfectly awful, it has quite upset me. I don't know what to do. If

we can manage somehow or other to get around this corner, you must arrange in the future to handle us a *great deal* easier or you will ditch the Contract Company beyond all hope of picking up the wreck.

As soon as he had finished this letter to Hawkins, Graves wrote another one, again emphasizing his unhappiness and concern over the contents of Hawkins's cable.

I must tell you that the strain on us to meet your calls during the past two months has been something almost indescribable. It has become my duty to warn you, in the plainest language, that our financial position is being tested beyond its strength when such telegrams as yours come in. We have now gone quite beyond the limits of our financial plans. London has gone back on me, and I can hardly blame them for feeling discouraged, in view of the fact that the railroad is blocked, construction suspended by weather and a strike, earnings small, operating expenses large. If this extra $100,000 you want immediately is to be provided at all I shall have to raise it here in Chicago on my own credit. It is absolutely necessary if we are to avoid having a financial crisis and the bottom dropping out of the whole thing, that for the future we shall not be called upon for such enormous sums of money. At the present time every dollar is as big as a cart wheel.[31]

His outburst over, Graves started to view the matter in practical terms. His first move was to cable Hawkins in Seattle to test his figures.

THE 50,000 TO BE PROVIDED ON MARCH 16, AS AGREED AT OUR MEETING, IS TO COVER YOUR FEBRUARY PAYROLL. WHY DO YOU REQUIRE $100,000 MORE? WHY SHOULD YOU WANT TWICE AS MUCH MONEY WITH THE MEN ON STRIKE AS YOU EXPECTED TO NEED WHEN THEY WERE WORKING? WHAT IS THE LEAST YOU CAN DO WITH? ANSWER QUICK.

Hawkins reworked his figures and cabled Graves.

WILL HAVE TO MAKE ALL NECESSARY PREPARATIONS TO PAY WITHOUT DELAY $50,000 WORTH OF STRIKERS OLD PAY CHECKS. STRIKE AND SNOW BLOCKADE HAS REDUCED EARNINGS 66 2/3%. FOR THIS REASON WILL REQUIRE $40,000 IN EXCESS OF THE MARCH 16 $50,000. EARNINGS WILL RUN ABOUT $2000 to $4000 DAILY WHEN SNOW BLOCKADE OVER.[32]

Graves breathed a sigh of relief. Hawkins was now asking for only $40,000, a significant reduction but still stiff. He wrote on March 14:

I am much relieved to learn that your requirements for an additional
$40,000 only. The March 16 remittance of $50,000 plus the additional
$40,000 will be forwarded to you today in one remittance of $90,000,
and I sincerely trust that you will succeed in keeping down your future
calls to the lowest possible notch.[33]

Graves's position had been precarious throughout the crisis. The Pacific
Contract Company, which was building the railway, had exhausted its financial
resources and virtually all of its borrowing power in London and Chicago. It
had also mortgaged the funds it was entitled to receive from the Trustees
through the submission of Trustee Engineer's Certificates. Future certificates,
therefore, would not free fresh funds for construction but would merely pay
back money already advanced.

At this stage of the railway's development, there was no market whatever
for its shares. Graves underscored the railway's precarious position in another
letter to Hawkins:

> We have been counting on making a market for the Railway Com-
> pany's shares as soon as it was showing big earnings and prosperity
> which we have all along been telling people would result the moment
> we were open to the Summit for traffic. The delay in reaching the
> Summit and the railway's lack of earnings has had a most discouraging
> effect on London. But now that we have reached the Summit the
> situation for the time being seems to be worse instead of better.
>
> I do not want to frighten you unnecessarily as to our financial condi-
> tion. I still believe that with extremely careful nursing we can somehow
> or other keep things going until the line is opened to Bennett in some
> kind of shape sufficient to run cars over, after which the question of
> improving the road will be comparatively easy.

Graves could not, however, resist concluding his letter without enunciating a
few hard facts.

> On the other hand, it is absolutely essential in order to avoid a catas-
> trophe, that you should understand once and for all that we are not so
> robust financially as we used to be and that our constitution is now so
> exhausted that a sudden jolt like the one you gave us yesterday is pretty
> certain to kill us altogether, instead of bringing you the money you
> require.[34]

Hawkins responded by apologizing to Graves for his frequent demands for money. He acknowledged the difficulties Graves faced in raising large sums of cash, but he made it quite clear that he was equally pressed and that his requests for cash were totally justifiable. "We called for one hundred thousand upon request of Mr. Siegley," he wrote. "Subsequently, after going over the situation we were able to reduce the demand from one hundred thousand to forty thousand. Of course," he emphasized, "the one hundred thousand requested was actually needed."[35]

Hawkins returned to Skagway on March 21, leaving his Seattle staff to reduce the number and quantity of purchases. Commissary supplies were slashed, lumber orders were cut to the bone, rail and track iron inventories were checked and further orders suspended until the railway's financial position improved. "In view of Mr. Graves' urgent request that we curtail expenses, we have cut down essential orders as much as one third," the Seattle office manager, Hussey, informed Hawkins on March 22, "and I trust that this action will conform to your wishes."[36]

In Skagway Hawkins found that the railway was still being buffeted by storms, construction was lagging, and the strike was continuing in full force. Now this new financial crisis added to his woes. He wrote to Graves again, assuring him that he would do everything in his power to keep expenses down during the current emergency. "If necessary," he said, "I am ready to go to New York, or elsewhere, and aid in making personal arrangements for finances." Then, in an act of generosity and loyalty to Graves and the railway, he offered Graves all of his Pacific Contract Company stock. "I wish this placed to the credit of the company and when things get in better shape, I will then ask for its return at your convenience." As a further demonstration of his loyalty to the railway, Hawkins offered to reduce his own salary of $1000 per month until the company's financial position improved.[37]

AFTER TWO WEEKS off the job, the strikers had failed to achieve any of their objectives. Cracks were appearing in their united front, and many men were openly critical of the strike leadership. Some construction workers were still on the job, although they were under constant threat from the more militant members of the strike committee. Many strikers wanted nothing better than to abandon the strike and return to work, but they were held in line by a small but determined group of angry strike leaders. "It has been a hard task to hold on to the hot-headed agitators, and in a crowd like this there are a lot of them," wrote strike committeeman, Clarence D. Baker, to his father.

"The seeds of discontent have been sown by twenty-five anarchists, aided and abetted by chronic disturbers," declared the *Skagway News*.

These men quit work at the advent of springtime after working through the howling blasts of winter. They quit work for the reason that the price of common labor was reduced from 35 to 30 cents per hour. By April 1 they would have been permitted to labor eleven hours daily for $3.30, leaving them, after deducting $1.00 *per diem* for board, $2.30 for their work.

Is there another place today on the American continent where a common laborer is paid $2.30 and board *per diem?* . . .

Skagway has no sympathy with the strikers for the reason that there is no reason to strike. The men, by a very large majority, realize this fact and are anxious to resume work and be independent as becometh all men.

Arrest and ship a few of the leaders out of the city and the angel of peace will spread her white wings over the territory from tide water to the summit within twenty-four hours.[38]

At the start of the strike there had been a degree of sympathy among the townspeople for the men. Petitions had been circulated, donations sought, food distributed, and beds provided. But much of Skagway's goodwill had been eroded by the drunken antics and anti-social behaviour of a small number of the strikers and by the sophistry of the strike leaders.

In a desperate attempt to maintain the momentum of the strike, as well as force the last of the workers to join the walkout, a group of between eighty-five and a hundred strikers decided to raid Camp 1 north of town and demand that all remaining workers leave. On Monday, March 14, the group set out for Camp 1, determined to eject every man from the railway's property and bring the entire operation to a halt.

The Reverend Mister Sinclair heard the unruly strikers tramping along the street and ran out to ask them where they were going. He was told that they were heading for Camp 1 to deal with the men who had refused to go on strike and force them off the job. Sinclair sprinted to the front of the boisterous throng and confronted the men, pleading with them to listen to his words. Out of respect they stopped, but with undisguised impatience.

"One or two unscrupulous agitators are leading you astray," he shouted. "Abandon these leaders, listen to reason, and seek solutions to your problems by more rational means." He warned them of the consequences of the unlawful act they were about to commit, the damage it would do to their cause, and the injuries that would inevitably result from a physical confrontation.

By the force of his presence and the power of his words, Sinclair succeeded in ramming some common sense into most of the strikers. Slowly, in twos and threes, many of them melted away into the early darkness of the winter afternoon.

The remaining thirty-five strikers were unimpressed. Led by J. Robert White, they refused to abandon their attack. With a shout of encouragement from White, supported by two strike leaders, Fowler and Dick, each of whom directed sixteen men, the determined strikers marched on towards Camp 1.

Sinclair's delaying tactic not only reduced the number of strikers bent on attacking the camp, but it also gave Hislop time to warn Heney, who was in the Camp 1 area.

Commissioner Sehlbrede had witnessed the strikers' march and asked Captain R.T. Yeatman of the United States Army to provide a military presence and give aid to the civil power. Yeatman responded by detailing twenty-three men from Company B, 14th Infantry, and three men from the Hospital Corps, to proceed immediately to the centre of Skagway where they would operate under his direct command. Sehlbrede then ordered Deputy Marshal Tanner to close all of the town's saloons. Soldiers were posted near each one to ensure that no "side-door" liquor reached the streets.

An ugly tension was gripping the town.

White's strikers had already entered the Camp 1 area and were distributing notices that stated, "Quit this camp. By Order of the Alaskan Confederation of Labor." Workers who resisted the order were unceremoniously driven from the camp, their blankets and belongings thrown to the ground.

"If this camp is not abandoned by seven tomorrow morning it will be blown up with dynamite," shouted one of the hot-headed leaders.

Without knocking, they entered Roadmaster Middaugh's house and searched the rooms in an attempt to find "the boss," who, by this time, had already joined Heney and Dr. Whiting at the railway's shops and roundhouse. White and his mob then turned their attention to the shops.

As a defensive measure, Heney had run two locomotives out onto the spurs, with their headlights pointing down the most likely avenues of the attack. Beside the locomotives stood Heney, Dr. Whiting, and Roadmaster Middaugh. Heney and Dr. Whiting were each armed with a Winchester rifle, Middaugh with a heavy wooden club. It was no longer a matter of defending the shops, but of personal survival.

The minutes ticked by. Soon they could see the strikers approaching through the gloom, occasionally caught in the yellow beams of the two head-

LOOKING DOWN THROUGH CUTOFF CANYON FROM HALF MILE BELOW WHITE PASS SUMMIT MAR 20-99.

The White Pass looking south from near the summit, showing Sawtooth Mountain, the Brackett road north of White Pass city, a solitary pack train, and the railway grade slicing across the mountain slope (upper left).

96. LOOKING UP WHITE PASS SUMMIT FROM HALF MILE BELOW   MAR. 20-99.

The Brackett road winding toward White Pass summit. Near the summit "notch," the snow
(upper right) has been discolored by construction debris dumped from the grade.

The railway's first passenger train reached the summit of White Pass over the completed line on 20 February 1899.

The first passengers to reach the summit were royally treated by railway officials, who repeatedly stopped the train to allow the "Kodakers" to take pictures of the magnificent scenery.

The railway's first snowplow was capable of slicing through the huge
snowdrifts that had shut down the railway for days on end.

Clearing the track of snow at White Pass summit was a daily task in the winter months.

At White pass summit, freight was transferred from the railway's boxcars to wagons and sleighs of the Red Line Transportation Company for onward shipment to Bennett City.

Lake Bennett, with hundreds of boats lining the shore. The railway grade (left) has almost reached Bennett City, the head of Yukon River navigation.

The first train to Bennett City, 6 July 1899.

Driving the Bennett last spike on 6 July 1899. This marked the
completion of the railway's "First Section."

Sternwheel steamers met the trains at Bennett city to ship freight onward to
Canyon City on the Yukon River.

After Lake Lewis was inadvertently drained, one-horse dump carts hauled gravel and dirt to create a fill across low spots on the exposed lake bed.

One of the two 600-foot
bridges under construction
near the outlet of drained
Lewis Lake.

After its accidental draining,
Lewis Lake was reduced to a
string of shallow waterways.
In places the railway grade
was built below the
old lake bed.

How to cut the grade through
the permafrost north of
Carcross stumped the
builders until they treated it
as rock and blew it to bits
with dynamite or
black powder.

The rails approach Whitehorse, Yukon.

HEGG #83, UNIVERSITY OF WASHINGTON

The old wooden tramline around Miles Canyon and White Horse rapids. Steamers connected with the temporary railhead at Bennett City until the railway was completed.

BARLEY, AUTHOR'S COLLECTION

Building the grade beneath a mud escarpment just south of Whitehorse.

The grade and rails reach Whitehorse on 6 June 1900.

The first official train arrived in Whitehorse on 8 June 1900. Yukon riverboats (left) provided an ongoing freight and passenger service from the end of rail to the Klondike. Sleighs replaced the boats when the river was frozen.

Heney's Red Line Transportation Company hauled freight and construction
material to the grade until the last spike was driven. Here, a combined
Red Line and construction camp readies for the final push from
Bennett to Carcross. Heney, with his two dogs, is front right.

A boisterous crowd of Alaskans and Yukoners witnessed the driving of the "Golden Spike" at Carcross, Yukon on 29 July 1900.

By August 1900, the railway was open from Skagway to Whitehorse, riding on
spindly legs as it hugged the moutainsides. Today, the grade is cemented and
bolted to the rockface, and the clean rockcuts are as stained and weathered as
the mountains from which they were blasted.

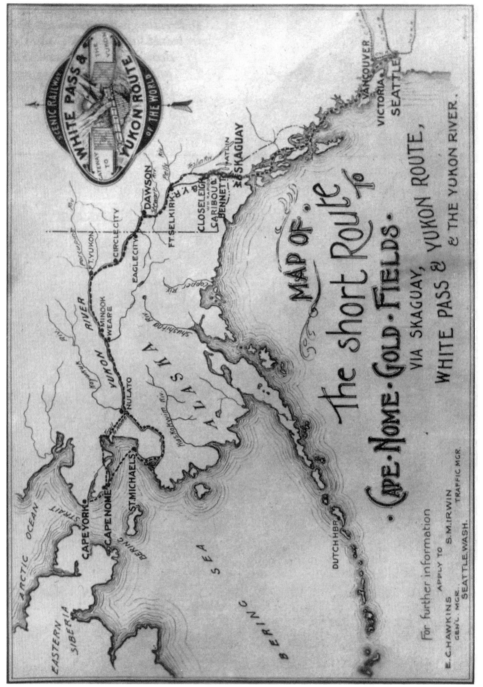

lights. Three men against thirty-five strikers did not afford healthy odds. Heney had been promised help from Deputy Marshal Tanner and some hastily sworn deputies, but they had not arrived.

As they emerged from the darkness, the strikers were suddenly caught in the full glare of the headlights. White, a powerfully built Englishman, ordered his men to halt and he advanced confidently, alone, drawing his revolver from its holster as he came. Dr. Whiting moved out to meet him. In a flash, Whiting struck White on the head with his Winchester rifle, breaking the stock. White crumbled to the ground. The strikers stood by horrified, their eyes riveted on their fallen leader, who was writhing helplessly on the frozen snow.

Heney, Whiting, and Middaugh stood facing the mob, flanking the fallen White. They challenged the strikers to attack again. There was no move. They had had enough. Leaving White, they vanished into the night just as the Deputy Marshal and his posse arrived on the scene, too late to take part in the action. Three men, two rifles, and a club had already stopped the strikers cold.

The three carried the strikers' fallen leader to the commissary, where Dr. Whiting reversed his role and did everything possible to relieve White's suffering. Then White was placed on a handcar and removed to the city jail.

"All of this is wrong," lamented the *Skagway Alaskan* on the day following the attack, "and unless the strikers change their methods the better it will be for all concerned. The strikers have nothing to lose, whereas the city of Skagway has everything to lose. The citizens received the strikers in good faith and yesterday's action was a poor return for all the kindness extended to them."[39]

White was later charged with assault and sentenced to six months in prison, which he served at Sitka, Alaska.

The battle of Camp 1 was the beginning of the end. By March 15, more than a hundred men had returned to the grade shouting "Anarchists be damned!" More followed on March 16, and by March 17 the entire strike organization had collapsed. "INTELLIGENT MEN CONFESS THEIR GRIEVOUS MISTAKE," headlined the *Skagway News*. "These respectable, law-abiding men allowed themselves to be dictated to by a few agitators and anarchists who have no doubt devoted more time to raising hell than providing for their families."[40]

The day after his arrival in Skagway, Hawkins wrote to Graves: "You will be pleased to learn that the strike is a thing of the past; no damage done and we are in as good standing with the community as before the strike began. Skagway is very much disgusted with the strike and the manner in which it was conducted."

The strike now behind him, Hawkins turned his attention to the problem of releasing the grade from the grip of winter and pushing the rails into Bennett by the first week in July.

Sixteen

ON TO BENNETT CITY

THROUGHOUT MARCH the main problem facing the railway was snow. It was now too deep on the ground to justify the enormous cost of paying men to remove it. "Abandon all attempts to open up new work in the snow," Hawkins instructed Heney in a sudden effort to economize. "Reduce your force to about 300 or 350 men and do not exceed this number until you get further orders."[1]

Within a week of receiving Hawkins's instructions, Heney cut manpower north of the summit to 275 men. Some fifty men were sent south to put the finishing touches on thirty-seven bridges, which had a combined length of 4,095 feet.[2] When weather permitted, they were also kept busy clearing the snow off the completed twenty-five miles of main line, sidings, and switches, and building two more warehouses to accommodate the increasing amount of freight. Ship after ship unloaded freight on Skagway's wharves and the beaches of Dyea. Tempers flared as shippers ran between packers, tramline operators, railway freight agents, and Brackett, urgently seeking any means of transporting their supplies. The railway's freight-handling facilities were not yet in place, and the movement of goods beyond the summit to Log Cabin and Bennett by horse-drawn sleighs over the winter roads often proved to be more than Heney's Red Line Transportation Company could effectively handle.

Nevertheless, an immense amount of freight was moved inland by all of the existing modes of transportation. But because of the snowstorms, the railway could not always deliver its share. This seriously affected the railway's income. Even the earnings expected from the Brackett road failed to materialize. During the last weeks of winter, when the railway was often snowbound, thousands of tons of freight were transported through the White Pass by independent packers, who had successfully outflanked Brackett's toll-gates. "This was made possible," Hawkins explained to Graves, "by the vast accumulation of snow and ice which piled up in the canyons and ravines, giving first class sledding over what is normally an impassable canyon and what helped the packers injure the railway. For the past few weeks the Brackett Wagon Road has earned us nothing." He assured Graves, however, that "next year when our snowsheds are erected and we have a rotary snowplow, we shall have no such conditions to contend with."[3]

With the approach of spring the freight situation and the weather gradually improved. The railway started to deliver freight to the summit on a fairly regular basis and transfer it to the Red Line Company. Heney's overland freight operations, however, became virtually immobile when the spring sun started to melt the snow road and the lake ice along the route turned to mush.

In letter after letter to Graves, Hawkins emphasized the need to eliminate the cumbersome horse-drawn sleighs and wagons operating between the end of steel and Bennett. "It is of the greatest necessity to push our construction and get the tracks to Bennett, and when the snow melts we should have the largest possible force of labourers that can be procured." Hawkins pleaded with Graves to arrange the finances required to support this expanded work force. These men, he insisted, should be on the ground not later than the first of May. "Of the uncompleted line there are seven miles of heavy rock work between the summit and Lake Bennett and we must cover the ground fully with labourers. In the meantime we will hold our manpower to 300 until the snow melts and we can get to the ground."[4]

Hawkins offered to travel to Seattle, or even Chicago, to discuss the manpower issue personally with Graves. He explained in a progress report that Heney and his workers beyond the summit were faced with the burden of drilling, dynamiting, and moving in excess of 110,000 cubic yards of rock, to say nothing of building the grade and laying the track. And, in addition to the normal grade work, more than 3,000 linear feet of bridges would have to be built across the deep canyons near Summit Lake before a foot of track could be laid -- all to be completed by July.

Heney had been hauling timbers and material over the snow to the bridge sites ever since the end of the strike, and by the middle of April he had supplied the right-of-way between the summit and Bennett with tons of construction material, including timbers, rail, ties, and track iron. These preconstruction deliveries would make up for the delays suffered in 1898 because of Heney's inability at that time to deliver material to the bridge sites until each canyon and ravine south of the summit had been reached by the railway track.[5]

Hawkins was worried. He was overworked, a situation that aggravated his recurring stomach trouble. He was frustrated because at times quick answers were required from Graves but often did not arrive in time. Supportive as Graves was, he was thousands of miles away from the action. Graves's activities were centred in Ottawa, Washington, and Chicago, with occasional trips to Seattle. Close Brothers, the final arbiters of all major questions, were even further from the scene. This wide network of decision centres was loosely knitted together by the telegraph and postal services of three countries. The weak link was the relatively slow steamship service betwen Skagway and the telegraph office in Seattle. Five days could elapse before a telegram dispatched from Skagway would arrive in Seattle for transmission to Graves in Chicago. Graves's answer could take another five days to reach Skagway, even if a ship departed on the day his answering telegram arrived in Seattle. Both men were dealing with important questions with a communications system that, even under ideal conditions, caused a ten- to twelve-day gap between message and reply.

ALTHOUGH GRAVES insisted that expenses be kept to a minimum and construction reduced to a crawl, Hawkins continued to push the decimated work force to the limit of its endurance. Fortunately Heney, whom Hawkins now referred to as "the contractor," was a master at extracting the best his men had to offer. He directed, inspired, coaxed, and demanded a level of performance beyond the experience of his unskilled crews. And when he heard of a slowdown, or a reluctance to carry out a difficult job because of danger or fear, Heney would motivate the men by tackling it himself.

There was no question that Hawkins was the engineer-in-chief and general manager, responsible in every respect to Graves for the results expected by Close Brothers and the shareholders. But it was Heney who directed the men who blasted the rock, tunnelled the mountain, bridged the canyons, shovelled the snow, and ripped the grade out of miles of granite. And now Heney had not only delivered the construction material, he had completed 6.3 miles of grade north of the summit and had cleared the bush, timber, and snow off an additional mile and a half of surveyed line, making it ready for future grading operations.

Heney seemed tireless. A tent and bed were reserved for him at every construction camp. When passing through he often would indulge in a shot or two of whisky, a meal, a few hours' sleep, and then, mounting a fresh horse, he would ride off to deal with construction problems involving rock cuts, blasting plans, bridges, fills, the delivery of construction material to key work sites, and the health of his men. As well, he was responsible for moving the railway's commercial freight from the end of rail at the summit to Log Cabin and Bennett, by way of his Red Line Transportation Company – an organization that was, by agreement with Hawkins, transporting the railway's construction supplies at cost. Heney was accomplishing more than could be expected, given the limited resources he had. But with construction work curtailed by foul weather, snowdrifts, and a reduced workforce, rumours began to circulate that the railway could not possibly reach Lake Bennett until late August or September. There were even stories that the project might not reach Bennett at all. These persistent rumours dismayed some shippers, who decided to transport their freight to Dawson and the Klondike via St. Michael and the Lower Yukon River steamboats – the original all-water route that the railway was supposed to eliminate by offering a faster and less expensive system.[6]

This was Hawkins's dilemma. Until the weather improved it was not realistic to employ a large work force, even if the funds were available. Graves, influenced by signals from London, was insisting that Hawkins keep his expenses down "to the lowest possible notch." But until the railway reached Lake Bennett, its earnings would be minimal – hardly enough to pay operating expenses, let alone finance the construction of the railway. To reach Bennett would require the infusion of a large amount of fresh capital, a prospect that London wished to avoid. One thing was certain, unless a way could be found to finance the completion of the railway to Bennett, other than from freight earnings, it was unlikely the railway could reach there before the advent of winter. By that time shippers would have written off the railway as a realistic route to the Klondike.[7]

Already the three Chilkoot aerial tramlines, now combined and operating as the Chilkoot Railroad & Transport Company, were becoming a threat to the White Pass Railway. Managed by Brackett's arch enemy, Huch C. Wallace, the reorganized aerial operation was offering freight service across the Chilkoot Pass to Crater Lake, and a packer service from the end of the tramline to Lindeman Lake and Lake Bennett at a rate lower than the railway's. The *Skagway-Atlin Budget* was helping their efforts by publishing anti-White Pass and anti-railway stories. Southern shippers, who knew next to nothing about conditions within the passes or the extremely limited capacity of Wallace's new aerial operation, were starting to send freight through the Chilkoot Pass. As a consequence, the tramline was receiving more freight business than it could handle.

During April, Wallace announced his intention to increase the capacity of the aerial tramline by extending it from Crater Lake at Chilkoot Summit to Lake Bennett, providing a complete aerial transportation link from Dyea to the head of Yukon River navigation, an impressive undertaking that was expected to cost $300,000. This figure, added to the $200,000 spent on the construction of the three original tramline systems, would result in a $500,000 outlay. Because of the enormous investment required to construct the White Pass Railway, this relatively low investment could give the tramline a distinct advantage should a freight war develop between Wallace's tramline and Hawkins's rails.

The threat of the Chilkoot Pass tramline operations was a worry not only to Hawkins but also to Graves. In a sharp letter to Hawkins he said, "having heard from many sources that the Chilkoot tramline is taking a lot of freight from us, it is time we produced a comparative statement of the freight being carried by the railway, the packers, and the Chilkoot tramline. I have no means of knowing whether the railway is taking twice as much as the tramline, or whether the tramline is taking twice as much as the railway, or whether the packers are taking as much as both of them together. What I want are the actual facts."[8]

The facts were staring Hawkins in the face. Hundreds of tons of freight were leaving West Coast ports destined for the Klondike via Dyea and the Chilkoot tramline. Further, the Skagway wharves were alive with the tramline's agents, who were snatching freight from under the noses of the packers and the railway. They hauled it by barge to Dyea, where it awaited its turn to be carried over the Chilkoot Pass by the revitalized tramline system.

Hawkins was still convinced that the railway would ultimately emerge as the prime transportation route to the Yukon interior, but he recognized that, at this crucial time, the tramline was needed to help move the huge quantities of freight that were piling up at Skagway, Dyea, and at the summits of both passes. The truth was that neither the tramline nor the railway was in a position to deliver the quantity of freight or the quality of service that they both ultimately hoped to achieve.[9] At times snowstorms, ice, wind, or fog shut them down for days on end. The tramline frequently broke down and the railway was burdened by the effort to construct it and use it to haul freight at the same time.

Hawkins reacted to the shippers' demands and the tramline's growing threat by instructing Superintendent Whiting to use every effort to transport freight to the summit the same day it was received, "even if an extra train crew is put on and you have to go from Skagway to the summit with one engine and two freight cars."[10]

Weather and freight, construction and manpower, were not Hawkins's only problems. He also faced the difficulties of marketing a freight service that was incomplete and the harsh realities of adverse public opinion moulded by the power of the press.

The *Skagway-Atlin Budget* for months had devoted its talents and energies to attacking the White Pass Railway at every opportunity. "This foreign transportation system," it claimed, "has a knife at Skagway's business throat," and quoted the railway's advertisement in West Coast papers as proof. These ads, insisted the *Budget*, were telling prospectors they should purchase their outfits in Seattle or elsewhere before coming north.

"This persistent advertising," the paper stormed, "means nothing else but an attempt to sidetrack our local merchants. This railway now spreads its tentacles not only over business of all kinds, but goes abroad to head off the little business that might come to local businessmen and pocket that as well." Having ripped into the railway's advertising, it turned its editorial guns on the railway's senior personnel. "The officials of this monopoly sit on church and civic councils, but never fail to act in the interest of their masters. Beware of them," it wrote, "and beware of their supporters who willfully encourage the railway in every scheme against Skagway's interest."

Not only was the *Budget* condemning the railway, but it was doing its best to champion Dyea and Wallace's Chilkoot tramline, claiming that it was superior in every way. It claimed that, in a test of both passes, goods were landed at Bennett from Dyea via the Chilkoot tramline in thirty-six hours, the same tonnage taking fifty-four hours from Skagway to Bennett by the railway.

> The *Budget* has learned, that many shippers have gone to Dyea on learning the conditions existing on the White Pass & Yukon Railway. The tramline is delivering goods promptly, and does not pile them up at a point midway on the line. This fact has become generally known, and shippers are moving their freight by the Chilkoot route as fast as they can. All of this is the result of the hoggish methods of the railway which has thrown down every industry in Skagway.[11]

The railway's general traffic manager, L.H. Gray, was furious. "These libelous articles are doing us great harm," he informed Hawkins. "The *Budget* is being urged on by the Dyea Tramway people, who purchase many copies of the papers and send them broadcast throughout the country stating that it is the sentiment of a recognized Skagway newspaper."

The paper was indeed doing the railway a great deal of harm. Many southern shippers accepted the *Budget*'s claim that the White Pass railway was blocked by snow and inefficiency and that it was incapable of promptly moving freight. When Gray's agents tried to convince shippers that the *Budget*'s stories were untrue they would not listen. "They insisted," Gray informed Hawkins, "that where there is smoke there must be some fire."[12]

The *Daily Alaskan* was livid. HOW SKAGWAY IS BEING VILIFIED it headed its rebuttal to the publisher of the *Budget*'s attack.

> Commercial Interest of the Town Injured and Jeopardized by a Series of Lying, Malicious Articles Issued by a Libelous Grafter Who Has Sold Himself Body and Soul to Skagway's Enemies. Dyea and its Tramline Boosted for Pay to the Detriment of Skagway Merchants Whom the Treacherous Scoundrel is Knifing in the Back While Working his Grafts. Special Copies Mailed Away by Dyea and Tramline People – What will Skagway People Do About it?
>
> How do the citizens and businessmen of Skagway who are exerting every legitimate means to build up this community like to have their hard-earned efforts destroyed, their business interests jeopardized and the good name of Skagway traduced day in and day out by a contemptible blackmailing sheet that is a disgrace to journalism.
>
> Skagway's best interests are being injured by a newspaper without shame or character. So long as it confined its blackmailing to the White Pass railroad no one in the community felt called on to interfere. Those attacks were systematic efforts to squeeze blood money out of the railroad company. The railroad, however, has persistently refused to be bled, and this crawling publication, whose whole life has been one of slime and grafting, now turns on Skagway and her citizens.
>
> The Daily Alaskan departs from its fixed rule of avoiding any and all mention of this scurrilous sheet. . . . We feel called upon, however, after repeated urgings from prominent citizens, to let the public know just what the Budget is doing. If the citizens and merchants are satisfied to see Skagway's best interests and future growth ruined by this paper, then they must take the consequences. We at least feel that we have done our duty.[13]

Skagway's weekly newspaper, the *Skagway News*, was equally upset by the *Budget*'s constant attacks on Skagway and the railway's integrity. Commenting on why many citizens of Haines, Alaska, had stopped purchasing their supplies in Skagway, the *News* quoted Frank F. Clark, a Haines businessman, who said, "The Budget has queered this city. Ever since it started abusing Skagway we transferred our business to Juneau."[14]

Maintaining its reputation for firing from the hip, the *Budget* responded by suggesting that the *Daily Alaskan* was actually controlled by Hawkins and his group, thus accounting for the *Alaskan*'s apparent support of the railway. Roaring back in an editorial, the *Alaskan* said that the *Budget* was under the control of a blackguard.

> The Alaskan is not today, and never has been owned or controlled by the railroad company, the obscene sheet to the contrary notwithstanding. But we owe it as a duty to the citizens to defend the railroad company when false statements are published for facts that tend to paralyze and destroy the business and property interests of every person in the community. By its systematic and scurrilous attacks the Budget is doing more injury to Skagway and her commerce than it is doing to the railroad.[15]

Hawkins was dismayed. The ongoing newspaper war was creating ill-feeling between both the citizens of Skagway and Dyea and between their respective business communities. Some members of the public were even questioning the railway's integrity and this, in turn, was adversely affecting its reputation and level of business. But Hawkins could only ignore the growing bitterness between the two cities and do what he could to convince shippers that the *Budget*'s stories about the railway's ineffectiveness were entirely false. Final proof of the railway's capacity and reliability would, of course, be established only after the track reached Bennett. On that day, the railway's problems with shippers and the tramline would be over – or so Hawkins thought.

WITH APRIL CAME the start of the 1899 construction season. Hawkins had allowed the work force to expand to 500 men, and Heney sent his men to work on both sides of the summit, most of them working on bridge-building, blasting rock, shovelling snow, or reballasting sections of the existing track that had been laid on top of the snow.

Despite his persistent warnings about controlling costs, Graves was sympathetic to Hawkins's position. There was no doubt in either Hawkins's or Graves's mind that the railway would be built to Bennett. The question was how fast. Hawkins was in the unenviable position of being asked to make haste slowly while Close Brothers assessed the situation based on information provided by Graves.

The first break came on April 17, when Graves cautiously urged Hawkins to push the work as fast as he could, although no *carte blanche* release from his restrictions was offered or implied. He also admonished Hawkins over the state of his health:

I can easily understand that last winter was a very trying one for you in every way, both physically and mentally. On top of that, the financial worries coming in the spring have apparently been too much for you. If you do not take better care of yourself you will be breaking down and then we shall all be in a fine fix. . . . If you are not more careful I shall have to go out there and look after you. But at present the pot is beginning to boil and I don't want to be as far away as the Pacific coast if I can help it. But . . . if I find that you are not taking better care of yourself I am liable to start from here at anytime at the drop of the hat.[16]

Graves then left for Ottawa in search of government assistance to extend the railway beyond Bennett. Without a government grant, Graves was sure there would be little likelihood of any construction beyond Bennett during 1899. "I am quite sure," he informed Hawkins, "that you will be safe in assuming this, and hence you should do whatever you see fit towards working down our engineering staff and other forces . . . to the lowest notch, consistent with the quick and efficient completion of the work to Bennett."[17]

Completing the work to Bennett while keeping expenses down was proving to be easier said than done. Rock-blasting costs were soaring. General construction and snow-removal expenses were well above estimates. Hawkins ordered the line foremen's wages cut from forty-five cents to forty cents an hour in an effort to curb these skyrocketing costs. This effectively reduced their monthly income to approximately $100.

The rising costs were a curse, and the hoped-for blessings of spring were becoming a nightmare. The winter snow road between the summit and Bennett was being churned into a quagmire. Superintendent Whiting complained bitterly to Hawkins that Heney's teams were moving an average of only three boxcar-loads of freight from the summit to Log Cabin and Bennett each day. As a result, Whiting's summit freight facilities were in a shambles. "We have at present 200 tons of freight stored in the summit warehouse, and another 200 tons stored in 17 boxcars on the summit siding. We have 75 additional tons parked on the siding at Glacier Station, with 100 more tons jammed into the warehouse at Skagway."

Heney was in a bind. The freight rate he received from Hawkins to transport both construction and commercial freight from the summit to Log Cabin and Lake Bennett was so low that it barely covered Red Line's overhead. Nevertheless, to support the railway and keep the freight moving, Heney had been hiring teams of horses from the packers to augment his own, which now numbered more than 200. But the dreadful conditions on the winter road had led the packers to increase their rates. Heney could not meet their demands.

Superintendent Whiting, who was ultimately responsible for the movement of freight, told Hawkins that "Heney is somewhat to blame. He should either have a proper rate made for him to deliver this freight so that he can be compelled to buy sufficient teams to handle it, or we shall find that the public will soon be going via the Dyea tramlines."[18]

The appalling conditions beyond the summit and the continuing flood of freight were shortening everyone's temper. It had been a vicious winter, and now the warm penetrating rays of the sun were turning the trails and winter road into mush. The lake ice was rumbling and rotting, flooding the road where it crossed Summit, Fraser, and Portage lakes. "I question very much whether the Mounted Police will allow people to risk their property and lives in attempting to pass over the lakes," Whiting told Hawkins in a letter informing him that there were now 350 tons of freight stacked all over the summit, an additional sixteen carloads of freight on the summit siding, and another 300 tons at Skagway waiting to be transported north to the summit.[19]

The one White Pass official who always appeared cheerful and optimistic was the General Traffic Manager, L.H. Gray. His tendency to ignore adverse operating conditions often sent Whiting into rages of epic proportions. Time after time Whiting appealed to Hawkins for protection from Gray's infuriating practice of promising shippers firm freight delivery dates from Seattle to Log Cabin or Bennett. Setting shipping schedules in a warm Seattle office was a simple matter for Gray. But it was Whiting in Skagway who had to deal with the shippers' wrath when they realized Gray's firm promises meant little because the railway was blocked with snow.

Gray was a man who sought the headlines. Good-natured exaggeration was his style, and the promotion of the railway as *the* route to the Yukon was his goal. "Fully ninety-nine percent of travel will pass through Skagway this summer," he announced to the *Daily Alaskan* early in May, "and the bulk of the freight will come this way." Commenting on Gray's exuberance, the *Alaskan* said, "Mr. Gray is in town and, as usual he is full of business in the interest of his railway, as well as plans for the future." Gray preferred to speak in broad concepts and generalities, and his vision of Skagway as a great northern port, servicing both passengers and freight, was attractive and convincing.

"Tourists recognize the fact that Muir glacier has lost its supremacy as a great Alaskan attraction since the White Pass Railway has been written up in all the prominent newspapers and magazines in United States and Europe," he said. He announced that the railway was advertising extensively, and that it was maintaining a close contact with the tourist agencies such as Thomas

Cook, Raymond and Whitcom, Phillip Judson, and others. "As a result these agencies are selling coupon tickets to all points reached by our railway and connecting systems. In fact," he said, "we expect the first Alaska excursion here on June 15, and we are making preparations to handle passengers and freight with promptness and dispatch."[20]

WHILE HENEY and Superintendent Whiting faced a construction grade that was awash with slush and water, Close in London, and Graves in Chicago, tussled with the problem of financing construction beyond Bennett.

Their initial approach was to find out what assistance the Canadian government could offer them. In a letter to Hawkins, Graves said, "While in Ottawa I will find out what the prospect is for getting any government aid for extensions of our railway this season, but we have practically determined not to make any special push for it. Hence, unless the government voluntarily offered it to us – which seems unlikely – we will take it for granted that there will be no extension of the road in 1899 beyond Lake Bennett."[21]

Hawkins, with Graves's approval, had already informed Hislop that construction would stop at Bennett, but that it would most likely continue from Carcross to Whitehorse Rapids during 1900, "leaving the expensive section along the shore of Lake Bennett for future considerations."

The land at Whitehorse Rapids on the Yukon River had already been surveyed for rail yards and terminal facilities and steamship wharves. Applications for the required tracts, complete with plats, had been forwarded to Ottawa for approval.

To ensure that the railway had sufficient space for its operations at Carcross, Hawkins instructed Hislop to proceed to the north end of Lake Bennett and survey the land required for railway yards, a depot, and a good steamboat landing, "all within the grounds to be occupied by the railway." Thinking of the future, Hawkins added, "If there is available ground for a townsite adjoining the track I think it would be well to have it surveyed and filed upon."[22]

Hawkins could do no more. The future rested with London.

By the middle of May the winter road was impassable. The North-West Mounted Police had stopped travel across the lakes to prevent the loss of property and life. Gray telegraphed all of his agents telling them of conditions north of the summit and ordering them not to promise freight delivery dates that the railway could not meet. Heney fought rivers of gushing water that were flooding over stretches of his prepared grade, ripping it to pieces. Whiting faced irate customers who demanded service, despite the washouts, snowslides, and overused and underpowered locomotives that had been bucking snowdrifts for months on end. Hawkins struggled to reconcile conflicting interests, increase income, move freight, and control costs.

Everything depended on reaching Bennett, where some 1,000 miners were camped waiting for spring breakup. Their supplies were packed and ready. Hundreds of small, hand-made boats and half a dozen snub-nosed, steam-powered riverboats, built during the winter, lined the shore. Men and horses were constantly on the move, freighting supplies, lumber, machinery, and logs from the surrounding hills. Permanent structures were springing up, the largest being the British Columbia government office building. The Portland Hotel was open for business, and the Merchants' Bank of Halifax was providing a full banking service. Mizony's store was buying and selling anything that would turn a dollar. And in a framed wooden structure covered with a large white tent, the *Bennett Sun* printed its first issue on Queen Victoria's birthday – May 24, 1899. After a loyal bow to "Our Most Gracious Sovereign The Queen," the paper announced that it would be independent, print the news, and turn its "withering heat on those of a dishonest or grafting nature."

Extending the hand of fraternal friendship, the *Daily Alaskan* offered the fledgling paper (which would one day become the *Whitehorse Star*) its hearty congratulations and warm wishes for its continuing success. An expanding Bennett, reasoned the *Daily Alaskan*, would be good business for Skagway and its growing business community.[23]

The apparent spirit of community fellowship that existed between Skagway and Bennett was not always reflected, however, by the governments of Canada and the United States. An unexpected order from Ottawa to the North-West Mounted Police effectively prevented American customs officers from accompanying bonded goods beyond White Pass summit – a point that Ottawa unofficially accepted as the boundary between Canada and Alaska. "Strange to say," Hawkins advised Graves, "this order does not apply on the Chilkoot or the business of the tramway. As far as I can see, it is a continuation of the same procedure which started last summer to prevent our construction beyond the summit." Hawkins insisted that there was no excuse for such an order. "It has been acknowledged that Log Cabin is the common meeting ground for both Canadian and American customs officers. We are losing many large shipments to the Tramway where they encounter no such trouble and prohibitory order." Hawkins asked Graves to "do something in Ottawa to have this order revoked."[24]

Graves appreciated Hawkins's problem with the Ottawa order but he did not give it a high priority. He was giving his full attention to Close Brothers' telegrams requesting the cost of completing the railway to Whitehorse Rapids on the Yukon River. Graves telegraphed Hawkins, "Ascertain soon as possible estimated cost and mileage to extend railway from Caribou Crossing to foot of Whitehorse Rapids. London expects to be able to finance this construction after completion of railroad to Lake Bennett."[25]

Graves admitted that he had not thought it possible that new construction would be attempted during 1899, "but our London people seem to begin to see daylight in connection with the financing of the Second Section of the Railway between Caribou and White Horse," he wrote to Hawkins. He took pains to explain, however, that the final decision would rest on the railway's earnings. "If the receipts are poor they will wait until there is an improvement before attempting to finance construction beyond Bennett."

There would be problems constructing and operating two sections of railway that would be separated by the twenty-seven-mile length of Lake Bennett. Graves thought that the two sections could be temporarily joined by ferries during the summer months and an over-ice sleigh and wagon road during the winter. "The cheapest way for us would be to build large scows of steel, with a shallow draught and a large deck space which would carry a number of freight cars." He envisioned the scows being towed by tugs. "It is at any rate obvious that during the work of construction of the Second Section, tugs and scows would be the proper way to get the material to the front."[26]

London's interest in the second section lifted Graves's spirits. It had been an anxious winter, full of setbacks and alarms. His English associates had not always been pleased with the general progress of the project, particularly with the railway's inability to finance its own construction at the level expected. Now, Hawkins's reports were indicating a small but steady rise in freight earnings. During April, income from freight was about $3,000 a day. Once the rails reached Bennett, however, this figure was expected to increase substantially, provided the railway's rival, the Chilkoot Tramlines, did not siphon off too much of the business. Encouraging news arrived from Washington announcing that Paul Mohr, the original surveyor of a rail route along the east side of the White Pass, had allowed his survey to lapse, leaving the Tancred-Hawkins-Hislop survey free of encumbrances.

Hawkins responded enthusiastically to London's request for information on construction costs and mileage from Carcross to the foot of Whitehorse Rapids. "I will start parties cutting a preliminary line as soon as the ice goes out and we can get men down Lake Bennett in boats," he informed Graves.

Hawkins instructed Hislop to organize the Carcross-Whitehorse Rapids survey with A.B. Lewis, a railway civil engineer, in charge. He insisted that both Hislop and Lewis see that strict secrecy be maintained. "I do not, at this time, wish this to become public. If news gets out, our right-of-way will probably be filed upon by town site boomers." He instructed Hislop to ship the required pack mules to Carcross in boats, "in such a way that the public will not know for what purpose they are intended."[27]

Graves was relieved to learn that the second section survey was under way. He now felt reasonably confident, although his new-found buoyancy was somewhat tempered by the growing threat of the Chilkoot tramline. From all reports, it was capturing a far greater share of the northbound freight than either Hawkins or Gray had expected. Hawkins had repeatedly registered his concern about its irritating ability to survive and prosper despite reports from Gray and others that its demise was imminent.

When Hawkins suggested to Graves that it would be to the railway's advantage to purchase the tramline and shut it down, he was given authority to open negotiations with the tramline's officials in Seattle, with the understanding that the final agreement would be made by Graves himself.

In Seattle, Hawkins learned that most of the tramline's directors were opposed to Wallace's proposal to extend its facilities to Bennett, although they stated that its present operation from Dyea to Chilkoot summit was viable and could continue operating for years to come. Countering this argument, Hawkins suggested that as soon as the railway reached Bennett, the tramline's ability to attract volume freight would be substantially reduced. He argued that the tramline's shareholders could recover a portion of their capital by selling the entire aerial operation to the railway for a reasonable sum, a proposal that appealed to J.D. Farrell, a major investor in the Chilkoot Tramline system who now doubted its ability to survive. Patterning his proposal on the Brackett road agreement, Hawkins suggested that the purchase price, yet to be agreed upon, could be paid to the tramline's shareholders by applying a "tonnage tax" based on each ton of freight transported to Bennett by the railway. Farrell agreed, subject to arriving at an acceptable purchase price for the three combined tramlines, which, together, had cost $200,000 to build.

Hawkins wrote to Graves stating, "I feel convinced that the purchase of the tramline will add materially to our strength, from a financial point of view. I hope that you can make a deal with Mr. Hugh Wallace."[28]

During May, Wallace, Farrell, and Teal, each official representing one of the original three tramlines, completed a deal with Graves and Hawkins. The railway bought the three aerial tramline companies for $100,000 to be paid by a "tonnage tax" of five dollars per ton transported by the railway after July 10, 1899 – coal, lumber, and ore exempted. Should a balance remain at the end of one year, it was to be cashed out by the railway in one single payment. All payments were to be made to the joint account of the three tramlines and distributed in proportion to their respective investments.

Wallace, the peppery manager of the combined tramlines, balked at the deal. He insisted that the combined tramlines could successfully compete with the railway and produce a handsome profit for their shareholders if his plan to extend the operation to Bennett was realized. But the voices of Farrell and Teal prevailed. Wallace was silenced and the agreement approved. All that remained now was for the railway to take possession of the tramlines' property and equipment.[29]

Everyone connected with the purchase of the tramlines had been sworn to secrecy, and all meetings had been held behind closed doors. But within a few days, the story of the purchase had leaked out. Writing to Graves, Hawkins said, "You will be greatly vexed to learn that in spite of the precautions which we had taken, the whole scheme was elaborately unfolded in the *Seattle P-I*, and now everyone knows about the affair, so there is practically no use in attempting to keep the matter quiet."

Hawkins was livid. No one would admit to breaking the silence. Wallace claimed that the information had been leaked by Gray, although this was never proved. Hawkins was a private man, and an honest man, but he had yet to learn that trying to manage the news is a mug's game.

Despite the unwanted publicity he was glad that the problem was solved. "The tramway could have made a very formidable rival," Hawkins wrote to Graves, "and I cannot express to you the feeling of relief to have this thing closed up. I think that it will be better to leave everything just as it is for the present; we can take it down later if we find that we can dispose of the machinery."[30]

The tramline's champion, the *Skagway-Atlin Budget*, blasted the sale. "It is now so arranged that tribute must be paid to this English Company for every pound of goods that is moved from the wharves of Dyea and Skagway to Bennett." Even George Brackett, who was now associated with the railway through the sale of his road, was targeted as an enemy of Skagway. "Through the machinations of George Brackett, the wagon road is controlled by the railway which," the *Budget* ranted, "was built by British money and manned by a band of pirates."[31]

BY EARLY JUNE, 1899, all rock work between Fraser Lake and the outskirts of Bennett was completed. All through the winter months, Heney's gangs had been drilling and blasting their way through the heavy rock formations that barred the way to Bennett. Little work had been done along Summit Lake. The grade line along its rocky shore was still covered in snow, and the winds that funnelled through the pass never seemed to stop.

By noon each day the warm sun had melted the snow, creating torrents of water that rampaged over the grade, causing washouts and floods that, in places, brought work to a standstill. At night the temperature dropped, and by morning the work would be once again encased in ice. The deep ravines were filled with snow, forcing Heney's construction crews to shovel them out before they could be bridged or filled with rock. "At times," Hawkins said, "it is a puzzle to know whether it is better to shovel the snow, or simply wait for the sun to melt it."

Hawkins at first believed that, with luck, Heney could complete the line to Bennett by July 1, but the weather forced him to revise his estimate. "I think it will be impossible to finish track laying to Bennett by July 1," he advised Graves, "but we believe that we can reach there sometime between the 12th and 15th of July." Then he added, "At the present time, I sincerely wish that we did not have a pound of freight to handle until we reach Lake Bennett with our trains."[32]

The tempo of construction gradually increased as the weather warmed and the dregs of winter flowed from beneath the rotting and collapsing drifts. Manpower recruitment was reinstated, although the results were not encouraging. Knowledge of the railway's plans to build the second section had not been made public. Thinking that work would cease after the rails reached Bennett, the men refused to travel north for only two months' employment. Many men already on the payroll were planning to leave for either the Klondike or Atlin gold-fields as soon as the mining season opened. The exodus would decimate the work force, as it had done the previous year during the Atlin excitement.

On top of this, there was now a possibility of another strike. A Seattle private detective hired by Hawkins reported the old strike organization still existed in part, and that it was being encouraged by the *Skagway-Atlin Budget*. Referring to it as a scandalous and libellous sheet, Hawkins grumbled that "its sole object is personal revenge, that every item is so magnified and distorted as to be hardly recognizable."[33]

Although burdened with construction, financial, manpower, and freight problems, and indifferent health, Hawkins never neglected the simple tasks that came his way, such as meeting General William Booth's daughter, Commissioner Evangeline Cory Booth of the Salvation Army, who had arrived in Skagway on a northern tour of inspection; or arranging for passes for the Reverend Mister Sinclair, his books, and portable organ, which he used to minister to the miners on the trail; or providing free transportation for the Victorian Order of Nurses, who were on constant errands of mercy between Skagway and Lake Bennett and beyond; or donating an American flag and a flagpole to the Skagway Chamber of Commerce to be raised on the summit of White Pass near the North-West Mounted Police pole, which was flying the Union Jack. "I will furnish the necessary cords and pulleys," he told the Chamber president, "as well as provide transportation for your committee when you raise the flag."

He was capable of executing broad and complicated undertakings with consummate skill and a deft hand. Yet he was a frugal man concerned with detail. To achieve a proper departmental distribution of the monthly electricity bill, he instructed A.L. Berdoe, the company auditor, to produce a list showing "how much candle power has been consumed each month" by the various railway offices in Skagway.[34] And he possessed great foresight. When a midnight fire started in E.S. Brown's shoe store, Hawkins and his staff were out spraying the railway depot with water, using a system of fire hoses he had earlier ordered installed in case of such an emergency. The fire quickly destroyed seven of Skagway's principal commercial buildings. Exploding cases of benzine, dynamite, and small-arms ammunition added to the confusion, scattering the crowds of onlookers and endangering the lives of the firemen. Sparks flew from the roaring flames, landing on the surrounding roofs. By early morning a block of buildings was nothing but a jumble of burned timbers and mounds of smouldering ash.[35]

He detested his own excuses as much as he did others'. "I can not begin to tell you how much I dislike to make explanations or apologies," he wrote to Graves, "but the cold fact is it is going to be difficult to reach Lake Bennett by the middle of July." The main problem was snow at the summit. Its depth averaged twelve feet for more than six miles, and to achieve the proper slope, the cut through it would have to be forty feet wide at the top. "You can see to shovel out this vast quantity of snow, which is very hard in places, would be a costly and difficult undertaking; and by the time we employed hundreds of men to shovel it out it would be melted out by the sun."[36]

Snowdrifts prevented construction for six miles north of the summit, and the rotting ice on Summit Lake could no longer support the heavy freight convoys. This left Heney facing a gap between the summit and the start of his incomplete railway grade, which he was already using as a replacement for the now impassable winter road. To fill the gap, he dynamited the ice on Summit Lake, creating a channel for a steam tug and scows, which he had procured in Seattle, transported on the railway to White Pass summit, and manhandled to the ice-encrusted lakeshore. Freight was transferred from trains to wagons and hauled to the scows, which were then towed to the north end of the lake. Two miles of quagmire separated the lake from the railway grade. "We have put in a great deal of work on this trail," Hawkins informed Graves. "We have changed it from a pack trail to a sleigh road, and then back to a pack trail, and every day it gets worse." At the northern end of the lake, freight was transferred from the scows to pack trains for onward shipment along the mucky pack trail to the railway grade. Here the freight was transferred again, this time to wagons, which rumbled over the usable portions of the grade to Log Cabin and Bennett. It was a tedious and costly operation that lost money for both Heney and the railway.[37]

It was imperative that the shattered gap between the summit and Bennett be closed by rail without delay. It was June 6, and Hawkins had had enough of pack trains, sleighs, wagons, steam tugs, and a winter road that had been churned into mud by the pounding feet of the horses and piercing rays of the sun.

On June 7, Hawkins dispatched two telegrams over the railway's telegraph system. The first to John Hislop: DO UTMOST TO CARRY TRACK TO BENNETT BY JULY 1 REGARDLESS OF QUALITY OF WORK. The second to Heney: VERY NECESSARY TO COMPLETE LINE TO BENNETT BY JULY 1. DO YOUR BEST.

Neither Heney nor Hislop needed urging. They were as anxious to reach Bennett as Hawkins. Heney was ready. He had been planning the final push for months. The material was on the ground, the camps were established, and except for six miles of slowly melting drifts north of the summit, the grade was clear of snow, although it was still rough in spots and large areas were either under water or had been washed out by the rampaging spring floods.

Eight hundred and seventy-one men were spread out along the grade. The powdermen and drillers were concentrated at Summit Lake, shattering a mile and a half of rock along the lakeshore. With each blast, showers of rock, snow, and debris spattered across the surface of the lake, disturbing the open water, cracking and discolouring the remaining ice.

Heney suggested that, to save time, several bridges could be eliminated by replacing them with rock fills. Hundreds of tons of rock were blasted from the surrounding outcroppings and hauled by wagons to the canyons and hollows to provide a base for the grade.

Two hundred men were dispatched to the summit to shovel snow. Some men complained that the combined weight of the snow and their shovels was too heavy to handle by the middle of a ten-hour shift. Without Heney's knowledge, the blacksmith obliged many of them by trimming three inches of metal off their shovels during the final all-out attack on the summit drifts.

By the middle of June, a rough and ready grade had been completed from six miles north of the summit to Bennett, and a heavy concentration of men was removing the last of the snow from the summit grade line. The rock work along Summit Lake was almost complete. The work was fast and furious. One man had been killed and two seriously injured in a snow slide. After the dead man and his two injured companions were removed from the snow, the work continued – the incident vividly remembered by some and soon forgotten by others.

On June 20, Heney announced that he had opened up six miles of grade on the summit section and that the first four miles were almost ready for rails. Much grade construction north of the summit remained incomplete, but the opening of the summit section created a rough grade line from the unofficial boundary to Lake Bennett.

Traffic on the railway between Skagway and the summit was temporarily suspended, and all of the railway's manpower was dispatched to the summit to help remove the last of the snow and distribute ties, rail, and track iron to the construction front.

On June 21, the men started laying track towards Bennett. By the evening of June 22, the rail was three and a half miles beyond the two White Pass flagpoles. Hawkins was both ecstatic and relieved. "By the first of July we expect to have our tracks to Log Cabin and sometime between the sixth and tenth of July we will, in all probability, be running trains direct to Bennett," Hawkins informed J.H. Greer, the railway's traffic agent in Victoria. "You can make bets with your friends who have been prophesying that we would not reach Bennett before the first of August, the first of September, or even the first of October."[38]

Already, construction work trains were moving back and forth north of the summit, delivering track iron to the gangs who were laying steel at a rate of a mile a day. By the night of June 28, the track was more than eight miles into British Columbia. The gangs gradually increased speed, and by June 30 they were a few hundred yards south of Log Cabin. They worked around the clock.

The Sunday no-work rule was ignored. Speed was the only consideration. Little attention was paid to the quality of the work. That could come later. "We will be busy all summer getting the track surfaced and ballasted, and brought to grade and alignment," Hawkins reported to Graves.[39]

Hawkins informed Graves by letter that his preliminary estimate of the construction cost of the Carcross to Whitehorse extension would be $751,825. "This estimate is based on doing the job in a favourable season of the year and before the frost and snow. If done during the winter," he said, "the work will cost twice as much as this amount."

Lewis, the divisional engineer, was of the opinion that the line could be constructed without long loops and curves, and that the grades would not exceed 105 feet to the mile. "There will be very little rock work," concluded Hawkins, "and a large proportion of the line can be constructed by teams and scrapers after clearing off the brush."[40] This was a totally unrealistic assessment that failed to recognize that hidden beneath the surface of Lewis's preliminary line were large interlocking tracts of permanently frozen ground.

Heney directed construction from dawn to dusk and on into the grey light of the northern night sky. He rode the summit to Bennett grade on horseback, hitched rides on the supply wagons, travelled with the work trains, and waded through water and muck to reach the work sites ahead of the advancing rails. He cajoled and coaxed, urged and ordered, and, when necessary, demanded a level of performance that exceeded the expectations of Hawkins and the men themselves. This final drive to Bennett firmly placed the mantle of leadership around Heney's shoulders. Wherever there was a serious problem, he was there with his high boots covered with mud and a cigar gripped between his teeth. With the help of engineering drawings spread out on the ground, the corners anchored with stones, he conferred with Hawkins, Hislop, and his construction foreman about everything from bridge construction and curvatures to the locations of construction camps.

There were constant distractions that demanded Heney's time and energy; some pleasant, some not. On June 30, two motion-picture photographers, Thomas Crahan and R.K. Bonine of the Thomas Edison Company of New Jersey, arrived to take "kinetoscopic views" of the Klondike gold rush, which included shooting motion pictures of the railway and the construction between the summit and Lake Bennett. Heney found time for them, although as always, they interrupted the rhythm of the work in their eagerness to capture the essence of the action and the drama of the scene.[41]

A more pleasing distraction was a letter from Hawkins inviting him to bid, as an independent contractor, on the construction of a section of the railway beyond Bennett. "I have received confidential advice from Chicago," Hawkins wrote, "that our London people are expecting to go on this season with the construction of the railway from Caribou Crossing to a point near Whitehorse Rapids."

Hawkins expressed his confidence in Heney's ability to handle the contract. "It will be our policy to give you preference as against other contractors making the same bid." He told Heney that the Pacific Contract Company would no longer construct the railway as it had in the past, but that it would sub-contract sections "of such lengths as can be guaranteed by the Contractor to finish in a certain length of time."

Hawkins advised Heney that the company would be prepared to sell him any supplies and construction material it had on hand after reaching Lake Bennett. "This will probably not require cash but could be paid for in easy monthly payments, as the work progresses," he said. Heney was warned not to make the information public.[42]

This was the day Heney had been waiting for. If the Whitehorse extension was authorized, and he was given the contract to build it, he would become the contractor – the position he had been hoping for ever since that meeting more than a year ago in the St. James Hotel.

By July 1, the railway tracks had passed through Log Cabin, which was glutted with freight, horses, and men. The railway line was rough near the construction front, and work trains had to crawl along to prevent derailment or a serious accident that could delay construction. But already Heney's gangs were busy aligning and ballasting the track from the summit forward, readying it for freight and passenger operations.

The track was within three miles of Bennett on July 3, when progress was temporarily halted by an unfinished bridge. Working through the night, the bridge gang finished it on the morning of July 4, and by noon the track gangs had laid rails across its deck. The work trains immediately passed through.

More than 1,000 men were now labouring on construction – 100 of them south of the summit and 900 strung along the right-of-way from the summit to Bennett. Two ten-hour shifts kept construction moving at a relentless pace. The whistles of the work trains and the resounding clang of steel against steel echoed from the hills as the work gangs followed the descending grade to the lakeshore and the bustling town of Bennett.

July 6, 1899, dawned bright and clear. The sun-tipped mountain peaks gave promise of a glittering summer day. This day would mark the completion of the White Pass and Yukon Railway from Skagway to Bennett, "an event," said the *Daily Alaskan*, "that would mark a never to be forgotten era in the history of Alaska." The article went on:

> Heretofore, Bennett has been the fixed star of the pilgrims. It was the packer's Mecca for there he unburdened his load, having accomplished a long and perilous journey. No matter whether the summit was crossed by the White Pass or the Chilkoot, Bennett was his goal. Now, with the completion of the railroad from salt water to the head of Yukon navigation the terrors of the two passes will be known no more.
>
> There now remains but one way to reach the interior from Lynn Canal and that is by the railroad. What was formerly an all winter's job for the gold seekers can now be achieved in four hours' time and for less than one-tenth of the financial outlay. Mind and money has scored a triumph over the past. The groans of the overburdened pack horses and the curses of the mule train conductors have died away along this route forever. Today the defiant snort of the iron horse reverberates through the White Pass that is strewn with the whitening bones of the pack animals who died in harness along a bloody and profane trail.
>
> To Skagway, Bennett, and the entire valley of the great Yukon, as well as Atlin and the whole northwest country, this is the most important day since the discovery of gold in the Klondike.

Hawkins could hardly disagree with the newspaper's sentiments. Supported by his two outstanding lieutenants, Hislop and Heney, he had successfully reached the railway's first objective, and he had attained it despite the weather, despite the terrain, and despite the often perplexing activities of arrogant men.

Hawkins had ordered that a fitting ceremony be organized for the driving of the Bennett last spike, and that thirty of Skagway's most prominent and influential citizens be invited as guests of the railway.

At eight in the morning, the congenial party, which included Hawkins's wife, boarded the regular passenger train at the Skagway depot and, after a short ride up Broadway, they entered the coastal forest. As the train gained Inspiration Point, seventeen miles north of Skagway, it passed beneath a ragged row of splintered mountain peaks that seemed to have burst through the glacial ice. Beyond, on the opposite side of the pass, could be seen countless waterfalls dropping gracefully into space, and occasionally there were spectacular glimpses of the Skagway River as it rushed down its narrow gorge to the sea.

At the summit, the guests were given lunch. Superintendent Whiting ensured that everyone present was provided with food from a bountiful table as well as generous lashings of the finest liquor that money could buy.

Because the track beyond the summit had yet to be properly aligned and ballasted, the guests were transferred after lunch from the railway's well-sprung passenger coaches to hard-riding flat cars equipped with wooden benches and little else. With a blast of the locomotive's whistle they were off.

After a brief stop at Log Cabin, the train continued its lurching, pitching journey towards Bennett, arriving at its southern outskirts at two o'clock. There, the guests found that the track was still 300 yards short of its final destination. Ahead of them, gangs of sweating men were feverishly laying track on the barren grade. Hundreds of Klondikers and Bennett citizens lined both sides of the track, cheering the workers on – many of them leaping onto the grade to lend a hand.

When they finally arrived, the guests were escorted to Heney's commissary tent. There a banquet was served consisting of oyster soup, choices of devilled fowl, lamb cutlets, and green peas, roast sirloin of beef, boiled leg of mutton with caper sauce, asparagus, new potatoes, and string beans. For dessert there was meringue pudding, strawberry or lemon jelly, compotes of fruits, oranges, bananas, raisins, and peaches, followed by tea, coffee, wine, and spirits.

The satiated guests then joined the growing crowd of onlookers to witness the driving of the Bennett spike. At five o'clock, Hislop tapped the spike into the last tie. He handed Mrs. Hawkins a spike maul and invited her to give it a few symbolic taps. She was followed by Frank Walters, Heney's walking boss, Captain Jarvis of the North-West Mounted Police, and Heney. "In turn, each one of them," the *Daily Alaskan* reported, "gave the spike a lick for luck."

When the spike had been hammered home the sternwheel steamers *Gleaner*, *Clifford Sifton*, and *Australian*, with other small craft standing off shore, blew their whistles, joining the piercing wails of the locomotives and the spirited acclaim of the crowd. Heney's powdermen shot off twenty-one earth-shaking dynamite explosions in the mountains in rapid succession. As the thunder of the blasts rolled across the lake, Heney's teams, neatly lined up with their wagons in four columns, reared up but were reined in by the drivers.

The noise subsided. Private stocks of spirits appeared from hip pockets and lunch buckets, and the railroad was toasted on the shores of Lake Bennett by Heney's construction workers – the grunts who levered the rock and shovelled the snow, the unskilled labourers who lifted the ties and spiked the rail, the workers who shivered and sweated on the railway's emerging grade, the hourly rated employees with calloused hands who respectfully moved aside when the bosses came to inspect the work, to issue orders, or simply to remonstrate because the work was behind schedule or some standard of performance had not been met.

All that was behind them for the moment. This was a different kind of day, so they openly drank to the railroad they had built. Most of them cheered, raising their bottles, their shovels, and their mauls in the air, not because they loved the railroad, but because they felt more than a little pride in what they had accomplished.

The Reverend Mr. Sinclair, an abstainer of note, watched the milling scene. He saw Hislop lever the spike out of the tie and present it with due ceremony to Mrs. Hawkins as a memento of the day. The official guests returned to Heney's tent to toast the railway with a glass of iced champagne and prepare for the journey home.

At six o'clock the train pulled out of Bennett with many more passengers than it brought in. Early in the day, before the spike ceremony, the steamers *Gleaner* and *Australian* had landed 200 outward-bound Klondikers at Bennett – many of them loaded with gold. These rich gold-seekers had not only participated in the ceremony – for them a happy surprise – but most of them had purchased tickets to ride to Skagway on several hastily attached flat cars procured from Heney's work train. With them came a half a million dollars in gold dust. Another hundred or so Klondikers, who had been waiting at Bennett for the rails to arrive, joined the celebrating party.

The overloaded train rocked its way down the rough unballasted track. As the train passed the construction camps, the workmen cheered the boisterous Klondikers, who had provided themselves with ample stocks of beer, whisky, and rum before leaving Bennett. Because Hawkins had declared July 6 a holiday, the railway builders were in a jovial mood. And Heney, breaking his own rule regarding liquor in the camps, had distributed thirty kegs of beer along the line, which put almost every man in complete harmony with the occasion.

At the summit, the official guests were given a light snack and refreshments, while the Klondikers went in search of fresh supplies of spirits, which they had no trouble in finding among the summit's accommodating entrepreneurs.

After a short break, the train was reloaded and started its slow descent into Skagway. Laughter and the sound of bottles breaking against the rock cliffs punctuated the night, and the hooting and shouting and singing competed with the steady cadence of the locomotive's pistons. It was a night to remember. "If any Klondiker walks up the track barefooted this season," cautioned the *Skagway-Atlin Budget*, "they will cut their feet to ribbons for there is now a streak of broken glass from Bennett to Skagway."

The train pulled into the depot by the sea at eleven o'clock. Someone called for three cheers for the railroad and a chorus of 300 voices obliged, splitting the night sky with a final tiger.

"The day was one to be remembered," said the *Budget*. "All honour and all hail to Mr. Hawkins and his associates," commented the *Daily Alaskan*. "An imposing sight – one that tells the story of the onward march of civilization," wrote the *Skagway News*.

Seventeen

HENEY'S SEVENTY MILES

THE DAY AFTER they pounded home the Bennett spike, the railway finally was in business. It had forty-one miles of track, twenty miles ballasted and aligned, the rest roughly laid on an uneven grade. Eight hundred men were working to bring the grade to operating standard.

Four days later, Hawkins took over the physical assets of the three Chilkoot tramlines, and on July 13 he shut them down. He told Graves that he was allowing Wallace to transport any freight that was on hand. "I think the tramline property is worth the money . . . and I believe we can realize something on the plant by selling it."[1]

Now that the railway was complete to Bennett and the tramline's competition had been eliminated, the railway's income from both freight and passengers rose sharply. Its influence over the steamboat operators on Lake Bennett also jumped significantly, as it was now their only source of freight. No other major transportation system existed between Skagway and Bennett, other than the Brackett road, which was firmly under the railway's control.

Half of Heney's Red Line wagons and teams were set to work between the summit and Bennett supporting the work force that was upgrading the track. The rest were shipped by barge and steamboat to Carcross at the north end of Lake Bennett, where a major construction base camp was being developed for the Carcross-Whitehorse extension.

Hawkins faced the summer days with a sense of relief. The grand plan was gradually emerging. Superintendent Whiting was working to reduce the huge backlog of freight that had accumulated during the breakup of the winter road. This was his priority, but he was placed in a difficult position by Heney, who demanded that his construction freight be given priority over commercial freight. Whiting, of course, felt obliged to respond first to his customers, who insisted that they should receive the preferred treatment. Further, Heney did not always appreciate the fact that much of his construction material had to be processed by Canadian customs officials, all of which required documentation, inspections, and, at times, Whiting's personal intervention. This often caused serious delays in the delivery of critical material to the construction sites and raised the level of ill-feeling that was developing between Heney and the railway's superintendent.

"I wish to say to you," Whiting wrote to Hawkins, "that Mr. M.J. Heney and others in connection with the construction department are very desirous of placing me in a bad light, and they are, as I know from various sources, placing blame on me which is neither just nor honorable. You of course will take your own view on these matters, but I make the statement because I deem it no more than just to myself."[2]

Hawkins pleaded with him to do his best to accommodate Heney, but the tension between the operating and construction departments continued throughout the summer months.

It was understandable that dissension existed. The means of communication available to the railway's operating and construction officials were still primitive. There were still gaps in the telegraph lines, and the telephone system was so overloaded that its use had to be restricted in order to lengthen the life of its bank of dry-cell batteries.

Hawkins, nevertheless, was satisfied that the accomplishments to date would merit Graves's approval and London's endorsement. The general plan was evolving as originally perceived. Lewis and his surveyors were making headway with their line of location north of Carcross. The grade and track improvements between the summit and Bennett were progressing rapidly, allowing the locomotives to travel faster and deliver a greater volume of freight. Heney's gangs were at work building barges to carry commercial and construction freight from Bennett to Carcross, and a part of his Red Line Company was established at Carcross, ready to move material and equipment to the construction front should London finally approve the Whitehorse extension.

Hawkins had every reason to feel buoyant, particularly as London was looking favourably on extending the railway. Graves, too, was heartened by the possibility. "If we go on with the Second Section," Graves had said, "you will be able to keep your men together and go right on with the work." Continuing construction during 1899 seemed even more assured after the rail reached Bennett and income from freight and passengers had begun to increase. In anticipation of the Whitehorse extension being authorized, Graves had again written his views about the ferries that would be required to operate between

Bennett City and Carcross – a temporary measure to close the gap between the two sections of railway.

Hawkins began to prepare for the construction of the Whitehorse extension, hoping that London did not call a stand-down at the last moment, but within a few days, his worst fears were realized. On July 15, a message from Graves informed him that London had decided against constructing the extension to Whitehorse during 1899. Close's telegram was emphatic. "CANNOT POSSIBLY UNDERTAKE TO FINANCE SECOND SECTION OF RAILWAY TO FOOT OF WHITEHORSE RAPIDS IN ABSENCE OF SATISFACTORY TRAFFIC."

Graves's message also provided the surprising news that Close himself was sailing from England early in August, and that he would be coming to Skagway to inspect the railway and discuss future construction. "Under the circumstances you had better postpone activities beyond Bennett," Graves warned.[3]

The conflicting signals from London, as interpreted by Graves, were making it difficult for Hawkins to give the project a consistent sense of direction. After considering his options, he decided to complete the work in hand. He could not ignore London's restraints, but he chose to disregard them for the time being in order to maintain momentum and keep the construction work force intact. He allowed Lewis to continue plotting the Whitehorse extension, and he placed no restrictions on the building of Heney's construction camp at Carcross. He was on fairly firm ground. News of the railway's increased business and earnings had not yet reached Chicago, let alone London.

"There is no reason for our London people to be discouraged with the earnings for the month of June," Hawkins wrote to Graves. "Since reaching Bennett earnings have run about five thousand dollars per day, and we have freight enough on hand to keep up this average for some time to come. On July 10 alone we brought in $11,436.00."

As further evidence of future business, Hawkins cited the discovery of copper near Whitehorse Rapids. Exploration work was under way on the Pueblo, Carlisle, and Copper King claims. "I find that the mineral resources here are tremendous. Just before leaving the interior I learned on the very best authority of the location of three hundred thousand tons of high grade copper ore a short distance from White Horse."

Hawkins was confident that, with Graves's assistance, he could convince Close that the Whitehorse extension should be constructed without delay. "If work were commenced in a short time we could get the grading all done this fall and the track laid during the winter and in operation to White Horse by the opening of navigation." Furthermore, he was ready to propose that the twenty-seven-mile gap between Bennett City and Carcross should be closed with track along the lake's eastern shore at the same time the forty-one-mile Whitehorse extension was constructed. This would provide the Yukon and northern British Columbia with a railway approximately a hundred and ten miles in length by July 1900 – a full year ahead of Close's current timetable.[4]

Hawkins was most concerned about the overall development of the railway, but he still had to deal with the flood of details that crossed his desk. Whiting was complaining that the turntable at the summit had not been installed, which forced his locomotives to be backed more than a mile down the track to the switchback before they could be turned around, a procedure that was causing excessive wear on his locomotives' rear wheels. Complaints from shippers about goods damaged by the Red Line Transportation Company were more often than not addressed to Hawkins. "It was not to our profit that these goods were carried beyond the summit," he informed Heney, "but all of the shippers seem to be holding the railway reponsible for the affairs of the Red Line Transportation Company."[5] The railway had no sooner started to build a series of snow sheds in preparation for winter operations when work was suspended because of forest fires. Gangs of men were mobilized to fight the fires and save the snow sheds. A Boston professor, who was on an Alaskan excursion, observed that the company was not only fighting fires, but that some men were at work ballasting the track. He made a point of informing Hawkins that he would not, under any circumstances, purchase stock in a railroad that worked its men on the Sabbath. Close sailed from England on August 2, accompanied by Cowley Lambert, Chairman of the Pacific Contract Company. "I want you to meet our party in Seattle and accompany us north," Graves had written in a memo to Hawkins, "so that our English friends will have the opportunity of hearing your views about the railway in your own words. I am therefore extremely anxious that you should be with them as much as possible."[6]

Nothing could have suited Hawkins better. The group would be together aboard ship for four or five days, giving him ample time to present his case for continuing construction through the winter months. Hawkins was sure his estimate of freight the railway would carry between August and freezeup, more than 6,000 tons, would help convince Close.

Skagway welcomed Close and his party on August 20. Whiting, on Hawkins's instructions, had prepared the railway's Skagway facilities for inspection. The permanent depot was complete, the railway yards were spotless, and the wharf office building had been given a fresh coat of paint.

The next day, Close was made an Honourary Member of Camp Skagway, No. 1,

Arctic Brotherhood, a gesture that reflected Skagway's respect for the man responsible for the railway's existence, although there were some who regarded the English capitalists, with their fancy accents, as intruders to be treated with disdain.

Close and Lambert settled in the St. James Hotel where they talked to Skagway's leading citizens, who answered many of their questions about the railway's immediate future. Close quickly realized that the patterns of transportation through the White Pass and the Chilkoot Pass had changed forever the day the railway reached Bennett City. Graves's letters from Chicago and Hawkins's Trustee reports had repeatedly emphasized the importance of Bennett to the railway's freight earnings. But seeing the railway in action first hand provided both Close and Lambert with a fresh perspective, and they were encouraged by what they saw. Their original belief in the railway's success was confirmed. There was simply too much activity among the miners and prospectors, and too many reports of new discoveries of gold and copper and coal, to believe otherwise.

Close and his party, which now included Hislop and Heney, inspected the entire railway from Skagway to Bennett, the stalled extension from Carcross to Whitehorse Rapids, and the proposed rail route along the eastern shore of Lake Bennett that would link Bennett City to Carcross.

Close was particularly anxious to examine the two wooden-tracked, horse-drawn tramways, which transported boats, freight, and men around the thundering white waters of Miles Canyon and Whitehorse Rapids. They had been a source of worry since the summer of 1898. Close had received reports on the two tramways before he left England, and he had reluctantly agreed to their purchase, recognizing that the tramway service could have been a threat to the railway extension.

Norman Macaulay had built the first tramway on the east bank of the Yukon River during the winter and spring of 1898, and it was in full operation by the summer of that year. It was a primitive structure, which started at Canyon City, an unarranged muddle of log and tent-framed buildings that clung tenaciously to the river bank. Here, the lake sternwheel steamers, which could not navigate the canyon and rapids, transferred their freight to Macaulay's waiting tram cars.

Macaulay's operation was so successful that by the summer of 1899 he was contemplating the construction of a conventional railway to haul freight to his northern terminal below Whitehorse Rapids.

The success of Macaulay's tramway attracted the attention of John Hepburn, who constructed a competitive system on the west bank of the river. Hepburn's tramway virtually duplicated Macaulay's operation in every respect, but did not enjoy Macaulay's success. It was, however, a thorn in Macaulay's side. After lengthy negotiations, Macaulay had purchased Hepburn's line for $60,000. He now controlled both sides of the river for six miles between Miles Canyon and Whitehorse Rapids.

It was clear to Hawkins that the railway's Whitehorse extension would have to follow the Yukon River's west bank, part of which was already occupied by the Hepburn line. But purchasing the Hepburn operation from Macaulay would not completely solve the problem, as it would leave Macaulay operating on the east side of the river and in a position to outflank the railway.

There was only one answer – to purchase both of Macaulay's operations. After Close gave his approval, Hawkins handled the deal through C.E. Peabody, managing director of the Alaska Steamship Company – a subterfuge that concealed the railway's interest in the purchase. Peabody bought the two tramways for $185,000. Had the railway's involvement been revealed, the price may have been double that amount, or more.

Close was less than pleased about the cost of the purchase, but he accepted the inevitable. This was a practical problem with legal overtones that could only be solved by cash. He later justified the cost to the London shareholders by explaining the navigational hazards of Miles Canyon and Whitehorse Rapids, and how the lake steamers and the riverboats were linked by two tramways that outflanked these two formidable river obstructions. Without finding a way around them, he said, "the capacity of our railway would be limited to the capacity of the tramway," which was true but hardly the real problem.

Close was most impressed with the mining developments near the railway's proposed terminal below the rapids. "Had there been no river obstructions," he said, "I believe that these deposits warrant the railway building a short branch line to develop these copper properties and thus secure return traffic for our railway."[7]

To Graves and Hawkins's relief, it was obvious that Close was convinced that the construction of the extension should start without delay. At a final meeting at Bennett on August 23, 1899, Close told the railway chiefs, including Heney, that he was "perfectly happy about the permanency of the enterprise," and that he approved the construction of the extension from Bennett City to Whitehorse Rapids – a seventy-mile line he dubbed the "Second Section."

Close did, however, add one important caveat. Authorization to build the thirty-mile section along the lakeshore between Bennett City and Carcross would be withheld until arrangements to finance it had been completed in London. Close left Hawkins and Heney with the impression, however, that they would receive authorization for the Lake Bennett section before the end of the year.

A final decision involved Heney. He was selected as sub-contractor and made responsible for completing the railway to the specifications of the Pacific Contract Company, which was still controlled by the railway and managed by Hawkins. The chain of command would remain the same as before except that, for the first time since construction started, Heney was the contractor in his own right. Hawkins had recommended that Heney be hired as sub-contractor for the Second Section and later wrote that he was "an able and experienced contractor who had been in practical charge of construction of the first section."[8]

On August 24, Hawkins telegraphed Whiting from Bennett City, "WE RUSH CONSTRUCTION TO WHITE HORSE. INSTRUCT ALL AGENTS AND TRAIN CREWS TO PUSH ALL CONTRACT SUPPLIES AS RAPIDLY AS POSSIBLE."

Superintendent Whiting was uneasy. He anticipated demands being made of him that he had neither the time nor the equipment to meet. "I shall do my best to comply with the contractors' requests," he replied to Hawkins, "but I cannot do what I do not have the machinery to do with. Therefore, should there be delays . . . bringing complaints . . . you must bear in mind that I have forewarned you of their coming; and it will not be ill-will upon my part that makes the failure."

The battle between the railway operating department and the builders persisted, and the tensions between Whiting and Heney remained. "It will be almost an impossibility to handle any more freight than we are now handling," Whiting concluded. "We can hardly keep up with the freight, to say nothing of what the contractor will want."[9]

Voices of concern, or even dissent, were to be expected from time to time. But Heney was a builder, not a boxcar-counter or a record-keeper. He was a driving force who had achieved a reputation for being the one person most responsible for punching the railway through the White Pass and across the broad rocky uplands to Lake Bennett. Now he had sub-contracted to build two sections of railway, totalling seventy miles, from Bennett City to Whitehorse Rapids and he was not interested in protests or objections, no matter how justified they might be. He was determined that the demands of construction would prevail. Unless they did, he would not meet his date of completion, which he said would be no later than August 1, 1900. After that the commercial freight could flow without interruption.

Heney's most pressing problems were transporting men and materials from Bennett City to Carcross. The lake steamers could easily accommodate the men, but they were not equipped to move thousands of tons of rail, locomotives, ties, wagons, horses, dump carts, and camp supplies. Once again, Heney looked to Stikine Bill, this time to supervise the construction and operation of a large scow, which was to have a carrying capacity of 150 tons.

The scow, which was shaped like a cigar box, was built on the lakeshore near Bennett City. When it was finished, no one could tell which end was the bow and which was the stern. Stikine Bill examined his handiwork in the presence of the shipwright foreman. Finally he said, "I think that we will make this end the stern." The foreman, hoping to avoid future arguments, took a large piece of chalk and printed STERN in large letters on the chosen end. The other end became the bow. The shipwright and his men then installed the engines. When the vessel was finally launched, Stikine Bill took the helm. The ungainly craft, with steam up and her whistle blowing, engaged in trials, which were declared a great success. Her speed, however, left something to be desired. After thrashing her way back to shore with her three propellers churning at top speed, she was unceremoniously dubbed the "Torpedo Catcher." She was then loaded with rails for Carcross.

Stikine Bill backed his loaded craft away from the shore and attempted to swing it around by applying full ahead with his starboard engine, and full astern with his port engine. The "Torpedo Catcher" began to pivot. Around and around it spun, its momentum maintained by the weight of 150 tons of rail.

The crowd on shore watched with unrestrained glee as Stikine Bill attempted to bring his revolving craft under control. Someone on shore started to sing a popular song of the day, "Waltz me around again Willie," and everyone else soon joined in.

Stikine Bill stood on the deck of his whirling craft, took off his hat, and bowed repeatedly to his audience. Slowly, he brought the craft under control and pointed her "bow" to the north. Later that day, his cantankerous scow delivered the first of many cargoes of construction supplies and equipment for the Whitehorse extension and for operations along the lakeshore.[10]

HENEY WAS ready. His men were in place. Late in the morning of August 24, the long-awaited message to start constructing the grade to Whitehorse arrived at the Carcross construction camp by steamer from Bennett City. By early afternoon more than 500 men, and a hundred teams of horses pulling wagons and scrapers, were at work following Lewis's neat line of stakes, which led northward through the Watson Valley towards Whitehorse. Stikine Bill Robinson, now employed as Heney's master of horse and grading foreman, roared his commands. The line of graders ripped through the sand dunes north of Carcross and entered the scrub forest that carpeted the floor of the valley and the slopes of the surrounding hills.[11]

Far ahead, Lewis continued running his lines, searching for the most practical route for the railway through the low-lying hills, ridges, swamps, and lakes that would dictate both the integrity and direction of the grade.

There had been no time to sink sufficient soil test holes, but those that were drilled produced encouraging results. As the graders moved deeper into the valley, they found permafrost beneath the soil, something neither Hawkins nor Heney had anticipated. Its presence created unexpected delays and increased costs. "We ran into frozen ground beneath the surface," Graves later explained to the London shareholders. "It had been frozen to great depths by the intense cold of the glacial period."[12]

By September 4, thirty miles of the Whitehorse extension survey had been completed. Graves reported to London from the comfort of his Chicago office that the work was "a picnic" compared to the heavy work so far experienced. His comment might have applied to the Whitehorse extension during August and September, but Hawkins, who was often on the site, later reported that "all the material that could freeze was frozen solidly and required almost continuous blasting."[13] But Heney had the men, the material, the powder, and the contract to do the job, and the forty miles of winter ice and summer swamps were obstacles he was prepared to meet as a full-fledged contractor in his own right.

Heney's plan was to complete the grade and lay the track from Carcross to Lewis Lake, fifteen miles to the north, in time for this section of railway to be in operation before the advent of winter. This would provide him with rail transportation between his base supply camp at Carcross and the head of construction at the lake.

By September 12, the grade had reached a small canyon at the lower end of the lake, where preparations were under way to bridge the canyon with a small trestle that would lead the railway to the lake's western shore. Hawkins's engineers decided to lower the water level of the lake by ten feet to facilitate construction of the grade along the lake and to reduce costs. On September 14, after all of Lewis's engineering calculations had been completed, Heney's men began cutting a four-foot-wide trench through a 300-foot narrow, sandy ridge that contained the southern end of the lake.

By two o'clock that afternoon, they had opened a small stream about four inches deep and two feet wide, which allowed the lake water to flow across the retaining ridge towards the Watson River valley.

Soon the accelerating flow of water began to rip out a ragged ditch. As the flow increased, it tore more sand and gravel from the banks of the ditch, widening it into a channel of water that gushed through with tremendous force, creating an ominous flood a hundred feet wide and ten feet deep. By evening, the sides of the channel had collapsed, tossing trees end over end into the water. Huge boulders were gouged from the banks and spun into the roaring torrent.

The rushing waters thundered into a natural basin downstream, creating a second lake. Still the flood continued, inching the water level up towards the lip of the newly formed lake's lower retaining bank. Suddenly, without warning, the entire channel from the upper lake collapsed, releasing an immense quantity of water that swept everything in its path. Soon a 100-foot-high waterfall was pouring from the lower lake into the valley, flooding the Watson River with mud and debris.

A group of Indians, who were drying fish some miles away, were petrified with fright. One old Indian exclaimed, "The earth's going down. You pray."

Two days later Lake Bennett was brown with mud for fifteen miles south of Carcross, and the waters were stained all the way to the North-West Mounted Police Post at Tagish Lake. The Watson River valley was covered with mud from Lewis Lake to Lake Bennett.

When the builders returned to examine the results of their work, they found that they had unintentionally lowered Lewis Lake by seventy feet, sixy feet more than planned. What were once mounds of sand beneath its surface were now mud-caked hills.

"Lewis Lake has been drained to the bottom except for a few deep holes," lamented Hawkins to Graves. "We now have to cross the newly formed canyon by means of two bridges, each one nearly 50 feet in height and 600 feet long." To a friend in Toronto, however, he described the Lewis Lake calamity as a normal construction operation. "This lake has been drained by an earth cut and lowered seventy-five feet," he said, as if it had been done on purpose.[14]

In truth, it had been a complete disaster. Unless material for construction of the two bridges was delivered from Seattle to the bridge site before freezeup, grade construction beyond Lewis Lake would be stalled. Should the materials arrive late, they would be trapped behind Lake Bennett ice until May or even early June the following year. This could delay completion of the railway well into 1901, a year or more later than Heney's target date of August 1, 1900.

Hawkins's engineering staff worked overtime to design the bridges and draw up material requirements. These were dispatched to Hussey in Seattle with orders to purchase the piles, bents, timbers, and construction iron and send them immediately to Skagway. From there, they would be rushed by train to Bennett City and loaded on lake steamers for delivery to Carcross. At Carcross, the materials would be transported to the bridge sites by work trains operating over Heney's recently laid track. In desperation, Hawkins, Hislop, and Heney appealed to the lake steamer captains to delay beaching their ships for the winter as long as possible – and to be ready to force them through surface ice if necessary.[15]

The railway was reaching a critical period in its development. Winter was only a few weeks away. The level of freight was dropping. The influx of miners had virtually ceased for the season. Revenues were down. Construction costs were up, and the Lewis Lake problem was absorbing the energies of senior engineers whose time and talents were required elsewhere.

By the end of September, Lewis's surveyors were forty miles north of Carcross, and on October 10 they entered the broad gravel bench below Whitehorse Rapids and drove in their final stake. The line survey from Carcross to Whitehorse was now complete. On the same day, Hawkins officially received the completed first section of railway between Skagway and Bennett City from the Pacific Contract Company. The railway's engineering and standard of construction had been approved by government inspectors and it was now authorized to function under the respective laws that governed the operations of railways in Canada and the United States.

Hawkins's sense of fulfilment, however, was marred by the news that a competitive transportation system – the Dyea and Chilkoot Railway Company – was preparing to begin the construction of a railway from Dyea to Whitehorse via the Chilkoot Pass. Included in the project was a proposal to drive a 3,800-foot tunnel beneath Chilkoot Pass summit.

The *Daily Alaskan* reported that it was generally conceded that "should the Chilkoot tunnel be pushed to completion and the proposed railroad be built over the pass from Dyea, the line thus created would prove a lusty rival to the White Pass & Yukon Railway, forcing it to act on the defensive, as it did in the case of the Chilkoot Tramlines – and buy out the impending rival."

North-West Mounted Police Superintendent Wood reported that the tunnel was to be twelve feet high, ten feet wide, and three-quarters of a mile long. Local newspapers reported that eleven men were already at work on the tunnel, which would cost $250,000 to build.

Hawkins dispatched engineer Alfred Williams to Dyea with instructions to determine the scheme's validity. "Perhaps we should have someone obtain employment there to observe and report on any construction activities," suggested Hawkins. It seemed that everyone had an opinion about the tunnel scheme. Rumours were spreading rapidly through the cafés, bars, and gambling joints – all of them giving rise to newspaper speculation and editorial comment. Some thought the project was backed by riverboat captains operating on the Upper Yukon River and Lake Bennett, who were determined to force the White Pass Railway to abandon its preference for the Canadian Development Company's steamers. Others reasoned that it was nothing but a wildcat scheme put forward by Dyea businessmen to "create some excitement" in what was regarded as a dying city. Many in Dyea were convinced that a deal had been struck between Canada and the United States, and that Dyea was on the brink of becoming a Canadian port. Should this be the case, they said, the tunnel-railway promoters would be in a position to earn huge returns on their investment.

Hawkins had to take the railway project seriously, although he had doubts about its design and engineering and about its suitability as a transportation system. But, for the moment, Hawkins could do little more than hold a watching brief, and hope that another transportation system was not emerging to compete with his White Pass Railway.

ON OCTOBER 20, 1899, London telegraphed Graves: "INSTRUCT BY TELEGRAM E.C. HAWKINS CAN COMMENCE CONSTRUCTION ALONG LAKE BENNETT. CLOSE."

Hawkins received the telegram on October 26. He was both elated and concerned. "I am very glad to get this very welcome word," he wrote Graves, "but for once I am a little unprepared to carry on with this work. Because of the difficult London money market I had supposed that we could do nothing until the first of next year."[16]

Hawkins could do nothing but make the best of it. He telegraphed his lieutenants instructing them to meet him at Heney's construction headquarters at Bennett City at noon, October 27. At the meeting, Hawkins acquainted Heney, Hislop, Lewis, and senior engineers with the surprising instruction he had received from London, which called for a change in plans and an acceleration of the work.

Agreement on the main thrusts of future construction was quickly reached. Lewis and his surveyors were to start immediately a line survey for the railway along the eastern shore of Lake Bennett – work that would continue through the winter months. Special attention was to be paid to the first seven miles north of Bennett City, where exceptionally difficult rock work would be encountered.

Heney would henceforth operate on two fronts – the Whitehorse extension and the twenty-seven-mile Lake Bennett railway link. His first priority would be to complete the Whitehorse extension by early June, 1900, but, at the same time, he would deploy a gang of drillers and powdermen to blast out a rough grade through the heavy rock formations along Lake Bennett's eastern shore. By late spring, when the Whitehorse grade was to be completed, his graders would be moved, gang by gang, to the Lake Bennett link, where, with picks, shovels, scrapers, and horses, they would drive towards Carcross. After the track gangs had reached Whitehorse, they would be transferred to Bennett City, where they would start laying rail on the completed sections of the Lake Bennett grade. The ferries linking the two sections of railway would then no longer be required. The connecting link would be by rail, not water.

Hussey in Seattle was instructed to secure an additional twenty-seven miles of rail and track iron for the Bennett link. By chance he located 1,700 tons of rail in Vancouver, British Columbia, which had originally been purchased to build the Mackenzie and Mann railway through the Stikine River valley. By the time the rail had reached Vancouver from the United States manufacturer, the all-Canadian route had collapsed. Subsequently it had been sold to a Japanese firm, but had never been delivered. The rail was eventually bought from the Japanese by a Seattle firm, which sold it to the White Pass railway. Thus, the rail originally manufactured for an all-Canadian route into the Yukon interior still fulfilled its destiny by becoming part of the White Pass and Yukon Railway.[17]

Hussey had proved his worth as a competent purchasing agent. He not only knew his sources of supply and how to strike a bargain, but he had the knack of anticipating requirements, often having stock available before it was ordered from Skagway. But now, once the supplies arrived in Skagway, they moved painfully slowly as winter returned to the White Pass. "When the lake freezes over and before it is sufficiently solid to support teams with loads, it will be impossible to supply the camps along the lake section, or make any progress on the work," Hawkins advised Graves, "hence it will be the middle of December or possibly the first of the year before much of a showing can be made."[18]

To keep the construction material flowing, Hawkins instructed the railway's agent at Bennett City to notify the steamboat captains that "we can keep them busy hauling railway supplies for a month or as long as navigation is open."[19]

The captains obliged, and by the middle of November, Hawkins was able to report that the lake steamers and the "Torpedo Catcher" had succeeded in delivering a huge quantity of supplies and equipment to Carcross. "We have an engine, train, coal, eighteen miles of track and track iron, and we expect to get the track to Lewis Lake this fall," Hawkins informed Hussey.[20]

The temperature was between ten and fifteen degrees below zero. Heney's work force of nearly 600 men and 130 teams was cutting and filling through the frozen sand and the cement-hard permafrost below the surface. Rail was being laid on the advancing grade north of Carcross and Heney's Red Line was delivering piles and timbers for the two bridges that would carry the railway across the boulder-strewn chasm created by the disastrous lake-lowering operation. A pile driver had been floated to the northern tip of Lake Bennett, where a 150-foot swing bridge with 260 feet of wooden approaches was being built to carry the track across the Nares River into Carcross.

Just as fall construction was gaining momentum late in October, Superintendent Whiting submitted his resignation. Hawkins accepted, but asked that he stay with the railway as mechanical superintendent in charge of the shops. Whiting declined, but agreed to remain in his position until his replacement was appointed. His resignation shocked many of the train crews and members of his staff, particularly those who had worked closely with him. Sixty of his employees organized a banquet in his honour, where he was fed a sumptuous meal and presented with a gold watch and chain. When making the presentation, Conductor Murray Miles said in part, "In presenting this watch and chain to Mr. Whiting, the employees of the road wish him to remember every time he consults it that he has the affectionate regard and esteem of each and everyone of the donors. It was a pleasure and an honour to have worked for him."[21]

The day following his departure, Whiting was replaced by J.P. Rogers. "You come amongst us with a hearty welcome," Hawkins wrote on November 30, "and I am confident your experience in railway matters will enable you to take hold of affairs in a satisfactory matter. I do not wish changes made except for cause, but no employees will be retained who become intoxicated or who gamble or are discovered in any form of dishonesty." That is the way Hawkins lived his own life, and he had little patience with anyone who did not behave in a similar manner.[22]

Hawkins then left Skagway to inspect the work on the Whitehorse extension with Hislop. As usual, he was inundated with work and interviews. "We had a time trying to get him some lunch before he left," explained his assistant and chief clerk, J.W. Young, to Hussey. "There were people chasing him like chickens after good warm corn."[23]

It was an extremely busy time for Hawkins and everyone else engaged in the construction and operations of the railway. Five new locomotive stalls were being added to the roundhouse and new railway stations were being constructed at Bennett City, White Pass, and Log Cabin. Hundreds of yards of snow fences, to control drifting snow, were being erected in the most exposed areas along the operational portions of the track. Bunkers were being designed for coal storage at strategic locations, and long snow sheds to protect the track at slide areas were being built.

The Chilkoot tunnel proposal remained a worry to Hawkins. It was reported that the Pacific Coast Steamship Company had delivered fifty-five mules as well as scrapers, dump carts, and other construction equipment to Dyea for C.H. De Witt, a packer and general contractor who had signed a $45,000 contract to construct a railway grade to the mouth of the proposed tunnel. But little was being accomplished. Hawkins was partly reassured by a report that only five men were at work on the grade and tunnel. "They have no powder, and the pack trains with supplies have failed to reach them for several days," Hawkins informed Hussey.

Graves proposed that Hawkins should consider purchasing the Dyea wharf that was being used by the railway-tunnel promotors. Hawkins rejected the proposal. "Even if we should buy it that would not prevent the proposed railway from building another wharf." He argued that owning just a portion of Dyea's waterfront facilities "would not give us any advantage in the transportation business."[24]

Speculation was rife, much of it created by bluster and promotional statements made by Michael King and L.D. Kinney, who were both deeply involved in the railway-tunnel proposal. But despite the publicity they were creating, nothing of consequence was happening. A shortage of cash was miring the project in a sea of unpaid bills. De Witt had not been paid, and sensing that something was seriously wrong, he travelled to Juneau to discuss the faltering railway-tunnel with its supporters, some of whom were members of the Juneau Chamber of Commerce. Hawkins followed him to Juneau in an attempt to assess for himself the facts surrounding the much-publicized Chilkoot tunnel scheme. There, Hawkins soon determined that the whole project was being promoted by men with champagne ideas and nothing but beer money. No settled plan of action had been adopted. No surveys were under way. No engineering studies had been completed.

De Witt threw up his hands. He was unable to collect his money from Kinney, so he pulled his outfit out of Dyea, taking his horses and equipment to Bennett City, where he set up business in association with the owners of the *Nugget Express*.

The incompetence of the scheme was later confirmed by Hawkins's chief clerk, J.W. Young, who reported that he had learned that Kinney now proposed to run his line of railway from Dyea to the steep face of Chilkoot Pass.

Here, he planned to use the power of a waterfall to lift his trains, car by car, a thousand feet in the air to the portal of the tunnel. From there, the trains would be re-assembled and passed through the tunnel to open country and on to Bennett City.

North-West Mounted Police Superintendent Wood was also keeping a watchful eye on the Chilkoot tunnel scheme. He reported to his superiors that "The manager, Mr. Stotko, on being interviewed by the Chilkoot Summit detachment, refused to divulge the names of the Syndicate – whether American or English. I notified him by letter that unless he had a proper charter, he could not tunnel under British possessions."[25]

By early December, Hawkins was satisfied that the Chilkoot railway-tunnel was a confused and improbable proposition that had little chance of succeeding under its present management and financial backers. He took the precaution, however, of asking for regular reports on any railway-tunnel activities taking place in Dyea or within the Chilkoot Pass. The tunnel's future appeared doubtful, but it could not be ignored. He had already been forced to purchase the Chilkoot tramlines, which at first glance had seemed to offer no competition but subsequently had become a threat to the railway. Now another Chilkoot transportation scheme was emerging at a critical time, and he knew that any transportation system that competed with the White Pass Railway would have the support of the independent steamship captains, who could see an advantage in having two competitive sources of freight for their ships.

During this period, Alaska was starting to come into its own. Governor John Green Brady was urging Congress to consider Alaska's future. "It is time for us to become a state." he said. "Our territory is large enough for many states, and should not only be admitted to statehood as it now stands, but it should be admitted with the understanding that it might be divided up into smaller states as the population of various portions increase."[26]

Alaska wanted recognition, as well as the federal government's understanding of its needs and its potential. "We want more United States courts, land laws, and telegraphic communications. It is not right that our telegrams should have to pass through hundreds of miles of British possessions intervening between the lower states and Alaska." But Brady's plea fell largely on deaf ears. To most people in the United States, and to the rest of the world, Alaska was a hostile land of ice and snow – a distant frontier filled with mists and misery.

In mid-December the world's popular view of Alaska came close to being realized. The heaviest snowstorm ever recorded in the area was raging from Lynn Canal to Carcross, encompassing Dyea, Skagway, and the two passes.

Captain Moore stated that it was the worst storm he had ever experienced since his arrival at Skagway Bay in 1887.

Construction came to a halt. The White Pass was all but closed by heavy drifts that covered the track from Skagway to Bennett City. Led by the railway's recently acquired rotary snowplough, which was pushed by two locomotives, a train consisting of flat cars, boxcars, and two coaches carrying twenty passengers took five hours to travel twenty miles through the snow from Bennett City to White Pass summit. South of the summit near the switchback, the rotary bored into a huge snowbank that formed the foundation of a deep, wind-blown mass of snow, which clung precariously to the steep mountainside. As the rotary churned into the base of the drift, the high-banked channel it was creating collapsed, burying the rotary and its two locomotives. The snow smashed through the rotary windows, trapping the crew in a cabin filled with steam. The train, travelling well behind the rotary, escaped the avalanche.

Forty men from the White Pass Division maintenance section, who had been assigned to the passenger cars to deal with just such an emergency, rushed to the buried rotary and locomotives and attacked the mounds of snow with their shovels, assisted by volunteers from among the passengers. They soon rescued the crews, but it took hours of more work to extract the equipment.

After an all-night battle the train finally reached Skagway at seven the following morning. Once again the railway had withstood the sharp edge of winter and won the battle. The rotary snowplough was proving its worth, as was Charlie Moriarity, a red-headed Irishman whose exploits as a rotary operator had earned him the title of "Snow King" – an epithet he jealously guarded.

Graves had great respect for the rotary men. "One's ears are deafened by the noise of the machinery and the roar of the snow," he told the London shareholders. "Clearly it is no place for a weakling. Your oil cups freeze, your feet freeze, and you have been on your legs for 48 hours and the worst is yet to come. But you stick to it like a bulldog and you get the train through. And you do – if you are a White Pass rotary man."

The rotary was a great asset to the railway's ongoing fight with winter, and the snow fences and snow sheds were also proving their worth. The unprotected areas of the railway were still subject to serious drifting, but Hawkins was sure that the day would come when snow would no longer defeat the rotary men.[27]

Throughout December 1899, railway operations between Skagway and Bennett City were constantly interrupted by violent snowstorms that raged for days on end. Almost every morning the rotary faced drifts from eight to twenty feet deep. Avalanches brought down large rocks and trees, making it difficult for the rotary to operate without damage to its revolving blades. Passengers travelling between Skagway and the summit faced white crystal walls of snow a foot beyond their coach windows, created by the biting blades of the rotary as it sliced through the drifts. Mr. Rogers, the railway's new superintendent, observed that the deep channels of snow "made parts of the railway look like snow sheds without any roof."[28]

As the winter storms subsided in the interior, Heney's construction crews stepped up their work. The Whitehorse track out of Carcross was laid towards Lewis Lake at a rate of a mile a day. Along the eastern shore of Lake Bennett, 150 of Heney's rockmen were blasting their way along Lewis's surveyed line, creating a rough grade that would be completed during the spring and summer of 1900.

With Heney now in charge of construction, Hawkins took steps to reduce the activities of the Pacific Contract Company. "I wish to close all of its departments except the forwarding of construction material to Carcross," he informed Hislop. "The Contract Company is now an item of great expense and after the present snow sheds are finished we will have no further business on hand."[29]

While the Contract Company was, by and large, becoming inactive, it was still the corporate instrument that held the primary contract for the construction of the railway and the day-to-day administration of its expenditures.

Building the railway was now Heney's responsibility, although every foot of his line would still have to meet the specifications set out in his sub-contract with the Pacific Contract Company, of which Hawkins was still chief engineer and superintendent. The new contract arrangement changed nothing of a practical nature. Hawkins, Hislop, and Heney continued to work as a team for the railway, with little thought given to the intricacies of its corporate structure. In any event, most of the shareholders of the railway companies were also shareholders of the Contract Company. "It was like making an agreement with ourselves," Graves had explained to Hawkins early in 1899.[30]

Lake Bennett was now frozen solid, so Heney's supplies, materials, and equipment were delivered from Bennett City to Carcross over the ice by his Red Line Transportation Company, which was also moving commercial freight towards frozen Whitehorse Rapids.

Stikine Bill Robinson, who had relinquished command of his now beached "Torpedo Catcher," had become Heney's grading foreman north of Carcross – a position that was already adding to his considerable reputation as a taskmaster whose bulk and mastery of profanity could provoke the most indolent toiler into spirited action.

The grade was easier between Carcross and Whitehorse and little rock work was necessary, but the temperatures plunged lower than any experienced during construction in the White Pass. It was cold working and it was cold living. The main construction camps at Carcross and Lewis Lake were rough-and-ready towns composed entirely of canvas. Out of each canvas structure emerged a blackened chimney, the smoke rising straight up in the cold, still air. The branches of the surrounding evergreens hung low under the weight of the snow. The penetrating frost hardened tent tops and stiffened fingers. Beyond the camp, deep in the trees, were the horse lines, each horse covered with a blanket during the night and hitched to a wagon, a sleigh, or a stone-boat during the day.

Stikine Bill's first love was the horses. He believed you could not pay too much for a horse, nor could you work a horse too hard, nor feed him too well. His basic test of a horse's value was the balance between the amount of oats you could get it to eat and the amount of work you could get it to do.

North of Bennett City, Heney's rock men continued to drill and blast through the rocky points that jutted into the deep waters of Lake Bennett, creating numerous cuts through which the grade would eventually pass. The shattered rock was hauled by teams and tipper carts and dumped into the heads of the numerous bays that intersected Lewis's surveyed grade line, creating solid embankments to support the coming grade. Blast and fill, fill and blast, was the Lake Bennett crew's rhythm of work, a repetitive and taxing procedure designed to eliminate hundreds of curves that would have resulted from following the lake's eastern shore.

Hawkins made preparations to report on the work's progress to Graves in Seattle. First he travelled to Bennett City, where a saddle horse was kept for his use. Together with Heney, he inspected both the Lake Bennett section and the Whitehorse extension. He was impressed with the quality of Heney's work and the rapid progress he was making in spite of the harsh winter weather.

In his report to Graves, Hawkins expressed his complete satisfaction with Heney's performance as the sub-contractor. "Mr. Heney has performed the work with great care," he said. "The work has been excellently put together and is as pretty a piece of railway grading as you could find in any part of the land. I think he takes even more pain in doing a pretty piece of work under contract than when engaged as practically a foreman of the Company."[31]

Heney's status had taken another leap forward, and before him was seventy miles of railway to construct – the first section of which, stretching from Carcross to Whitehorse Rapids, he said would be completed by June 1, 1900. Meeting that deadline would be Heney's critical test. Only then would Hawkins's faith in his competence – and his own belief in himself – be fully justified.

Eighteen

---◆---

THE BENT SPIKE

O N JANUARY 2, 1900, the railway confidently advertised in Dawson City's newspapers that "THE WHITE PASS AND YUKON RAILWAY WILL BE COMPLETED TO WHITE HORSE BY JUNE 1."

Superintendent Rogers's plans to ferry freight and passengers from Bennett City to Carcross by lake steamers were well advanced. All that remained was to complete the Whitehorse extension by the date announced and wait for the lake ice to break up and release the steamers, the "Torpedo Catcher," and two other steam-powered scows that Heney had ordered built during the winter. It was expected that the Yukon River system would be largely free of ice by June 1.

With the railway-ferry link in place and operating, rail construction could continue along the eastern shore of Lake Bennett to close the gap between Bennett City and Carcross by Heney's target date of August 1.

Ten days after the railway's Dawson City announcement, a series of violent snowstorms swept through the White Pass and across the rocky uplands beyond, shutting down the railway for eighteen days. Temperatures during the storms ranged from twenty-two below at Skagway with a sharp wind blowing, to sixty-four below at Whitehorse.[1] A rotary crew under the direction of Snow King Moriarity mounted an expedition to rescue a train trapped at Bennett. After ploughing day and night on the mountain and beyond the summit for thirty-seven hours the rotary snowplough broke through to Bennett on January 30. The exhausted members of the rotary and locomotive crews were welcomed as heroes, as they were the first railwaymen to reach Bennett in more than two weeks.

The rotary and its three locomotives then reploughed the heavy grade south of Bennett City, attacking heavy drifts that had been re-formed by the howling winds. Behind the rotary came the trapped train, keeping well back to give Moriarity room to reverse his equipment so that he could ram the drifts again and again until he and his crews had carved a clean cut through which the ice-encrusted rotary and train could pass.

The rotary and the rescued train finally arrived in Skagway early the following morning. Moriarity and his crews had been on duty for fifty hours without relief.

The storms had brought the railway to a standstill. Freight was piled high on Skagway's docks and in the warehouses. Forty boxcars of freight bound for Bennett sat on a siding, and in the railway's pens and corrals north of town were 105 head of cattle and seventy-five horses. Hundreds of people had been trapped in Skagway by the snow, and the town's fourteen principal hotels were packed full of impatient salesmen, miners, gold-seekers, missionaries, and journalists, all anxious to depart for the Atlin and Dawson City gold-fields.[2]

V.I. Hahn, the railway's chief draftsman, was completing engineering drawings for additional snow sheds to control the drifting snow. It was now obvious to Hawkins that, unless the construction of snow sheds was given the highest priority, winter storms would become an annual problem that could seriously affect the railway's reliability. He instructed V.I. Hahn to draw up plans for additional snow sheds to control the drifting snow along the exposed stretches of the line. Eventually, 2,685 feet of snow sheds between Skagway and Summit Lake were built. This enabled the rotary to keep the trains moving in all but the most violent snowstorms.

The snow beyond Carcross was minimal, but the temperatures were, at times, forty below zero. In spite of the cold, Heney's crews picked, shovelled, and blasted their way towards Whitehorse. Hislop, who spent six days with Heney inspecting the work, reported that Heney was making a large number of cuts "through ground that has never known the sun's warmth." Hislop had never heard before of a railway grade being cut through such perplexing formations. "The frost in the ground seems to have been there for ages. We can make the cuts in no way save blasting."

One worry Hislop shared with Heney was a particularly difficult stretch of quicksand several hundred feet in length. "It promises to give us considerable trouble after the sun is permitted to shine upon the exposed surface," he said. "It may be that the dry earth that we have placed on top of it will keep the buried quick sand hard enough to sustain the track and the trains."

Bridge-building crews, under the direction of Sam Murchison, were at work on several bridges, including the two 600-foot bridges at Lewis Lake, where pile-driving continued day and night. But the pile driver was helpless against the permafrost. "In setting the piles we first have to blast out six feet of frozen earth," Hislop complained.

Now only four miles of grade remained to be built on the Carcross-White-horse section. "The grade is almost as level as a floor," Hislop reported. "It will require simply the throwing up of earth on which to lay the rails."

Heney's work train began moving material forward from Carcross, slowly advancing along the grade as the rails were laid towards the incomplete Lewis Lake bridges. But on the Bennett-Carcross section, the weather was even colder than in the White Pass. Here, Heney's crews of rock men were blasting cuts through the heavy black fingers of weathered granite that jutted into the lake.

By the end of February, two miles of heavy rock work north of Bennett City had been completed. "All of the work along Lake Bennett division is in granite and some of the cuts through it are 20 feet deep," reported Lewis, who had still to finish locating the grade line from Bennett City to Carcross. "The grade from one end of Lake Bennett to the other will run just about four feet above the high water mark," he said.[3]

Hawkins recovered his confidence as soon as freight began to move inland once again and construction was back on schedule. Two large coal bunkers were being designed – one for Skagway and one for Bennett City. Further encouraging news came from the United States Customs Office, which reported that goods worth $2,247,000 had been shipped into the interior through the port of Skagway in the previous six months, and virtually every pound had passed over the White Pass and Yukon Railway.

The communications system had also been greatly improved. A telegraph line from Bennett City to Whitehorse and Dawson had been constructed by the Canadian government and was finally working. And now, seventeen sleighs piled high with wire, insulators, and other telegraphic equipment had arrived in Atlin to extend the line from Bennett City to Quesnel, British Columbia. "This," the *Daily Alaskan* predicted, "will connect the Dawson line, and incidentally Dawson and Skagway, with the world at large."[4]

The construction of the railway's new office building at Skagway was making rapid strides. Five new company cottages were almost complete, and Superintendent Rogers's cottage was ready for occupancy as soon as his furniture arrived from Seattle.

But amid the good news of development and progress, death intervened. A labourer named McAllister fell from a snow embankment near the summit, striking his head against the wheels of a passing train. He was killed instantly. And on a sharp curve a coupling snapped, overturning a caboose in which eight Indians were riding. One was killed, one mortally injured, and the remaining six were seriously hurt.[5]

EARLY IN MARCH, 1900, hundreds of tons of steel rail and track iron landed in
Skagway from Seattle and Vancouver for the completion of the railway. Two
ships docked on March 6, carrying between them 500 tons of rail, 100 tons of
coal, 60,000 bricks, and 11,000 feet of lumber. A few days later, the steamer
Amur discharged 450 tons of rail, 25,000 feet of lumber, and 150 tons of coal.

The flood of supplies continued throughout March, but most of it had to be
piled in Skagway awaiting the abatement of winter's final storm. The storm
had trapped a train, consisting of two locomotives, two cattle cars loaded with
horses, two baggage cars, and four passenger coaches, in the snow 1,500 feet
south of the switchback.

The railway's maintenance-of-way men hauled blankets, hay, and oats from
Glacier through the swirling snow to cover and feed the horses. Food and a
case of whisky were delivered to the train for the passengers and the crews. All
of the passengers survived, but one horse died of exposure and others suffered
injury and illness.

When the train finally reached Bennett City after fighting snow for more
than sixty hours, more than a hundred of the 135 passengers signed a testimonial thanking Moriarity and his rotary crew for their courage and perseverance
in getting them safely to Bennett.[6]

Within the week, Heney predicted that he would have 1,500 men at work
north of Carcross and along the shore of Lake Bennett. "We are determined to
put on a big force right away," Heney announced to the *Daily Alaskan* on
March 18. "Several big camps will be established along Lake Bennett and up to
1,000 men employed there as soon as possible. These, with the men on the
division beyond Caribou Crossing, will make a total of 1500."

He told the newspaper that grading between Carcross and Whitehorse was
practically complete and that he was now waiting for an opportunity to lay the
rails. "The actual rail laying will not begin until after the opening of Lake
Bennett, as we desire to take the rails in by boat." He confirmed his prediction
that the Whitehorse extension would be ready for use by the first week in June.
"The idea is to get the track thrown around Lake Bennett as soon as possible. I
intend to have it there and trains running to Whitehorse direct from Skagway
by July 30."[7]

Not everyone agreed with Heney. Engineers, who claimed to have railway
experience, stated that he could not possibly reach Carcross by July 30. One
railway builder with eighteen years' experience claimed that the Lake Bennett
section could not possibly be completed before December, 1900.[8]

By the end of March, 6,000 tons of rail had been delivered to Skagway by the
coastal freighters, and by early April it was on its way to Bennett City, ready

for delivery to Carcross and the construction supply dumps along the lake-shore.

The grand plan was unfolding as Hawkins believed it should. On the heels of Heney's confident announcement came the news that Captain William Moore had sold his interest in the Moore wharf. This transaction marked the end of a long legal battle that had occupied the Moores, the Syndicate, and Hawkins for months.

In the summer of 1898, the Moores had made an agreement with the railway regarding the use of their wharf, in which the Syndicate still held a 55 per cent interest. Captain Moore and his son Bernard, who together owned the remaining 45 per cent, had found themselves on opposite sides of an argument over both the contract and the management of the wharf. Bernard had sup-ported the Syndicate's appointment of C.E. Wynn-Johnson as manager and he had argued that the agreement Wynn-Johnson and the Moores had made with the railway should be honoured. Captain Moore, however, not only had dis-agreed with the Syndicate's interpretation of the contract but had argued that, as founder, he should manage the wharf. To make his point, he had taken the matter to court, fighting the railway, the Syndicate, and Wynn-Johnson, as well as his son Bernard, in the process. After repeated court appearances and applications, the court had found for the Syndicate and had confirmed Wynn-Johnson's appointment as manager.

Shortly after the court victory Hawkins had written to E.E. Billinghurst stating, "you will be greatly pleased to learn that the long controversy between our company and Capt. Moore has been settled by a verdict in favour of our company. Mr. Johnson has gained full control of affairs in accordance with the intention of the contract ... which was left uncertain by its peculiar wording. This last decision is of the greatest possible benefit to our company. Had it been given to Moore we should have been obliged to have given up all use of the Moore wharf."[9]

The litigation and infighting had consumed hours of Hawkins's time and, in the end, had forced the railway to construct a wharf of its own south of the Moore installation. An expensive spur line on a narrow strip of land between Moore's wharf and the high rocky bluff overlooking Skagway Bay had also to be built to connect the new wharf to the railway's main line.

Captain Moore had lost his fight. At the age of seventy-eight, he packed up a few belongings and headed for Nome, Alaska, the scene of a rich new gold strike. He announced that he would order a ship to be loaded with goods in Seattle for Nome, "and in the meantime I shall start over the ice and be there in time to handle the goods upon their arrival."[10]

Hawkins was relieved by the departure of the troublesome but respected Captain Moore. This was one less problem of a long list of problems demanding his attention – the latest being the reappearance of the Chilkoot tunnel proposal.

Kinney, the original promoter of the tunnel scheme, reported to the *Seattle Post-Intelligencer* that financiers from Skagway, Juneau, Walla Walla, Boston, and New York were interested in the proposal. He said that their plans were to re-start construction of a preliminary tunnel 3,800 feet long, which would cost $115,000 to complete. Should this tunnel prove to be a success, Kinney explained, a second longer and larger tunnel would be constructed below the first at a cost of $1,500,000. His plans also included an electric railway from Dyea through the tunnel to Whitehorse Rapids. Kinney announced that the matter was now before the British Columbia parliament's railway committee, and he expected that he would soon receive a permit granting him authority to proceed with the construction of a tunnel beneath the still-contested Canadian side of Chilkoot Pass.

"With the prestige of such a permit," he said, "I do not anticipate a refusal of the parliament to grant a charter or any difficulty in interesting ample capital to carry out the whole plan." He said nothing, however, about permits to build his tunnel beneath the American side of Chilkoot summit.

On the face of it, the Chilkoot tunnel scheme seemed ludicrous to Hawkins, yet its ongoing threat could not be ignored. He took the precaution of instructing the railway's Victoria legal counsel to monitor the government's attitude towards the tunnel proposal.

Heney, who had arrived in Victoria on business, was immediately questioned by the newspapers whether his visit had any connection with possible railway legislation. "It certainly has not. I never heard about any such legislation until after I reached this city," he replied. "Since my arrival I have been told about the proposal to parallel our road, but I hardly think the legislature will take a course which will interfere with the supply of capital necessary for the completion of the White Pass and Yukon Railway." Driving home his point, he said, "Owing to the war in South Africa it is hard enough getting money for a railway in Alaska and northern British Columbia ... without handicapping the company with a rival charter."[11]

There was nothing Hawkins could do but await developments and hope that the railway would not be faced with new competition, or another buyout in the Chilkoot Pass.

HENEY WAS desperate for men. On April 1, 1900, he announced that he was looking for 2,000 men. "I have 750 men employed on the extensions at present and I have sent to Seattle for 2000 more. Every man that applies will be engaged."[12] Recruitment drives in the major cities of United States and Canada still only produced minimal results. Some men came to work on the railway, but most of them came for the gold. The dream of striking it rich far outstripped the reality of an assured thirty cents an hour shovelling snow and gravel for the railway. But, fortunately for Hawkins and Heney, many gold-seekers arrived broke and could not dismiss the chance to make a grubstake by working on the railway. Others simply changed their minds about searching for gold when they finally arrived in a mysterious land of bewildering rivers, mountains, lakes, and streams. Being lost and alone in an empty landscape was a frightening prospect, so they forgot the gold and sought the security of the grade.

Heney's men were now putting the finishing touches on two large barges, scheduled for completion on April 12. Both barges were constructed on the frozen surface of the lake, eliminating the need to launch them from the shore when the lake ice melted. They each had a carrying capacity of 150 tons and were built to be towed to the lakeshore construction camps by either a steam tug or a lake steamer; they would do double duty carrying construction and commercial freight from Bennett City to Carcross.

Superintendent Rogers's maintenance and repair shops in Skagway were turning out five new freight cars a week, each car equipped with the most modern braking system. Four new locomotives were due to arrive from Seattle by the end of April, a new baggage car was under construction, and two new passenger coaches were expected shortly from the eastern United States. "More engines, cars, and other fine rolling stock will be arriving soon, and they will be ready for the opening of the line to Whitehorse," Superintendent Rogers assured the *Daily Alaskan*.[13]

Heney was on his feet eighteen to nineteen hours a day, preparing for the final push. His battle was now on two fronts – the Whitehorse extension and the Bennett gap. The line to Whitehorse was almost complete. "Stikine" Bill Robinson had supervised construction and his presence alone was sufficient to galvanize the workers, who made a point of avoiding any confrontation with the demanding Stikine Bill.

Heney, with Hawkins's blessing, hired Charlie "Snow King" Moriarity to supervise the track laying on the Whitehorse grade. Now the winter storms were over, Moriarity was able to devote his considerable talents and leadership to driving men and steel towards Whitehorse – and arrive there by the first week in June. The *Daily Alaskan* boasted, "Moriarity will be the leader of the most northerly track laying work on the American continent and the western hemisphere."[14]

Moriarity was ready, but he had to wait for Sam Murchison and his crews to bridge the creeks, gaps, and gullies that intersected the Whitehorse grade and complete the two bridges at Lewis Lake. Without the bridges the rails could not advance.

Heney had only forty-five days left to complete the line to Whitehorse. The movement of men and supplies to the Klondike was on the increase; the railway's warehouses were bulging with freight and more arrived in Skagway each day; even the pens north of town were full of livestock. Heney was feeling the pressure.

By May 1, puddles of water were appearing on the surface of the slowly rotting lake ice, which rumbled and cracked as heavily loaded freight sleighs moved across its surface. In early May, a team of horses and a sled loaded with 4,000 pounds of machinery suddenly broke through the ice on Lake Bennett. The driver jumped clear, but neither the horses nor the sled were ever seen again.

The lake was no longer safe. Now, men and freight alike had to wait in Bennett until the ice broke up and navigation was re-established between Bennett City and Carcross.

Hawkins reported on May 10 that the two fifty-foot-high Lewis Lake bridges, aggregating 1,200 feet in length, were now complete. "Moriarity's track crews have laid rail across them and are working towards White Horse at a rate of two miles per day." Hawkins expected that all of the twenty-two miles of rail stocked north of Carcross would be laid within a few days. "Track laying beyond the 22 miles will have to be postponed until the lake opens. We have a large stock of rail and track iron at Bennett City ready to send forward on Heney's scows as soon as the Lake is clear."

Hawkins's estimation was that Lake Bennett would be open for navigation between the 25th and 28th of May. "Eight days of work after that will finish track laying into White Horse."

He told the *Daily Alaskan* that terminal facilities at Whitehorse were progressing rapidly. A railway depot, offices, and a locomotive roundhouse were on the drawing board and sites for their erection were being cleared. "This summer or fall we shall put in coal bunkers to serve our locomotives as well as the steamers on the Upper and Lower Yukon River."[15]

On May 24, the ice broke up on Lake Bennett, one day ahead of Hawkins's earliest prediction. The lake steamer *Australian* was loaded with freight and left Bennett City for Carcross at three in the morning on May 24. Heney's new steam scow, christened the *Omega*, had completed her trial run on the afternoon of May 23 and was being loaded with construction material and rails to complete the Whitehorse extension. The lake steamer *Gleaner* was loaded and scheduled to depart for Carcross on May 25 and the *Omega* was due out the next day.

"Now that the lake is open I shall rush track material to Caribou Crossing to complete that division," Heney said. "I hope to have the rails laid into White Horse ten days hence, and except for ballasting the extension will be complete."

Heney now had 560 men working on the Whitehorse extension and 900 along the shore of Lake Bennett, "but I could use 1,000 more," he lamented. "Many of the men have been quitting of late to go to the interior mines. Fifty left today." He noted that a number of malcontents among the crews were spreading discontent. "'They complain, but unjustly so. We ask only for an honest day's work and pay for it."[16]

The rock work along the shore of Lake Bennett was proving more costly than anticipated even by the most liberal estimates. Blast after blast was fired to break through the walls of granite that parallelled the lake shore and blocked the way. "At $250,000 for the mile, the shots presently being fired embrace the most costly mile on the line from White Horse to Skagway," Heney said. "The ordinary cost of a mile of road is $10,000 to $12,000."

The last of the current series of blasts had alone dislodged more than 8,000 cubic yards of rock. "It was one huge convulsion as though mother earth was in the agony of death," the *Daily Alaskan* extravagantly explained. "The irresistible force lifted off the face of the mountain for 200 feet and the loosened mass dropped with a mighty splash into the lake."

The blast was fired ten miles north of Bennett City along a sinuous cliff that stood two hundred feet above the surface of the lake. A tunnel had been driven thirty feet into the cliff. From the end of this tunnel, two more tunnels were driven, one twenty-five feet to the left and one twenty feet to the right, creating a giant "T" within the bowels of the rock. These tunnels were packed with powder.

"The first intimation we had of the shots going off was a tremor like an earthquake." said photographer Barley, who was present. "I would like to have got closer and watched the cliff in its torment."[17]

The blast, which created a tidal wave four feet high, was a fitting fanfare to usher in the celebration of Queen Victoria's birthday at Bennett City. A special train had brought 130 people from Skagway to help with the festivities. The feature of the day was a baseball game in which Skagway vanquished Bennett

City, sixteen to fifteen, on a rain-soaked field. The contests included rock drilling, pole vaulting, sprinting, horse races, boat races, and a tug-of-war, which, to Bennett's shame, was also won by the stalwarts from Skagway. At the end of the day, scores of Skagwavans and Bennettites – men, women, and children – gathered on the shore of Lake Bennett and sang "God Save the Queen."[18]

Supplies could now be moved without interruption to the construction camps that were strung out along the grade – fourteen camps between Carcross and Whitehorse and more under construction along the shore of the lake. Fifteen hundred men were labouring on the two sections of railway, consuming mountains of material and tons of food. Two boxcars loaded with potatoes left Skagway for Bennett City late in May to be delivered to the camps. "The shipments of so many spuds down the line," commented one Skagway merchant, "tells ... the nationality of the men who are helping Heney [and] Moriarity build the railroad."[19]

By the end of May, the railway's new Skagway office building was almost completed. Hawkins, Hislop, J.W. Young, who was Hawkins' chief clerk, and Miss Grace McFarlane, the office stenographer, who had faithfully served the railway since the start of construction in the spring of 1898, had already moved in.

Beyond Carcross, Stikine Bill's grade was being pushed through the sand bluff that skirts the Yukon River's entrance into Whitehorse. Working two twelve-hour shifts, the teams and scrapers moved thousands of yards of sand towards the river bank, creating a solid surface for the grade along the foot of the escarpment.

Ten miles back, Moriarity's crews were laying steel towards Whitehorse at a rate of two and a half miles a day. They worked with the measured cadence of a well-drilled team of jugglers. Day and night the hills echoed the sounds of the locomotive as it inched forward, pushing two flat cars loaded with rail and track iron onto the newly laid track. Crews lifted the rails from the flat cars, carrying them forward to the naked ties, which had already been positioned and marked to receive the thirty-foot lengths of rail. Then four gangs of men drove home the spikes – four spikes to the tie, thirty-six spikes to the rail, seventy-two spikes to each thirty feet of track. When the rails were down and spiked, the work train crept forward and the routine was repeated, hour after hour.

Lake steamers *Bailey*, *Gleaner*, *Clifford Sifton*, and *Reaper* were on constant duty transporting rail from Bennett City to Carcross. Four locomotives, a coach, and a combination of sixty boxcars and flat cars were freighted to

Carcross in Heney's barges and set out on the completed track ready to transport commercial freight as soon as the rails reached Whitehorse.[20]

Hawkins was feeling easier about the railway's progress, although the Chilkoot tunnel question had still to be settled. Michael King remained confident that the tunnel-railway proposal would succeed, offering shippers a choice of routes across the coastal mountains. Earlier in the year, the *Skagway-Atlin Budget* boasted that "everything about the scheme is practicable, and if the road is built it can be operated cheaper than the White Pass and Yukon Railway, and the latter will have its monopoly broken."

The *Budget* was still firing from the hip, hoping that one or more of its editorial bullets would hit the railway in a vital spot and do it damage. Although its publisher's hostility did not receive wide support, he never lost an opportunity to heap abuse on the railway and its officials – particularly the railway's general manager, to whom he often referred as "King" Hawkins.[21]

In March, however, Dawson's *Klondike Nugget* reported that the Chilkoot tunnel scheme "existed only in the minds of moneyless promoters."[22] This was encouraging news to Hawkins, although the rumour mill kept the dreaded proposal alive. Hawkins was still worried by the Chilkoot railway-tunnel proposal, but it did not hold him back from his drive to complete the railway by the announced dates. Shippers were relying on the railway, and the railway needed the income. A corrugated iron warehouse 500 feet by forty feet was under construction at Carcross, and material for one twice as long was on site for installation at Whitehorse.

Passengers, eager to reach Dawson as early in the season as possible, were leaving Bennett City in droves, taking lake steamers to Carcross and the train to the end of steel. There, Heney's wagons were waiting to carry them over the untracked grade to Whitehorse, where they could catch a riverboat to Dawson. The railway was now already providing a through-service by rail, lake steamers, and wagons from Skagway to Whitehorse.

Eighty per cent of the Whitehorse extension was railed, aligned, and ballasted – providing a first-class track. "It is therefore in condition for running trains fast time," announced Superintendent Rogers after a personal examination of the grade and track.

On the morning of June 6, Stikine Bill's graders reached Whitehorse, and Moriarity's track crews were working just five miles to the south. Hawkins, Hislop, Heney, and Rogers were there already. By the evening of June 6, the track was less than two and a half miles from Whitehorse. Each worker was invited to work as many hours as he wished, and some took the opportunity to earn as much as $5.00 a day for a seventeen-hour shift, less a dollar for board.

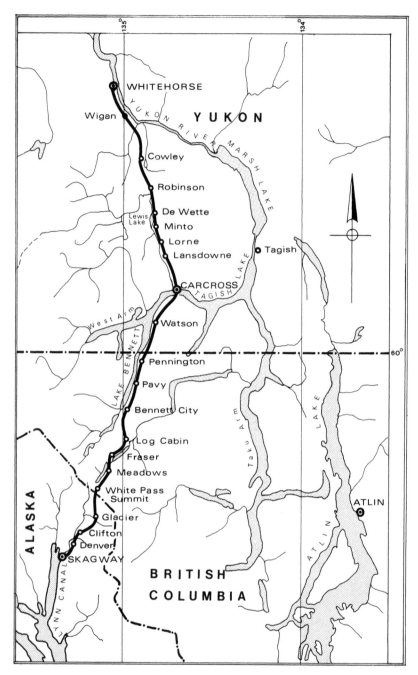

FROM SKAGWAY TO WHITEHORSE
The railway was built in three stages: first from Skagway to Bennett City,
then from Carcross to Whitehorse. The stage linking Bennett to Carcross
was the last to be constructed. Twenty-one stations originally served
the 110.7 mile railway.

On the morning of June 7, the track crews passed by Miles Canyon on their way to Whitehorse Rapids. The flat cars and locomotives followed the newly laid rails along the riverbank towards a knot of people gathered near two riverboats moored to the bank. As the trackmen appeared, the steamboats blew their whistles and were answered with a chorus of whistles and bells from the locomotives.

The Whitehorse welcome was short-lived. After a brief stop the locomotives retreated to haul sand and gravel to the 500 men spread out for nearly two miles aligning and ballasting the track. By three the following afternoon, the track was aligned and rock steady.

At four in the afternoon of Wednesday, June 8, 1900, the locomotives made their first official appearance in Whitehorse. They moved slowly down the track and stopped at the foot of Main Street. At a quarter past four, Mrs. Wood, the wife of North-West Mounted Police Superintendent Z.T. Wood, tapped in the Whitehorse extension's last spike in the presence of the railway's senior officials and a group of inquisitive citizens.

There was no ceremony. That would have to wait until the rails reached Carcross from Bennett City at the end of July. Then there would be a celebration. Graves had ordered it and announced that he would be there himself to help drive home the last spike.

ON JUNE 9, 1900, the White Pass and Yukon Railway could truthfully state that it operated a passenger and freight transportation service between Skagway, Alaska, and Whitehorse, Yukon. The system was still not by rail all the way. Lake steamers and Heney's barges and scows were still needed to fill the rail gap along the length of Lake Bennett. The lake link was reasonably efficient, but it still entailed transferring freight and passengers twice before reaching Whitehorse, a labour-intensive operation.

Closing the gap by rail by the end of July was now Hawkins's primary goal, and Heney's heavy responsibility. He was still searching for men. They came and worked for a while, but soon the lure of gold put fire in their bellies and then they were gone. But there were others who laboured for the railway because working for wages was all they knew and thirty cents an hour was the best wage they had ever earned. It was all that they wanted. Many of them had a real sense of pride in their work. For them, there were no horizons to search. They stuck to the grade, leaving the fantasies to others who were prepared to give up thirty cents an hour to chase a dream.

Stikine Bill Robinson and Snow King Moriarity were moved with their crews to the Lake Bennett section, Robinson to supervise the construction of the grade and Moriarity to lay the track.

Throughout the days and the bright, northern summer nights, lake steamers and Heney's scows nudged their stubby bows onto the beaches to discharge thousands of ties, tons of steel rail, and boxes of fish plates, track bolts, nuts, washers, and sacks of spikes. Back from the shore, nestled among the trees or high on the rocky plateaus, were the construction camps. Sleeping tents, dining tents, supply tents, and first-aid tents were scattered about. Beyond the camps were the horse lines, surrounded by wagons, ploughs, and scrapers. At a distance, protected from the cook-stove sparks, were boxes of dynamite, large tins of black powder, and coils of fuse.

At times the camps were noisy, but after a shift change they were quiet, with only the occasional sound of a concertina, a banjo, or a mouth organ drifting from a tent where a few tired workers had gathered to smoke their pipes, sing hymns, or, with Heney away, enjoy a drink from a hidden supply of bourbon or a cherished bottle of Scotch.[23]

Heney was always on the move, making his way from site to site by horseback, steamboat, or canoe. He conferred with his walking boss, the rock men, Robinson, and Moriarity. He remained in constant touch with Hislop. There were conferences with Hawkins's engineers, who had chosen the route and put down the survey flags for Heney to follow. There were disagreements and serious discussions. Heney would ask for modifications he believed would improve the grade, reduce the curvatures, save a day's construction, and speed the work. He checked the work force, pondered morale, pushed but never shoved. He seldom passed a crew without pausing to observe the work, offer encouragement, or suggest a better way.

Robinson's graders, now nearly 1,000 men, were working two shifts a day, 500 men to a shift. Each man was free to labour as many hours as he wished, subject to the maintenance of health and safety, which, under the circumstances, was difficult to monitor. By the end of the first week in July, five miles of grade out of Bennett City were ready for rails.

Moriarity's crews were assembled in Bennett and by Friday, July 8, they had laid two and a half miles of track.[24] The work was demanding. The straight track alignments were difficult enough, but the curves slowed the pace, ravaged the muscles, and bathed the workers in sweat. As the track approached the curves, the steel rails, each one as straight as a ramrod, were bent by the sheer brute force of men, inch by inch into a curve, and spiked to the ties. Then they were joined together with fish plates, two plates to the joint, one on each side. Track bolts were shoved through holes in the fish plate and through corresponding holes in the rail, and each bolt was secured with a nut and a lock washer.

An intense rivalry developed between Robinson's graders and Moriarity's track layers. The issue came to a head when Moriarity accused Robinson of holding him back. Robinson rose to the challenge and bet Moriarity a new suit of clothes that the track layers would never catch up to his graders. Moriarity accepted the bet and the fight was on.

The two gangs soon learned of the bet and joined in the battle, their pride and competitiveness overruling their judgement. Soon, the workers along the Bennett grade were working harder than Heney, Robinson, or Moriarity thought possible, or had a right to expect. They were also betting heavily on who would be the winner. Graves reported, "the betting became ruinous."

At one critical point, Moriarity claimed that he and his men had their rails projecting beyond Robinson's grade, a claim Robinson vigorously denied. But by the time Moriarity had his rails spiked and fish-plated, Robinson's grade had once again advanced beyond the track layers' reach. Fortunately for the graders, the track layers fell behind while waiting for the work train to bring forward a fresh supply of track iron, ties, and rails.

The gangs were working feverishly, and the same excitement was gripping Skagway, Bennett City, and Whitehorse. Reports of the railway's progress appeared almost daily in the Skagway press. They were studied by shippers, who were anxiously awaiting the day when they could freight from tidewater to the interior by rail all the way. Skagway's warehouses were full, and on July 15, four large sea-going freighters and a barge docked at Moore's wharf – the latest in a constant round of arrivals that was taxing Skagway and the railway to the limit. The *Daily Alaskan* reported that "an army of longshoremen was employed rushing the freight from the vessels to the warehouses." Three of the four ships were British, it said, "and their sky-piercing masts, picturesque funnels, bright house flags, and the huge bulk of the ships themselves made up a sight of a typical seaport."

Once again, the flood of freight was more than the incomplete transportation system could handle. By early July, 1,600 tons of freight had accumulated at Whitehorse – most of it under canvas on the river bank. The Yukon River steamboats were simply unable to cope with the hundreds of tons of machinery and supplies being hauled to Whitehorse. It did not take Hawkins and Graves long to recognize that the fleet of independent riverboat operators sailing between Whitehorse and Dawson City were incapable of providing the reliable Yukon River service required to support the railway's advertised through service from Skagway to the Klondike. In Graves's opinion, the railway was being forced to turn its freight and passengers over at Whitehorse to "an irresponsible mob of river steamers that competed for the business in much the same fashion as cab drivers outside an ill-managed railway station." He said that, after a thorough investigation of the Yukon riverboat services, they had found that "Innocent passengers were fought over, through shipments and goods split up, customs papers lost, goods stolen on the boats, and, in short, perfect anarchy prevailed."

Graves's opinion was not without substance. Many of the boat owners were financially strapped and disorganized. When tickets were not honoured or when goods were damaged, passengers and shippers, more often than not, made claims against the railway and received compensation. This left the railway with the task of recovering the cost of the claim from the delinquent boat owners, most of the time without success.

Graves made plans to rationalize the Yukon River operations by driving out the independents. He purchased all ships that flew the flag of the Canadian Development Company – an organization that had been closely associated with the railway for more than a year – and turned them over to Hawkins. Hawkins entered a raging Yukon River rate war, declared by some of the independents who were fighting for their survival. Some of them were offering passage from Whitehorse to Dawson City first class for $15, the regular price being $60. Hawkins, with superior steamboats and premium service, reduced the rate to $30 and retained most of his business. This fledgling service was dubbed the White Pass River Division to distinguish it from the railway, which was already being referred to as the Rail Division of the White Pass & Yukon Route.[25]

This river link served the Yukon interior, but the Atlin gold-fields and their lucrative freight business were not forgotten. The railway purchased the northern assets of John Irving's Canadian Pacific Navigation Company, which was operating steamers on the Yukon River, as well as Lake Bennett, Taku Arm, and Atlin Lake. The lake steamers, combined with John Irving's horse-drawn railway across a two and a quarter mile portage between Taku Arm and Atlin Lake, provided a direct route to Atlin's gold-fields.

Known variously as the "Atlin Southern," "Taku Central," and the "Taku Tram," this important railway link between the two lakes was provided with its first locomotive by Hawkins in July, 1900. Known as the "Duchess," it was unloaded from the *Danube* at Skagway and forwarded by rail and lake steamer to Taku, where ten days later it was fired up and put to work hauling freight and passengers across the short Taku isthmus.[26]

The pieces were falling into place, including some that had not been part of the original plan. Certainly, operating steamers on the southern lakes and the Yukon River was never part of the grand design. But having developed a river division, there remained no pressing reason to construct the railway to Fort Selkirk. This extension could no longer be justified now that the bulk of the freight could be moved to Dawson City during the summer season by a combination of rail and river steamers. So it came as no surprise when Graves announced that there were no plans to extend the railway beyond Whitehorse in the immediate future.[27] The construction of a branch line from Log Cabin to serve the Atlin district was also shelved.

The railway's shareholders were still concerned about the future of Yukon mining. To date they had invested some $10 million in the railway alone, to say nothing of the cost of acquiring the lake and river steamboats. Without a strong, ongoing mining base, the investment could be in jeopardy.

There appeared to be little reason for concern. Gold shipments from the Klondike through Skagway for 1900 to the first week in July totalled more than $7 million. "This tide of treasure," bragged the *Daily Alaskan*, "makes Skagway one of the greatest gold shipping ports in the world." The steamer *Victorian* alone left Skagway on July 4 with $1,450,000 in gold in her strong box. The previous week the *Yukoner* and the *Columbian* had left with $950,000 and $700,000 in their safes.[28]

The interior country was also burgeoning. Whitehorse was growing rapidly. More than thirty businesses were now operating – most of them out of tents. Five hotels were either completed or under construction. P. Scharschmidt of the *Bennett Sun* was busy transferring his operation from dying Bennett City to Whitehorse, where he was beginning to publish the *Whitehorse Star*. Lumber had been in short supply, but now it was arriving by the carload from mills at Carcross, Bennett, and Taku. Restaurants were flourishing; an electric light plant was being planned; a board of trade had been organized; an athletic club was in business; a post office had been opened; and streets were being cut through the spruce and cottonwoods. Main Street, at the town's centre, was a generous hundred feet wide.

Whitehorse was no longer an obscure settlement in the wilderness. It had become a legitimate community – the northern terminus of a railway on the verge of completion and the logical operational headquarters for the White Pass River Division's growing fleet of sternwheelers plying the Upper Yukon River and its major tributaries.[29] The grade between Whitehorse and Carcross was in its final stages of refinement. The trains could run faster as track alignment and ballasting approached full operating standards.

Hawkins, who was in Seattle conferring with Graves, received a steady stream of construction reports – each one rushed to him from the ships as they arrived from Skagway. His particular interest was construction progress along Lake Bennett. Heney had eleven days to meet his end-of-July deadline, and both Graves and Hawkins planned to be present during the driving of the golden spike at Carcross.

They arrived in Skagway on July 25. This was Graves's first visit to Skagway during 1900, and he planned to remain in the North throughout the month of August, visiting all the major centres and inspecting the railway and the recent riverboat acquisitions.

Heney now had six days to the end of July. The major rock work had been completed, and a hundred horses were at work along the Bennett grade, some hitched to graders, some to wagons, while others dragged rail, length by length, to the track gangs that were laying rail across short bridges. Robinson worked desperately to stay ahead of Moriarity as the graders and track gangs worked in two shifts around the clock.

On July 26, the end of steel was some eight miles south of Carcross. Heney signalled that he would be in Carcross by late afternoon, July 29, a message Hawkins was profoundly relieved to receive.

Graves was in a buoyant mood. "We are pleased to announce that we have never been better equipped to handle traffic," he informed Skagway's reporters. "With the large fleet of White Pass steamers meeting the train at White-horse, the service given is quite commensurate with the demands that come in from the field." He believed that Skagway was the logical point for a smelter, should one ever be required. He was proud of Skagway and the contribution the railway had made to its growth. "The railway has made Skagway and it desires to help the port all it can." He insisted that "the gold that is coming from the Klondike is one of the greatest advertisements the north has ever had." He said that with the completion of the railway "the day of the hard luck stories about the Klondike is past."[30]

"AN EPOCH in transportation affairs of the north will be marked when the first train makes its run all the way from the great Pacific port of Skagway to the busy new inland town of Whitehorse," wrote the *Daily Alaskan* on July 27. "The last few miles of rails are now being laid, closing the last link which skirts the shore of Lake Bennett."[31]

The Carcross bridge was finished, complete with track. Graders from Carcross were driving south along the shoreline, and by the morning of July 27 they were within shouting distance of the main grading and track-laying forces who were pushing north. That night the two grades met and by the morning of July 28, the track was only six miles from the Carcross bridge.

Heney informed Hawkins that the rails would reach Carcross by late afternoon on Sunday, July 29, and that Whitehorse residents had been offered a complimentary ride to Carcross on a special train to celebrate the completion of the railway and the driving of the last spike.

Three miles of track were laid on July 28, Robinson's men consistently managing to bring their rough grade to a standard high enough for Moriarity's men to lay their rails. Construction continued through the night of July 28, and by early the next morning the track was only two miles from Carcross. Behind Moriarity, 1,300 men laboured to bring the track's alignment and ballast to an initial operating standard.

Sunday, July 29, was cool and sunny. A stiff breeze from the south was blowing whitecaps on the lake and ripples in the surrounding sand dunes. By early afternoon fifty visitors had arrived in Carcross by ship from Bennett City, and later they were joined by fifty more from Whitehorse. The track was not in sight, although smoke from the work trains could be seen in the distance, and the sharp ring of the spike mauls could be heard when the wind was right.

Graves and a party of guests, including a number of employees from Skagway, were on the lake aboard the sternwheel steamer *Australian*. As the ship neared Carcross, Graves could see the graders and track layers at work along the shore. He checked his watch. It was half past four, and the track was still half a mile from Carcross. He was stirred by the intensity of the work. "The men drove the spikes in a cyclone of sledge hammers," he recalled, not realizing that calling a spike maul a "sledge hammer" would be forgiven by only the most tolerant of railway men. The metronomic cadence of sounds grew louder as the work train approached the long curve leading to the bridge.

Hot white steam, venting under pressure from the locomotives' cylinders, was now in plain sight. Sparks from glancing blows of the spike mauls could be seen as the bridge and grade rails were joined.

The locomotive's whistle and bell, and the sounds of its pumps, silenced the crowd in Carcross. With a screech of brakes, it slowed to cross the Nares River and came to a stop in the middle of the span, its flat cars still heavy with unused rail and ties.

There it stood, black and daunting.

Kodakers, as they liked to be called, swarmed over the King's Mill building. One climbed half way up a sixty-foot pole to get a better view and record the scene with his camera. Others climbed to the top of the pile driver that had rendered sterling service during the construction of the Lewis bridges and the

Carcross swing bridge, which was at this moment carrying its first locomotive across the river to Carcross.

Graves, Hawkins, Heney, and their guests approached a specially marked tie. The rails were down, and all of the spikes driven in – except one.

The guests and more than 1,000 workers crowded in around the designated tie. A small round clearing was left in the middle, like a target's bull's-eye. It was within this tiny orb, protected by Major Primrose and Dr. Parree of the North-West Mounted Police, that the principal actors were expected to perform the task of driving home the last spike.

The onlookers stood on logs, piles of lumber, and spare rails that had accumulated beside the track. There were heavy-booted labourers in waterproof pants, bank clerks in natty black suits, grey-suited men with dark waistcoats and watch chains of gold. The crowd was so packed, only the celebrants' hats could be seen. There were miners' hats, straw hats, bowler hats, fedoras, stetsons, and caps of many colours. And around the fringe of the crowd were the fine ladies' hats, which had withstood the rigours of the wind and the convivial mood of the crowd.

"This is the last spike; a spike of gold," shouted "Stikine" Bill Robinson as he held up a miserable-looking iron spike. The crowd roared in jest, mocking Robinson's grandiose announcement.

Graves raised his arms for silence and invited Heney to say a few words, "but he dodged," Graves recalled, so he said a few words himself. He was followed by Hawkins, who quickly realized that "no one wanted speeches," so he also kept his remarks brief.

Graves turned to the spike, which had already been tapped into place by Moriarity, who, expecting an amateur performance, was suppressing a grin.

Because the event was taking place on Canadian soil, Graves handed the maul to the Colonel commanding the United States troops in Skagway and Dyea and invited him to "strike the first blow." The Colonel swung, hitting the wooden tie inches wide of the mark. The crowd, which was in high spirits, roared its disapproval of the Colonel's performance.

Warned by the Colonel's fate, Heney tapped the spike gently and backed away, leaving the impression that, as contractor, he would have no difficulty with the spike but was deferring to others the honour of driving it home.

John Hislop, who was present in his capacity of mayor of Skagway, took the next turn, but failed to distinguish himself or the town he represented. The crowd revelled in his embarrassment and cheered him on to greater effort.

An unnamed dignitary, who Graves claimed had been "straightening his eye" behind a tent, had overdone it and saw two spikes. "Greatly to his credit," recalled Graves, "he hit one of them a wallop on the side and knocked it flat."

The spike was battered and bent, having resisted all attempts to drive it home.

Now it was Graves's turn. Moriarity could not conceal a smile of anticipation as Graves, maul in hand, approached the spike. Graves said, "I knew he was thinking of the box of cigars I would owe him, as would any luckless railway man who missed the spike." Graves swung the maul and to his joy "it connected with that disreputable spike." Everybody cheered, and then there were handshakes all round, and the Kodaks clicked until they ran out of film.

Later, when the festivities were in full swing, Moriarity sneaked up with a spike puller and removed the delapidated spike. He then marked the hole with a piece of white chalk for the attention of the track men. Graves watched Moriarity with pride. "I was rather pleased with this evidence of his strict attention to business even in the midst of pleasure."

Soon the ceremony was over and the crowd dispersed. The Skagwavans returned by ship to Bennett City, where they boarded their special train for home.

Before the Whitehorse special could return, it was forced to wait for a long train of southbound "empties" that had been hauling freight on the Whitehorse extension. Now that the line was complete, they were being returned to Skagway for full freight service.

This was the first train to pass over the line from terminal to terminal – justifying an Irish trackman's remark, "Be Jakers, the first thrain into this country was a thrain OUT!"[32]

Two days later, on July 31, 1900, the *Daily Alaskan* proclaimed "FIRST PASSENGER TRAIN THROUGH": "The first passenger train over the Lake Bennett division of the White Pass & Yukon Railway, and the first to make the continuous run from Skagway to Whitehorse accomplished the feat yesterday. Everything works O.K."

The railway was in business.

Heney left the following day – his contract at an end.

EPILOGUE

AFTER THE LAST-SPIKE CEREMONY, Graves and Hawkins made plans to leave for Dawson on the *Canadian*, a sternwheel riverboat on the Whitehorse-Dawson run. Their departure was delayed, however, after they were told that "the boys" had organized a farewell dinner for Heney.

To prevent Heney from bolting from the affair, the organizers led him to believe that the dinner was to honour Graves.

"We had a great dinner," Graves recalled, "and Heney didn't smell a mouse – though he seemed to think it hardly the thing for me to take the chair at a dinner given in my honour."

After dinner, Hislop proposed a toast to Heney, saying that "the boys who are soon to part wish to mark their appreciation of your never failing kindness and courage through all the dangers and troubles of the past year."

Graves said that Hislop's speech "was one of the finest tributes to the good qualities of an old and tried comrade that could be put into language."

Heney was perplexed and somewhat confused by the attention being suddenly showered upon him. He rose and stood in silence before attempting to reply. Then he thanked them all for the honour it had been to work with such a fine body of men, and to wish them all Godspeed and happiness in the future.

Hislop presented Heney with a gold watch and chain – a gift from Heney's many comrades – and an illuminated Souvenir Tribute depicting Heney's work as Superintendent, and later as Contractor, during the construction of the White Pass and Yukon Railway.

Graves, Hawkins, Hislop, and Heney then went their separate ways. What happened to each one of them is, in a way, a part of the story – the closing chapters of four busy and productive lives.

Samuel Haughton Graves

Samuel H. Graves remained president of the White Pass and Yukon Railway through the first decade of the twentieth century. In 1911, however, he prepared segments of his routine work to distribute among his senior officials, a first step towards his retirement.

On November 11, 1911, he arrived in Ottawa with four members of his senior management to meet with government officials regarding the railway's current and future operations. They checked into the Aylmer Hotel and, after being assigned rooms, they went to the Rideau Club, where Graves ate what was later described as "rather a hearty meal."

He remained at the club until half past eleven that night visiting with business friends. Fifteen minutes later, he arrived back at the Aylmer Hotel with his officials, leaving them with an invitation to meet for breakfast at nine.

The following morning, vice-president O.L. Dickinson and corporate secretary F.C. Elliot knocked on Graves's door. There was no reply, so they proceeded to the dining room, where they expected to find him. He was not there. They returned to Graves's room, where they found the door locked from the inside. With rising concern, they called the porter, who climbed through an outside window and unlocked the door. When they entered the room, they found Graves dead in bed.

Dickinson reported that Graves's belongings were in perfect order, "indicating that he was still feeling all right when he retired." The covers on the bed were undisturbed, "and it was quite evident from his posture that he had not moved a muscle."

A doctor was called, who theorized that "something he ate formed a gas which pressed against his heart until it stopped beating."

Graves's remains were taken to Chicago, and on Saturday, November 18, 1911, they were cremated at Graceland Cemetery, in accordance with the provisions of his will.

"As to the future," wrote Dickinson, "I can see no reason why the former policies pursued by Mr. Graves in the past should not prevail in the future, and I feel that all of us should undertake to manage the property in such a way as to carry out his current plans to ultimate termination, if possible, with the result he would like to have attained."

Graves was fifty-nine years of age.

Michael James Heney

Heney wandered rather aimlessly about the world after completing the White Pass and Yukon Railway, passing the time until a new challenge caught his fancy.

He was rich and he could afford the pleasures of life – travel, society, gentlemen's clubs – but they were poor substitutes for the joys of blasting a railway grade through the Alaskan mountains. While he cut quite a figure with his handsome features, high white collars, and evening clothes, he was happiest when he was wearing high boots, iron pants, a flannel shirt, and a slouch hat.

By chance, in the fall of 1905 Heney read a newspaper reporter's interview with David Guggenheim, which told of the construction of a railway from Valdez, Alaska, to important copper claims in which a partnership consisting of J.P. Morgan and M. Guggenheim and Sons had a substantial interest.

The interview revealed that the Valdez trail was chosen as the most practical route for the railway, the Copper River route being discarded because of insurmountable engineering difficulties.

Heney wasted no time. That winter, accompanied by J.R. McPherson, an engineer, Jack Dalton, a famous Alaska packer, and three Indians, he landed at Valdez and disappeared into the mountains.

A few weeks later, Heney met with the Guggenheims in New York and informed them that their choice of the Valdez route was a mistake. He then presented them with an alternate route – his own officially recorded survey of the rejected Copper River route.

The Guggenheims did not accept Heney's recommendation. But because of a recent coal discovery they sent out M.K. Rogers, an engineer, to re-evaluate the situation. This resulted in the Valdez being abandoned in favour of Katalla as the base for the railway because it would provide access to the coal-fields. Rogers's report was adopted and a million dollars was set aside to finance the Katalla project.

With the aid of outside capital, Heney began to build his own railway towards the developing copper fields along his own surveyed route. As Heney had predicted, the Katalla project proved to be a failure. The artificial breakwater that was required to protect the harbour was swept away by the fierce storms that lash the Alaska coast during the winter months.

The Morgan-Guggenheim partnership was appalled by the continuing problems that were plaguing the project. As a last resort they retained E.C. Hawkins, most likely at Heney's suggestion, to examine the railway problem and come to a realistic decision. Morgan made it clear to Hawkins, "Whatever the route we've got to bring that copper and coal together."

Hawkins's survey confirmed that Heney's Copper River route was the only one capable of bringing the copper and coal together. And the only recorded survey of this route was the one owned by Heney himself. The Morgan-Guggenheim partnership had no alternative but to purchase Heney's right-of-way for a quarter of a million dollars and give Heney the contract to build the railway.

Heney was once again in his element. Hawkins joined him as chief engineer; so did Dr. Whiting and others of the old White Pass team. Together, they worked to build the Copper River and Northwestern Railroad, a 131-mile line running from Cordova to Chitina, with a sixty-five-mile branch line to the Kennecott mine.

Sadly, Heney did not see the completion of the railway. On August 29, 1909, the steamer *Ohio*, on which he was travelling north, struck a reef after leaving Millbank Sound on the northern British Columbia coast, and sank. Heney worked ceaselessly during the ordeal, rescuing passengers, releasing trapped horses, and spending much time in the water. He had always said that you could never trust the sea – only rivers could be trusted. His long exposure to the cold left him exhausted. A deep chest cold resulted from which he never recovered.

The following year, on October 4, 1910, he died in San Francisco of pulmonary tuberculosis.

He is buried in Calvary Cemetery, Seattle, Washington.

He was forty-six years of age.

Erastus Corning Hawkins

Hawkins remained as the railway's general manager until 1902, when, with Thomas O'Brian and W.H. Parsons, he promoted and built the Klondike Mines Railway – a short line based in Dawson City, which served the Klondike goldfields. On its completion, he joined the engineering staff of the Union Pacific Railroad, where he remained for nearly five years.

After the Guggenheims' unsuccessful attempt to construct a railway from Valdez and Katalla to their Alaska copper properties, Michael J. Heney signed a contract to construct the railway along a route of his own choice – one in which both he and Close Brothers and Company had an interest. Heney sent for Hawkins, who became the chief engineer of the project. He was later appointed the railway's vice-president and general manager.

Known as the Copper River and Northwestern Railroad, its completion was seriously doubted, particularly as Hawkins was required to bridge the Copper River between Miles Glacier and Childs Glacier – an engineering feat that was regarded by many experienced engineers as an impossible undertaking. But consistent with his past accomplishments, he bridged the river, an achievement that made him known as "the engineering genius of the Alaska Mountains."

He left the North in October 1911, carrying an engraved testimonial that stated that he was the modern founder of Cordova and that he was "the guiding genius who accomplished the most wonderful engineering achievements in the nearly four years that he was here."

In late February 1912, he travelled to New York to submit his final report to the directors of the Copper River and Northwestern Railroad, which had been in operation for a year.

On arrival, he started to feel ill and he was taken to hospital, where, on April 9, 1912, he died after an operation.

He was fifty-two years of age.

John Hislop

After the completion of the White Pass railway, John Hislop requested one year's leave of absence, which was granted, commencing December 1, 1900.

On December 2, 1900, he left Skagway for Chicago where he married his fiancée, Mary Edith Young, in January 1901.

He then returned to Chicago to visit with his bride's relatives and to keep a number of business appointments, one of which concerned the construction of a short-line railway near Valdez, Alaska.

On February 22, 1901, four weeks less a day after his marriage, he left the home of his bride's brother to attend a business meeting in downtown Chicago. At the Englewood railway station he saw the Rock Island suburban train leaving, slowly gaining speed. He ran forward and grasped a coach handrail as he leaped onto the coach steps. At that moment, his coat caught on a protruding trestle beam. He was jerked from the train and flung under the wheels. His right leg was severed above the knee and his skull was crushed.

The train was brought to a stop. Hislop was taken to the Englewood Union Hospital, where he was pronounced dead on arrival.

He was forty-five years of age.

BIBLIOGRAPHY

While I was researching and writing this book, the White Pass and Yukon Corporation gave me free and unhindered access to available files, maps, and drawings relating to the construction of the railway. It was also my good fortune to stumble upon a number of old documents relating to the early days of northern transportation that were destined for the trash pile. I retrieved a number of papers that helped greatly in completing my analysis of the events that transpired in Skagway, the White Pass, and along the gold-rush trails during the stampedes to the Klondike and the gold-fields of Atlin.

UNPUBLISHED SOURCES

Anon. "Memorandum and Articles of Association of the British Columbia Development Association Limited, 5 December 1895." The Companies Acts, 1862-1898. Public Records Office, Chancery Lane, London, England. Red BT31/6575, and "Extract from Minutes of Board Meeting, 6 September 1897. The British Columbia Development Association Limited, London." Public Records Office, Chancery Lane, London, BT31/6575.

————. "Draft Prospectus, White Pass and Yukon Railway Company, Limited," 2 April 1898. White Pass and Yukon Railway Company Limited files. (Privately held.)

————. "Memorandum of Association, White Pass and Yukon Railway Company." 30 July 1898. The Companies Acts, 1862-1898. The Companies House, London, England.

————. White Pass and Yukon Railway Company Limited files. (Privately held by author).

Brackett, George A. Papers. Manuscript Collection, Minnesota Historical Society, St. Paul, Minnesota.

Cartwright, F.L. "Annual Report of Inspector F.L. Cartright, N.W.M.P., White Pass Detachment, 1898." Appendix 1. In Annual Report of NWMP, Part III, Yukon Territory, 1898. RCMP Archives, Ottawa.

Christie, C.G. "Report by C.J. Christie, C.E., on the Route of the White Pass and Yukon Railway to the Directors of the Pacific Contract Company." (Papers privately held).

Gauvreau, Narcisse Belleau. "Exploration of the North-West Portion of the Province." Crown Land Surveys. PABC, Victoria.

Hawkins, E.C. "Report of the Chief Engineer on the Construction of the First Portion of the Railway," Part I, 31 March 1900; Part II, ca. 15 August 1900. Papers among White Pass and Yukon Railway files. (Privately held.)

Hislop, John. Papers. (Privately held by Robert E. and Helenita Harvey.)

Laurier, Sir Wilfrid. Letter, Mitchell to Laurier, 20 March 1897. Papers, PAC.

Moore, William, and Moore, J.B. Papers. Skagway City Hall. Records.

Ogilvie, William. "Report, Exploratory Survey of the Yukon River District." PABC, Victoria.

Rogers, Clifford J. Papers. (Privately held by author.)

Sifton, Clifford. Letter to George R. Patullo, 14 April 1899. Papers, PAC.

Steele, S.B. "Annual Report of Superintendent S.B. Steele." Annual Report of N.W.M.P., Part III, Yukon Territory, 1898.

Stretch, R.H. Vistas of Life, 1906-07.

Tancred, Sir Thomas S. "White Pass & Yukon Railway. Report of the Directors of the Pacific Contract Company Limited." April, 1899. Close Brothers Company files. (Privately held.)

Wood, Z.T. "Annual Report of Superintendent Z.T. Wood, Appendix A, North-West Mounted Police Annual Report, 1 November 1898-1900." RCMP Archives, Ottawa. BT31/6575.

ORAL HISTORY INTERVIEWS
   (with R.S. Minter)

Barteau, Ernest.	June, 1963
Boss, Fred.	1960
MacBride, W.D.	1957-1968
Murchison, Alice.	April, 1964
Rogers, Clifford J.	1957-1970
Shiels, Archie.	November, 1966
Sweet, Walter.	June, 1963
Watson, Matthew.	1957-1960

GOVERNMENT DOCUMENTS

Canada. Parliament. *Senate Debates*, Official Report (Hansard). Ottawa, 3rd Parliament, 5th Session, 1878.

———. Parliament. *Senate Debates*, Official Report (Hansard). Ottawa, 3rd Parliament, 5th Session, 14 April 1899.

———. Parliament. *Senate Debates*, Official Report (Hansard). Ottawa, 3rd Parliament, 5th Session, 28 April 1899. Special Committee Report on opening up Direct Communication between the Railway System of Canada and the Navigable Waters of the Yukon.

———. Department of the Interior. Report Respecting the Yukon District. By Major J.M. Walsh. Ottawa, 1898.

————. *House of Commons, Sessional Papers*, No. 15, 1899. "Report of the North-West Mounted Police, 1898, Part II, Instructions to and Diary of J.D. Moodie in charge of Patrol from Edmonton to the Yukon, 1897." Ottawa: Queen's Printer, 1899.

British Columbia. *British Columbia Sessional Papers*, 6 January 1888. "Report Upon Yukon Country, 1888." PABC, Victoria.

————. *Statutes of British Columbia*, Chapter 49, 8 May 1897. "An Act to incorporate the British Columbia-Yukon Railroad Company."

————. Legislative Assembly of British Columbia. 1 April 1897. "Twenty-Second Report, Select Standing Committee on Private Bills and Standing Orders."

————. Legislative Assembly of British Columbia. *Journals, Sessional Papers*, 1873-4. "William Moore's Charter." PABC, Victoria.

Beardslee, L.A. *Report of Captain L.A. Beardslee, U.S. Navy, Relative to Affairs in Alaska*. Executive Document, 1st Session, 47th Congress, Washington, D.C.: Government Printing Office, 1882.

Bearss, Edwin C. *Proposed Klondike Gold Rush: Historice Resource Study*. Washington, D.C. Office of History and Historic Architecture, 1970.

Dawson, George M. Report on an Exploration in the Yukon District, N.W.T. and Adjacent Northern Portion of British Columbia, 1887. Ottawa: Printer to the Queen's Most Excellency, 1898.

Ogilvie, William. Information respecting the Yukon District from the Reports of Wm. Ogilvie, Dominion Land Surveyor and from other sources. Ottawa: Government Printing Bureau, 1897.

————. *Yukon Handbook*. Ottawa: Minister of the Interior, 1898.

Spude, Robert, and Gordon Chappell. *Skagway's Railroad Headquarters: the Broadway Depot and General Offices of the White Pass and Yukon Route*. Historical Data Section, Historic Structures Report. Anchorage: National Parks Services, 1984.

Great Britain. House of Lords. *Assets Development Company Limited*, n.d. (Extract from official "Minutes of Proceedings" of the House of Lords on 7 August 1903: Close Brothers & Company -vs- Assets Development Company Limited et e contra.)

United States. U.S. Department of Commerce. *Pacific Coast Pilot-Alaska: Coast and Geodetic Survey*, 2 vols. Washington: Government Printing Office, 1883.

————. U.S. Department of the Interior. *Alaskan Boundary Tribunal: the Counter Case of the United States*. Washington: Government Printing Office, 1903.

————. State of Alaska, Division of Lands, Department of Natural Resources. *The Chilkoot Trail: Trail of '98*. 1968.

NEWSPAPERS

Skagway-Atlin Budget	Skagway, 1899-1900
Daily Alaskan	Skagway, 1898-1913
Daily British Colonist	Victoria, 1866
Daily Colonist	Victoria, 1897-1902
Daily News	Victoria, 1902

Daily Standard	London, 1897
Daily Times	Victoria, 1902
Dawson News	Dawson, 1902, 1913
Financial News	Toronto, 1898
Globe	Toronto, 1897-98
Globe-Democrat	St. Louis, 1898
Journal	Minneapolis, 1898, 1910
Monetary Times	Toronto, 1898
Morning Leader	Superior, Wisconsin, 1898
News	Skagway, 1897-98, 1901
Klondike Nugget	Dawson, 1899
Oregonian	Portland, 1899
Post-Intelligencer	Seattle, 1897-98
Province	Vancouver, 1898
Rocky Mountain News	Denver, Colorado, 1889
Scheme	Yukon, 1897
Star	Whitehorse, 1974
Sun	Bennett City, 1900
Sun	Dawson, 1900
Sun	Vancouver, 1964
Times	Seattle, 1898
World	New York, 1898

PUBLISHED DOCUMENTS

Adney, Tappan. *The Klondike Stampede*. New York: Harper & Bros., 1900.

Alaska Section American Society of Civil Engineers. *Alaska's Engineering Heritage: Bridge from Past to Future*. Juneau, Alaska: Alaska Section American Society of Civil Engineers, 1976.

Andrews, C.L. "Biographical Sketch of Captain William Moore," *Washington Historical Quarterly*, 21, 1 (January, 1930). Part 1, pp. 195-203; 21, 1 (January, 1930), Part 2, pp. 217-80; 22, 1 (January, 1931), Part 3, pp. 32-41; 22, 2 (April, 1931), Part 4, pp. 99-110.

Barkhouse, Joyce C. *George Dawson, the Little Giant*. Vancouver: Clarke, Irwin, 1974.

Barry, Mary J. *A History of Mining on the Kenai Peninsula*. Anchorage: Alaska Northwest, 1973.

Bearss, Edwin C., and Bruce M. White. "George Brackett's Wagon Road: Minnesota Enterprise on a New Frontier," *Minnesota History*, 45, 2 (Summer, 1976).

Becker, Ethel Anderson. "Monument at Dead Horse Gulch," *Alaska Sportsman* (May, 1957).

Bennett, Gordon, "Yukon Transportation: A History," Canadian Historic Sites: Occasional Papers in Archeology and History, No. 19. Ottawa: Public Information Branch, 1978.

Berton, Pierre. *Klondike: the Life and Death of the Last Great Gold Rush*. Toronto: McClelland and Stewart, 1958.

Betts, William James. "Captain Bill Moore, the Dreamer Who Lost a Town," *Alaska*

Sportsman (July, 1964).

Burch, Franklin W. *Alaska's Railroad Frontier: Railroads and Federal Development Policy, 1898-1915*. Washington: Catholic University of America, 1965.

Chase, Will H. *Reminiscences of Captain Billie Moore*. Kansas City: Burton, 1947.

Conkey Co. *Official Guide to the Klondike Country and the Gold Fields of Alaska*. Chicago: Conkey, 1897.

Crofutt, W.A. "A Railroad to the Yukon," *Frank Leslie's Popular Monthly*, 1 April 1900.

Dalby, Milton A. *The Sea Saga of Dynamite Johnny O'Brien*. Seattle: Lowman & Hanford, 1933.

Dall, William H. *Alaska and Its Resources*. Boston: Lee and Sheppard, 1870.

Emerson, Harrington. "The Engineer & the Road to the Yukon Gold Fields," *Engineering Magazine* (March, 1899).

Friesen, Richard J. *The Chilkoot Pass and the Great Gold Rush*. History and Archeology 48. Ottawa: Minister of Supply and Services, 1981.

Graves, S.H. *On the "White Pass" Pay-roll*. Chicago: Lakeside Press, 1908.

Green, Lewis. *The Boundary Hunters: Surveying the 141st Meridian and the Alaska Panhandle*. Vancouver: University of British Columbia Press, 1982.

Harris, A.C. *Alaska and the Klondike Gold Fields Containing a Full Account of the Discovery of Gold*. Philadelphia: Philadelphia National, 1897.

Herron, Edward A. *Alaska's Railroad Builder, Mike Heney*. New York: Julian Messner, 1960.

Hinton, A. Cherry, with Philip Godsell. *The Yukon*. Toronto: Ryerson, 1954.

Hulley, Clarence C. *Alaska: Past and Present*. Portland: Binfords & Mort, 1958.

Ingersoll, Ernest. *Gold Fields of the Klondike and the Wonders of Alaska*. Philadelphia: Edgewood, 1897.

Jennings, W.T. "Report of W.T. Jennings, C.E.," *Routes to the Yukon*. Ottawa: Queen's Printer, 1898.

Kirk, Robert C. *Twelve Months in the Klondike*. London: William Heineman, 1899.

Kitchener, L.D. *Flag Over the North: the Story of the Northern Commercial Company*. Seattle: Superior, 1954.

Krause, Aurel. *The Tlingit Indians*. Seattle: University of Washington Press, 1956.

Ladue, Joseph, *Klondyke Facts*. New York: American Technical Book Co., 1897.

Lawrence, Guy. *40 Years on the Yukon Telegraph*. Vancouver: Mitchell, 1965.

Lung, Edward B. *Black Sand and Gold As Told to Ella Lung Mastinsen*. New York: Vantage, 1956.

MacBride, William D. "Soapy Smith – Scourge of the Klondike," *Northwest Digest* (March, 1952).

MacDonald, Alexander. *In Search of Eldorado: A Wanderer's Experience*. London: Unwin, 1906.

Martens, A.H. *The Colourful History of Close Brothers*. London: Hepburn & Sons, 1964.

McIntosh, R.I. "The New Route to the Klondike," *Wide World Magazine*, 1 (1897).

McLain, John Scudder. *Alaska and the Klondike*. New York: McClure, Philips, 1905.

Mildred, Sister Mary. *The Apostle of Alaska: Life of the Most Reverend Charles John Seghers*. Paterson, N.J.: St. Anthony Guild House, 1943.

Miller, Mike. *Soapy*. Juneau, Alaska: Alaskabooks, 1970.

———. *Alaska Book*. Juneau, Alaska, 1970.

Moore, J. Bernard. *Skagway in Days Primeval*. New York: Vantage, 1968.

Morgan, Edward P., and Henry F. Woods. *God's Loaded Dice*. Caldwell, Idaho: Caxton, 1948.

Munn, Henry Toke. *Prairie Trails and Arctic Byways*. London: Hurst, 1932.

Newell, Gordon R. *The H.W. McCurdy Marine History of the Pacific Northwest*. Seattle: Superior, 1966.

Newell, Gordon, and Joe Williamson. *Pacific Coastal Liners*. Seattle: Superior, 1959.

Ogilvie. William. *Early Days on the Yukon*. Toronto: Bell & Cockburn, 1913.

Robertson, Frank C., and Beth Kay Harris. *Soapy Smith: King of the Frontier Con Men*. Toronto: Saunders, 1961.

Satterfield, Archie. *Chilkoot Pass: Then and Now*. Anchorage: Alaska Northwest, 1973.

Schwatka, Frederick. *Along Alaska's Great Rivers*. New York: Cassell, 1895.

Secretan, J.H.E. *To Klondyke and Back*. London: Hurst and Blacett, 1898.

Seggar, Martin. *The British Columbia Parliament Buildings*. Vancouver: Arcon, 1979.

Sherwood, Morgan B. *Explorations of Alaska 1865-1900*. New Haven: Yale University Press, 1965.

Shiels, Archie W. *The Purchase of Alaska*. College, Alaska: University of Alaska Press, 1967.

Sinclair, James M. *Mission: Klondike*. Vancouver: Mitchell, 1978.

Sporr, Josiah E. *Through the Yukon Gold Diggings, A Narrative of Personal Travel*. Boston: Eastern, 1900.

Spude, Robert L.S. "Skagway, District of Alaska, 1884-1912: Building the Gateway to the Klondike," Anthropology and Historic Preservation, Cooperative Park Studies Unit, Occasional Paper No. 36. Fairbanks: University of Alaska Press, 1983.

Steele, Samuel B. *Forty Years in Canada*. Toronto: McGraw-Hill, Ryerson, 1972.

Stumer, Harold Merritt. *This was Klondike Fever*. Seattle: Superior, 1978.

Tancred, Sir Thomas S. "White Pass & Yukon Railway," *Railway and Shipping World* (October, 1898).

The Chicago Record. *Klondike: The Chicago's Book for Gold Seekers*. Chicago: Chicago Record, 1897.

Walden, A. *A Dog-Puncher on the Yukon*. New York: Houghton Mifflin, 1928.

Warman Cy. "Building a Railroad into the Klondike," *McClure's Magazine* 14 (March, 1900).

Watt, Bob and Nancy. *Skagway*. Skagway: Skagway Historical Society, 1969.

Whiting, F.B. *Grit, Grief and Gold*. Seattle: Peacock, 1933.

Wickersham, James, ed. *Alaska Reports*, Vol. 1. St. Paul, Minnesota: West, 1903.

Wright, A. *Prelude to Bonanza*. Sidney, B.C.: Gray's, 1976.

NOTES

CHAPTER 1

1. Ogilvie, *Early Days on the Yukon*, pp. 36-37.
2. *Ibid.*, p. 30.
3. Ogilvie, as quoted by *Victoria Daily Times*, 27 July 1902.
4. Morley, "B.C.'s Greatest Explorer Was a Little Man – But He Stood Tall," *Vancouver Sun*, 18 April 1964.
5. Dawson, *Report on an Exploration in the Yukon District*, p. 2.
6. Ogilvie, as quoted by *Victoria Daily Colonist*, 27 July 1902.
7. Chase, Reminiscences of Captain Billie Moore, p. 12.
8. Andrews, "Biographical Sketch of Captain William Moore," *Washington Historical Quarterly*, p. 38.
9. State of Alaska, Division of Lands, *The Chilkoot Trail*, p. 40.
10. Ogilvie, *Report*, p. 64.
11. Ogilvie, *Early Days*, p. 37.
12. *Ibid.*, p. 39.
13. *Ibid.*, p. 40.
14. Ogilvie, as quoted by *Victoria Daily Times*, 27 July 1902.
15. Berton, *Klondike*, p. 41.
16. Moore, *Skagway in Days Primeval*, p. 35.
17. Ogilvie, as quoted by *Victoria Daily Colonist*, 27 July 1902.
18. Captain William Moore, as quoted by the *Daily Alaskan* and *Dawson News*, 22 April 1913.
19. Ogilvie, *Yukon Handbook*, p. 18.
20. Moore, *op. cit.*, pp. 15-16.
21. *Ibid.*, pp. 90-91.
22. Ogilvie, as quoted by *Victoria Daily Colonist*, 27 July 1902.
23. *Ibid.*
24. *Ibid.*
25. Ogilvie, *Yukon Handbook*, p. 22.
26. *Ibid.*, p. 26.
27. Ogilvie, as quoted by *Victoria Daily Colonist*, 27 July 1902.
28. William Moore to Lieutenant-Governor C.L. Cornwall, 22 and 26 February 1883. *Canadian Correspondence, 1882 to 1878*. Moore Papers, PAC.

29. Ogilvie, as quoted by *Victoria Daily Colonist*, 27 July 1902.

30. Moore, *op. cit.*, p. 82.

31. William Moore & Son to F.G. Vernon, "Report Upon Yukon Country," p. 496.

32. Moore, *op. cit.*, p. 92.

33. *Ibid.*, p. 94.

34. *Ibid.*, p. 95.

35. *Ibid.*, p. 102.

36. *Ibid.*, p. 102.

37. *Ibid.*, pp. 111, 122.

38. *Ibid.*, p. 110.

CHAPTER 2

1. Memorandum of Association of the British Columbia Development Association, Limited, 14 December 1895, Public Record Office, BT 31/6575.

2. Gavreau, "Exploration of the North-Western Portion of the Province," *Crown Land Surveys*, pp. 483, 497, 499.

3. William Moore to Lieutenant-Governor Edgar Dewdney, 6 March 1893, "Roads in the Yukon District," *B.C. Sessional Papers, 1893*, p. 672.

4. Moore, as quoted by *Victoria Daily Colonist*, 1 December 1895.

5. William Moore, with attachments, to the Honourable Forbes G. Vernon, Chief Commissioner of Lands and Works, Victoria, 3 May 1892, "Roads in Yukon District," *B.C. Sessional Papers, 1892*, pp. 667-69.

6. Moore, as quoted by *Victoria Daily Colonist*, 1 December 1895.

7. Deposition of Capt. William Moore, 23 March 1903, *Alaskan Boundary Tribunal*, p. 417.

8. Green, *The Boundary Hunters*, pp. 54, 55.

9. *Victoria Daily Colonist, Supplement*, 5 August 1900.

10. Author's correspondence with James Nesbitt.

11. *Victoria Daily Colonist*, 9 August 1959.

12. *Ibid.*

13. Personal communication from W.D. MacBride.

14. Moore, *op. cit.*, p. 178.

15. *Victoria Daily Colonist, Supplement*, 5 August 1900.

16. *Ibid.*

17. Kitchener, *Flag Over the North*, p. 195.

18. Berton, *op. cit.*, p. 22.

19. Close to Pennington, 18 December 1897.

CHAPTER 3

1. Burke & McGilvra to Drake, Jackson & Helmcken, 17 June 1896. House of Lords, *Assets Development Company, Limited*.

2. Moore, *op. cit.*, p. 178.

3. Green, *op. cit.*, p. 54.

4. "Annual Report of Superintendent Z.T. Wood, Appendix A," North-West Mounted Police: Annual Report, 1898, p. 35.

5. Moore, *op. cit.*, p. 201.

6. Ogilvie, *Early Days*, p. 157.

7. *Ibid.*, p. 158.

8. *Ibid.*, pp. 158, 159.

9. Green, *op. cit.*, p. 43.

10. Personal communication from Patsy Henderson, Indian resident, Carcross, Yukon.

11. Adney, *The Klondike Stampede*, p. 280.

12. *Ibid.*, p. 287.

13. Ogilvie, *Early Days*, p. 130.

14. *Ibid.*, p. 130.

15. Adney, *op. cit.*, p. 288.

16. Ogilvie, *Early Days*, p. 130.

17. Berton, *op. cit.*, p. 48.

18. *Ibid.*, p. 50.

19. *Ibid.*, p. 51.

20. *Ibid.*, p. 52.

21. *Ibid.*, p. 59.

22. Ogilvie, *Early Days*, p. 212.

23. Berton, *op. cit.*, p. 74.

24. Close to Pennington, 18 December 1897. House of Lords, *Assets Development Company, Limited*.

25. Townsend to Wilkinson, 15 November 1897. *Ibid.*

26. The British Columbia Development Association, Limited. Extract from minutes of Board Meeting, 6 September 1897.

27. Legislative Assembly of British Columbia, 1 April 1897. Select Standing Committee on Private Bills and Standing Orders. Twenty-Second Report.

28. *Statutes of British Columbia*, Chapter 49. An Act to Incorporate the British Columbia-Yukon Railway Company, 8 May 1897.

29. Bennett, *Yukon Transportation*, p. 46.

30. Mitchell to Laurier, Ottawa, 20 March 1897. Laurier Papers, PAC.

31. House of Commons, *Journals*, Vol. 32, 1897.

32. "Petitioners' List for Incorporating the British Yukon Chartered Company," in *Victoria Daily Colonist*, 1 May 1897.

33. *Globe*, 22 April 1897; *Victoria Daily Colonist*, 1 May 1897.

34. *Victoria Daily Colonist*, 15 May 1897.

35. *Times*, 22 May 1897. *Victoria Daily Colonist*, 30 May 1897.

36. *Victoria Daily Colonist*, 30 May 1897.

37. Secretary of the Interior, Washington, D.C., to Messrs Struve, Allen, Hughes & McMicken, 30 September 1897. Lands and Railroad Division, National Archives, Washington, D.C.

38. *Victoria Daily Colonist*, June, 1897.

39. *Ibid.*, 3 May 1897.

40. *Ibid.*
41. *Ibid.*

CHAPTER 4

1. Adney, *Klondike Stampede*, pp. 1, 2.
2. *Ibid.*, p. 1.
3. *Ibid.*, p. 2.
4. Berton, *op. cit.*, p. 107.
5. *Seattle Post-Intelligencer*, 17 July 1897.
6. *Monetary Times*, 31, 3 (16 July 1897), p. 114.
7. Kirk, *Twelve Months In Klondike*, pp. 10, 11.
8. Adney, *op. cit.*, pp. 48, 49.
9. *Ibid.*, p. 47.
10. Watt, *Skagway*, pp. 2, 3, 5, 6.
11. Adney, *op. cit.*, pp. 53, 54.
12. Author's correspondence with Robert L. Spude, Regional Historian, United States National Park Service, Alaska Regional Office.
13. Betts, "Captain Bill Moore," *Alaska Sportsman*, p. 56.
14. Adney, *op. cit.*, p. 74.
15. *Ibid.*, p. 67.
16. Kirk, *Twelve Months in Klondike*, p. 23.
17. *Ibid.*, p. 43.
18. Adney, *op. cit.*, p. 114.
19. Memo as to Stamping the Various Instruments, 11 January 1898; Close to Pennington, 18 December 1897; Memorandum of Option, 29 October 1897; Minutes of Board Meeting, British Columbia Development Association, Limited, 9 September 1897.
20. Martens, *The Colourful History of Close Brothers*, p. 64.
21. Draft of the Contemplated Contract for Loan of 10,000 pounds to C.H. Wilkinson, 17 November 1897. House of Lords, *Assets Development Company, Limited*.
22. Longbourne Stevens & Co. to Close Brothers & Company, 15 December 1897. *Ibid.*
23. Close to Pennington, *et al.*, 18 December 1897. *Ibid.*
24. Draft, 17 November 1897. *Ibid.*
25. Midgely to Wilkinson, c. early December, 1897. *Ibid.*
26. Midgely to the Secretary, Exploration Company, Limited, 27 January 1898. *Ibid.*
27. Close to Wilkinson, 24 January 1898; Magner to Wilkinson, 12 February 1898. *Ibid.*

CHAPTER 5

1. Brady to the Secretary of the Interior, as quoted by *Victoria Daily Colonist*, 21 August 1897.
2. MacDonald, *In Search of Eldorado*, p. 3.

3. Mann, *Prairie Trails and Arctic Byways*, p. 75.
4. Steele, *Forty Years in Canada*, pp. 295-96.
5. Quoted by Alaska-Yukon historian, William D. MacBride, during a conversation with the author.
6. Green, "First Christmas in Skagway," *Alaska Sportsman* (December, 1967), p. 51.
7. *Ibid.*, p. 3.
8. Brackett to Acklen, 29 December 1897. Brackett Papers.
9. McIntosh, "New Route to Klondike," *World Wide Magazine*, 1 (1897), p. 69.
10. *Ibid.*
11. Rowan to the Secretary of the Interior, 26 July 1897. "Interior Department, Territorial Papers, Alaska, 1869-1911." National Archives Microfilm Publication 430. Records Center, Seattle, Washington.
12. *Ibid.*, 7 August 1897.
13. Biographic Directory of American Congress, 1774-1961.
14. Adney, *op. cit.*, p. 35.
15. *Ibid.*, pp. 44, 45.
16. Moore, *op. cit.*, pp. 167, 168.
17. Hielscher, "Over Chilkoot Pass," *Daily Alaskan*, 3 February 1898.
18. Acklen to Brackett, 26 October 1897. Brackett Papers.
19. *Victoria Daily Colonist*, 27 January 1898. (Reprint of article on Yukon Railroads originally published in *Toronto Mail and Empire*.)
20. George W. Mitchell to Sir Wilfrid Laurier, 20 March 1897. Laurier Papers, PAC.
21. "Report of W.T. Jennings, C.E., *Routes to the Yukon*.
22. Burch, *Alaska's Railroad Frontier*, p. 81.
23. *Railway and Engineering Review*, XXXVI (19 September 1896), p. 531.
24. Burch, *op. cit.*, p. 81.
25. *Monetary Times*, 25 February 1898, p. 1118.
26. *Victoria Daily Colonist*, 27 January 1898.
27. *Skagway News*, 15 October 1897.
28. "Agreement between the Alaskan and North Western Territories Trading Company of West Virginia and Assets Development Company of London, England, 11 November 1897." House of Lords, *Assets Development Company, Limited.*
29. Hartman to Acklen, 29 November 1897. Brackett Papers.
30. Acklen to Brackett, 29 November 1897. *Ibid.*
31. Brackett to Acklen, 7 November 1897. *Ibid.*
32. *New York World*, 20 December 1898; *Minneapolis Journal*, 10 April 1910.
33. Bearss and White, "George Brackett's Wagon Road," *Minnesota History*, 45 (1976), p. 47.
34. Brackett to Acklen, 29 December 1897. Brackett Papers.
35. Brackett to Senator Davis, 29 October 1897. Brackett Papers.
36. Crofutt, "A Railroad to the Yukon," *Frank Leslies' Popular Monthly* (April 1900), p. 617.
37. Robertson and Harris, *Soapy Smith*, pp. 27, 66, 67; "J.R. Smith," *Skagway News*, 9 July 1898. MacBride, "Soapy Smith – Scourge of the Klondike," *Northwest Digest* (March, 1952).

38. Robertson and Harris, *op. cit.*, p. 158.
39. *Rocky Mountain News*, 30 July 1889.
40. Robertson and Harris, *op. cit.*, p. 159.
41. *Ibid.*, p. 20.
42. *Ibid.*.
43. *Ibid.*, p. 9.
44. *Ibid.*, p. 159.
45. *Seattle Post-Intelligencer*, 25 February 1898.

CHAPTER 6

1. Brackett to Acklen, 10 November 1897. Brackett Papers.
2. *Ibid.*
3. *Ibid.*
4. Acklen to Brackett, 26 October 1897. Brackett Papers.
5. *Ibid.*
6. *Ibid.*
7. Acklen to Brackett, 24 November 1897. Brackett Papers.
8. Acklen to Brackett, 29 November 1897. *Ibid.*
9. Samson to Brackett, 30 November 1897. *Ibid.*
10. Bearss and White, *op. cit.*, p. 49.
11. *Ibid.*, p. 50.
12. Brackett to Acklen, 29 December 1897. Brackett Papers.
13. *Minneapolis Journal*, 8 June 1898.
14. Brackett to Acklen, 7 November 1897. Acklen to Brackett, 24 November 1897. Brackett Papers.
15. Brackett to Senator Davis, 7 December 1897. *Ibid.*
16. Croffut, *op. cit.*, p. 649.
17. Brackett to Acklen, 29 December 1897. Brackett Papers.
18. Telegram, Van Horne to Brackett, 7 January 1898. *Ibid.*
19. *Minneapolis Journal*, undated news clip (c. 1892). Brackett Papers.
20. *Ibid.*
21. Bearss and White, *op. cit.*, p. 51.
22. Brackett to Horne, 13 January 1898. Brackett Papers.
23. Van Horne to Brackett, 13 January 1898. *Ibid.*
24. Brackett to Horne, 12 January 1898. *Ibid.*
25. Van Horne to Brackett, 29 January 1898. *Ibid.*
26. Emerson, "The Engineer and the Road to the Yukon Gold Fields," *Engineering Magazine* (March, 1899).
27. Bearss and White, *op. cit.*, p. 55.
28. Brackett to Van Horne, 8 March 1898. Brackett Papers.
29. A.S. Kerry's letter, "To whom it may concern," 26 February 1898. *Ibid.*
30. Brackett newspaper advertisement, *Seattle Times*, 15 March 1898. *Ibid.*
31. P. Humbert, Jr., to Brackett, 27 February 1898. *Ibid.*
32. Brackett newspaper advertisement, *Seattle Times*, 15 March 1898. *Ibid.*
33. *Skagway Times*, undated item. *Ibid.*

34. Wallace newspaper advertisement, *Seattle Times*, 15 March 1898. *Ibid.*

CHAPTER 7

1. Illustration and advertisements, *Seattle Post-Intelligencer*, 4 August 1898.
2. Author's interview with Archie Shiels, who was once Heney's field secretary.
3. Herron, *Alaska's Railroad Builder*, p. 40.
4. Barry, *A History of Mining on the Kenai Peninsula*, p. 32.
5. Stretch, Chapter 16 of his unpublished manuscript. Courtesy personal files of Mike Butler, Seattle, Washington.
6. *Seattle Times*, 15 February 1898.
7. *Victoria Daily Colonist*, 21 February 1898.
8. *Seattle Times*, 10 February 1898.
9. *Daily Colonist*, 17 February 1898.
10. Whiting, *Grit, Grief and Gold*, p. xiii; Herron, *op. cit.*, p. 78.
11. Personal communication with Mrs. C. Cassidy, Heney descendant, Ottawa, Ontario.
12. PAC., RG 12, Vol. 1897, Sections 3356-31 (1-5), Contracting General 2-1.
13. Whiting, *op. cit.*; Herron, *op. cit.*, *passim*; *Ottawa Journal*, 18 December 1954.
14. *Seattle Times*, 17 January 1898.
15. *Seattle Times*, 12 March 1898.
16. Personal communication with residents and former residents of Skagway.
17. *Seattle Post-Intelligencer*, 27 March 1898.
18. *Seattle Times*, 12 March 1898.
19. *Ibid.*, 27 February 1898.
20. *Daily Alaskan*, 3 September 1898.
21. *Seattle Times*, undated news clip, March, 1898.
22. Warman, "Building a Railroad into the Klondike," *McClure's Magazine*, 14 (March, 1900), p. 243.
23. Becker, "Monument at Dead Horse Gulch," *Alaska Sportsman* (May, 1957).
24. *Ibid.*
25. "Annual Report of Inspector F.L. Cartwright, N.W.M.P., White Pass Detachment, 1893."
26. Personal communication, RCMP historian S.W. Horrall, 19 May 1983.
27. "Annual Report of Superintendent Z.T. Wood, N.W.M.P."
28. "Annual Report of Inspector F.L. Cartwright, N.W.M.P., White Pass Detachment, 1898."
29. "Annual Report of Inspector R. Belcher," *Annual Report of N.W.M.P., Part III, Yukon Territories, 1898*, RCMP Archives, Ottawa.
30. "Annual Report of Superintendent Z.T. Wood, N.W.M.P."

CHAPTER 8

1. Townsend to Midgely, 15 November 1897. House of Lords, *Assets Development Company, Limited*.
2. Midgely to Wilkinson, 12 February 1898. *Ibid.*

3. Telegram: Magner to Wilkinson, 17 February 1898. *Ibid.*
4. Telegram: Magner to Wilkinson, 18 February 1898. *Ibid.*
5. Telegram: Wilkinson to Magner, 18 February 1898. *Ibid.*
6. "Memorandum of Association, Pacific Contract Company, Limited, 8 March, 1898," Public Records Office, Chancery Lane, London.
7. Midgely to Close, 12 March 1898.
8. Magner to Wilkinson, March, 1898.
9. Prichard to Wilkinson, telegram, 26 February 1898.
10. *Financial News*, 6 December 1898; *Railway and Shipping World* (January, 1899).
11. *Monetary Times*, 11 February 1898; 25 March 1898.
12. Midgely to Close, 5 March 1898. House of Lords, *Assets Development Company, Limited*.
13. Sir Charles Tupper, quoted in a speech on the "Canadian Yukon Railway" by Hon. Clifford Sifton, MP, House of Commons, Ottawa, 15 February 1898. *Senate Debates, Official Report* (Hansard), 15, 16 February 1898.
14. Speech by Sir Charles Tupper, House of Commons, Ottawa, pp. 20, 23. *Senate Debates, Official Report* (Hansard), 14 April 1899.
15. *Vancouver Province*, 26 March 1898.
16. *Globe*, 30 March 1898, as reprinted in *Victoria Daily Colonist*, 31 March 1898.
17. Clifford Sifton to George R. Patullo, 14 Aprill 1899, Sifton Papers, PAC.
18. Legislative Assembly of British Columbia, 1898. *Journals*.
19. *Ibid.*
20. Whiting, *op. cit.*, pp. 3-4.
21. Wilkinson to Magner, 3 March 1898. House of Lords. *Assets Development Company, Limited*.
22. Moore, *op. cit.*, p. 21.
23. U.S. Secretary of the Interior to the Commissioner of the General Land Office – re John G. Price vs. Bernard Moore, 7 January 1901, Vol. 28, No. 49, in the Moore Papers. City of Skagway, City Hall Records, File 1044, p. 1.
24. *Ibid.*, pp. 4-5.
25. *Ibid.*, p. 6; *Skagway News*, 31 January 1901.
26. *Seattle Post-Intelligencer*, 23 June 1898.
27. Hawkins to Berdoe, 29 February 1899. Author's file.
28. Hawkins, "Report," 31 March 1900. *Ibid.*
29. *Daily Alaskan*, 14, 15 June 1898; *Seattle Post-Intelligencer*, 23 June 1898.
30. Tancred, "*White Pass & Yukon Railway Report*," April, 1898. Courtesy Close Brothers & Company Files, London, England.
31. *Seattle Post-Intelligencer*, 21 April 1898.
32. *Oregonian*, 15 April 1898.
33. Hawkins, "Report," 31 March 1900.
34. Whiting, *op. cit.*, p. 5; Tancred, *op. cit.*
35. Whiting, *op. cit.*, p. 4.
36. Hawkins, "Report," 27 April 1898.
37. Whiting, *op. cit.*, p. 5.
38. *Ibid.*, p. 6.
39. *Ibid.*, p. 7.

40. *Ibid.*, p. 13.
41. Hawkins, "Report," 31 March 1900.
42. Whiting, *op. cit.*, p. 12.
43. Hawkins, "Report," 31 March 1900.

CHAPTER 9

1. Tancred, "White Pass & Yukon Railway Report," April, 1898. Courtesy Close Brothers Company Files, London, England.
2. Hawkins, "Report," 31 March 1900.
3. Tancred, *op. cit.*
4. *Victoria Daily Colonist*, 21 April 1898.
5. *Ibid.*, 23 April 1898.
6. Tancred, "White Pass & Yukon Railway," *Railway and Shipping World*, (October, 1898), p. 203.
7. Hawkins, "Report," 31 March 1900.
8. C.J. Christie, "Report on the Route of the White Pass and Yukon Railroad," April, 1898. Author's file.
9. Whiting, *op. cit.*, p. 12; Hawkins to Berdoe, 18 November 1898. Author's file.
10. Graves's address to the first General Meeting of the White Pass and Yukon Railway, Limited, 5 December 1898. *Ibid.*
11. *Financial News*, 6 December 1898.
12. Graves to Hawkins, 20 March 1899. Author's file.
13. *Memorandum of Association, White Pass and Yukon Railway Company, Limited*. The Companies Acts, 1862-1893, Companies House, London, England.
14. *Monetary Times*, 18 March 1898.
15. *Seattle Post-Intelligencer*, 21 May 1898.
16. Whiting, *op. cit.*, p. xv.
17. E.C. Hawkins to J.P. Rogers, 1 November 1899; E.C. Hawkins to F.B. Whiting, 8 April 1899. Author's file.
18. F.H. Whiting to George H. Buss, 16 February 1899. *Ibid.*
19. *Seattle Post-Intelligencer*, 24 May 1898.
20. Warman, "Building a Railroad," p. 240.
21. Hawkins, "Report," c. 15 August 1900. Author's file.
22. Skagway Ordinance No. 6, signed by H.E. Battin, President of the Council, 31 May 1898, and by E.C. Hawkins, Chief Engineer and General Manager, on 23 June 1898; *Skagway News - Supplement*, 3 June 1898; *Daily Alaskan*, 3, 14, 15 June 1898; *Daily Alaskan Graphic*, 27 July 1898. Hislop Papers.
23. Graves, *On the "White Pass" Pay-roll*, p. 43.
24. *Ibid.*, p. 47; Warman, "Building a Railroad," p. 240.
25. *Seattle Post-Intelligencer*, 26 May 1898.
26. *Skagway News - Supplement*, 3 June 1898.
27. *Daily Alaskan*, 14 June 1898.
28. *Ibid.*, 15 June 1898.
29. *Ibid.*

CHAPTER 10

1. Graves, *op. cit.*, p. 42.
2. Hawkins, "Report," 31 March 1900. Author's file.
3. Hawkins to Hon. T. Peterson, Canadian Minister of Customs, 3 July 1899.
4. Graves to Hawkins, 2 May 1899. Hawkins, "Report," 31 March 1900. Author's file.
5. *Ibid.*
6. Author's interview with construction worker Walter Sweet of Atlin, B.C., and construction accountant Ernest Barteau; unidentified Seattle newspaper clip, 12 March 1899; *Skagway News*, 3 March 1899; diary entry of John Hislop, Hislop Papers.
7. Graves, *op. cit.*, p. 63.
8. *Daily Alaskan*, 18 June 1898.
9. Hartman to Rowan, telegram, 20 June 1898. Brackett Papers.
10. Rowan to Hartman, 21 June 1898. Brackett Papers.
11. Brackett to Van Horne, 9 November 1898. Brackett Papers.
12. Now called State Street.

CHAPTER 11

1. Watt, *Skagway*, p. 12.
2. Graves, *op. cit.*, p. 18.
3. *Daily Alaskan*, 1 July 1898. Hislop Papers.
4. Robertson and Harris, *op. cit.*, p. 203.
5. *Skagway News - Supplement*, 2 September 1898; *Morning Leader*, London, 1 September 1898.
6. Hawkins to Brackett, 12 December 1898. Brackett Papers.
7. Graves, *op. cit.*, p. 61.
8. Newspaper clip, *St. Louis Globe-Democrat*, 8 September 1898.
9. Graves, *op. cit.*, p. 58.
10. *Ibid.*, pp. 47, 48; author's interview with Walter Sweet.
11. Hawkins to Heney, 15 February 1899; *Victoria Daily Colonist*, 8 March 1899.
12. *Financial News*, 6 December 1898.
13. "Soapy Smith's Last Bluff," *Skagway News*, 8 July 1898.
14. Graves, *op. cit.*, p. 19.
15. *Ibid.*, p. 21.
16. Miller, *Soapy*, p. 108.
17. *Skagway News*, 8 July 1898.
18. Graves, *op. cit.*, pp. 23, 24, 25; *Skagway News*, 8 July 1898; *Seattle Post-Intelligencer*, 15 July 1898.
19. Coroner's Report signed by C.W. Cornelius, M.D., 9 July 1898.
20. Graves, *op. cit.*, pp. 28-30.
21. *Daily Alaskan* newsclip, undated. Hislop Papers.
22. *Daily Alaskan*, 22 July 1898.

23. Emerson, "The Engineer & the Road to the Yukon Gold-Fields," *Engineering Magazine* (March, 1899).

CHAPTER 12

1. *Skagway News*, 20 July 1898; *Victoria Daily Colonist*, 30 July 1898.
2. *Skagway News*, 20 July 1898.
3. Newsclip, 22 July 1898. Hislop Papers.
4. *Victoria Daily Colonist*, 24 August 1898.
5. Warman, *op. cit.*, p. 243.
6. Hawkins to Brackett, 12 December 1898; Hawkins, "Report," 31 March 1900. Brackett Papers.
7. Graves, *op. cit.*, p. 49.
8. Newsclip, October, 1898. Hislop Papers.
9. Personal communication with Walter Sweet.
10. *Seattle Post-Intelligencer*, 3 August 1898; *Victoria Daily Colonist*, 14 August 1898.
11. *Tacoma Evening News*, 31 July 1899; author's interviews with Skagway families.
12. *Skagway News*, 29 July 1898; unidentified Seattle newspaper clips, Hislop Papers.
13. *Seattle Post-Intelligencer*, 3 August 1898; *Victoria Daily Colonist*, 14 August 1898; Graves, *op. cit.*, p. 59.
14. Warman, *op. cit.*, p. 242.
15. Hawkins to Brackett, 12 December 1898; newsclip, 17 August 1898. Hislop Papers.
16. Hawkins, "Report," 27 April 1898; *Daily Alaskan*, 17 August 1898. Hislop Papers.
17. Graves's quote, *Railway and Shipping World* (August, 1898).
18. Hawkins, "Report," 27 April 1898. Author's file.
19. Graves, *op. cit.*, pp. 10, 20.
20. *Seattle Post-Intelligencer*, 15 August 1898.
21. Graves, *On the "White Pass Pay-roll"*, p. 116.
22. Hawkins to Brackett, 12 December 1898; the figure of $120,000 per mile represents approximately $2,500,000 in 1986. Brackett Papers.
23. Unidentified newspaper clip, 17 August 1898. Hislop Papers.
24. Graves, *On the "White Pass Pay-roll"*, p. 50.
25. Robert Brydone-Jack, trustee's engineer, to D.C. Fraser, MP. Author's file.
26. Author's correspondence and interviews with Mrs. Katherine Rendell, Miss Faith Rendell, Mr. Jack Rendell, Mrs. Francis (Bernice) Brydone-Jack, Mr. Vaughan Brydone-Jack; military documents, "Diploma of Graduation," Cadet Robert Brydone-Jack, 29 June 1887; *Daily Alaskan*, 14 February 1898; Graves, *op. cit.*, p. 50.
27. *Victoria Daily Colonist*, 13 October 1898.

CHAPTER 13

1. Warman, *op. cit.*, p. 241.

2. *Seattle Post-Intelligencer*, 28 October 1898.
3. *Victoria Daily Colonist*, 12 October 1898.
4. Hawkins, "Report," 27 April 1898. Author's file.
5. Hawkins, "Report," 31 March 1900.
6. *Victoria Daily Colonist*, 4 January 1899.
7. Hawkins to Graves, 29 January 1899. Author's file.
8. Hawkins to Hussey, 11 February 1899. *Ibid.*
9. Hawkins to Graves, 11 February 1899. *Ibid.*
10. Author's interview with Walter Sweet, former employee of White Pass during construction, Atlin, B.C.
11. Undated newspaper clip. Hislop Papers.
12. Graves, *op. cit.*, p. 51.
13. Unidentified newspaper clip, 11 October 1898. Hislop Papers.
14. *Ibid.*

CHAPTER 14

1. Brydone-Jack, "Report to Trustees," 17 November 1898. Author's file.
2. Hussey to Hawkins, 28 November 1898; Brydone-Jack, "Report to Trustees," 3 December 1898; Graves to Hawkins, 2 May 1899. *Ibid.*
3. Clarence D. Baker to his father, 22 January 1898. *Ibid.*
4. Brydone-Jack, "Report to Trustees," 1 December 1898. *Ibid.*
5. Brackett to Van Horne, 9 November 1898. Brackett Papers.
6. Agreement of sale, 9 November 1898. *Ibid.*
7. Brackett to Van Horne, 9 November 1898. *Ibid.*
8. *Financial News*, 6 December 1898; *Railway and Shipping World* (January, 1898); Graves's "Report to the Shareholders," 5 December 1898. Courtesy Close Bros. Company files.
9. *Skagway News*, 2 December 1898; unidentified newspaper clip, 2 December 1898. Hislop Papers.
10. Unidentified newspaper clip, 14 December 1898. *Ibid.*
11. *Victoria Daily Colonist*, 4 January 1899.
12. Daily Alaskan, 16 January 1899.
13. Hawkins to Hussey, 11 February 1899. Author's file.
14. Hawkins to Graves, 29 January 1899. *Ibid.*
15. Brydone-Jack, "Report to Trustees," 19 January 1899. *Ibid.*
16. Advertisement, *Victoria Daily Colonist*, 20 December 1898.
17. *Ibid.*
18. Gray to Hawkins, 9 February 1899. Author's file.
19. Hawkins to Gray, 15 February 1899. *Ibid.*
20. Hawkins to Graves, 2 February 1899. *Ibid.*
21. Hawkins to Hislop, 6 April 1899. *Ibid.*
22. Hawkins to Hussey, 14 February 1899. *Ibid.*
23. *Skagway-Atlin Budget*, 14 February 1899.
24. Unidentified newspaper clip, 16 February 1899. Hislop Papers.

CHAPTER 15

1. Hawkins to F.H. Whiting, 15 February 1899. Author's file.
2. *Seattle Post-Intelligencer*, 27 February 1899.
3. *Daily Alaskan*, 21 February 1899.
4. Hawkins to Flood, 31 January 1899. Author's file.
5. Secretary Bliss to William S. King, Brackett's agent, 16 May 1899. Brackett Papers.
6. *Daily Alaskan*, 24 January 1899.
7. *Ibid.*, 4 February 1899.
8. Hawkins to Graves, 29 January 1899. Author's file.
9. *Seattle Post-Intelligencer*, 3 December 1900; Provincial Disallowed Acts 1872-1978; Clarence D. Baker to his father, 12 February 1899. Author's file.
10. Hislop to Governor Brady, 31 January 1899. Hislop Papers.
11. Hawkins to Graves, 29 January 1899. Author's file.
12. Brydone-Jack to D.C. Fraser, MP, 29 January 1899. *Ibid.*
13. Hawkins to Gray, 15 February 1899. *Ibid.*
14. Hawkins to Heney, 15 February 1899. *Ibid.*
15. Hawkins to Hussey, 11 February 1899. *Ibid.*
16. Hawkins to Graves, 2 February 1899; Hawkins to Macaulay, 22 July 1899; Heney to Hawkins, 30 May 1899; "Annual Report of Superintendent Z.T. Wood," 1 November 1898, RCMP Archives, Ottawa; *Daily Alaskan*, 2 February 1899.
17. Hawkins to Hussey, 11 February 1899. Author's file.
18. F.H. Whiting to Gray, 24 February 1899. *Ibid.*
19. F.H. Whiting to Hawkins, 23 February 1899. *Ibid.*
20. *Daily Alaskan*, 13 February 1899.
21. Graves to Hawkins, 13 March 1899. Author's file.
22. F.H. Whiting to Hawkins, 15 March 1899. *Ibid.*
23. *Skagway News*, 17 March 1899.
24. *Skagway-Atlin Budget*, 28 February 1899.
25. Sinclair, *Mission: Klondike*, p. 170.
26. F.H. Whiting to U.S. Marshall Shoup, 4 March 1899. Author's file.
27. Sinclair, *op. cit.*, pp. 170-73.
28. *Victoria Daily Colonist*, 18 March 1899; *Daily Alaskan*, 9 March 1899.
29. Hawkins to Graves, 6 April 1899. Author's file.
30. Graves to Hawkins, 14 March 1899. *Ibid.*
31. *Ibid.*
32. Exchange of cables between Graves and Hawkins. Cables repeated in Graves's letter, 13 March 1899. *Ibid.*
33. Graves to Hawkins, 14 March 1899. *Ibid.*
34. *Ibid.*
35. Hawkins to Graves, 6 April 1899. *Ibid.*
36. Hussey to Hawkins, 22 March 1899. *Ibid.*
37. Hawkins to Graves, 27 March 1899. *Ibid.*
38. *Skagway News*, 17 March 1899.
39. *Victoria Daily Colonist*, 18 March 1899.

40. *Skagway News*, 17 March 1899.

CHAPTER 16

1. Hawkins to Heney, 25 March 1899. Author's file.
2. Hawkins to Graves, 7 April 1899. *Ibid.*
3. Hawkins to Graves, 27 March 1899; Hawkins to Hussey, 27 March 1899. *Ibid.*
4. Hawkins to Hussey, 27 March 1899; Hawkins to Graves, 3 April 1899. *Ibid.*
5. Hawkins to Graves, 5 April 1899. *Ibid.*
6. Hawkins to Graves, 3 April 1899. *Ibid.*
7. *Ibid.*
8. Graves to Hawkins, 11 April 1899. *Ibid.*
9. Hawkins to Graves, 22 March 1899. *Ibid.*
10. Hawkins to Whiting, 24 March 1898. *Ibid.*
11. *Skagway-Atlin Budget*, 9, 10, 12 May 1899.
12. Gray to Hawkins, 13 May 1899. Author's file.
13. *Daily Alaskan*, 14 May 1899.
14. *Skagway News*, undated newspaper clip. Hislop Papers.
15. *Daily Alaskan*, undated newspaper clip. *Ibid.*
16. Graves to Hawkins, 24 April 1899. Author's file.
17. *Ibid.*
18. Whiting to Hawkins, 4 May 1899; Whiting to Brown, 4 May 1899; Whiting to Heney, 4 May 1899. *Ibid.*
19. Whiting to Hawkins, 25 April 1899. *Ibid.*
20. *Daily Alaskan*, 10 May 1899.
21. Graves to Hawkins, 24 April 1899. Author's file.
22. Hawkins to Hislop, 25 March 1899. *Ibid.*
23. Undated newspaper clip, *Daily Alaskan*, May, 1899, Hislop Papers; *Monetary Times*, 12 April, 1899; *Victoria Daily Colonist*, 4 June 1899.
24. Hawkins to Graves, 3 April 1899. Author's file.
25. Graves to Hawkins, via Hussey, 22 May 1899. *Ibid.*
26. Graves to Hawkins, 23 May 1899. *Ibid.*
27. Hawkins to Hislop, 31 May 1899. *Ibid.*
28. Hawkins to Graves, 19 June 1899. *Ibid.*
29. "Minutes, Board of Directors' Meeting," Pacific and Arctic Railway and Navigation Company, Seattle, 21 July 1899; Graves to Hussey, 19 July 1899; Graves to Hawkins, 30 June 1899. *Ibid.*
30. Hawkins to Graves, c. July, 1899. *Ibid.*
31. *Skagway-Atlin Budget*, 12 July 1899.
32. Hawkins to Graves, 24 May 1899. Author's file.
33. Hawkins to Graves, 30 May 1899. *Ibid.*
34. Berdoe to Superintendent F.H. Whiting, 14 June 1899. *Ibid.*
35. *Daily Alaskan*, 4 May 1899.
36. Hawkins to Graves, 29 May 1899. Author's file.
37. Hawkins to Greer, 30 May 1899. Hawkins to Graves, 29 May 1899. *Ibid.*
38. Hawkins to Greer, 23 June 1899. *Ibid.*

39. Hawkins to Graves, 28 June 1899. *Ibid.*
40. *Ibid.*
41. Hawkins to Maitland Kersey, 13 May 1899. *Ibid.*
42. Hawkins to Heney, 31 May 1899. *Ibid.*

CHAPTER 17

1. Hawkins to Graves, 11 July 1899. Author's file.
2. Whiting to Hawkins, 10, 11 July 1899. *Ibid.*
3. Hussey to Hawkins, 8 July 1899. *Ibid.*
4. Hawkins to Graves, 18 July 1899. *Ibid.*
5. Hawkins to Heney, 22 July 1899. *Ibid.*
6. Graves to Hussey, 19 July 1899. *Ibid.*
7. *Victoria Daily Colonist*, 10 March, 30 November, 8 December, 4 June 1899.
8. Hawkins, "Report," 15 August 1900. Author's file.
9. Whiting to Hawkins, 24 August 1899. *Ibid.*
10. Graves, *op. cit.*, pp. 88-91.
11. Hawkins to Close Brothers and Company, 13 November 1899. Author's file.
12. Graves, *op. cit.*, p. 65.
13. Hawkins, "Report," c. August, 1899.
14. J.E. Beatty to R.E. Stretch, 2 October 1899. *Daily Alaskan*, 3 October 1899; H.T. Harper to Hislop, Hislop Papers; *Railway and Shipping World* (December, 1899); personal communication Ernest Barteau; *Star* (Whitehorse), 13 January 1984.
15. Young to Hawkins, 10 October 1899. Author's file.
16. Hawkins to Graves, 26 October 1899. *Ibid.*
17. *Railway and Shipping World* (November, 1899).
18. Hawkins to Graves, 26 October 1899. Author's file.
19. Hawkins to Bennett Agent, 7 November 1899. *Ibid.*
20. Hawkins to Hussey, 30 November 1899. *Ibid.*
21. *Daily Alaskan*, 17 December 1899.
22. Hawkins to J.P. Rogers, 30 November 1899. Author's file.
23. Young to Hussey, 31 October 1899. *Ibid.*
24. Hawkins to Hussey, 21 November 1899. *Ibid.*
25. "Annual Report of Superintendent Z.T. Wood," *Daily Alaskan*, 16 September, 21 November 1899; Hawkins to Williams, 19 October 1899, and Hawkins to Hussey, 14 November 1899; Young to Hawkins, 21 November 1899; Young to Hawkins, 8, 14, 23 December 1899. Author's file.
26. *Daily Alaskan*, 1 December 1899.
27. *Ibid.*, 1, 20 December 1899; Graves, *op. cit.*, p. 125.
28. Young to Hawkins, 19, 21, 22, 26, 28, 29 December 1899. Author's file.
29. Hawkins to Hislop, 19 November 1899. *Ibid.*
30. Graves to Hawkins, 18 May 1899. *Ibid.*
31. Hawkins to Graves, 14 November 1899. *Ibid.*

CHAPTER 18

1. Graves, *op. cit.*, p. 121.
2. *Daily Alaskan*, 31 January 1900.
3. *Ibid.*, 27 February 1900.
4. *Ibid.*, 7 February 1900. Lawrence, *40 Years on the Yukon Telegraph*, p. 36.
5. *Klondike Nuggett*, 30 January 1900; *Daily Alaskan*, 6 February 1900.
6. J.W. Young to Hawkins, 12 March 1900. Author's file.
7. *Daily Alaskan*, 18 March 1900.
8. *Yukon Sun*, 24 April 1900.
9. Hawkins to Billinghurst, 30 June 1899. Author's file. *Daily Alaskan*, 11 March 1900.
10. *Daily Alaskan*, 11 March 1900.
11. *Yukon Sun*, 10 March 1900.
12. Unidentified newsclip, 1 April 1900. Hislop Papers.
13. *Daily Alaskan*, 5 April 1900.
14. *Ibid.*, 7 April 1900.
15. *Ibid.*, 10 May 1900.
16. Unidentified newsclip, 24 May 1900. Hislop Papers.
17. *Daily Alaskan*, 18, 24 May 1900.
18. *Ibid.*, 25 May 1900.
19. Unidentified newsclip, 25 May 1900. Hislop Papers.
20. *Daily Alaskan*, 2 June 1900.
21. *Skagway-Atlin Budget*, 19, 25, 27 January 1900.
22. *Klondike Nuggett*, 10 March 1900.
23. Personal communication from Matthew Watson.
24. *Daily Alaskan*, 11 July 1900.
25. Graves, *op. cit.*, p. 141; *Daily Alaskan*, undated newsclip, c. 1 August 1900.
26. MacBride, W.D., *Northwest Digest*, April, 1950; personal communication from Archie Shiels.
27. *Daily Alaskan*, 26 July 1900.
28. *Ibid.*, 18, 19 July 1900.
29. *Victoria Daily Colonist*, 26 July 1900.
30. *Daily Alaskan*, 26 July 1900.
31. *Ibid.*, 27 July, 1900.
32. Graves, *op. cit.*, p. 79.

INDEX

Abt rail system, 129

Acklen, Joseph Hayes, 88-93, 95, 101-4, 105, 106, 111-13, 115-17, 123, 140

Adney, Tappan, 76-77, 79, 232

Ajax (barge), 218

Alaska and Northwestern Railway, 98

Alaska Magazine, 239

Alaskan (steamboat), 35

Alaskan and North Western Territories Trading Co., 51-52, 54, 59, 63, 80, 85, 90-91, 92, 102, 196

Alaskan Government, 155, 157

Alaska Panhandle, 39, 52, 98

Alaska Railroad & Transportation Co., 93

Alaska Steamship Co., 166, 320

Alger, Russell A., 122, 200

Alice (riverboat), 55

Al-Ki (steamer), 70, 185

Alsek River, 97

American Episcopal Church, Skagway, 88

American Review of Reviews, 243

Amur (steamer), 338

Anchor Point, Alaska, 128

Ancon (steamer), 19, 20, 22, 23

Anderson, Col. Thomas M., 122

Angus, Richard B., 117

Arctic Ocean, 19

Arkins, Col. John, 108

Ashcroft, B.C., 97

Associated Press, 236

Athenian (steamer), 215

Atlin gold field, 228, 229, 235, 243, 250, 254, 261, 262, 272, 273, 274, 277, 305, 311, 336, 337, 350, 351

Atlin Lake, B.C., 99, 350

Australian (steamer), 212-13, 342-43, 353

Aylmer Hotel, Ottawa, 357

Bailey (steamer), 344

Baker, Clarence B., 250, 279, 286

Bank of Montreal, 114

Barley, Harry C., 207-8, 223-24, 268, 343

Batten, Mr., 183, 184

Battleford, 131

Beasley, F.W., 279

Beeton, Henry Coppinger, 62, 175

Bennett, 184, 190, 192, 228-29, 232, 236, 246, 250, 277-78, 283, 285, 289, 290, 291, 293, 295, 297, 298, 300, 301, 302, 303-4, 305, 307, 308, 309, 310, 311, 312-13, 315, 316-17, 318, 319, 320, 321, 322, 325, 326, 328, 329, 330, 331, 333, 335, 337, 338, 341, 342, 343-44, 345, 347, 348, 349, 351, 353, 355

Bennett Sun, 301, 351

Berdoe, A.L., 306

Bering Sea, 29, 170

Big Delta, Alaska, 15

Big Salmon River, 21, 78, 171

Billinghurst, Ernest Edward, 34-38, 39, 40-43, 44-48, 51, 60, 62, 66-67, 68, 72, 82, 106, 140, 154, 339

Billinghurst, Henry Farcome, 40, 63

Bishoprick Mill Creek, 189

Bishop Rowe Hospital, Skagway, 216
Bismark, N.D., 104
Bjax (barge), 218
Black, James A., 265
Black Cross Rock, 226
Bliss, Cornelius, N., 65, 91
Board of Trade (Vancouver), 168
Board of Trade (New Westminster), 169
Board of Trade Building (Victoria), 40
Bonanza Saloon, Skagway, 74
Bonine, R.K., 309
Booth, Cory, 306
Booth, John Patton, 62
Booth, Gen. William, 306
Boulder, 205, 220
Bowers, "Rev." John, 108, 109, 209, 215
Brackett, A.L., 270
Brackett, George Augustus, 89, 103-6,
    111-12, 113, 114-23, 125-26, 129, 137, 154,
    156, 180, 190, 195, 196-99, 200, 205,
    251-52, 270-72, 290, 293, 304
Brackett, James, 89, 116
Brady, John Green, 86, 330
Bray and Enniskerry Railway, 40
Bridal Veil Falls, 77
British Columbia, 14, 19, 20, 26, 27, 28,
    34, 36, 39, 42, 50, 52, 62, 64, 91, 98, 101,
    129, 133, 144, 152, 168, 192, 228, 235,
    236, 245, 266, 308, 318, 340, 359
British Columbia Development Assoc.,
    Ltd. (the syndicate), 34, 39, 40, 43-44,
    46, 49-50, 52, 59-66, 72, 76, 80-81, 83,
    88, 90, 91, 92, 93, 95, 98, 102, 105, 106,
    114, 127, 137, 140, 147-48, 149, 154, 155,
    172, 175, 177, 179, 196, 234, 339
British Columbia Government, 60, 62,
    150, 152-53, 157, 169, 192, 269, 272-73,
    293-94, 301
British Columbia Northern Railway, 97
British Columbia-Yukon Railway, 62,
    63, 85, 102
British Government, 149, 157
British Pacific Railway, 97
British Yukon Chartered Co., 63-64
British Yukon Mining, Trading and
    Transportation Co., 65, 80, 82, 85

Broadway Street, Skagway, 74, 181,
    186-88, 189, 194-95, 204, 218, 220, 311
Brooks, Mr., 245
Brooks, J.H., 271-72
Brooks, Samuel, 81
Brooks, William, 81
Brooks Locomotive Works, 191
Brown, D.M., 106, 112, 113
Brown, E.S., 306
Brown, Melville C., 21
Bryant, Dr. 188
Brydone-Jack, Robert, 233-35, 245-46,
    250-51, 258, 260, 263-65, 266, 269, 277
Burkard's Hall, Skagway, 87
Burke, Shepherd & McGilvra, 51
Burns, Archie, 79-80, 95, 183
Bush, Samuel S., 94

Cadman, Mr., 88
Cady, "Troublesome Tom," 108
Calgary, 131, 132
California, 21, 146, 150, 163
Call (San Francisco), 69
Calvary Cemetery, Seattle, 359
Camp 1, 220, 287-89
Camp 2, 220
Camp 3, 215, 220, 221, 222, 223
Camp 5, 215
Camp 6, 231
Campbell, Rev. Dr., 183
Canada, 39, 52, 59, 98, 104, 120, 141,
    151-53, 160, 203, 236, 242, 246, 301, 325,
    341
Canadian (riverboat), 356
Canadian Army, 13
Canadian Development Co., 326, 350
Canadian Government, 15, 54, 60, 63-65,
    67, 98, 99, 101, 117, 119, 120, 129-30,
    140-41, 144, 150-52, 157, 192, 193, 231,
    236, 237, 249, 269, 301, 337
Canadian Pacific Airlines, 15
Canadian Pacific Navigation Co., 50, 350
Canadian Pacific Railways, 42, 85, 97,
    117, 121, 131, 133, 140, 176
Canyon City, 125, 319
Carcross, Yukon, 146, 300, 302-3, 309,

315, 316-17, 318, 320, 321, 322, 323, 324,
   325, 327, 328, 330, 332, 333, 335, 336-37,
   338-39, 341, 342, 343, 344-45, 347, 351,
   352-54
Caribou Cassiar Railway, 37
Caribou Crossing, 302, 310, 338, 343
Caribou Region, 42
Carlisle claim, 317
Carr-Glynn, Sidney, 175, 253
Cartwright, Capt. F.L., 236
Cassiar Region, 21, 97
Carmack, George Washington, 23-24, 54,
   55-57, 58
Carmack, Kate, 24
Central News agency, London, 64
Chamberlain, Joseph, 63
Chamber of Commerce (Juneau), 329
Charlie (schooner), 23
Chicago, 360
Chicago Daily Record, 48
Childs Glacier, 359
Chilkat Pass, 97, 99
Chilkoot Indians, 21-22, 23, 24, 79
Chilkoot Pass, 14, 19, 20, 21-22, 23, 24-25,
   26, 28, 29, 30, 32, 36, 37, 41, 44, 45-46,
   47, 48, 67, 77, 78-80, 88-89, 93-95, 98,
   103, 118, 123-26, 136, 146, 153, 156, 167,
   169, 246, 248, 260-62, 293, 319, 325,
   329, 330, 340
Chilkoot Pass Route, 260-62
Chilkoot Railroad & Transport Co., 94,
   102-3, 123, 293-96, 299, 301, 302, 303-4
Chilkoot tramlines, 80, 93-95, 102-3, 118,
   123-25, 136, 146, 156-57, 236, 246, 248,
   260-62, 279, 293-96, 299, 301, 302,
   303-4, 315, 325, 330
Chilkoot tunnel, 325-26, 329-30, 340,
   345
Chinese workers, 246-47
Chitina, Alaska, 359
Christie, C.J., 171-72
Chronicle, San Francisco, 69
Chrysler, Francis H., 62, 65, 106, 192
Church, Mr., 182
Cigar Factory, Fortymile, 49
Circle City, Alaska, 43, 48-49, 59

City of Kingston (steamer), 70
City of Seattle (steamer), 70, 89, 176, 179
City of Topeka (steamer), 70
Civil War (U.S.), 104
Clark, Frank F., 296
Cleveland (steamship), 134
Clifford J. Rogers (motor vessel), 15
Clifford Sifton (steamer), 312, 344
Close, Frederick, 81
Close, James, 81
Close, William Brooks, 81, 82-85, 106,
   147-48, 149, 151, 154, 157, 169, 173, 174,
   175, 176, 179, 300, 317-18, 320-21, 326
Close Brothers & Co., 81, 90
Close Brothers & Company, 81, 118, 129,
   147, 148-49, 150, 151, 153, 155, 164,
   172-73, 174, 175, 196, 269, 273, 277, 292,
   297, 301-2, 359
Closeleigh (later Whitehorse), 228, 250
Coal, 358
Colorado, 163
Colorado (barge), 218
Columbia & Puget Sound Railway, 191
Columbian (ship), 351
Committee of One Hundred and One,
   201-3, 211, 212
Comox, B.C., 153
Constantine, Charles, 49
Copper, 317, 358
Copper King claim, 317
Copper River, 358-59
Copper River and Northwestern
   Railroad, 359-60
Cordova, Alaska, 359, 360
Cornelius, Dr. J.C., 214
Cornforth, Joseph T., 123-24
Cornwall, C.F., 27
Costello, J.A., 138-39
Cottage City (ship), 239
Crahan, Thomas, 309
Crater Lake, B.C., 94, 261, 293
Creede, Colorado, 108
Creede Candle, 108
Croffut, W.A., 105
Crow's Nest Pass, 235
Cuba, 173, 174

Cunliffe, Roger, 81
Cunliffe and Brooks Bank, 81
Customs Office (U.S.), 337

Daily Alaskan, 87, 200-1, 236, 266, 268,
    269, 274, 284, 296-97, 299-300, 301,
    311, 312, 314, 337, 338, 341, 342, 343,
    349, 351, 352, 355
Dalton, Jack, 358
Dalton Post, 97
Dalton Trail, 97, 98, 148
Danube (ship), 350
Davidson, Gus, 270-71
Davis (desk clerk), 161, 162
Davis, Senator Cushman K., 114
Davis Creek, 57
Dawson, George Mercer, 19, 20
Dawson City, 15, 83, 97, 98, 111, 129, 146,
    171, 176, 235, 250, 262, 293, 335, 336,
    337, 345, 349, 350, 351, 359
Dawson Creek, B.C., 15
Dead Horse Gulch, 140, 242
Denver, Colorado, 107-8
Denver Glacier, Alaska, 185
Dewdney, Edgar, 35
de Wette, Auguste, 175
Dewey, Admiral, 173, 222
De Witt, C.H., 329
Dick (striker), 288
Dickey, Rev. Mr. Robert McCahan, 87,
    88
Dickinson, O.L., 357
Dickson, George, 22-23
Discovery Claim, Rabbit Creek, 56-57
District Land Recorder's Office
    (Juneau), 154, 155
Dixon Entrance, 179
Dodwell, Carlow & Co., 94
Drake, Jackson & Helmcken, 34
Driard Hotel, Victoria, 41
Drucker, Adolph, 62
Dugas, l'Aime, 236
Dugdale, James, 175
Dyea, Alaska, 14, 19, 21, 22-24, 29, 30, 31,
    32, 44, 46, 47, 52, 67, 78, 79, 80, 86, 87,
    89, 93-94, 95, 97, 99, 102-3, 119, 121,

123-26, 127, 128, 136, 150, 156, 158, 180,
    182, 183, 186, 203, 210, 220, 248, 261,
    279, 290, 293-94, 295, 296, 297, 304,
    325-26, 329, 330, 340
Dyea and Chilkoot Railway Co., 325-26
Dyea-Klondike Transportation Co., 93,
    102-3, 236

Edmonton, 97
Edwards, D., 57
Edwards, David, 56
Eldorado Creek, 58, 69
Elkhorn, Man., 132
Elliot, F.C., 357
Emden, Germany, 21
Engineering and Mining Journal, 70
Engine No. 2, 191
England, 80, 114
Englewood Union Hospital, 360
Ennis, Mr., 275
E.R. Peoples' Undertaking Parlor, 214,
    264
Escolme, John Henry, 63, 66, 67, 76, 78,
    90-91, 92, 102, 106, 115, 119
Esquimalt, B.C., 40
Excelsior (steamer), 69
Exclusion Act, 272-74
Exploration Co. Ltd., 84-85, 147-48

Farallon (coastal vessel), 227
Fargo, N.D., 104
Farnham, F.C., 103
Farr, Jack, 271
Farrell, J.D., 303-4
Finnegan's Point, 79
First Bank of Skagway, 155
Firth of Forth Bridge, 153
Five Fingers Rapids, 97
Flood, F.B., 259, 269
Foot, J.H., 75
Ford, White Pass, 270
Ford, Bob, 108
Ford Cudahy, 49
Fort Selkirk, Yukon, 62, 97, 129, 143, 146,
    149, 157, 160, 170, 171, 177, 192, 228,
    233, 236, 258, 351

Fortymile, Yukon, 28, 29, 43, 49, 54, 55, 57, 59, 99
Fortymile River, 21, 43, 48
Foster, "Slim Jim," 108, 215
14th Infantry Regiment, 136
Fowler, Mr., 288
Foy, Hugh, 193, 194, 206, 225, 235, 259, 265, 266, 267, 274, 276-77
Francis, Duke of Teck, 34
Frank H. Brown (motor vessel), 15
Fraser, Duncan Cameron, 63
Fraser Lake, 144, 238, 245, 257, 299, 305
Fraser River, 97, 133

Galt, Ontario, 153
Garden, Mayor, 168
Gaudreau, N. Belleau, 34-36, 45, 46
General Land Office (U.S.), 62
Geological Commission (U.S.), 171
George V, 34
Georgian Bay Branch (CPR), 131
Gerrow, Mr., 220
Glacier Creek, 57
Glacier Station, 276, 298, 338
Gleaner (steamer), 312, 313, 343, 344
Glenora, 169
Globe, Toronto, 151-52
Godson, John, 141
Gold, 48, 54, 55, 56
Gold Bottom Creek, 55, 56
Golden North Hotel, Skagway, 213
Gold rush, 13, 19, 20, 21, 27, 56-57, 66-68, 70-75, 98, 127-28, 139, 143-45, 243, 254, 309, 339
Gordon, Dr. Charles William (Ralph Connor), 88
Gordon, John, 281
Graceland Cemetery, Chicago, 357
Grand Army of the Republic, 217
Grand Trunk Railroad, 175
Grant, General, 216
Graves, Samuel H., 81, 148, 149-50, 153, 164, 169, 170, 171-75, 176, 179, 184, 192-93, 195, 197-99, 200, 203-5, 206, 207-9, 210-11, 212, 213, 214-15, 216, 222, 231, 232-33, 234, 238, 240, 242, 243,
245, 246, 247, 249, 251-56, 262, 264, 272, 273, 275, 277-78, 283-86, 289, 290-92, 293, 294, 297-98, 300, 301-2, 303, 304, 305, 306, 307, 309, 315, 316-18, 319, 320, 323, 324, 326, 327, 329, 331, 333, 347, 349-50, 351-52, 353, 354-55, 356, 357
Gray, L.H., 261-62, 265, 275-76, 295-96, 299-300, 303, 304
Great Britain, 52
Great Northern Railway, 51, 104, 116
Greeley, Horace, 118
Greer, J.H., 308
Grotto saloon, Skagway, 74
Guggenheim, David, 358-59
Guggenheim and Sons, M., 358

Hahn, V.I., 336
Haines Mission, Alaska, 22, 296
Hall, Capt., 134
Hanson, Edward, 175
Haro Strait, 19
Harper and Bros., 76
Harris, Bronco, 130-31, 132
Hartman, C.G., 236-38
Hartman, John P., 103, 120, 121, 196-97
Hartshorn, Bert, 139
Hawkins, Mrs., 312, 313
Hawkins, Erastus Corning, 149, 153-81 *passim*, 184, 190-200 *passim*, 204-12 *passim*, 215, 217, 219, 220, 221, 222-23, 225, 228, 229-30, 231-32, 233, 234, 238, 240-57 *passim*, 260-78 *passim*, 282-86, 289-311 *passim*, 313-34 *passim*, 336, 337, 339-40, 341, 342, 344, 345, 347, 349, 350, 351-52, 353, 354, 356, 358-60
Hayes, President, 91
Hayne, J.T., 213
Healy, Mrs., 30, 31
Healy, Capt. John Jerome, 22-23, 31, 32, 36, 43
Healy and Wilson Trading Post, 22, 30-31, 41, 45
Hearst, William Randolph, 69
Hegg, Eric A., 268, 269

Helmcken, H. Dallas, 42, 44, 47, 52, 62, 72, 106, 225-26, 235, 247
Henderson, Bob, 55-56, 58
Heney, John, 131
Heney, Mary, 132
Heney, Michael James, 127-46 *passim*, 161-70 *passim*, 172, 176, 178-79, 180, 188, 189-90, 192, 193-95, 204-12 *passim*, 215, 217, 219, 221, 222, 223, 225-26, 228-29, 230-32, 234, 235, 236, 238, 241-43, 244-47, 249, 250, 254, 256-58, 259, 265, 266, 268, 274-75, 276, 277, 279, 282, 288-89, 290-91, 292-93, 297, 298, 299, 300, 305-28 *passim*, 332-45 *passim*, 347-49, 352, 353, 354, 355, 356, 358, 359
Heney, Patrick, 169
Heney, Peter, 132
Heney, Thomas, 131, 132
Heney Station, 233, 235, 238, 239, 240, 243, 246, 251, 263, 274, 278, 283
Hepburn, John, 319, 320
Hill, James J., 116, 118-19
Hislop, John, 153-54, 157, 160-65, 169, 174, 179, 180, 184-85, 190-91, 192, 193, 203, 204, 207, 209, 210-11, 212, 215, 217, 219, 221, 225, 226, 228-29, 231, 232, 234, 236, 238, 245-46, 254, 259, 263-65, 269-70, 272-73, 278, 279, 280, 300, 302-3, 307, 309, 311, 312, 313, 319, 325, 326, 328, 332, 336-37, 344, 345, 348, 354, 356, 360
Hobart, J., 70
Holmes, Capt., 71
Holmquist, Gus, 270-71
Homestead Act, 174-75
Hootlingua River, 21, 97, 171
Hornsby, Mr., 183, 186-87
Hudson's Bay Co., 62, 64
Hukell, Mr. 281-82
Humbert, Jr., Pierre, 125
Humbert Transportation Co., 125
Hunter, Capt. J.C., 19
Hussey, Mr., 264, 286, 324, 327, 328, 329

Idaho, 78

Illinois Steel Co. of Chicago, 177
India, 42
Indian River, 55
Inside Passage, 20, 207
Inspiration Point, 242, 311
Interior, Dept. of the (Canada), 101
Iowa (tug), 218
Irving, John, 350
Irving, Capt. John, 50

Jackson "Dr." W.H., 109
James, Jesse, 108
Jarvis, Capt., 312
Jeff Smith's Parlors, 209-10, 211, 213, 215
Jennings, Mr. 180-81, 183-88
Jennings, W.T., 99-101
Johnny, Capt. "Dynamite," 127, 133, 134
Johnson, Mrs. C.S., 259
Johnson, Judge C.S., 272
Johnson, Richard Byron, 63
Johnston, 104
Juneau, 23, 31, 32, 44, 48, 220, 271, 272, 296, 329
Juneau City Mining Record, 48
Juneau Wharf, 212-13

Kane, Elmer, 271
Katalla, 358
Keelar, F.T., 183
Kelly, Charles E., 89
Kenai Peninsula, Alaska, 128
Kennecott mine, 359
Keer, Mr., 176
Kerry, A.S., 123
Killashandrea, Ireland, 131
Kimball, C., 57
King, Michael, 329, 345
King, Col. William S., 117
Kinney, L.D., 329-30, 340
Kirk, Robert, 79
Klondike (motor vessel), 15
Klondike, the, 13, 55, 56, 57-58, 67, 69-78, 82, 83, 88, 95, 97, 99, 106, 109, 111, 114, 118, 123, 127, 128, 129, 143-44, 145-46, 150-52, 167, 168, 169, 176, 243, 250, 254,

261, 272, 277, 293, 294, 305, 309, 342, 349, 351, 352

Klondike Mines Railway, 359

Klondike Mining, Trading and Transport Co. Ltd., 176

Klondike Nugget, 345

Klondike River, 54, 55, 57

Klondike Saloon, Skagway, 74

Kootenay region, 42

Lacey, John F., 117-18

Lake Bennett, 14, 25, 26, 27, 29, 30, 37, 49, 50, 52, 59, 60, 66, 67, 78, 88, 89, 91, 97, 98, 105, 118, 120, 121, 125, 128, 129, 137, 141, 143, 144-46, 159, 160, 166, 169, 170, 171, 177, 209, 228, 236, 245, 250, 257, 260, 274, 277-78, 291, 293, 298, 300, 302, 305, 306, 309, 310, 312, 315, 319, 321, 324, 326-28, 332, 333, 335, 337, 338, 342-43, 348, 350, 352

Lambert, Cowley, 175, 318, 319

Landers, Mr., 213

Laurier, Wilfrid, 63, 98, 152, 168

Law and Order Committee of Three Hundred and Three, 202-3

Leadville, Colorado, 107

Lewis, A.B., 302-3, 309, 316, 317, 322-23, 325, 326, 327, 332, 333, 337

Lewis Lake, 323-25, 333, 336-37, 342

Liard River, 20

Liarsville, Alaska, 135

Lincoln, Abraham, 104

Lindeman Lake, 26, 78, 93, 125, 141, 145, 293

Little Salmon River, 21

Log Cabin, B.C., 142, 144, 163, 203, 228, 235, 236, 238, 245, 247, 248, 274, 290, 293, 298, 301, 307, 308, 310, 312, 328, 351

Lokowitz, Mr., 188

London, 72, 91, 106, 176

London, Brighton and South Coast Railway, 175

London Chronicle, 76, 232

London Morning Post, 63

Longpré, Aime, 236

Louisiana, 91

Lovell & Jennings, 179, 180-81

Lower Yukon River, 43-44, 59, 62, 128, 171, 293, 342

Lynn Canal, Alaska, 19, 20, 21, 22, 25-26, 31, 39, 41, 42, 45, 48, 49, 51, 52, 60, 66, 78, 82, 86, 87, 97, 109, 129, 158, 179, 185, 242, 261, 311, 330

Lynn Canal and Dalton Railway, 97

McAlister, Mr., 337

Macauley, Mrs., 116

Macauley, Norman, 319-20

McConachie, Grant, 15

McConnell, Richard George, 20

Macdonald, Alexander, 86

McEvoy, James, 20

McFarlane, Grace, 344

McGill University, 153

McGilvray, Daniel, 56

McInnes, Marshal, 134

McKay, David, 56

Mackenzie, William, 101, 106, 130, 150, 151-52, 275, 327

Mackenzie Mountains, 19

Mackenzie River, 20

McKinley, William, 173, 200

McKinney, Dave, 74

McLagan, J.C., 168-69

McLeod, Mr., 145

McMicken, M., 62

McNeil, J., 279

McPhee, Bill, 57

McPherson, J.R., 358

Macrae, Colin, 175

Magner, M., 147-48, 149

Mahoney, Mr., 272

Main Street, Whitehorse, 347, 351

Manila, 173, 222

Manila Bay, Battle of, 173

Mann, Donald, 101, 106, 130, 150, 151-52, 275, 327

Mann, Capt. Henry, 86

Maris, Omer, 48

Marsh Lake, Yukon, 27

Mary (Queen), 34

Mayo, Yukon, 16
Meen, Mr., 219
Memphis, 91
Merchants' Bank of Halifax, 301
Mexico, 153, 178
Mexico (steamer), 35
Meyer's Hall, Skagway, 188
Middaugh, Mr., 288-89
Midgely, Edwin, 82, 84-85, 147, 149, 151
Miles, Murray, 328
Miles Canyon, Yukon, 29, 146, 319-20, 347
Miles Glacier, 359
Millbank Sound, 359
Miller, Joaquin, 87
Miller Creek, 57
Minneapolis, 104, 117
Minneapolis Journal, 118
Minnesota, 104, 117, 118
Mitchell, George W., 62-63
Moffat, J., 57
Mohr, Paul, 175, 302
Monahon, Edward, 56
Monetary Times, 101
Montana, 163
Montreal, 117, 129
Moody, C.S., 155-56, 183
Moore, Capt. William, 20-21, 22, 23, 24-33, 34, 35-39, 41-44, 45, 46, 47-48, 51, 54, 55, 58-59, 66, 67-68, 72, 74-76, 77, 78, 90, 91, 92, 106, 111, 115, 137, 140, 154-55, 156, 196, 234, 331, 339-40
Moore, Dr., 214
Moore, Mrs., 54, 75
Moore, Bernard, 21, 27, 28, 29-33, 39, 42, 54, 74-75, 90, 91, 92, 94, 111, 137, 154-55, 156, 196, 234, 339
Moore, William "Billie," 21, 22, 23, 24, 27, 28
Morgan, J.P., 358-59
Moriarity, Charlie "Snow King," 331, 335-36, 338, 341-42, 344, 345, 347-49, 352, 353, 354, 355
Mountain Flats trio, 88
Mount Dewey, 185
Mozambique, 153

Muir Glacier, 299
Murchison, Sam, 259, 336, 342
Murphy, J., 75, 213

Nanaimo, B.C., 153, 218
Nares Lake, 27
Nares River, 328, 353
Nashville, Tenn., 91, 106
Nationalists' Society, 169
Needham, George, 174-75
Newman, Jack, 139
Newton, H.A., 201
New York, N.Y., 59, 72, 91, 112, 149
Nome, Alaska, 339
Noonan, Georgia, 106
North American Transportation and Trading Co., 36, 43, 48, 49
Northern and Yukon Railway, 97
Northern Pacific Railroad, 94, 104
North London Railway, 175
North West Highway System, 13
North-West Mounted Police, 86, 141-42, 143, 144, 145, 192, 193, 203, 231, 235, 236, 269, 299, 300, 301, 306, 312, 324, 325, 330, 354
North West Staging route, 15
Nowell, Thomas, 93
Noya (steamer), 110
Nugget Express, Bennett, 329
Nugget saloon, Skagway, 74

O'Brian, Thomas, 359
Ogilvie, William, 19-28 *passim*, 35, 54-55, 59, 88
Ohio (steamer), 359
Omega (scow), 343
O'Neil, Father, 87
Ontario, 131
Oregon, 21, 146, 150
Oregonian, 158-59
Orleans Club, Creede, 108
Ottawa, 59, 71, 106, 149, 150, 357

Pacific and Arctic Railway and Navigation Co., 52-54, 60-62, 65-66, 85, 175, 225, 256

Pacific and Yukon Railway, 97
Pacific Clipper Line, 218
Pacific Coast Steamship Co., 93, 329
Pacific Contract Co. Ltd., 149, 164, 172,
    193, 195, 209, 219, 231, 234, 235, 242,
    250, 254, 266, 274, 276, 280, 282-86,
    310, 318, 321, 325, 332
Pacific Hotel, San Francisco, 41
Pacific Steamship Co., 19
Pack Train saloon, Skagway, 73, 74
Parree, Dr., 354
Parsons, W.H., 359
Peabody, C.E., 320
Peace River, 97
Peale, Mr., 236
Pearce, G.B., 94
Pells Brothers Packers, 226
Pelly River, 20, 21, 48, 71
Pennington, Frederick, 175
Peterson, Peter H., 94-95
Philippines, the, 173
Phillip Judson agency, 300
Pinkerton agency, 257
Placer Mining Act (1899), 272
Porcupine Hill, 137
Porcupine Ridge, 77
Portage Creek, Yukon, 145
Portage Lake, 299
Port Blakely, Wash., 186
Portland, Wash., 71, 171, 219
Portland (steamer), 69-70, 127-28
Portland Canal, B.C., 52, 97
Portland Hotel, Bennett, 301
Poudrier, Omer, 35
Price, John G., 155, 188
Price, Joseph, 175
Primrose, Major, 354
Prince Rupert, B.C., 101
Pueblo claim, 317

Quartz Creek, 55
Quebec, 131
Queen Charlotte Islands, 179
Queen Mexico (steamer), 70
Quesnel, B.C., 337
Quinlin, Deputy, 134

Rabbit Creek, 54, 55, 56, 57-58
Railway and Shipping World, 231, 247
Railway Share and Trust Co., Ltd.,
    233-35
Rainer-Grand Hotel, Seattle, 176
Raymond and Whitcom agency, 300
Reaper (steamer), 344
Red Line Transportation Co., 274-75,
    278, 290-91, 293, 298, 315, 318, 328, 332
Reid, Frank H., 74-75, 110, 201, 203, 211,
    212-14, 216-17, 218
Reliable Packers, Skagway, 110
Rice, George M., 178
Rice, Herbert, 67
Richardson Mountains, 20
Rideau Club, Ottawa, 357
Right of Way Act (1875), 65
Roberts, Capt., 227
Robertson, D., 57
Robinson, William (Stikine Bill), 275,
    322-23, 332-33, 341, 345, 347-49, 352,
    353, 354
Rocky Mountain News, 108
Rocky Mountains, 140
Rocky Point, 205, 219, 220-24, 230, 232
Rogers, J.P., 328, 332, 335, 337, 341, 345
Rogers, M.K., 358
Roosevelt, Teddy, 200
Rosalie (steamer), 164, 166, 169, 258,
    265, 277
Rowan, D. Noble, 52, 59, 72, 90-91, 115,
    118, 149, 196-97
Rowe, Bishop, 87
Royal Military College, Kingston, 235
Royal Navy, 40
Runnalls, Dr. R.B., 89
Runnalls Street, Skagway, 120, 198-99
Russia, 15, 19, 52

St. James Hotel, Skagway, 135, 136,
    153-54, 165, 319
St. Louis, 104
St. Michael, Alaska, 19, 36, 42, 43, 48,
    49, 59, 62, 70, 128-29, 158, 170, 293
St. Paul, Minn., 116, 118
St. Stephen's Church, Winnipeg, 88

Salvation Army, 306

Samson, David, 89, 113

San Francisco, 36, 41, 48, 49, 69, 71, 119, 208, 218, 219, 230, 359

San Francisco Examiner, 69

Saporatas, Billy, 183, 213

Sardonyx (steamer), 32

Sarle, Sir Allan, 175

Scales, The, 125, 261

Scharschmidt, P., 351

Schwabaker's dock, Seattle, 128

Seattle, 36, 51, 70-71, 103, 106, 113, 116, 119, 121, 125, 127, 130, 139, 169, 171, 173, 176-77, 178, 191, 197, 203, 206, 207, 208, 216, 219, 222, 249, 258, 276, 277, 292, 299, 303, 338, 341

Seattle Post Intelligencer, 70, 128, 137, 176, 201, 232, 236, 248, 304, 340

Seattle Times, 137, 139

Seghers, Archbishop, 29

Sehlbrede, Judge, C.A., 210-12, 214, 271, 288

Shaughnessy, Thomas G., 117

Shay, William, 227

Sheep Camp, 79, 125, 261

Shirley (barge), 89, 104, 218

Sibley, General, 104

Siegley, Earl E., 282-3, 286

Sifton, Clifford, 88, 98-101, 106, 151, 152

Sinclair, Rev. Mr. John A., 216-17, 264, 268, 277, 279, 280-82, 287-88, 306, 313

Singfelder, Charles, 212

Sitka, Alaska, 215, 271, 289

Skagway, 13, 14, 15, 24, 27, 28, 31, 32-33, 36, 37, 44, 47-48, 51, 52, 54, 59, 66-67, 72-76, 78, 80, 82, 86-88, 89, 90, 91, 92, 95, 98, 99, 102, 103, 104-5, 106, 109-10, 111, 112-13, 116, 118, 119, 120, 121, 123, 125, 127, 128, 129, 133-37, 140, 143, 146, 149, 150, 153-55, 156, 157-58, 164, 166, 167, 170, 174, 176, 177, 178, 179-91, 193, 195, 196, 198, 200-3, 204, 205, 206, 207, 208, 209-14, 218, 219-20, 226-28, 232, 233, 234, 235, 242, 246, 248, 249-50, 256, 260, 261, 262-63, 264, 266, 268, 271, 272-73, 275, 277, 278, 279, 280,

282, 286, 287, 290, 292, 294-97, 299, 301, 304, 306, 311, 313, 319, 325, 327, 330, 331-32, 335, 336, 337, 338, 341, 342, 343, 344, 345, 347, 349, 351, 352, 353, 354, 355

Skagway Alaskan, 289

Skagway and Lake Bennett Tramway Co. Ltd., 102, 137, 156, 179, 180-81, 187, 191, 204-5

Skaway & Yukon Transportation & Improvement Co., 103, 114

Skagway-Atlin Budget, 278, 293, 295-97, 304, 305, 314, 345

Skagway Bay, 28, 29, 38-39, 46, 47, 50, 92, 133, 136, 221, 331, 339

Skagway News, 125, 182, 204, 216-17, 219-20, 227, 247, 256, 287, 289, 296, 314

Skagway River, 21, 46, 77, 105, 122, 138, 164, 180, 181, 184-85, 190, 204-5, 220, 222, 226, 227, 270, 311

Skookum (barge), 186, 207, 218

Skookum, Jim, 21, 22, 23, 24, 25-26, 54, 55-57

Sky Pilot, The, 88

Slippery Rock, Alaska, 239-41, 243

Smith Mrs., 106

Smith, Edwin Bobo, 108, 109

Smith, Hamilton, 85, 129, 147, 148, 176

Smith, Jefferson Randolph "Soapy," 106-10, 159, 174, 183, 194, 200-3, 209-14, 216, 217, 220

Smith, John U., 74

Smith, Norman R., 89-90, 92, 103-4, 105-6, 112-13, 114

Snag, Yukon, 15

South Africa, 42, 144

Southampton, 59

Spain, 173

Spanish-American War, 173, 174, 175-76, 200, 203, 207

Sperry, Mr., 183, 212

Stanley, John, 183

Steele, Major Samuel B., 86

Stevens, John, 132-33

Stewart, A.B., 62

Stewart, Gregory, 56
Stewart, John D., 209-10, 211
Stewart River, 21, 48
Stikine Bill, *see* Robinson, William
Stikine River, 20, 35, 36, 97, 98, 99-101,
    130, 150, 152-53, 167-68, 169, 176, 275,
    327
Stonecliffe, Ont., 131
Stone House, 79
Strait of Georgia, 19
Stretch, Richard Harper, 128
strikes, 278-82, 284, 286, 305
Struve, H.G., 52, 62, 72, 106
Sullivan, Mr., 145
Summit Lake, 52, 144, 238, 244-45, 291,
    299, 305, 306, 307, 308, 336
Sweet, Walter, 225
Sylvester Hall, Skagway, 202, 212
Syndicate, The, *see* British Columbia
    Development Assoc. Ltd.

Tacoma (tug), 186, 218
Tacoma, Wash., 71, 94, 219
Tagish Charlie, 23, 54, 55-57
Tagish Indians, 24
Tagish Lake, B.C., 24, 27, 29, 30, 141, 324
Tagish Post, 141, 145
Taiya River, 23, 30, 45, 79
Taku Arm, B.C., 184, 350, 351
Taku Inlet, Alaska, 99
Taku River, 36
Tancred, Sir Thomas, 148, 149, 153-54,
    155, 156-57, 159-64, 166-68, 169-71, 172,
    173, 175, 179-80, 190, 196, 269, 302
Tanner, J.M., 213
Tanner, Marshal, 279-80, 288-89
Taylor "Old Man," 107
Taylor, Marshal S.S., 210, 214, 215
Teal, Mr., 236, 303-4
Teck, Duke of, 63, 64
Telegraph Creek, 35, 97, 101
Teslin Lake, 97, 99-101, 141, 168-69, 176
Texas, 106
Theater Royal, Skagway, 182, 183
Thomas Cook agency, 299-300
Thomas Edison Co., 309

Tlingit Indian Nation, 21
Toronto Mail and Empire, 95-97
"Torpedo Catcher" (scow), 322, 327, 335
Tosi, Father Pascal, 29
Townsend, Walter, 60-61
Transvaal, 153
Treaty of St. Petersburg (1825), 19, 39, 52
Trenaman, Professor, 88
Trinidad, Colorado Lumber Co., 177
Tripp, "Old Man," 108, 215
Tunnel Mountain, Alaska, 239-41,
    243-44, 259
Tupper, Sir Charles, 114, 151
Turkey, 153
Turner, Premier, 152
Turner, Capt. J.C., 214
Turn Point, B.C., 19
Tutshi River, 171

Unik River, 39
Union Church, Skagway, 216-17, 264
Union Pacific Railroad, 359
United States, 30, 39, 52, 59, 65, 81, 98,
    104, 111, 126, 141, 144, 153, 160, 167, 171,
    203, 208, 233, 236, 247, 325, 330, 341
United States Army, 15, 104, 122, 214,
    288
United States Government, 15, 48, 51, 54,
    60, 67, 86, 87, 90-91, 98, 111-12, 115,
    117-18, 122-23, 144, 150, 153, 157, 174-75,
    177, 203, 204, 207, 301
United States Navy, 173
Upper Gate, 270-72
Upper Yukon River, 43, 58, 326, 342, 351
U.S. Hotel, 268
Utopia (steamship), 127, 130, 133, 176,
    179

Valdez, Alaska, 358, 360
Vancouver, 15, 71, 106, 119, 139, 153,
    168-69, 218, 258, 327, 338
Van Horn, Sir William, 117, 119, 120, 121,
    123, 252
Vermillion, Jack "Shoot-your-eyes-out,"
    108
Victoria (Queen), 301, 343

Victoria, B.C., 19, 28, 32, 39-41, 66, 67, 71, 91, 106, 114, 150, 153, 168, 171, 176, 219, 258, 276
Victoria Colonist, 17, 64, 101, 152, 168, 239, 263
Victoria Hall, Skagway, 277
Victorian (steamer), 351
Victorian Order of Nurses, 306

Wallace, Hugh C., 94, 123, 125-26, 261, 262, 293-94, 295, 303-4, 315
Walsh, Major James M., 99
Walters, Frank, 312
War Department (U.S.), 122
Warman, Cy, 108, 139, 229
Warm Pass, 184-85
Warner, Edwin Hall, 192
Washington, D.C., 106, 108, 111, 174
Washington (state), 52, 146, 150, 177
Washington and Alaska Steamship Co., 94
Washington Government, 157
Washington National Bank, 113
Watson, Mr., 182
Watson Lake, 15
Watson Valley, 323-24
Waugh, Harold, 56
W.D. Hofius & Co., 173, 177
Webb, C.L., 62
Webster, Basley A., 102
White, J. Robert, 288-89
White, Thomas, 19, 20, 26
Whitehorse, 13, 14, 15, 228, 309, 315, 316-18, 326-27, 328, 332, 333, 335, 336-7, 338, 341, 342, 343, 344, 345, 347, 349-50, 351, 352, 353, 355
Whitehorse Rapids, 29, 129, 146, 300, 302, 310, 317, 319-20, 321, 325, 332, 340, 347
Whitehorse Star, 301, 351
Whitehorse tramway, 319-20
White Pass Airways, 15
White Pass City, 121, 122, 137, 138-39, 195, 208, 211, 229, 232, 235, 238, 240, 247, 249, 251, 259, 270, 274, 278, 328
White Pass River Division, 350, 351
Whiting, Dr. Fenton B., 178, 221, 223-24, 238, 259, 265, 288-89, 359
Whiting, Frank Herbert, 178, 179, 180, 181, 183, 184, 186, 187, 188, 194-95, 213, 214, 235, 263, 265, 266, 275-76, 278, 279-80, 282, 294, 298, 299, 300-1, 312, 315-16, 318, 321, 328
Whitten, Thomas, 213
Wigan, Edward Alfred, 175
Wilder, George, 215
Wilkinson, Mrs., 80
Wilkinson, Charles Herbert, 34, 39-43, 44, 47-50, 51-54, 59-66, 67-68, 71-72, 80-85, 90, 98, 102, 106, 111, 118, 129-30, 140, 147-48, 149, 151, 154, 172, 175, 177, 196
Willamette (steamer), 71
Williams, Alfred, 325
Wilson, Edgar, 22, 23, 28, 31, 32
Windy Arm, Yukon, 185, 228
Winnipeg, 104
Wood, Mrs., 347
Wood, Zackery T., 141, 325, 330, 347
Wooden, Rev. Mr., 217
Word, T.M., 114
World, 70
Wrangell, Alaska, 35, 97, 99, 220
Wynn-Johnson, C.E., 339

Yeatman, Capt. R.T., 288
Young, J.W., 328, 329, 344
Young, Mary Edith, 360
Yukon and Pacific Railway, 97
Yukon (ship), 351
Yukon Order of Pioneers, 99
Yukon River, 14, 19, 20, 21, 27, 28, 29, 36, 38-39, 41, 43, 48, 49, 54, 55, 57-58, 59, 63, 67, 70, 82, 97, 117, 128-29, 141, 143, 145, 146, 160, 163, 167, 168, 170-71, 184, 228, 230, 250, 294, 300, 302, 311, 320, 335, 344, 349-50, 351
Yukum, Rev. Dr., 88

The White Pass
Designed by Linda Gustafson
Photoset by Pickwick Typesetting Limited
in Garamond Medium
The display type is a version of
Modified Gothic XX Condensed – a late
nineteenth-century American wood type